Reading Territory

KATHRYN WALKIEWICZ

Reading Territory

Indigenous and Black Freedom, Removal, and the Nineteenth-Century State

The University of North Carolina Press *Chapel Hill*

This book was published with the assistance of the Authors Fund of the University of North Carolina Press.

Set in Arno Pro by Westchester Publishing Services
Manufactured in the United States of America

Library of Congress Cataloging-in-Publication Data
Names: Walkiewicz, Kathryn, 1981- author.
Title: Reading territory : Indigenous and Black freedom, removal, and the
   nineteenth-century state / Kathryn Walkiewicz.
Description: Chapel Hill : The University of North Carolina Press, [2023] |
   Includes bibliographical references and index.
Identifiers: LCCN 2022035685 | ISBN 9781469672946 (cloth ; alk. paper) |
   ISBN 9781469672953 (paperback ; alk. paper) | ISBN 9781469672960 (ebook)
Subjects: LCSH: Settler colonialism—United States—History—19th century. |
   States' rights (American politics)—History—19th century. | Five
   Civilized Tribes—Government relations—History—19th century. | Five
   Civilized Tribes—Land tenure. | Indian Removal, 1813–1903. | African
   Americans—Relations with Indians—History—19th century. | African
   Americans—Social conditions—19th century. | Mass media—Political
   aspects. | United States—Territorial expansion—History—19th century. |
   United States—Race relations—History—19th century.
Classification: LCC E179.5 .W327 2023 | DDC 305.896/07309034—dc23/eng/20220824
LC record available at https://lccn.loc.gov/2022035685

Cover illustration: Yatika Starr Fields (Osage-Cherokee-Muscogee), *Osage shield, reclamation* (2022, oil on canvas). Used by permission of the artist. Please see the artist's statement on this work on page xiii.

Contents

List of Figures vii

Acknowledgments ix

Cover Artist's Statement xiii

A Note on Terminology xv

Introduction: Un-tied States 1

CHAPTER ONE
The Boundary Line 31

CHAPTER TWO
Surveying the Swamp 71

CHAPTER THREE
Kansas Bleeds into Cuba 112

CHAPTER FOUR
Sequoyah and the Stakes of Statehood 151

Conclusion: Unmaking the State 201

Notes 213

Bibliography 261

Index 279

Figures

0.1 Louis Dalrymple, "School Begins," *Puck*, January 25, 1899 9

1.1 Front page, *Cherokee Phoenix* (New Echota), February 21, 1828 45

1.2 Second page, *Federal Union* (Milledgeville), September 11, 1830 54

1.3 Third page, *Federal Union* (Milledgeville), September 11, 1830 55

1.4 James F. Smith, "A Map of the 4th District 2d Section of Originally Cherokee, Now Cherokee County" 64

1.5 Seal of Atlanta 69

1.6 *Cherokee Phoenix* masthead 69

2.1 Andrew Ellicott, insert no. 8, in *The Journal of Andrew Ellicott* 72

2.2 Front page, *Florida Gazette* (Saint Augustine), July 28, 1821 77

2.3 Title page, *An Authentic Narrative of the Seminole War: Its Cause, Rise, and Progress, and a Minute Detail of the Horrid Massacres of the Whites, by the Indians and Negroes, in Florida, in the Months of December, January and February* 88

2.4 "Massacre of the Whites by the Indians and Blacks in Florida," in *An Authentic Narrative of the Seminole War: And of the Miraculous Escape of Mrs. Mary Godfrey, and Her Four Female Children* 89

3.1 Front page, *Kansas Free State* (Lawrence), March 17, 1855 118

3.2 "Map of Eastern Kansas," front page, *Kansas Free State* (Lawrence), March 17, 1855 119

3.3 William C. Reynolds and J. C. Jones, *Reynolds's Political Map of the United States* 120

3.4 J. L. Magee, *Liberty, the Fair Maid of Kansas in the Hands of the "Border Ruffians,"* 1856 122

3.5 J. L. Magee, *Forcing Slavery down the Throat of a Freesoiler*, 1856 124

4.1 Map of Indian Territory Oklahoma, 1892 154

4.2 United States Indian Service, Union Agency, "Department of the Interior Public Notice," *Muskogee Phoenix*, May 23, 1905 160

4.3   Front page, *Indian Journal* (Eufaula), July 25, 1902 168

4.4   Advertisement, *Indian Journal* (Eufaula), July 25, 1902 171

4.5   Front page, *Boley Progress*, July 13, 1905 179

4.6   *All-Black Towns of Oklahoma* 183

4.7   Front cover, *Sturm's Statehood Magazine* (Tulsa), October 1905 189

4.8   *Map of the Proposed State of Sequoyah, circa 1905* 191

4.9   Front page, *Muskogee Cimeter*, October 26, 1905 194

Acknowledgments

The acknowledgments are unquestionably my favorite part of any book. They breathe life into the rest of the words and ideas in ways other parts can't quite do. They gesture toward the intimate moments of idea-making, questioning, and thinking together that we cannot witness on the page per se but can affectively feel in the richness of any project. Acknowledgments are reminders of just how collaborative most ideas worth writing down really are and serve as a beautiful archive of the care networks that make a book possible; they are the best form of citation.

In the case of this book, I found just as much pleasure in writing my own as I do in reading others'. Finishing a book project during a global pandemic brought unexpected challenges, and I am indebted to the communities of people and chosen family that kept me afloat. I have been fortunate that over the many years working on this project, I got to meet and love many incredible people who have undoubtedly made possible the most insightful parts of it. Any errors or missteps are entirely my own. I also apologize in advance for anyone I fail to name here.

First, I am grateful for Jesse Alemán's mentorship and support while I was a master's student at the University of New Mexico. Without his encouragement, I would never have applied to PhD programs. I am also grateful to the mentorship and guidance of Janet McAdams and Geary Hobson. I learned so much from working with them on *The People Who Stayed*. I started graduate school at the University of Illinois Urbana-Champaign at just the right time and place to meet and work with an exceptional group of professors and graduate students; this book began as a dissertation meaningfully shaped by the community I found there. Much thanks to my dissertation committee, Trish Loughran, Jodi Byrd, Fred Hoxie, Robert Dale Parker, and Robert Warrior. Trish was a phenomenal adviser. Not only was she present and involved, but she knew exactly when to challenge me and when to be supportive. She is still one of the most brilliant thinkers and careful readers I have ever met, and I am thankful for her continued friendship. Jodi's seminar on critical Indigenous studies, and the hours we spent talking in her office and over coffee about Indigenous studies, video games, current events, and politics, indelibly shaped my thinking as a scholar. At critical points in my graduate career,

Siobhan Somerville, Antoinette Burton, and Justine Murison all provided generous support and feedback on my work.

The Transnational Indigenous Studies graduate student group was a unique space of intellectual community and friendship. I'm especially grateful to Theresa Rocha Beardall, Rico Kleinstein Chenyek, Raquel Escobar, Eman Ghanayem, Kyle Mays, and T.J. Tallie. Thanks as well to friends who willingly read and offered feedback on my work, especially Ben Bascom, Silas Moon Cassinelli, Stephanie Seawell Fortado, and John Musser. In particular, Ben, Silas, and T.J. continue to be some of my closest chosen family. Along the way, there have also been a number of friends and intellectual interlocutors who have made this journey all the better, including Hi'ilei Hobart, Renee Hudson, Douglas Ishii, Ashley Smith, Lisa Tatonetti, Myra Washington, and Maria Windell. Huge *wado* to Pete Coser for being a lifelong friend and reminding me of the necessity of centering what's important. Special thanks to Tiffany Lethabo King, Shaista Patel, and T.J. Tallie for the Native American and Indigenous Studies Association 2020 conversations we shared in Aotearoa/New Zealand. They were profound, and I continue to reflect on them and work toward the kind of world(s) and communities we imagine. I am also thankful for the Think Tsalagi ᏔᎳᎠᏈᏍᏗᎵ ᏣᏫᏯ collective of Cherokee academics, which is a nourishing space of community and support.

I'm thankful to the many UC San Diego and Kennesaw State University colleagues who read chapters, tossed around ideas, and encouraged my writing. I am enormously grateful for the guidance and wisdom of Sara Johnson, Lisa Lampert-Wessig, Rosaura Sanchez, Shelley Streeby, Meg Wesling, Rebecca Hill, and Robbie Lieberman, all of whom served as mentors, friends, and models of how to do academic work with grace and integrity. I do not know how they always manage to make time to uplift and inspire so many others. I have the privilege of working with many people who are both colleagues and beloved friends. Much thanks especially to Kazim Ali, Theresa Ambo, Amanda Batarseh, Gloria Chacón, Joo Ok Kim, Simeon Man, Wendy Matsumura, Andrea Mendoza, Sal Nicolazzo, Shaista Patel, Roy Pérez, Ariana Ruíz, Brandon Som, Erin Suzuki, and Ameeth Vijay. The Native American and Indigenous studies community at UC San Diego has also been a space of reprieve. Special shout-out to Andrew Jolivétte for his efforts to amplify Native American and Indigenous studies on campus and to Elena Hood and Corinne Hensley-Dellefield for all their dedication to building community through the Intertribal Resource Center. Finally, I thank the graduate students I have the privilege of working with at UC San Diego. They are, without question, one of the best parts of my job. I am especially indebted to conversations with current and former graduate students, including Joanmarie Bañez-Clancy, Manu Carrion-Lira, Grace Dunbar-Miller, Bianca Negrete-Coba, Heather Paulson, Greg Pōmaikaʻi Gushiken, Muhammad Yousuf, Laurie Nies, and Isidro Pérez-García.

Thank you to Roy Pérez for the online writing group during COVID, and thanks to everyone who showed up at nine(ish) every morning, especially Andrea Mendoza, Bianca Murillo, Shaista Patel, Tommy Pico, and Ameeth Vijay, for being there during the stressful months of fall 2020. There were many days when the group was the only thing that kept me working on this project. T.J. Tallie and Xine Yao, you are a fantastic reading group duo. Our Fridays were such a needed moment of joy during the pandemic. Thanks to both of you for years of friendship and your incisive analysis of both the pop-cultural and the academic (and seamlessly interweaving the two through the most delicious conversations). Much appreciation goes to Renee Hudson and Juliann Anesi, the best fall 2021 writing accountability crew you could ask for, and to the incomparable Sara Johnson, who helped me push through the final stretch of revisions.

This project benefited from the support of numerous fellowships and grants. As a graduate student, the Newberry Consortium in American Indian Studies Summer Institute seminar Territory, Commemoration, and Monument led by Jean O'Brien and Coll Thrush was pivotal. So was the Other Languages, Other Americas seminar organized by Kirsten Silva Gruesz and Anna Brick-house at the American Antiquarian Society in 2017. The First Book Institute at Penn State provided an invaluable opportunity to learn what it actually takes to write a book. Much thanks to Sean X. Goudie and Priscilla Wald for their tireless efforts to create such a special space. Also, thanks to the friends and colleagues I met there, especially Chris Perreira, Sunny Xiang, and Xine Yao. A UC San Diego Institute of Arts and Humanities grant provided support for indexing and feedback on my manuscript, and a UC Humanities Research Institute Junior Manuscript Forum grant enabled me to assemble an intellectual powerhouse collective of scholars: Derrick Spires, Brigitte Fielder, Sandra Harvey, Carrie Hyde, Sara Johnson, and Xine Yao. Their willingness to share their time and their generous feedback on my manuscript changed this project in critical ways that I believe make it stronger. I am particularly thankful to Brigitte for her suggestion of the term "printscape." Alyosha Goldstein, Daniel Heath Justice, and the anonymous second reader at the University of North Carolina Press all provided robust feedback on the manuscript along the way. I am especially thankful to Alyosha for the reading list he provided—it helped me fill in some of the gaps in my thinking—and to Daniel for his unparalleled generosity and care for junior scholars. *Wado.*

A Hellman Fellowship and UC San Diego Faculty Research Grants provided financial support for research travel and research assistance funding. The completion of this project was made possible by a National Endowment for the Humanities Long-Term Fellowship at the American Antiquarian Society. Special thanks to Nan Wolverton, Kim Toney, Amy Tims, and Laura Wasowicz. Joanmarie Bañez-Clancy, Manu Carrion-Lira, and Katie Neipris worked as summer graduate research assistants, checking sources and catching my many typos. Staff at numerous special collections and archives were invaluable to this project as well. I am especially grateful to the Oklahoma Historical Society, the Oklahoma State University Special Collections and Archives, the University of Oklahoma Western History Collections, the Hargrett Rare Book and Manuscript Library at the University of Georgia, the George A. Smathers Libraries' Special and Area Studies Collections at the University of Florida, and the Florida Historical Society. Thanks as well to Ideas on Fire for their beautiful indexing and to MK Yoon at Humanities First and Kim Icreverzi for their patience and guidance as manuscript editors. Special thanks to Kim for suggesting the title *Reading Territory.*

I am grateful for the opportunity to collaborate with Yatika Starr Fields on a cover for this book. Who knew over twenty-five years ago when we talked about art, movies, and music that we would still be working and thinking together decades later? I am very grateful for your friendship and for the beauty and power you put into this world through your uncompromising commitment to Indigenous art and activism. To Mark Simpson-Vos, Thomas Bedenbaugh, María Garcia, and entire editorial team at the University of North Carolina Press, you were a dream to work with and made the process seamless.

Finally, an enormous *wado* to my partner, my mother, my brother, and my sister. Your love and your laughter make all good things possible.

Cover Artist's Statement

Flags are emblematic of identities, social crests to state and country. They are often imbued with settler colonial overtones, usually within the perimeters of the states' appraised narratives. In 1925, through a contest, Oklahoma revealed its new flag; an Osage shield was selected as the central symbol, along with other symbols taken from the previous iteration, Choctaw blue, pipe, and olive branch, all to symbolize something not so accurate.

Oklahoma is a place of agriculture, oil, and Route 66, the expansion of the West for commerce and capital. A landscape that once held Great Plains ecosystems sustaining Indigenous people, landscape, and bison is now replaced with cattle, farming, and the construct of property and boundaries accorded to settler wealth. Sprawling urban developments linked by wires, landscapes in grids are terrains we aspire to.

As an Osage artist, I wanted to have agency over this flag in reclaiming it as something sacred. I see it being used as a symbol of contradiction in many ways. The olive branch is broken to represent the state of Oklahoma's continued assault on tribal sovereignty. I have painted a more traditional Osage pipe adorned with barbed wire wrapping around it as a symbol of protection. It has a double meaning as well. With sacred lands taken from us and fenced in, we are banished in our own ancestral lands. Our fight continues every day to reclaim them with the LandBack Movement.

I am Osage, Cherokee, and Muscogee. I know this shield is a sacred object that once was used to protect our people in battle and attributed to community wellness, both physical and spiritual. As a tribe, we had to put the shield to rest, buried with other ceremonial articles. As we were forced to relocate like many tribes across North America, our way of life was over in some regards. Now, the Oklahoma flag and shield symbol is upon all, used as candid merchandise across Oklahoma and misused daily, even showing up as the first flag to breach the U.S. capitol on January 6, 2021.

Yatika Starr Fields
(Osage-Cherokee-Muscogee)

A Note on Terminology

The terms I use throughout *Reading Territory* are intended to delineate identities without being prescriptive. Language is constantly in flux, and the names people use to describe themselves change to attend to the particularities of historical moments and sets of relations. The terminology I use here will likely be imperfect or inaccurate at later historical moments (or even by the time this book is published) and differs from some of the most common terminology used in the nineteenth century; like territory and print, language use adapts to the needs of a particular place and time. I am also mindful that the U.S. nation-state and U.S. federated states routinely weaponize taxonomies of identity that either grant individual rights or take them away, especially for Black and Indigenous people. Therefore, when specific self-identifying terminology has been used by a group to legally or politically assert their autonomy, I do my best to use that language as well. Concomitantly, I use terms suggested by in-group scholars as much as possible, with the understanding that there are often internal disagreements about such things. I intentionally allow for some slippage across categories to highlight the complexity these words attempt to hold but cannot contain.

I prioritize the use of specific tribal names, with a preference for the twenty-first-century names tribal nations use for themselves if those names are markedly different from the ones used in the nineteenth century. The one exception is my use of the abridged "Creek Nation" for "Muscogee Nation," previously Muscogee (Creek) Nation. I use "Creek" in chapter 4 because it is how Muscogees publicly described their Nation at that time. I also occasionally include "Creek" in parentheses after "Muscogee" for continuity of terminology and to aid those readers less familiar with the histories I narrate. However, when I write about the Nation in the twenty-first century, I use "Muscogee Nation." Throughout the book, "Black" denotes individuals of African descent and "Afro-Native" refers to individuals of both African and Native descent. I use "African American" to describe Afro-descended people living in or from the United States whose primary political affiliation is the United States. My use of "Freedpeople" refers specifically to Afro-descended individuals whose ancestors or who themselves were enslaved by the Five Tribes (Cherokee, Chickasaw, Choctaw, Muscogee, and Seminole Nations).

While "Freedmen" is prevalent in official government documents, I use "Freedpeople" to account for gender diversity and the often overlooked experiences of formerly enslaved women. Many people who self-identified or were state-identified as Freedpeople were Afro-Native. I assume this to be true throughout, especially given what we know about enslavement and racialization in the United States. The one exception is my use of "Black Seminole" because I found this to be a preferred term of many Black Seminole people. I also use Black Seminole in chapter 2 because in the first half of the nineteenth century, people in these communities were not yet Freedpeople; most of them were still enslaved.

Indigeneity often complicates logics of racialization because Indigeneity is not inherently a racial category, although phenotypic racialization has historically been used to dispossess Indigenous communities and to delegitimize Afro-Native identity. Indigeneity, at least in the communities I write about in this book, is understood first and foremost as a kindship-based, culturally-informed political identity. I use "Indigenous" and "Native" interchangeably, with a preference for "Indigenous" when thinking more globally and "Native" when thinking about the peoples who call Turtle Island home. As caretakers of the land with cosmologies that dictate how to be in good relation to the more-than-human world of Turtle Island, Native people have what Leanne Betasamosake Simpson (Michi Saagiig Nishnaabeg) describes as a "grounded normativity" that settler colonialism seeks to break or contain, "so that it exists only to the degree that it does not impede land acquisition, settlement, and resource extraction."[1]

I almost exclusively use the term "Indian" to reference non-Indigenous depictions of Indigenous people that dehumanize Indigeneity by attempting to flatten Indigenous differences, abstract Indigenous subjectivity, and depersonalize settlers' participation in colonization. However, I acknowledge that "Indian" is a common in-group term still used by many people, especially Elders, and honor the ways Native people have taken back the word for themselves. When I discuss anti-Blackness, I am thinking especially about structures of power and discourses that challenge Black subjectivity and Black freedom. By "anti-Indigenous," I mean the willful desire to impede, if not destroy, Indigenous grounded normativity, and thus Indigenous people. Racialized Blackness and Nativeness continue to operate along continuums that routinely adapt to the growing needs of the colonial state. Additionally, and most importantly, because colonizers have concertedly worked for hundreds of years to divide Black and Native people into distinct, different groups, I invite slippage between the terms throughout my book. As one example, I describe militarized resistance to U.S. colonization in Florida as Afro-Native.

I capitalize "Black," "Indigenous," "Maroon," and "Native" to acknowledge "a distinctive political status of peoplehood."[2] It affirms "the status of a subject with agency, not an object with a particular quality."[3] I do not capitalize "white" because white supremacist settler colonialism already positions whiteness as the ultimate sovereign subject. I understand "land" more capaciously than most settler definitions, as a way to understand the vibrancy of the more-than-human world and not as a way to denote physical space that is possessable.

Reading Territory

Introduction

Un-tied States

On February 1, 2021, Oklahoma governor Kevin Stitt closed his State of the State address by cautioning the state legislature and the people of Oklahoma that "the U.S. Supreme Court's ruling in *McGirt v. Oklahoma* questions the sovereignty of the state as we've known it since 1907."[1] The *McGirt* ruling found that Oklahoma statehood did not legally dissolve the reservation lands of the Muscogee Nation in Indian Territory.[2] As a result, the U.S. federal government and the State of Oklahoma must once again acknowledge the reservations of the Quapaw and the Five Tribes (the Muscogee [Creek], Cherokee, Chickasaw, Choctaw, and Seminole) and their tribal jurisdiction over those lands. While these Native nations do not need Supreme Court recognition to know that their reservations were never legally dissolved, the ruling sets a precedent for Native nations across Indian Country to challenge thefts of land seen as illegal under U.S. federal law. For state actors like Stitt, the acknowledgment of tribal sovereignty articulated in the *McGirt* decision poses an existential threat for states because their ability to colonize Indigenous lands in perpetuity is an essential component of statecraft. But perhaps the more significant threat ushered in by the *McGirt* decision is the proposition of imagining a future in which state boundaries are compressed and tenuous and in which other spatialities come to the fore.

Unlike most studies of U.S. empire that focus on the nation-state as a whole, *Reading Territory: Indigenous and Black Freedom, Removal, and the Nineteenth-Century State* argues that states' rights logics are the glue that holds the U.S. colonial project together because states affirm white male possession of rights and land. In order to dismantle the violent networks of U.S. occupation and extraction across the globe, we must understand how Indigenous dispossession and anti-Blackness scaffold the white possessive project of states' rights.[3] The logic of Indigenous and Black exclusion, which I term "Removal," is why decolonization and Black and Native liberation can never be possible at the geopolitical scale of states. We may already know this at an abstract level, but we must also be attentive to this fact when faced with state policies that profess greater equity and inclusion by attesting to how they structurally continue to secure anti-Indigeneity and anti-Blackness. Paying close attention to nineteenth-century state formation and its Black and Native refusals is necessary for denaturalizing U.S. settler belonging. Nineteenth-century state formation was about *imagining into being* states under contradictory, inconsistent logics that stood in opposition to relational forms of territoriality and belonging practiced by Indigenous communities and others who found themselves in the wake of U.S. occupation.

In *Reading Territory*, "Removal" denotes more than nineteenth-century Indian Removal; it signals how the modern world order, forged through the global projects of enslavement and colonization, made bodies marked as Black or Native movable in order to secure capitalist-colonialist accumulation. Removal attends to the shared experiences of Black and Indigenous peoples, as well as how Blackness and Indigeneity have been positioned against each other, especially in the United States, by Enlightenment definitions of rights that always exclude Blackness and Indigeneity because, as Sylvia Wynter reminds us, Blackness and Indigeneity mark the limits of the Enlightenment human; they denote what he (Man) is not.[4] In the chapters that follow, I take up particular moments of state-making in so-called Georgia (chapter 1), Florida (chapter 2), Kansas and Cuba (chapter 3), Oklahoma, and Indian Territory (chapter 4), with emphasis on Removal and the Five Tribes.

I use "imagined into being" intentionally when describing nineteenth-century statehood to register that state identity is as much an imaginary project as it is a material one, one that cohered through nineteenth-century justifications for U.S. settler expansion. To put it simply, statehood was a method for producing geopolities where they did not belong. U.S. state boundaries were emphatically unnatural formations whose borders rarely followed topographical distinctions such as rivers, mountains, or deserts and instead were shaped by enslavement, Indigenous dispossession, racialization, capitalist accumulation, and white-propertied patriarchy. As I show, moments of statehood served to shore up white male possession of people, places, and things, *especially* when the rationale for statehood was increased inclusion across difference.

In *Reading Territory*, I apply a literary method of analysis to nineteenth-century print and visual culture, paying close attention to the newspaper and the printed survey as critical for U.S. placemaking. I describe the spatial and ideological work of these particular forms of print as "sovereign printscapes."[5] Russ Castronovo coined the term "printscape" to describe the "proliferation" of printed and written materials produced in the late eighteenth century that shaped the political and cultural contours of the emergent U.S. nation-state.[6] For him, "dissemination served as the principal aim of printscape, facilitated by such common practices as reprinting newspaper essays in pamphlet form or copying and circulating letters among committees of correspondence."[7] While Castronovo's definition of "printscape" foregrounds relationships between and across texts in the late eighteenth century, I modify the term slightly to place greater emphasis on how print materially shaped physical and cultural place in the long nineteenth century, and I pluralize the term to emphasize the multiplicity of territorialities produced by nineteenth-century texts. By repurposing the term in this way, I take a page (pun intended) from Black and Native newspaper editors, typesetters, writers, and others involved in the printmaking process to disrupt the white supremacist logics undergirding print forms, including the newspaper and land survey, to assert their own sovereign printscapes.

I employ the modifier "sovereign" to highlight the placemaking work of print, with special attention to the ways Black and Native people used print to assert notions of community and belonging that were often distinct from dominant U.S. ones. My use of sovereign invokes the capacious and complex understandings of the term deployed by Indigenous scholars such as Joanne Barker (Lenape, citizen of Delaware Tribe of Indians) and J. Kēhaulani Kauanui (Kanaka Maoli), who acknowledge the coloniality of sovereignty as a concept while also recognizing the usefulness of the term for asserting Indigenous a priori relationships to land that precede coloniality.[8] I use "sovereign printscapes" to denote Black and Native assertions of placemaking, relationality, and nationalism that operated in spite of, and often pointedly in distinction from, a U.S. settler project and its *colonial printscapes*. As a concept, "sovereign printscape" allows us to simultaneously understand two things. First, how newspapers and printed land surveys taught readers to read a particular story of place that secured white belonging and naturalized the U.S. map. Second, how Black and Native newspaper editors, community leaders, writers, and political activists wielded their own sovereign printscapes and reading praxes that aggressively worked to disrupt the dominant U.S. state map.

Land surveys were especially critical to the *story* of U.S. expansion. These scientific pursuits of knowledge cataloged place to reflect settler organizations of territory. Their gridded, mathematical construction presented territory as a thing that could be known, quantified, and owned. Territory conjointly became something that could easily circulate through print culture, like maps and land lotteries. While many nineteenth-century periodicals with regional circulation reprinted much of their content from other publications, especially throughout the first half of the century, they also served as important venues for detailing localized discourses of placemaking and belonging. My understandings of the political and ideological power of nineteenth-century print culture, especially for marginalized communities, are indebted to the scholarship of Kirsten Silva Gruesz, Noenoe K. Silva, Derrick R. Spires, and many others. Because many in the United States felt stronger regional affiliations than national ones throughout the first half of the century, this helps us glean a sense of how settler belonging took shape.

In some cases, newspapers served as recruitment tools to entice settlement. In others, they served as venues for debating Indigenous sovereignty, Black freedom, and U.S. expansion. Issues of states' rights and Indigenous and Black autonomy were certainly taken up in other places as well, but the hegemonic discourse of states' rights could be found throughout the pages of regional print. It cohered around affluent white Southern patriarchy, which argued that both enslavement and Removal were "states' rights." Attending to these forms of print provides a glimpse into the complexity of statehood debates that helps us understand just how artificial and fragile the state is, and the role storytelling played in bolstering state or territorial identity.

As importantly, periodicals and ephemeral forms of print were deployed to serve the needs of Indigenous and Black struggles for justice in ways that other forms of print, such as the book, could not always achieve, given periodicals' lower costs, (semi)regular publication, and ability to circulate work by multiple authors. Moreover, periodical culture invited a sense of collectivity and community that was not necessarily focused on the singular, liberal reading subject.

However, *Reading Territory* is not a recovery project. I am less interested in highlighting understudied materials than I am in how we read them. I argue for ideological depth in what we find on the printed page through close reading and visual analysis of both form and content that is based on a reading of over 2,000 full issues of newspapers from this era. In order to do this work, I suggest a reading praxis I term "territorial hermeneutics," influenced by the work of Indigenous and Black studies scholars like Maile Arvin, Barker, Mishuana Goeman, Shona Jackson, Kauanui, and Tiffany Lethabo King. They argue for the necessity of thinking spatially in registers outside the white supremacist state. In other words, the state encourages us to read space and text in one way, and I am asking us to read in another. I understand territorial hermeneutics as a literary reading praxis that encourages us to untie ourselves from the logics of state-based hegemony and open ourselves to other ways of being in relation to one another by reading literarily—meaning an approach attentive to the fictiveness of the worlds print constructs, including how metaphor, allusion, form, and so on are as critical as the content it conveys. This includes letting go of our attachments to states we might feel lovingly toward or strongly identify with and making room to imagine other spatial relations, turning toward un-tied states rather than united states, if you will. In an effort to denaturalize the state, I only include the city, not the abbreviated state or nation, next to the name of a newspaper title in my citations. Convention explains that this parenthetical helps a reader locate a publication, but I urge us to query the spatial politics of that impulse. Alongside this hermeneutic, I engage what I term a matrilineal citational praxis. This means I foreground intellectual genealogies of Black and Indigenous feminist, femme, Two-Spirit, and queer scholars and scholarship. As a Cherokee person, I am mindful of the ways colonization attacked Cherokee matrilineal structures of kinship and gender and that the same patriarchal white logics that inform colonial political life are woven into the fabric of the U.S. academy. A matrilineal citational approach reminds me of the necessity of methodologically working against these logics.[9]

Southeastern Spaces

The chapters that follow all contend with geographies that resonated for Indigenous and Black thinkers in the nineteenth century and beyond, what King describes as "the spaces and cracks where Black and Indigenous life caress each other."[10] They stage significant ideological flashpoints for developing a U.S. narrative of white supremacy, race, and dispossession and foreground the territorialities of Southeastern peoples, especially the Five Tribes and Maroon, free, and enslaved Black communities. Locating these case studies in the Southeast and the Caribbean allows us to see in sharp relief how colonization, enslavement, and forced Removal were experienced across and between Indigenous and Black life. For example, the Five Tribes were enslaved and enslavers; they were Removed and Removers. They were also prominent subjects and agents of nineteenth-century print culture discourse. The states' rights rhetoric that would come to dominate U.S. discourses of statehood was not *exclusive to* but was critically *shaped by* the contestations I detail in *Reading Territory*. Attention to it makes evident how Indigenous and Black dispossession shaped state identity and discourses of U.S. settler space.

I use "Southeast" as a slippery geographic signifier less invested in plotting out a particular map than in describing a set of spatial relations, which shifted and changed throughout the nineteenth century. Forced migration would resettle many Black and Native people to Indian Territory—the same place where reservation boundaries were reinstated by the 2020 *McGirt* decision— through extensive campaigns of Removal, including segregation, lynching, and other forms of racialized violence that took hold (and were often justified under states' rights) following the U.S. Civil War. What we see across southeastern Black and Native communities, however, are varied but sustained efforts to challenge the central paradox of a liberal democracy engaged in genocidal Removal projects. Understanding this history contextualizes the 1905 Sequoyah statehood campaign lobbying for a Native-run state and clarifies what writers and editors saw as the stakes of statehood for Indian Territory (as discussed in chapter 4). It also reminds us that Indigenous nations and autonomous Black, Native, and Afro-Native communities thriving beyond the gaze of the state continue to endure in the so-called U.S. South, despite repeated attempts at their total elimination.

Most importantly, the geographies traversed in this book are tethered to my own story. While my hope is that this book's case studies open up a broader conversation about statehood and territory, my motivation in selecting the spaces I write about is also grounded in a sense of responsibility and accountability to my own relationships to place. I am an enrolled citizen of Cherokee Nation born and raised in so-called Oklahoma. However, I was not raised on the reservation (I grew up about an hour's drive west), and I was not raised in a culturally Cherokee household. Moreover, as a public state university professor, I am a state employee and financially benefit from state structures. Understanding myself in relation to the stories, places, and peoples I write about in the same way my home community understands me is an essential part of the difficult ongoing relational work necessary for decolonial commitments to Black and Native freedom.

Federated States

There is a general assumption that states are stable, are ahistorical, and exist in perpetuity, no matter their actual material and political conditions. This logic is central to narratives of U.S. empire. To put it another way, the process of statehood, which Dean Itsuji Saranillio describes as a "knowledge-making spectacle," is a biopolitical one that works to foreclose other spatial futurities, other ontologies.[11] However, as *Reading Territory* demonstrates, the state never entirely fulfills such a mission. Other spatialities and geopolities continually collide, contest, bubble up, and override the state, revealing its fictive autonomy.[12] Despite the many U.S. territories, military occupations, and commonwealths, the fifty states almost always serve as a spatial and discursive shorthand for the nation. We know that it is too simplistic to understand the United States exclusively via states, but it is precisely this ideological and visual sleight of hand that I am getting at. By the end of the nineteenth century, statehood as a de facto policy of incorporation became far less desirable a method of territorial incorporation than a more multivalent approach to territorial categories. This was due to uneasiness in the nation about the perception of the United States as an empire and even greater unease about how statehood for Puerto Rico, Guam, the Philippines, and Hawai'i might reshape the cultural and racial landscape of U.S. states.

While the Northwest Ordinance of 1787 established a pattern of increased self-government leading to eventual statehood, the pattern it proposed was not a consistent template—it was not imagined that all territorial acquisitions of the United States would result in the eventual statehood of the Northwest model, particularly in the second half of the nineteenth century.[13] The acquisition of Puerto Rico, Guam, the Philippines, and (to some extent) Cuba following the Spanish-American War (1898) led to a series of Supreme Court cases termed the Insular Cases whose cumulative decisions not only asserted the flexibility of the term "territory" but attempted to institutionalize such flexibility. There was little interest in eventual statehood for these territories, and they became categorized as "unincorporated"—neither foreign nor part of the United States proper.[14] As such, "territory" was legally defined as both part of and distinct from the United States. Because legal understandings of the United States are flexibly obtuse, understandings of territory are as well, allowing a wider range of strategic decisions in what constitutes the U.S. nation and in what capacities. In this way, U.S. territory has a protean quality that paradoxically operationalizes it as both terra nullius and U.S. property. While state-making locates power, territorial accumulation obscures valences of U.S. empire that may be diplomatically or politically suspect.

Again, states have never been the only form of regional identity formation or necessarily the one that all individuals most attach to, but they nonetheless do critical work to perpetuate the U.S. settler nation. Importantly, state government continues to be one of the most influential scales of political, social, and ideological influence over the quotidian lives of those who live within their borders. The notion of a federated assemblage of states was a hallmark of the emergent United States. While many scholars, particularly scholars of Latinx and Latin American studies, have highlighted the hemispheric invocations in the inclusion of "America" in the nation's name, also of note are the "united states" that precede it.[15] In conversation, the terms produce a discursive affinity between the federated state (the collective of states housed under the federal government) and the hemisphere, gesturing toward a national identity that imagines itself as inherently multiscalar.

As scholars of federalism have demonstrated, federalism and state sovereignty were not seen as distinct scales of political power (i.e., the notion that a federal authority needed to cohere across a vast domain that states alone could not manage) but are in fact necessarily connected.[16] By the 1780s and the codification of U.S. federalism, the colonies already understood themselves as polities with the right to enslave and the right to colonize. Those legacies are knitted into the fabric of U.S. federalism. Moreover, federalism functions like a geolexicon and logic that rationalizes and normalizes U.S. settler empire as it epistemologically undergirds the thoroughfares of U.S. empire. By this, I mean that the organizing logic of federalism makes states beholden to the nation-state but also semiautonomous polities in ways that benefit empire and sustain settler colonialism. This occurs not only politically but ideologically and discursively. At the same time, federalism and state sovereignty, as the foundations of the U.S. nation-state, expose the limitations of such an arrangement. State sovereignty was formulated as a response to skepticism about the U.S. project, and while states' rights continue to uphold the federal state, they also reveal uncertainty about the viability of the project.

Animating States

Mel Y. Chen's concept of animacy is helpful in understanding the ideological and discursive work of states. For Chen, animacy is a "conceptually slippery" process by which seemingly nonliving, inanimate things, or less animate things, are understood biopolitically and in affective relation to culture.[17] Though federated states are outside the purview of Chen's book, its understanding of animacy "as an often racialized and sexualized means of conceptual and affective mediation between human and inhuman, animate and inanimate, whether in language, rhetoric, or imagery," helps us get at the animated nature of states.[18] While they are categorically geopolitical, they are also animated and animating containers semiotically imbued with signification. The cottage industries of California-marketed commodities, including T-shirts, jewelry, and state-shaped food, assert state sovereignty, even if the contours of that sovereignty are not universal; the outline and shape of the state alone signify cultural meaning. Federated states take on a life of their own, with a particular culture, a set of values, and signature songs, flowers,

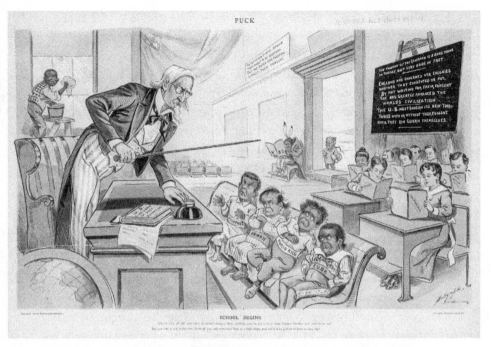

FIGURE 0.1 Louis Dalrymple, "School Begins," *Puck*, January 25, 1899, centerfold. Courtesy of Library of Congress Prints and Photographs Division (https://www.loc .gov/pictures/item/2012647459/).

flags, and birds that animate them as place but also more than place. States can take on a life, a personality—and often politics—that distinguishes them, and through that distinction, leaders of state government assert geopolitical control. However, states are semiotically slippery: meaning sticks to them but is not necessarily fixed or permanent.

Print and cultural production play an especially significant role in making cartography iconographic. The *Puck* cartoon "School Begins," published on January 25, 1899, evidences the kind of animation and animacy I am suggesting (figure 0.1). While most scholars have read this image in terms of territorial acquisition, what is equally salient in the illustration is the way state identity gets codified. In the magazine cartoon's visual and discursive cues, we see the animated and animating nature of these things called states. They become embodied, albeit malleable, representations of subjectivity. I want to take some time with this image to show how visual and print culture make the animating work of state identity legible.

The satirical image depicts Uncle Sam as a schoolteacher welcoming a new batch of pupils: the Philippines, Hawai'i, "Porto Rico," and Cuba. All but

Hawaiʻi were territories acquired by the United States following the Spanish-American War, and Hawaiʻi became an official territory following the illicit overthrow of the Hawaiian Kingdom. The territories sit disgruntled in the front row of the schoolhouse, depicted as caricatures of their homelands and meant to invoke known leaders from each territory, such as the Filipino revolutionary leader Emilio Aguinaldo and Hawaiʻiʻs queen Liliuokalani. The children shift uncomfortably, frowning up at Uncle Sam, who looms tall above them. Behind the new territories sit the incorporated territories of New Mexico and Arizona, the District of Alaska, and the states California and Texas. There are several striking distinctions between the depictions of the new pupils and the older class. While the new pupils are depicted as racially darker skinned, more colorfully dressed, and donning banners across their chests indicating their geographic home, the children behind them are visibly white (except for Alaska), and their geographic signifiers are written across the front of their schoolbooks. According to the illustration, with assimilation comes a whitening of the body politic, as well as a text-based, literacy-based relationship to the colonial nation-state. This emphasis on text and literacy is reinforced by a caricatured Indian sitting in a chair beside the schoolhouse door. While he seems to glance over at the studious class, he peeks behind a book of ABCs held upside down, indicating his own alleged illiteracy. He is relegated to the stereotypical dunce chair, excluded from the rest of the class.

It is a curious choice to include this presentation of Indigeneity in an illustration about territory because the two U.S. territories missing from the class are Indian Territory and Oklahoma Territory. In 1899 Indian Territory was an unorganized territory governed by Native nations. There, the Five Tribes had established schools, municipalities, and their own thriving print culture, many of which rivaled U.S. institutions, but here Nativeness is disentangled from spatial specificity, depicted instead as the "blanket Indian" stereotype.[19] Saranillio reads this elision of Native space in the image as a move from "masculine conquest to feminine domesticity."[20] While I agree with his reading of the ways gender operates in U.S. conquest, this still does not fully account for the exclusion of Indian Territory (or the masculinist depictions of the Black, Indigenous, and Asian figures). The absence of Indian Territory enables the cartoon to frame a narrative about territory that understands it in racialized terms in which governance, whiteness, civility, and territoriality are all synonymous. As I discuss in chapter 4, the rupture of this equivalency is one of the reasons Indian Territory leaders were unable to conduct their statehood campaign successfully; to admit a state of the union organized by

Native people would disrupt the foundational racialized logics undergirding the contours of U.S. national space.

The exclusion of Indian Territory makes sense if we follow the racialized spatial logics of the illustration. Yet those same logics fall apart when we return to Alaska, Arizona, and New Mexico, all of which had large Indigenous populations that were either entirely opposed to or at the very least wary of the impact U.S. statehood would have on their communities and ways of life. Moreover, Alaska was not an officially incorporated U.S. territory until 1912. How these figures are illustrated in the orderly classroom becomes less and less logical, and the lesson it aims to "teach" us is far less obvious the more we plumb out distinctions between on-the-ground political situations in each of these locales and *Puck's* rendering. In the breakdowns of a racialized, gendered logic of territory, we see fissures in the image's narrative of U.S. statehood.

Also included in the image is a male figure of Asian descent, depicted as the racialized stereotype promulgated by anti-Asian sentiments at the end of the century. The figure peers into the schoolhouse from just outside the doorway, a book clutched in his hand. An apparent reference to the Chinese Exclusion Act of 1882, the figure is occluded from (domestic) public space—while the door is open and he can glance inside, the door is not open for him. In the background, we see a Black figure washing the windows as he looks at the current lesson with delight, a positioning that denotes his place as a laborer and not a student in the schoolhouse. The image, therefore, works as a mapping and taxonomy of race and space, an *imperial printscape* that reveals how race and space were conflated in the nineteenth century and, in many ways, continue to be. Two logics seem to guide this taxonomy. First, in order to be fully incorporated into the United States, a space must be whitewashed. Second, African Americans, migrants of color, and Indigenous people cannot be fully incorporated into the U.S. colonial project. They are all excluded in some form or another, and they cannot be representative *of* or represented *in* statehood or incorporated territory. They are excluded from the larger body politic—individualized racialized bodies pushed to the edges of the U.S. political imaginary.

Across a poster and chalkboard are messages about governance and consent—or rather, inscriptions that argue *against* consent, using the examples of the Confederacy and the British colonies. The inscription at the bottom of the image reads, "Now children, you've got to learn these lessons whether you want to or not! But just take a look at the class ahead of you, and remember that in a little while, you will feel as glad to be here as they are!" Federal state power is described here in a rhetoric of consent that invokes sexual violence and violence against children as forms of coercion; civilization does not require civility on the part of the colonial power. The looming Uncle Sam, who dominates the foreground as he leans in over the children with his phallic pointing stick, reinforces the image's violence. And it unequivocally defines this violence as colonial, which is reinforced by the chalkboard message about England. In this conflation of liberal subjectivity, settler colonialism, migration, and racial capitalism, we see the "intimacies of four continents" described in Lisa Lowe's work, as well as the collusion of self-government rhetoric and U.S. empire.[21]

The image's political message and critique of imperial expansion are not entirely clear. Is it a satirical critique of U.S. imperial projects? Is it a satirical critique of the new colonies as unworthy of full inclusion in the U.S. political project? Or is it something more nuanced? The intended and received message of a newspaper or magazine could not be controlled any more than attempts to affirm the stability and legibility of U.S. states, and *Puck* published cartoons that parodied a variety of political perspectives throughout its run. For our purposes, the political stance of the cartoon is less important than the semiotics of territorial expansion and statehood that it gestures toward, and the ways in which it visually captures what María Josefina Saldaña-Portillo terms "racial geographies," the dialectical relationship by which space and race coconstitute national place.[22] The image hauntingly and violently stages U.S. settler empire in a one-room schoolhouse, collapsing multiple scales of political, social, and cultural geography inside the four walls in order to visually imagine them existing on the same spatial plane—or in the case of the Asian figure, excluded and just outside.

Statehood Innocence

As important in the image is the role of childhood and schooling. By staging the statehood process as akin to human development, the image naturalizes the state. Moreover, in the U.S. public school systems, state history is assigned to elementary and junior high classrooms. Students are often asked to rehearse simplified, sanitized narratives of statehood that imagine a smooth temporal transition from a something before to the present and future of statehood. This association of state narratives with childhood imbues them with a sense of innocence, ensuring the stories follow an uncomplicated progress narrative so as not to upset children, who are perceived as needing protection from the more violent and ugly truths of history.[23] In many states, fourth graders even reenact natal moments in the dominant state narratives, many of them precursors to statehood that seem to foresee its inevitability: the California mission system, the Alamo, or, in so-called Oklahoma, the 1889 Land Run. Although community pushback against some of these performances led to their decline in the first decades of the twenty-first century, these are salient narratives that serve as indoctrination into a particular sense of belonging.

It is also critical to remember that state governments wield significant control over all public schools' textbooks and curriculum, not just state histories. They assert enormous ideological and pedagogical influence over dominant narratives of U.S. history, as evidenced by Texas's outsize influence on textbook use across the United States. When the 1836 Project became Texas law in 2021, it demanded that all state landmarks, state museums, and public instructors in K–12 and higher education teach a "patriotic education," with penalties for anyone who does not do so.[24] The bill was initially proposed to challenge growing public critique of the Alamo myth—the notion that Texians (Anglo Texans) fought bravely to the death in order to protect the Texas republic from Mexican takeover. Omitted from this myth is the truth that white U.S. settlers were initially encouraged to immigrate to Texas to help the Mexican government fight Comanche, Apache, and other Indigenous warriors who challenged Mexican colonization with combat. Texians separated from Mexico and established their own republic over concerns about taxation and the abolition of enslavement in Mexico. In this lesser-known history, a history Texas politicians seek to obscure, we can see how Indigenous dispossession and enslavement shaped white belonging.

The Texas legislature's move to protect a myth and silence a far messier factual history is not new, nor is its emphasis on what gets taught to children in schools. As I suggested earlier, one of the ways the political work of naturalizing state sovereignty gets done is through educational maps and children's songs, which serve as a semiotic shorthand for the sedimentation of state identity. State power directly correlates to the project of mapping by creating a simplistic map that does not represent reality in its full nuance and detail but instead offers an uncomplicated version.[25] Through this process, the state reworks the reality it depicts, adapting to whatever representation favors the state at a given time. The malleability of this form of cartography helps one understand why a space like Kentucky could go through a variety of mutations, from the western frontier home of Daniel Boone in the early nineteenth century to a different kind of border state in the context of midcentury divisions over enslavement. The same borders plot the parameters of the federated state, but the space's meaning varies depending on its role in the larger nation.

This form of geographic training is evidenced in Harriet Beecher Stowe's *First Geography for Children* (1855), in which Stowe privileges the scale of the federated state in teaching her imagined young readers. In Catherine Beecher's preface to the 1855 version, she describes the book's goal as providing a "generalized and systematized" approach to geography that "afford[s] immense aid to a child both in acquiring and in retaining its details."[26] In order to do so, Beecher explains, her sister's book teaches geography through "association," or "connecting new ideas with those which have been made interesting."[27] Throughout the text, geographical places, especially states, are described through exceptional or unique qualities that are meant to help a child distinguish one from another.[28] By "generalizing and systematizing" geography in this way, Stowe provides a taxonomized rendering of the U.S. settler nation that is legible and logical and that utilizes the exceptional to signal federal inclusion.

While Stowe's most famous work of spatial and geographic critique narrates regional ruptures between North and South, *First Geography for Children* depicts an orderly, cohesive world easily accessible and legible to children. She produces a geographical assemblage, a printscape, that understands discourse and narrative to be as crucial to geographical understanding as maps, charts, and scientific measurements; it is the stories we tell about spaces, "associations" (to use Beecher's term), that solidify understandings of place. Perhaps the most intriguing of these state associations or mnemonics is the entry for Texas. Stowe's description of Texas's annexation and the U.S.-Mexico War is disembodied in ways that relieve the U.S. nation-state of direct culpability. She writes, "It was formerly a part of Mexico, but is now annexed to our country."[29] This version of Texas simplifies and pacifies the tumultuousness of nineteenth-century Texas history.

Stowe couples this brief history of the state with her association, her one-sentence mnemonic. Her association for Texas reads, "You may remember this state as the one that caused a war."[30] Texas becomes a historical actor anthropomorphized as cause, subject, and agent. Moreover, the structure of the sentence implies that Texas-as-state catalyzed a war, not Texas-as-republic or Texas-as-Mexico, which, intentionally or not, depicts statehood as permanently affixed to "Texas." Moreover, it distills temporality and geography onto a flat plane: the map of Texas and the narrative of its statehood offer a clean teleology that forecloses other pasts and other futures. For Stowe in the 1850s, Texas is the state that started a war; for some automotive companies in the twenty-first century, a "Texas series" of trucks invokes something slightly different, but the animated quality of Texas-as-state allows both invocations of "Texasness" to operate conterminously. While Stowe's geography was published almost fifty years before the *Puck* cartoon, they both demonstrate how print and popular visual culture actively participate in and do much of the cultural work of naturalizing and circulating imperial racialized terrains and forms of geographic reading practices that register along cartographic axes.[31]

Possession and Property

I want to return to what gets omitted in Texas's "patriotic education," which was legalized in 2021—namely, that a public reckoning with the history of enslavement, colonization, and racialization of "Mexicanness" in Texas is deemed unpatriotic and harmful, especially in a state where the Black, Indigenous, and of-color residents are projected to outnumber white residents in the very near future. In the nineteenth century, discussions of statehood often instantiated a dialogue between anti-Black violence and Indigenous genocide, revealing their dual necessity to the continued project of settler colonialism. Attention to state-making in the Southeast (itself a fraught geographical descriptor) lays out in stark relief not only how state sovereignty is dependent on Black and Indigenous exclusion but also how it works against Black and Native coalitional kinship. Central to the mythology is a temporal logic by which Indigeneity is imagined as a precursor to statehood and Blackness signals the racialized limits of inclusion that follow. Such a logic attempts to regulate both time and space to position Black and Indigenous freedom as antithetical to each other and Blackness and Indigeneity as distinctly separate. Throughout the nineteenth century, especially in places such as Indian Territory, Oklahoma, and Kansas, Indigenous sovereignty meant freedom *from* the state, and Black liberation was offered up *by* the state through the false promise of inclusion. However, because statehood reifies white masculinist control, real freedom is not possible for Black subjectivity within the state, and inclusion in the state requires that Native peoples deny their Indigeneity. Throughout *Reading Territory*, I pair "Indigenous and Black freedom" to describe a world that honors Black and Native life and understand the project as an interdependent one. My aim is to signal interconnections, distinctions, and intimacies in formulations of Blackness and Nativeness across Turtle Island.

Goenpul scholar Aileen Moreton-Robinson terms this mode of epistemological and ontological production of state stability (by which I mean both

the federated state and *the* state—i.e., the structural and institutional management of a nation and its subjects) as the "possessive logics" of patriarchal
white sovereignty by which the settler colonial nation-state continually reaffirms its "ownership, control, and domination" of Indigenous lands, particularly in the United States, Canada, and Australia.[32] In Moreton-Robinson's
discussion of the continued logic of the "naturalness" of settler colonial occupation, she argues that patriarchal white sovereignty instantiated projects
of racialization indelibly tied to dispossession and colonization. Moreover,
she argues that "the episteme of Western culture," forged through modern
constructions of race and gender, developed three ontological categories:
"owning property, becoming propertyless, and being property."[33] In her influential essay "Whiteness as Property" (which Moreton-Robinson pulls from
heavily in articulating the possessive logic of patriarchal white sovereignty),
Cheryl Harris outlines how whiteness as property is contingent on the exclusion of Black and Indigenous people, particularly under U.S. law.[34]

What the work of Moreton-Robinson and Harris reveals is that while Indigeneity and Blackness are both vital to the production of white supremacy—
because of or even though they also threaten its continuation and expose its
social, political, and cultural construction—they have historically been understood as not only distinct from one another but also antithetical. While
Blackness is circumscribed as whiteness's racial antithesis, Indigeneity is
deemed necessarily propertyless in an attempt to affirm continued occupation of Indigenous land. Such a logic shifts the gaze from the shared experiences of Black and Native people in the "New World" and the ways the liberal
human, whom Wynter describes as "Man," has been formulated to exclude
them.[35]

Studies of nineteenth-century Southeastern Native people, such as those
by Barbara Krauthamer, Tiya Miles, Celia E. Naylor, and Alaina E. Roberts,
reveal the necessity of working against these possessive logics by demonstrating the ways Black and Native histories are complex and interconnected.
Cherokee, Chickasaw, Choctaw, Muscogee, and Seminole participation in chattel slavery in the eighteenth and nineteenth centuries and the divisive impact
of allotment at the end of the nineteenth century are just two examples that
reveal a far more complex constellation of property and kinship relations. Additionally, U.S. racial taxonomies like blood quantum actively encouraged a
fracturing between Indigeneity and Blackness, productively disrupting Afro-
Native alliances and attempting to invisibilize Afro-Native subjectivity.
Blood quantum erases kinship as the essential way of understanding identity
and relationality and ties Black and Native peoples to white supremacist

logics of race and racialization. As Sharon P. Holland and Miles explain, the one-drop rule and blood quantum biologize Black and Indigenous identity and position Blackness as contaminating and Indianness as easy to contaminate.[36] Not only does the logic of blood quantum racialize Indigeneity, but it also posits Indigeneity as subsumable. When this concept is combined with the racialist logic that one drop of Black blood makes a person Black, Afro-Indigeneity becomes mathematically impossible. The racist arithmetic of these blood logics situates whiteness as able to modify either Blackness or Indigeneity but imagines Blackness and Indigeneity as incompatible.

What Holland and Miles highlight in legal and cultural logics of race also casts light on a pervasive problem in both Black studies and Native studies of analyzing identity in relation to the white settler state rather than in relation to one another (or to other racialized or marginalized groups).[37] These grammars of race and Indigeneity extend to disciplinary boundaries and have historically made it difficult to engage questions of race, colonization, Blackness, and Indigeneity in scholarly work without privileging one subject position at the expense of another. While many scholars have adeptly demonstrated that anti-Black racism and settler colonial occupation are coconstitutive, to engage in dialogue that does not treat one as supplementary continues to prove discursively challenging. I would argue that this is because the logic of possessive white sovereignty is further affirmed by perpetual obfuscation of its machinations, what Jodi Byrd (Chickasaw Nation) terms cacophony, or the "competing struggles for hegemony within and outside institutions of power" that repeatedly and tactically encourage discord among the settler colonial state's subjects, including those most disenfranchised by the state, and repeatedly demand complicity in the colonial project in efforts to assert liberal subjectivity.[38]

It should be no surprise, then, that federal (and sometimes state) recognition of tribes often depends on proximity to Blackness, which has proved especially true for numerous Indigenous communities in New England and the Southeast. Their perceived Blackness means their Indigeneity is more rigorously scrutinized by the settler state than that of Indigenous people phenotypically read by the (nation-)state as non-Black; recognition aligns with proximity to whiteness. Because the racialization of Blackness was codified through a logic of Blackness *as* an "object of property" in the eighteenth and nineteenth centuries and Indigeneity denoted a racialized propertyless subject, discursively race and Indigeneity operate on separate planes in white supremacist colonial ideologies.[39] The language with which to refer to both in the same breath is made almost unspeakable because the ability to do so would undermine the infrastructures of a racial order and colonial occupation, both of which are foundational to the upkeep of white settler patriarchy and U.S. empire.[40]

Maile Arvin (Native Hawaiian) further elaborates on how whiteness is organized around relations to both Blackness and Indigeneity through what she terms "possession."[41] It is critical to understand how whiteness also attempts to control kinship networks and mediate Blackness and Indigeneity through distinct forms of white heteropatriarchy that regulate sexuality, sex, and gender by making the two seemingly polarized ontologies. This is why women's, children's, and gender-nonconforming people's bodies have been key to the management of racial taxonomies, sexual violence, and the disruption of alternative kinship structures for Black and Native peoples.[42] Therefore, racial markers of Blackness and Nativeness become distinctly aligned with enslavement and colonialism, respectively, in ways that posit the two as antithetical to each other and flatten multiracial, diasporic identities that more accurately depict formulations of survival, kinship, and endurance in the face of violence and historical trauma. Federal Indian policy throughout the nineteenth century, including blood quantum and allotment, demanded racial logics— logics predicated on anti-Blackness—be used to determine Indigeneity and kinship. As a result, whiteness is centered as the fulcrum on which racial formations turn. Such a logic makes Afro-Native subjectivity a seeming impossibility—despite the fact that it is inarguably not—because it defies the logic of blood quantum in a legal U.S. context.

Cherokee Nation's infamous disenfranchisement of Freedpeople, the descendants of people enslaved by Cherokees before the U.S. Civil War, led to a series of contentious legal fights. While Cherokee Nation's official position was that determining tribal citizenship was an essential form of sovereignty, Freedpeople descendants argued that exclusion violated their rights under Cherokee and U.S. law. Eventually, in 2017, after intervention from the U.S. federal government and public disputes, Freedpeoples' citizenship was finally reinstated in Cherokee Nation, citing its post–Civil War Treaty of 1866. While Indigeneity is meant to denote political and cultural affiliations rather than race, the example of the Cherokee Freedpeople demonstrates how colonial logics of race, specifically anti-Blackness, have influenced rights and recognition.[43] Moreover, the 1866 treaties all Five Tribes negotiated with the federal government detail the reservation borders affirmed by the *McGirt* ruling. The treaties continue to have a profound influence on Black and Native sovereignty and citizenship. However, as of the writing of this book, Cherokee

Nation is the only one of the Five Tribes that currently recognizes full citizenship for Freedpeople descendants.

Territory beyond the Map

How do we commit to grappling rigorously with the world-altering experiences of genocide, enslavement, and colonization that are still fresh and raw as interconnected and entangled? How might we understand Removal as not just about the apocalyptic forced Removal of Indigenous people from homes, from other-than-human relatives, from kinship structures, from grounded cosmologies, but also as a way to address the equally cataclysmic forced Removal of Indigenous Africans from their homelands to the Americas? How do we bear witness to the Removals that followed for enslaved people from families, from communities? That tore Native children from their homes and placed them in boarding schools? How can Removal hold space to mourn the trauma of those people enslaved by the Cherokee, Chickasaw, Choctaw, Muscogee, and Seminole who were forced to move as well? I capitalize "Removal" to signal the ways it has operated as a violence across space and time; Removal from one world into another, forcible interpellation into a "new world." The forced taking from spatial ontologies and epistemologies marks the shared violence of Black and Native being in the Americas. But Removal gestures toward structural violence that seeks to distance Blackness and Indigeneity. Removal attempts to strip bodies of their prior selves and supplant other cosmologies, other worlds, with that of a white possessive world order. Removal is not a freedom of movement—it can also mean being forced to stay still. In a U.S. context, Removal continues to operate as a foundational tenet of states' rights—the right to move, the right to contain, the right to displace, the right to incarcerate, the right to kill. Removal is the ongoing project of Black and Native genocide, but it continues because the drive, not its fulfillment, is critical to U.S. racial empire.

When initially confronted with the totality of Black and Native interwoven histories, Tiffany Lethabo King describes the experience as one for which she could find no language. Such grappling necessitated an affective response that language could not adequately account for, revealing the ways discourse can work against reckoning. However, she insists that "genocide and slavery do not have an edge. While the force of their haunt has distinct feelings at the stress points and instantiations of Black fungibility and Native genocide, the violence moves as one."[44] It is a shared experience beyond words, an "edgeless distinction" that is "a haptic moment shared, and a ceremonial Black and Indigenous ritual."[45] As such, we must attend to the ways language, or at least the language we have now, fails to account for that which is beyond it, that which is felt in the body, including when "Black and Indigenous life caress each other."[46]

Attending to the haptic is essential when thinking about print culture and the nineteenth century. What stories were not captured (I use this word intentionally) or preserved in written language? *Reading Territory* focuses on written, material text to insist that even within the most limited archive, we see these stories emerge. It includes some examples, both historical and imagined, of Black and Native ritual. Often articulated through a shared Christian faith, through familial and kinship networks, or through articulations of Black and Native freedom, Indigenous and Black thinkers call out this "edgeless violence" and seek out one another. Here, I think of the correspondence between Samson Occom and Phillis Wheatley (Peters). Other than Wheatley's letter to Occom published in the *Connecticut Gazette; and the Universal Intelligencer* in 1774, the physical record is scant. Scholars speculate that the two developed a friendship, despite their age difference and despite Occom's relationship with Phillis's enslaver Susanna Wheatley, and grapple to imagine what they may have spoken about with each other. The gaps and fissures these missing letters create hold intimate exchanges omitted from us, the future readers. They deal with the latent power produced by the act of imagining what we might find nestled in those archival cracks. Without the letters as clues, what speculative histories are invited in?[47] In her poetry collection *The Age of Phillis*, Honorée Fanonne Jeffers constructs two "lost letters" between Occom and Susanna Wheatley, but in these, Jeffers does not disclose the conversations between Occom and Phillis Wheatley. Even in an act of imaginative speculation, they are shielded from the page. Jeffers's decision gestures toward the power of print to imagine otherwise, but also the necessary caution required in acknowledging its limitations.[48]

There are many more points of connection beyond the written word, kept safe through oral storytelling, song, recipes, familial and intimate relationships, humor, spiritual and medicinal practices, and other intentional efforts to avoid surveillance, but how do we attend to those in a discipline where citation necessitates proof or evidence? How do we hold space for literary studies work that thinks beyond the page and reads its absence not as a silence but as a story that needs to be held differently?[49] If we believe that our ancestors knew the power of Black and Native world-building and the intersections of their survival, then they undoubtedly knew the necessity of keeping stories safe. For as Afro-Indigenous activist and writer Amber Starks (Muscogee Nation) reminds us, "Black liberation and Indigenous sovereignty aren't mutually exclusive movements of resistance. They are instead, complementary refusals authored by Black and Native peoples which seek to define, interrogate, and dismantle our individual and intersectional oppression."[50]

I strategically include the "actualized" moments of collaboration in conjunction with the aspirational solidarities of writers and communities that hoped for Afro-Native alliances and understood their potential, even when those imaginings did not achieve their idealistic ends. Such aspirations serve as a reminder of the enduring belief that in Afro-Native alliance slumbers a radical potential to upend the colonial white supremacist state. This is one of the reasons Seminole-Maroon combat with the U.S. military in the mid-nineteenth century was framed by white politicians and Floridian settlers as such a pressing threat to the United States that troops and revenue were consistently funneled into Florida; their resistance was as much an ideological problem as it was a military one. Moreover, one of the most telling observations about the statehood and states' rights moments taken up in *Reading Territory* is that all of them reveal this racial logic at play and the threat posed to the U.S. settler nation when Blackness and Indigeneity collide and collude.

I have no illusion that *Reading Territory* will shore up these divides, but to continually highlight their existence and insist on challenging them seems a necessary step in bearing witness to the traumas of enslavement, colonization, and oppression that continue to mark the landscape of the so-called New World and move toward a decolonial something else. I therefore embrace how *Reading Territory* will fail to make good on these promises in an effort to participate in an imperfect dialogue that aims for the aspirational, the radical potential of listening to the discord in all its archival, embodied, and future complexity. Throughout this book, I highlight communities contending with these same problems of discord and their attempts to work through them, often aspirationally and imperfectly.

I do so also with an understanding of how my own story is complicit in these histories. According to family lore, my great-grandfather (believed to be non-Native and white) was one of the many terrorists who participated in the Tulsa Race Massacre of 1921, in which white Tulsans and their allies murdered Black Tulsans and attempted to destroy the Black neighborhood of Greenwood, also known at the time as "Black Wall Street."[51] It is an event that white Tulsans publicly silenced for almost a century and for which there has still been minimal justice. I wrote most of this book in the beautiful homelands of the Kumeyaay people, and one of the only things I knew about San Diego when moving here was that this same great-grandfather killed himself in this city. Allegedly, he suffered from PTSD following World War I, worked a number of itinerant jobs, and struggled with severe alcoholism. It is unclear if his death was accidental, but I wonder if he also could not escape the horrifying violence he committed against Black Tulsans twenty years before. While he was still a boy, my great-grandmother put my grandfather on a train by himself from Tulsa to San Diego to identify his biological father's body, a father whose surname he did not wear but whose legacy we continue to carry. My grandfather would travel to the Pacific again when he enlisted in the Marines at the age of sixteen; enlistment brought him a new legal last name and a new relationship to global projects of empire. During World War II, he would fight in Okinawa, another space of colonial conquest and occupation.

I do not share all of this to center my story, but rather as an attempt to be as honest as possible about the limitations of the story I tell. I do not mourn my great-grandfather, but I also cannot forget him; his legacy is part of my responsibilities. It is necessary for me to be clear that my whiteness allows me mobility and belonging in both the United States and Cherokee Nation that is historically predicated on Black exclusion. Omitting this fact would counter the sentiments of this project and contribute to the enduring silences surrounding anti-Black violence in the communities I write about. I identify as a white Cherokee person to call attention to the contradictory ways in which Indigeneity and race sit in tension in the United States. By identifying as white, I am not denouncing my Cherokee citizenship but rather performing an act of community with my Afro-Cherokee kin. I do so also to speak back to white supremacist logic that attempts to flatten race and Indigeneity by rewarding whiteness and white presentation (especially in the academy) while furthering anti-Blackness and making Nativeness something that is paradoxically both phenotypically legible and invisible (what does an Indian look like?). My position is in no way a commentary on or suggestion for how other scholars should situate themselves and their own work. I can only be as clear as possible about my own responsibilities, which depend on the specificity of who I am, where I am from, and when I am from—my relationality to all my human and other-than-human family existing now and otherwise. My hope in this book is to open up ways to think through and in space together, uncomfortably or painfully, when necessary, in an effort to make space for all of us in an aspirational pursuit of other worlds and lifeways beyond the state.

Territorial Hermeneutics

While this book works to denaturalize the state, it also aims to imagine other alterities by engaging the concept of territory as heuristic and hermeneutic. As I define it here, territory encourages movement and adaptability, rather than the settler definition of territory as a singular sovereign's land (or water) base. My invocation of the term is risky, though, given how colonizing powers, especially the United States and Europe, have monopolized its use. Nonetheless, the concept of territory as a spatial imaginary is not something inherent or exclusive to U.S. settler colonial mappings. Indigenous and Black understandings of territoriality shaped—and continue to shape—perceptions of space and power both within and beyond Indigenous and Black communities. Following a Westphalian model, U.S.-based definitions of territory affirm fixed borders denoted by possession, distinction, and difference rather than overlap or collaboration. Such a notion of territory is not just about securing borders of sovereign control, but also about securing sovereignty over the concept itself.[52] How to define "territory" in relation to the United States proper was roughly laid out in the U.S. Constitution and slightly more codified through U.S. Supreme Court cases and congressional debates, but it continues to be a nebulous, obtuse mapping of U.S. jurisdiction. Territory has its own animate and animating qualities—it is "diffuse" and adaptive; it is not just a signifier for property, it is as metaphysical as it is material.[53] Territory, however, can also be a way to both make visible borders and understand overlapping routes, movements, and migration patterns, be they discursive or material.

My efforts to acknowledge how Western empires attempted to colonize "territory" *and* to imagine spatial possibilities that emerge beyond the colonial, propertied definition of the term mean that there is slippage in how I use the word. Sometimes, I use it in the Westphalian sense to denote the physical holdings of a particular sovereign that are fixed and nonoverlapping, including U.S. legal definitions of territory, such as organized and unorganized territory (organized territory being territory with a governor, legislature, etc.) and incorporated and unincorporated territory (unlike federated states, which are all incorporated, unincorporated territories do not have the full constitutional rights). At other times, I use "territory" to signal Black and Native spatialities that are invariably informed by the previous two definitions, given hundreds of years of colonial occupation, but diametrically opposed to racial-colonial territoriality. Black and Indigenous thinkers and communities across North America have taken up "territory" as a way to describe what has always been and is still yet to be.[54] There is risk in using "territory" as a term. However, there are innumerable ways Black and Indigenous freedom struggles have taken concepts meant to harm and exclude and fashioned them differently and otherwise in ways that extend, complicate, and distract meaning as a means of world-building outside the grips of white colonial violence. For example, terms like "freedom," "liberation," "self-determination," and "sovereignty" have the potential to exceed colonial intent. Sylvia Wynter explains that Black territoriality is nearly impossible to imagine under the current global regime: "This is *the* dilemma, all this as a territory or issue that cannot be conceptualized to exist within the terms of the *vrai* or 'regime of truth' of our present order of knowledge." She defines Black freedom struggles (and other struggles of the oppressed) as "a hitherto unknown territory" that bursts through the current regime in fleeting moments recognizable in periods of dissent, including revolutionary political struggles of the late twentieth century.[55]

Similarly, in her essay "Territory as Analytic," Joanne Barker argues that territory as "an analytic or mode of analysis" nourishes a means of thinking against the state that centers Indigenous understandings of land as "a mode of relationality and related set of ethics and protocols for living social responsibilities and governance defined within discrete Indigenous epistemologies."[56] In order to do the work of reading beyond circumscribed boundaries, especially those of the state, I build on Wynter's and Barker's respective theorizations of territory and propose a territorial hermeneutics as reading practice, as a heuristic for engaging nineteenth-century extralegal narratives of relationality. Throughout the nineteenth century, the United States attempted to colonize the concept of territory in an effort to eradicate other forms of relationality. Turning to nineteenth-century cultural production by Black, Indigenous, and settler writers decenters legal narratives and brings into focus the ways the discursive, the imagined, and the literary are as central to placemaking as a legal and political doctrine, both in affirming U.S. conventions of belonging and in refusing them. If we are willing to take Mishuana Goeman's (Tonawanda Band of Seneca) call to "see *through* the concept of territory and understand the processes and concept as a social product," then we might be able to understand better how territory both as a proper noun and as ideology informed nineteenth-century state formation, the global reach of the settler nation-state, and Black and Indigenous ways of being that disrupt the U.S. colonial map.[57]

Understandings of territory in the context of Indigenous peoples' experiences of colonialism are invariably informed to some extent by Western notions of territory as the property of sovereign states—my own nation is currently structured to invoke nation-state legibility. However, Cherokees and other Indigenous peoples have always had ways of understanding territory and place beyond colonial geographies. This is why Indigenous scholars like Glen Sean Coulthard, J. Kēhaulani Kauanui, Audra Simpson, and Leanne Betasamosake Simpson argue against (nation-)state recognition as a viable form of Indigenous autonomy.[58] Black studies scholars like Tiffany Lethabo King, Katherine McKittrick, Fred Moten, and Christina Sharpe have all argued for the necessity of Black spatialities beyond the state as well, invoked through their respective theorizations of the shoal, demonic grounds, fugitivity, and the wake. All four emphasize the importance of the temporary, the fleeting, and the fluid in thinking about the radical geographies of Black space beyond the regime of patriarchal white supremacy. In her analysis of Octavia Butler's *Kindred*, McKittrick insists that "being materially situated *in place* is an inconclusive process."[59] To be in place is to acknowledge a field of relations that may shift and change. Thinking territorially allows us to more intentionally be in place together, especially with our more-than-human kin, while attending to a constellation of territorialities that are symbiotic, adaptable, and sustainable.

Physical boundaries or the material does not limit territory as an ideological framework. Rather, it functions as an assemblage of land, politics, economics, spirituality, kinship, culture, aesthetics, and the imaginary. Territory includes an assertion of spatial jurisdiction but is not limited by such. It is simultaneously spatial, ontological, and ideological.[60] Territory can be less geographically and legally codified, exposing the inability of settler colonialism to ever fully contain or control space, by which I mean its inhabitants, the land, and the stories embedded within the land; it is relational and affective. It does not inherently denote fixed borders but instead invites overlapping, cohabitative topographies and multiscalar engagements. It is not static. Territory can describe movement as much as it can fixity. It is a way to understand both human and other-than-human relations to space and describe the migration patterns of birds or the geographic reach of a species of tree or plant. Pacific gray whales, chinook salmon, and ruby-throated hummingbirds all travel great distances to make kin. Aspen trees are collectively one organism. These other-than-human relations show us how to share and honor space and movement. Territoriality pivots on a sense of relationality and interrelationality that is not necessarily propertied, even when connected to the land.

It also serves as a counterpoint to Removal. Territory not only provides a way to describe lands shared by multiple nations or communities as sacred space or for hunting, trade, or diplomacy. It also provides a way to think about relationships to land that are not formally acknowledged by the settler colonial government, as well as historical and autochthonous land-based relationships. By thinking "territorially," we can begin to understand the world we move through differently and move through the world differently together.[61]

Indigenous landholdings and self-determination in the face of continued colonialism are critical, but decolonization is not possible without Black freedom. Territory understood broadly serves as a way to insist on the necessity of including Black geographies in land-back movements across Turtle Island. Amber Starks reminds us that "white supremacy relies heavily upon us internalizing the myth that Blackness and indigeneity are incompatible. It depends upon us preserving the notion that Black-Native relationality is unnatural. And it thrives off us concluding that Afro Indigenous identities are inauthentic."[62] Given the ways Indigenous and Black collectivity challenges the "naturalness" of the white supremacist state, it is necessary in the work of letting go of the state to shift the ground toward Black and Native territorialities. By this, I mean both a willingness to let go of attachments to the (nation-)state and a commitment to an overlapping and complementary notion of territory that honors Indigenous peoples' roles as caretakers of the land and that sees Black epistemologies and geographies as place-based and necessary.

Balance is core to Cherokee and other Southeastern cosmologies. As Daniel Heath Justice (Cherokee Nation) explains, "If anything can be said to be a feature of contemporary and past Cherokee traditions, it is the quest for balance in all things."[63] Balance necessitates constant effort, adaptability, and renegotiation. In order to begin to think beyond the state in decolonial ways, I want to suggest the necessity of balance across the legacies of Black and Native experience in the Americas. Hence, my coupling of Indigenous and Black freedom in the book's subtitle. To find the balance that might heal and recenter this world, we must take both into account. It would mean acknowledging the cosmologies that have shaped this land since time immemorial and also recognizing the centrality of Black spatialities to the healing work that needs to be done, as well as the Indigenous African and Black place-based practices that found home in the Americas because of enslavement and forced Removal from Africa. Moreover, it reminds us to foreground Afro-Native territorialities and respect the powerful knowledge Afro-Native peoples carry with them that is critical to living and thriving beyond the state.

Chapters

There are many ways one could organize a study of nineteenth-century state formation, both spatially and temporally, but, as stated earlier, *Reading Territory* focuses on the territorialities of Southeastern peoples. By this, I mean Indigenous peoples with age-old connections to the region of land now occupied by the U.S. South. In particular, I focus on the Five Tribes, the Cherokee, Chickasaw, Choctaw, Muscogee (Creek), and Seminole people, which I acknowledge flattens and simplifies Southeastern peoples' experiences, as it leaves out a countless number of other Indigenous peoples and histories. While the book does follow a loose timeline, it is not truly linear. This is an intentional choice so as not to reinforce the problematic teleological tropes of Removal and westward expansion. As such, my book speaks to the work of Native South studies, especially the understanding that "South" is never a fixed region but rather a relational orientation and cultural ideology. While a project with a different geographical orientation could illuminate alternative aspects of territory and state formation, as there is much yet to learn at the interstices of nineteenth-century statehood, Indigeneity, Blackness, race, and territory, attention to the Southeast allows us to see incontestably the coconstitutive ways enslavement and Indigenous dispossession shaped states' rights. Chapters 1–4 take up the following configurations of Black and Native freedom and the state, respectively: Native contestation with the state; Afro-Native freedom outside the state; the false promise of Black freedom via statehood; and Black and Native freedom as statehood.

Chapter 1 begins with the midcentury territorial disputes between the Cherokee Nation and Georgia that pressed the question of whether states could directly challenge Indigenous sovereignty. Unlike previous scholars, I situate the Cherokee national newspaper, the *Cherokee Phoenix*, in conversation with Georgia newspapers and regional print circulation, not just those of a U.S. national network, with an emphasis on the relationship between the form of the newspaper and its emancipatory potential for Native and Black editors. Read this way, we can better understand how (and why) the Cherokee Nation used the form of the newspaper to assert its national sovereignty and combat Removal. Additionally, I explore how Georgia print reflected organizing structures of race, enslavement, and colonialism that would cohere the states' rights discourse Southern states used a few decades later to secede from the Union. Paying attention to the circulation (or noncirculation) of coverage of the Supreme Court case *Cherokee Nation v. Georgia* (1831) and David Walker's *Appeal* (1829) in these newspapers reveals how states' rights were solidified in the 1830s in relation to *both* Indigenous dispossession and enslavement.

Chapter 2 shifts to a study of combat and statehood in early nineteenth-century Florida, focusing on the years between the creation of Florida Territory (1821) and the end of the Second U.S.-Seminole War (1835–42). The U.S.-Seminole wars offer a counternarrative to the one typically told about southeastern Removal because they were official military campaigns. However, like other Removal efforts, they failed to fully achieve their objective—total elimination of Florida's Indigenous population. Because of the Seminole, Black Seminole, and Maroon alliances present in Florida, it represented a space of Afro-Native freedom beyond the United States that challenged prevailing notions of race and Manifest Destiny and fueled U.S. desires to "conquer" Florida. U.S. military failures raised existential questions about the dominance of white supremacy. I analyze print and visual popular culture surrounding the United States' acquisition of the Floridas and unpack how they mitigated and exacerbated attempts to contain the "swampiness" of the conflict in Florida. I also think through the limitations of print to account for Indigenous and Black freedom beyond the state and the ethical obligations of literary studies to deal with absence as a kind of radical presence that does not necessarily need to be filled.

Chapter 3 turns to the 1850s campaigns for Kansas's and Cuba's statehood, unpacking some of the ways statehood posited Black freedom as a rationale for state-making. In particular, I look at the writings of Martin Delany, John Brougham's play *el Filibustero!*, and John Brown's Black statehood proposal. Kansas, formerly part of Indian Territory, became a state. Yet the United States maintained a more unusual relationship to Cuba, "read" by the U.S. government and the press as a less amendable geopolitical space for the U.S. imperial project. As I discuss at some length in earlier chapters, statehood and states' rights were key colonial tactics for systematically delegitimizing and further discrediting Indigenous a priori land rights, and "reading" Kansas and Cuba together brings these truths to the fore. In the case of Kansas, popular sovereignty was staged as a fight over Black freedom, but in the end, statehood consolidated white male possessive power.

Chapter 4 turns to the 1905 State of Sequoyah movement, organized by leaders of the Five Tribes to create a Native-run state. This movement occurred only a few years after local Black leaders organized for the creation of a "Black state" from the territory. I use Sequoyah to anchor my discussion of a thriving and complex Indian Territory print culture that included official tribal organs and Black-run papers. At the end of the century, when Black and

Native political leaders lobbied for statehood to protect their communities, they defined their inclusion in U.S. statecraft in direct opposition to one another. The failures of *both* the Black and Native state campaigns reveal the limitations of state inclusion for Black and Native people and how white supremacy necessitated that both communities see their only means of survival as subjugation or Removal of the other. The pages of a thriving Indian Territory print culture stage all of these debates, and careful attention to these periodicals demonstrates how Native and Black editors used the orderliness of the newspaper form to argue for the stability and self-determination of their respective communities. While the State of Sequoyah movement was unsuccessful, the era's Black and Native print culture staged robust conversations about Black and Native land-based sovereignty.

The book's conclusion returns us to the *McGirt v. Oklahoma* decision of 2020. The U.S. federal government and the State of Oklahoma have emphasized that the decision primarily applies to criminal jurisdiction, policing and surveillance, and little else. By understanding *McGirt* in conversation with two of the most popular TV shows of 2019 and 2020, *Watchmen* (2019) and *Live PD* (2016–), we can think through the ways Indian Territory, especially Tulsa, figures in a larger twenty-first-century cultural imaginary that invokes long-standing discourses of U.S. intervention into tribal affairs, as well as the criminalization of Blackness and Indigeneity.

Indian Territory

Ralph Ellison observed that "the territory is an ideal place—ever to be sought, ever to be missed, but always there."[64] Understood in such a way, territoriality bends colonial conventions of time and space. It is both past and future. It is remembered and reproduced through story, through memory, and through possibility, and it cannot be delineated. It is significant that in the foregoing quote, Ellison is undoubtedly referencing the Indian Territory of his youth. All colonized continental lands occupied by the United States are Indian territory, and that specific understanding of territory—as *necessarily* Indian Territory—continued to inform U.S. imperial projects beyond the continent. Indian Territory is especially vital to this project.[65] Throughout the nineteenth century, Indian Territory, the land currently occupied by the state of Oklahoma, was a space of Removal and possibility for Indigenous and Black peoples.

In the nineteenth century, "Indian Territory" became the standard geopolitical marker used by the U.S. government to denote any region inhabited by

Indigenous peoples. Beginning with Thomas Jefferson's evocation of an "Indian colonization zone," Indian Territory was imagined as a liminal space both within and beyond the reach of U.S. federal control—a murky signifier of otherness.[66] What I find more compelling is what Indian Territory meant for Black and Native people. There, we see woven together the various threads of Black and Native Removal histories, as well as aspirational intentions for a different world. At the same, it was a space of oppression, discord, and violence, including Indigenous-practiced chattel slavery; of enslaved uprisings like the 1842 uprising in the Cherokee Nation; of civil wars; of allotment; of the murder of Native women and children for their land; of the lynching and racial segregation of Black people; of the illegal overthrow of reservations and the Tulsa Race Massacre.

It was a place of reparations where Cherokee Freedpeople would build some of the wealthiest Black communities in North America, including Greenwood in Tulsa. It was a place of Black towns made possible by the U.S. theft of Native land, but nonetheless spaces of some refuge for Black community. It was also a place with a thriving print culture where, on the pages of newspapers and magazines, Black and Native editors, journalists, artists, and community members grappled with many of the questions taken up in this book, with a keen interest in how they might work toward Native and Black futurity. At the turn of the twentieth century, there were clear divisions between many Native and Black male leaders in Indian Territory that would eventually benefit white men after Oklahoma statehood. Here, my turn to Indian Territory is speculative in its query of what might grow from these lessons of the past and how we might unlearn and uninhabit harmful patriarchal approaches and instead nourish Black and Native femme (Two-Spirit or queer) notions of territoriality, care, and healing that turn away from state structures of sovereignty and toward one another. The Indian Territory I imagine here has never been actualized. It gestures toward the possibility of Indigenous and Black freedom that is only possible beyond all forms of the state. The cover image for this book, Yatika Starr Fields' (Osage-Cherokee-Muscogee) painting *Osage shield, reclamation* (2022), gestures toward this kind of Indian Territory. As he explains in his artist's statement, Fields takes back Indigenous symbols used by the state of Oklahoma on the official state flag. The painting is a re-Indigenization of sorts. It defamiliarizes a pervasive symbol of state power by replacing the static, two-dimensional composition of the flag with vibrance, movement, and palpable energy. It is a reminder of what these important symbols (shield, pipe, and olive branch) can and should invoke.

CHAPTER ONE

The Boundary Line

Georgia State Route 225 links several historic Cherokee sites, including New Echota, the former capital of the Cherokee Nation, and the Vann House plantation, home of one of the most prominent Cherokee families before Removal. This part of SR 225, called the Chieftains Trail, was designated a State Historic Trail in 1988 by the Georgia General Assembly. It stretches over some of the routes taken by Cherokees during the Trail of Tears, and the aluminum signs that mark its path proudly declare as much. Explore Georgia, the official website of the Georgia Department of Economic Development, describes the trail as a "200-mile driving tour" through northwest Georgia that marks "our extensive Native American history."[1] The use of the plural possessive "our," the lack of an apostrophe in "Chieftains," and the emphasis on "history" in Explore Georgia's description lay bare the possessive logic of settler belonging: present-day Georgians have inherited a now-extinct Cherokee past.[2] Collectively, the tour emphasizes Removal as a totalizing and successful (albeit lamentable) erasure of Cherokee people and Cherokee territory from the region.[3] The Vann House, a symbol of the Cherokee Nation's complicity in Southern legacies of enslavement, is one of the most popular sites on the trail. Historian Tiya Miles convincingly suggests this is to some extent because it "is a distinctive place for the projection of southern visions of a landed aristocracy that nobly defended states' rights."[4] Through such logic, there is a misdirection of signifiers that brings Indigeneity to the fore only when it serves to anchor white supremacist belonging and alleviate white guilt through a shared complicity in enslavement and anti-Blackness. As a driving tour, the trail explicitly emphasizes movement rather than situatedness. Instead of highlighting the routes *between* Cherokee townships, communities, and sacred sites that wove together Cherokee space before the 1830s, the signage emphasizes movement *away* from the region. There are, for example, no obvious markers directing one just a couple of hours north by car to the Qualla Boundary, present-day home of the Eastern Band of Cherokee Indians.[5]

A collection of different federal and state agencies, as well as private clubs and community organizations, manages placards at historic sites along the trail. This jurisdictional assemblage highlights the jumbled scales of state power attempting to oversee and manage Indigeneity in Georgia specifically and across the United States more broadly. The cluster of entities that forms the state (by which I mean both the state of Georgia and the U.S. nation-state) controls the narrative told at the museums and on the historical markers across the trail, as well as how much funding is allocated to the sites and how involved the three federally recognized Cherokee nations can be in helping to craft the "official" story told. It is equally important to note that the trail is a state road, not part of the national highway system; its very existence is a marker of state power. I draw attention to this highway not because there is anything unique about it—one finds similar markers of Removal snaking throughout the Southeast—but to emphasize that the road's signage and the way it guides a driver (or passenger) through space crafts a particular story about Removal, and Georgia, through visual and discursive cues. Text, on highways signs, trail maps, and plaques, coalesces to produce a particular story of place.

Georgia state narratives have attempted to absorb Removal into a mythos that foregrounds state autonomy. While I am specifically referencing Indian Removal and the Trail of Tears here, I am also thinking more broadly about Removal as the forced mobility and exclusion of Black and Indigenous people from the U.S. state, which I define in detail in this book's introduction.[6] Removal becomes something that *belongs* to the state of Georgia, and it becomes an essential chapter in the story the state tells about itself. In this narrative, Georgia has a Native past that "indigenizes" the state of Georgia through an erasure of Indigenous people, making Georgians the necessary inhabitants.[7] It must also be noted that many of the state politicians who endorsed Trail of Tears commemorative projects in the 1960s were also the same politicians simultaneously fighting to maintain Jim Crow under the banner of states' rights.[8]

One can undoubtedly engage the official state narrative critically through a different territorial reading praxis, but I want to emphasize how text and mapping do a great deal to bolster state mythology. Their efficacy is indebted to an extensive history of textual production and sovereignty that have been critical to the *longue durée* of Cherokee-Georgia disputes. Turning to the Cherokee and Georgia print records of the 1820s–30s helps us better contextualize the visual and discursive registers we find along the Chieftains Trail, as well as how states' rights discourse, newspapers, and land surveys all encode racialization and Indigenous dispossession.

In this chapter, I foreground a study of Cherokee versus Georgia that is different from the infamous *Cherokee Nation v. Georgia* (1831) case, in which the court ruled that only the federal government can officially negotiate with

Native nations. I focus on print networks rather than U.S. Supreme Court cases to illuminate two key points. First, the development of Georgia's states' rights rhetoric established a template for *all* future states' rights claims that followed, one dependent on an interconnectedness of anti-Black violence and Indigenous genocide. Second, I argue that the very *forms* of print reinforced racialization and racial difference, and that such circumscription posed complex challenges for Native and Black editors and printers invested in the emancipatory possibilities of sovereign printscapes—namely, the ways print production and circulation might assert Native and Black politico-cultural spatialities.

The Cherokee Nation developed a relationship to print culture—newspapers and periodicals—that became a cornerstone of Cherokee intellectual and cultural life across the Cherokee diaspora. The *Cherokee Phoenix*, the official newspaper of the Cherokee Nation, asserted Cherokee nationalism and autonomy through the material circulation of the paper itself, in addition to the information it circulated. However, the *Phoenix*'s participation (and circulation) in Southern and U.S. print networks posed some problems in asserting Cherokee sovereignty. The paper's engagement in these networks and its similarities to the form and structure of the conventional white, middle-class newspaper threatened to muddy the distinction between the Cherokee Nation and the United States because the paper literally read along the same lines as most U.S. papers.[9]

This chapter focuses on the visual and textual analysis of two mediums, the newspaper and the survey, to better understand this quandary. The material and aesthetic representation of colonization are as crucial as the ideology that undergirds it. Through newspapers, maps, and other forms of visual and print culture, colonial expansion is made accessible to its subjects in ways that are not otherwise possible because of the geographic expanse of U.S. occupation—a map or a newspaper enables one to envision a whole in otherwise difficult ways. I focus first on how the form of the newspaper influenced Cherokees' ability to assert a *sovereign printscape* to combat Removal and develop an influential discourse of states' rights. Next, I show how Georgia newspapers' (non)citation of the *Phoenix* and what I term the "insurgent circulation practices" of David Walker's *Appeal* reveal the racializing structures embedded in the form and circulation of Georgia print culture. Finally, I turn to the way printed land lotteries operated as weapons of Removal. White, affluent Georgians, including Georgia governor Wilson Lumpkin, weaponized the *colonizing printscapes* of newspapers and lotteries to justify Removal. Reading newspapers and printed land lotteries in conversation exposes how these two technologies of power reinforced each other by promoting a shared reading praxis of race and place, not unlike the signage and roadways of the Chieftains Trail. The form and layout of newspapers affirmed colonial spatial logics demarcated in land surveys, while printed land surveys narrated state belonging through a U.S.-centric reading of territory. I argue that, while the newspaper proved a compelling tool for Black and Indigenous freedom struggles, the form of the mid-nineteenth-century newspaper—the newspaper as a form of print but also the formatting of the pages themselves—sometimes posed complex political and material challenges as well. Recognizing this complicates dominant assumptions about print culture's emancipatory potential for antiracist and anticolonial resistance.

The *Phoenix* and Regional Print

The *Phoenix*'s significance as the first Native American newspaper published in both a Native language and English by a Native nation has, since the inaugural issue, bestowed it with a sense of novelty, exceptionalism, and overdetermination. In response, a robust body of scholarship has emerged that analyzes how Cherokees used the *Phoenix* to assert their status as a nation by educating a far-reaching readership in their fight to protect their homelands, but there has been far less attention to how the *Phoenix* engaged U.S. Southern print culture. This gap is surprising given how much citation there is of Georgia newspapers in the *Phoenix* and vice versa. More importantly, though, a study of the *Phoenix* that engages Southern print culture reveals how print conventions reinscribed Indigenous dispossession and enslavement in both the content and the formal organization of the paper. In this, we can see how print, especially text and maps, was used to assert states' rights, enslavement, and colonization, as well as how Indigenous and Black writers and editors attempted to disrupt these logics through their own publication and circulation practices.

One reason for the dearth of regional analysis may be the assumption that the U.S. South was a far less literate, a far less print-friendly, space than other regional networks in the nineteenth century, leaving a spottier and more fragmented materialist shadow than, say, "Northern" spaces. While there is no question that Northern cities housed the industrial needs of print, there is growing evidence that the nineteenth-century South was far more literate and print friendly than previously assumed.[10] Acknowledging a more textured Southern print culture helps us better understand why the Cherokee Nation chose to publish a national newspaper as part of a broader campaign against the genocidal project of forced Removal and why white Southern politicians passed laws to prohibit Black literacy, all of which occurred in the same historical moment and on the same fields of print.

As a print archive, the *Phoenix* reveals the complex geopolitical scales at play in asserting Cherokee sovereignty and self-governance but also in white Georgians' insistence on the state of Georgia's right to Cherokee lands. Understanding how the *Phoenix* and Georgia journalism staged debates about colonization, enslavement, and Indian Removal helps us better glean the narrative of states' rights that white male newspaper editors and politicians developed in the 1820s–30s, a unified narrative dependent on anti-Indianness and anti-Blackness to formulate an understanding of state sovereignty. This states' rights discourse was developed in direct contrast to Cherokee assertions of nationhood. It imagined Georgia's "rights" as the rights to possession via enslavement, genocide, and economic self-determination. Print played a critical role in this formulation by making states' rights visually legible. Even the layout of the conventional regional U.S. paper, with its division of sections, pages, and columns, materially and discursively lays bare the ways Indigeneity and Blackness were often spatially rendered as distinct from each other. Black and Indigenous people were situated outside the modern subjectivity organized by a newspaper—they were content, not readers. In non-Native papers, Indian affairs often appeared in local or national news columns. Advertisements that advocated the seizure of self-emancipated people or the sale of enslaved people situated Black life as surveillable property.[11]

The possibility of a Black or Native reading subject posed an enormous threat to this racist social order, as evidenced so powerfully by the panic Walker's *Appeal* incited in the same Georgia newspaper editors and politicians who wrote scathingly about the *Phoenix* and Cherokee people. When the militia invaded Cherokee territory to forcibly Remove Cherokees from their territory and destroy their homes during the 1835 raid of New Echota, the Georgia Guard intentionally dismantled the *Phoenix* printing press; it was an act of violence that reaffirmed the symbolic import of print for Cherokees and Georgians alike. Moreover, paranoia that Walker's *Appeal* might incite enslaved people to rise up was used as a rationale by state politicians to justify draconian censorship policies in Georgia that were then implemented by other Southern states.

While early nineteenth-century U.S. newspapers were often organized according to white supremacist logics of space, time, and personhood, Black and Native community leaders nonetheless turned to the form of the newspaper to advocate for and educate their communities. Despite clear limitations, editors understood the newspaper's influence in shaping macro structures of race, freedom, and sovereignty. The initial issues of *Freedom's Journal* and the *Phoenix*, the first newspapers in the United States owned and operated by African Americans and Native Americans, respectively, were published less than a year apart and collectively demonstrated a keen awareness of the power of print.[12] They addressed complex and expansive reading publics while foregrounding in-group readers through their content and circulation. At the same time, they made political statements simply by existing. Both papers invoked the prevailing (liberal bourgeois) belief that the act of reading (and producing) a newspaper demonstrated one's liberal subjectivity in two ways: a reading person was someone capable of civic and cultural engagement, and the reading of the newspaper provided one with the necessary tools to contribute to public life.

However, these papers did not simply replicate white newspapers. Of the readership for *Freedom's Journal*, Elizabeth McHenry argues, "the 'imagined community' was racially bounded and its sovereignty was perceived as free from the control of whites."[13] Independence from white control was also paramount for the *Phoenix*. From the *Phoenix*'s inception, rumors spread that Samuel Worcester and other white missionaries ran the paper, a rumor the paper's editor Elias Boudinot (Buck Watie) repeatedly denounced in its pages. The editors of both papers refashioned the typical paper's format, layout, style, and content in ways that better fit their specific goals. These publications also served a distinctly nationalist purpose for Cherokee and Black readers and imagined themselves as part of broader Indigenous and African diasporas (the *Phoenix* would add *Indian Advocate* to its title in 1829, and *Freedom's Journal* imagined itself as part of a transnational, if not global, Black world).[14]

Despite the complexities the newspaper-as-form posed for circulating and articulating Black and Cherokee self-determination, it continued to be a key venue for staging political struggle throughout the rest of the century. Abolitionist and antiracist activists, including Frederick Douglass, Martin Delany, James McCune Smith, Mary Ann Shadd Cary, Zitkala-Ša (Gertrude Simmons Bonin), Susette La Flesche (Tibbles) (Inshata Theumba), and Ida B. Wells-Barnett (to name just a few), famously utilized the periodical press for political organizing. The newspaper also continued to be a significant vehicle for Native and Black political mobilization in Indian Territory, which bore a thriving territorial print culture at the end of the nineteenth century that was unquestionably influenced by the *Phoenix*'s legacy.[15]

As I stated earlier, there is scant *Phoenix* scholarship that focuses on the paper's local networks. However, when one turns to contemporaneous newspapers in Georgia, there are clear citational debates and reprintings from the paper. Despite dominant assumptions about Southern literacy and print culture, there were no fewer than a dozen Georgia papers circulating in the same years as the *Phoenix*, printing and reprinting articles about the Cherokee-Georgia debates.[16] Adding to this absence is a tactic I describe as "noncitation," meaning white Georgia editors' decisions intentionally *not* to cite the *Phoenix*. In fact, in the February 21, 1829, issue, Boudinot, then editor, explained that the price of the paper was determined according to the going regional rate: "In order that our paper may have an extensive circulation in this Nation and out of it, we have fixed upon the most liberal terms possible; such, in our opinion, as will render it as cheap as most of the Southern papers."[17] The *Phoenix* did not enter a print vacuum: it boldly entered a thriving journalistic conversation about the future of so-called Georgia.

Constituting the Nation

To better account for the Cherokee world that birthed the *Phoenix*, it is necessary to have some context for U.S.-Cherokee relations in the decades leading up to 1828, when the paper published its first issue. Cherokees had begun a process of national consolidation in the eighteenth century, following the midcentury Anglo-Cherokee War and the U.S. Revolutionary War, both of which resulted in severe causalities and the destruction of numerous Cherokee communities, as well as increased white squatter intrusion on Cherokee land. Fears of unending U.S. encroachment were amplified by regular demands from U.S. agents (including Wilson Lumpkin, discussed later in this chapter) to renegotiate the boundary line between Cherokee and U.S. territory, as white settlers aggressively pushed for more land.[18] No matter where the boundary line stood, white intruders continued to ignore tribal sovereignty and invade Cherokee territory.[19]

By the early years of the nineteenth century, Cherokees became increasingly convinced that the United States would attempt to Remove them from their ancestral homelands forcibly.[20] The decision by some Cherokees to move westward to Arkansas Territory with the promise of more land and freedom from white harassment had made some Cherokee leaders concerned that the U.S. federal government would try to entice all Cherokees to do the same. Principal Chief John Ross and other Cherokee elites felt that Cherokees were already as civilized as citizens of the United States proper, and thus not in need of improvement through displacement.[21] Ross and others redeployed the United States' "civilizing" approach to the Cherokees by restructuring the Nation in ways that emulated a modern nation to strengthen Cherokee autonomy and make it far more difficult for the United States to discredit Cherokee sovereignty and Remove them.

As a tactical response, the Cherokee National Council passed legislation in 1817 stating that only the council could cede Cherokee lands; any Cherokee individuals who attempted to do so would receive severe punishment.[22] This legislation was made possible because of the consolidation of a centralized national government. Since the mid-eighteenth century, Cherokees had begun a process of shifting from a township structure, in which towns functioned as autonomous communities that were part of a larger confederation, to a more centralized nation with a principal chief, a legislative branch, and a judicial system with a police force.[23] While centralization helped fuel cohesion across Cherokee communities in some ways, it came at a profound cost. Before national consolidation, towns were matrilineally organized, and Cherokee women held positions of political and diplomatic power. As township autonomy eroded and a smaller, predominantly male-run government gained authority, women's official roles in Cherokee politics and society dramatically diminished.[24] By the start of the nineteenth century, male elites represented the Cherokee as a unified nation in official dealings with the U.S. federal government, and more specifically a nation that echoed the tenets and rhetoric of U.S. political structures.

While this strategy made dealing with the U.S. federal government more effective, it had the inverse effect on relations with Georgia. Throughout the first three decades of the century, Georgia political leaders insisted that forcibly Removing all Native people from Georgia territory was a state right, under the terms of Georgia's admission to the Union. When the Cherokees established themselves as a democratic republic, it was more difficult to argue that they could easily be Removed. In 1827 Cherokee representatives finalized a national constitution—a move that, according to numerous Georgia politicians, served as a breaking point in Cherokee-Georgia relations.[25] Georgians argued that this was a case of *imperium in imperio*, a state operating within a state, and that the Cherokee Nation could not establish a credible constitution because the only reason Cherokees still lived in their ancestral homelands was because the State of Georgia allowed them to do so. It is telling that the formulation of a constitution—documentation that makes a nation discursively legible—was especially threatening to a sense of Georgia sovereignty.

This constitution would also be the first thing Boudinot published on the front page of the first issue of the *Phoenix*.

Reworking Cherokee governance as a means of protecting Cherokee homelands and Cherokee sovereignty created a structure that powerfully challenged U.S. interference but entrenched a racialized and gendered social order. It dramatically restructured the lives of many Cherokees, especially women, Afro-Cherokees, and enslaved people of African descent, and would have a devastating impact on the Nation for the next two hundred years. Article III, Section 4, of the constitution, outlining legislative power, placed explicit limitations on Cherokees of African descent and prohibited anyone of African descent from holding office in the Nation: "The descendants of Cherokee men by all free women, except the African race, whose parents may be or have been living together as man and wife, according to the customs and laws of this Nation, shall be entitled to all the rights and privileges of this Nation, as well as the posterity of Cherokee women by all free men. No person who is of negro or mulatto parentage, either by father or mother side, shall be eligible to hold any office of profit, honor, or trust under this Government."[26] The dual articulation of property outlined in Article I and Article III codified a racialized, racist structure of belonging that would not combat Removal.[27] Embracing chattel enslavement helped affluent Cherokee enslavers build their fortunes in ways that were anathema to precolonial legacies of prosperity, but this wealth did not help the Nation protect its homelands or secure self-determination.[28] Nor did the exclusion of Afro-Cherokees from holding public office. If anything, Cherokee practices of enslavement gave rise to an established class of Cherokees who consolidated power and furthered social divides by instituting new gender and racial norms that also exacerbated class divides. Cherokee participation in chattel enslavement disrupted matrilineally informed understandings of kinship, labor, and community responsibility. Intentionally or not, by embracing enslavement, elite Cherokee enslavers were undercutting what had always been women's contributions to their communities.[29]

Critically, the constitution also marked an official break with matriarchal forms of governance and kinship; only men could hold government appointments. The disempowerment of Cherokee women facilitated the disempowerment of Afro-Cherokees through the erosion of clan structure and matriliny and demonstrated the anti-Black violence of patriarchal heteronormativity.[30] According to the dictates of Cherokee matriliny, any child of a Cherokee woman was Cherokee with a specific clan relationship, regardless of the race or tribal affiliation of the child's father. Clans shaped every aspect of Cherokee life, from who one was to where one lived to one's communal responsibilities and situatedness in Cherokee cosmologies. Matriliny ensured that all community members, both human and more-than-human, were valued and cared for.[31] Cherokee home life was organized around a network of maternal figures, and homes were intergenerational; landholdings were communal. Husbands would move to their wives' homes, and when couples separated, husbands were expected to leave and return to their own matrilineal clans.[32] Maternal uncles, rather than biological fathers, were influential male figures in a child's life because of their shared clan ties.

On the one hand, matriliny thwarted the racist logics of white supremacy by determining Cherokeeness through clan and kinship and not by phenotype or biology. On the other, matrilineal kinship structures had the unintended effect of also reinforcing anti-Blackness under the plantation system. Before the constitution, children born of Cherokee fathers and enslaved Black mothers traditionally had no clan affiliation and therefore no place in Cherokee communities, but children born of Cherokee mothers and enslaved fathers were Cherokee. As the Nation shifted from a matrilineal township structure to a centralized nation, racial understandings of belonging and anti-Blackness were legally codified. After the constitution, however, all Afro-descended Cherokees were marginalized. Returning to the language of Article III, Section 4, in the constitution, children born to white women and Cherokee fathers were granted full citizenship under the new government, but Cherokees of African descent were not afforded the same inclusion.[33] For the few Cherokee men with white wives, like Elias Boudinot and his cousin John Ridge, this change ensured their children's full citizenship in the Nation.

Printing Cherokee Territory

In 1828 Boudinot was appointed as the *Phoenix*'s editor by Principal Chief John Ross and the National Council.[34] Boudinot came from a prominent Cherokee family and was part of the emerging class of Cherokee elites who gained significant influence in the Nation. Boudinot was of mixed European and Cherokee descent, but because his mother was Cherokee, he was Cherokee. Boudinot spent five years studying at the American Board of Commissioners for Foreign Nations (ABCFM) mission school in Cornwall, Connecticut, where he met his wife, Harriet Gold. He became very familiar with U.S. culture, but hostility toward his marriage with a white woman also made clear the vehemence of anti-Native sentiments in the United States.

In New Echota, a building was constructed for the print office not far from the courthouse and council house. Initially, two white printers were approved by the council to help, John Foster Wheeler and Isaac N. Harris. Eventually, John Candy (Cherokee) would also join the operation, and his fluency in Sequoyan Cherokee would become invaluable.[35] Creating an issue of the paper was a labor-intensive process. For one thing, the press required three people to operate, but even more challenging was the labor required to print in Cherokee. Boudinot was responsible for almost all of the translations between Cherokee and English in the paper, and, at least initially, Boudinot and Candy set all of the type themselves because Wheeler and Harris did not understand Cherokee.[36]

Much like the Cherokee decision to reorganize cultural and political life as a centralized republic with a written constitution, the Cherokee establishment of a national newspaper was motivated by a desire to make the Nation legible to its citizens, its supporters, and its opponents, in ways that mirrored the United States' legibility.[37] The two cohered in Boudinot's decision to showcase the constitution on the front page of the first issue of the *Phoenix*. The combination of the Nation's development of the constitution, a three-branch form of government, and a national newspaper emulated U.S. revolutionary era mythos—namely, the emergence of a democratic republic casting off an oppressive colonizer and coming into being through civic discourse disseminated through print. The establishment of a Cherokee newspaper was a conscious appropriation of this print culture origin story, but the limitations of print—the form of the newspaper and the material conditions of the print shop—all made it challenging to print a proper dual-language paper.[38] As a result, the conventions of the newspaper-as-form sometimes worked at cross-purposes with the Nation's aims. These challenges raise an important set of questions: Why did the Cherokee leadership advocate a national newspaper? Why was this the preferred medium for disseminating information about the Cherokee struggle? Why not focus solely on publishing and circulating pamphlets and legal documents bilingually, which would require less typesetting and less constant need for supplies than publishing a weekly periodical?

Something about the newspaper as a medium, especially its relationship to time and space, seemed particularly apt for the Nation's print culture aims. In his October 1828 annual message, Ross insisted that "the public press deserves the patronage of the people, and should be cherished as an important vehicle in the diffusion of general information, and as a no less powerful auxiliary in asserting and supporting our political rights."[39] Newspapers not only circulated more quickly and cheaply than, say, books, but the existence of the *Phoenix* challenged the anti-Indigenous belief that Indians were living in a premodern past and their lives were incommensurate with modernity. In addition, by 1828, when the paper began, newspapers circulated widely and cheaply and could thus reach readers both near and far through the initial material circulation of the paper itself and through the fervent reprinting practices of the era. A weekly newspaper, with its date printed in the masthead and its coverage of current events, asserted a presentness to Cherokee nationhood through its participation in "modern" industrial time; it asserted a sovereign printscape meant to reflect a sovereign nation.

In the sections that follow, I first discuss the symbolic import of printing in the Cherokee language. Then I explain some of the limitations the newspaper-as-form placed on the newspaper's message. I turn from formal analysis to a discussion of the paper's reception (or lack thereof) by Georgia newspapers alongside circulation of David Walker's *Appeal*, demonstrating how Georgia newspapers mediated and exacerbated Cherokee Nation–Georgia border disputes through a rhetoric of states' rights. The chapter ends by connecting the ideological work of Georgia newspapers to printed land lotteries and the creation of county lines. Collectively, these printed documents (the newspaper and the survey) construct a printscape of state sovereignty that stands in direct opposition to Native and Black freedom.

Bilingualism as Sovereign Printscape

Careful attention to the *Phoenix*'s bilingual approach demonstrates how Boudinot and the Nation asserted place-based national sovereignty through written language but also reveals how the paper's formatting worked against some of these same aims.[40] National political news was prioritized for Cherokee-language content, indicating that one impetus for the paper was to keep Cherokee citizens civically and politically informed. While a decision born out of pragmatism and necessity, the linguistic sectioning of the paper created a boundary line, both visually and discursively, that itself demonstrates the problems Cherokees faced in making sovereignty visible in a colonial context that actively refused the legibility of Indigenous nationhood. The material and structural problems Boudinot and the printers faced in constructing a Cherokee newspaper unintentionally reflected the political problems between the State of Georgia and the Nation that he hoped to narrate. Much like the boundary line between the United States and the Nation, the relationship between English- and Cherokee-language content kept changing. I do not mean to suggest that there was no room for Sequoyan Cherokee in the paper, but rather that the paper materially echoed the problems Cherokee leaders faced when asserting autonomy through a nationalized political structure that was meant to register legibility in Euro-American terms.

The decision to publish in both English and Cherokee made the constellation of audiences addressed by the paper visible, even to readers who did not understand both languages. Many scholars have rightly argued that an impetus for publishing in English and Cherokee, one stated frequently in the editorials of the *Phoenix* itself, was a desire to have the paper circulate among supporters of the Cherokee cause. There was a hope that white supporters in the United States could exert pressure on their own government to advocate for the Cherokees (and help financially fund the paper). Some Cherokees only read one language or the other, so publishing in both languages attracted a more diverse array of Cherokee readers, and, due to the linguistic violence of colonialism, English enabled access to a broader audience of Indigenous readers.[41] Moreover, publishing in both languages had the political benefit of demonstrating Cherokee abilities to speak the language of U.S. diplomacy and foreign relations (and a market economy, as a newspaper soliciting subscriptions). The Cherokee syllabary was itself a new form of Cherokee expression that had been used for less than a decade by the time Boudinot began publishing the paper, but Cherokees already viewed it as an influential symbol of the Nation. While it was used in the *Phoenix* and other printed materials, it was also used in manuscript form for personal letters, recipes, medical remedies, and other intimate and quotidian forms of communication.[42] In addition to its utility, the syllabary also served an identitarian function that was explicitly anticolonial in intent. It became a powerful symbol of Cherokee endurance and adaptation in Cherokee protests against forced Removal in the 1820s–30s and after the reestablishment of the Cherokee Nation in Indian Territory.

The syllabary was a Cherokee invention, one constructed by Sequoyah with the help of his daughter Ayoka (also spelled Ahyokeh).[43] Sequoyah grew up in a matriarchal Cherokee world and was a skilled blacksmith and silversmith.[44] Wurteh, his mother, who was from a prominent Cherokee family near the Overhill town of Tuskegee, raised him.[45] While Sequoyah grew up near trading posts and may have heard or understood some English, he only ever publicly spoke in Cherokee and demonstrated little interest in the English language. He married Sally Waters and developed the syllabary between 1810 and 1820 while living in Arkansas Territory. His daughter Ayoka was his best student, and she aided him in finessing the syllabary and presenting it to the National Council, which approved it as the official written language of the Cherokee Nation in 1821. Within a very short period of time, a majority of Cherokees were literate in Sequoyan Cherokee. In her study of the syllabary, Cherokee scholar Ellen Cushman importantly reminds us that "the first learners of Sequoyan would have linked the meaning, logic, perspective, location, and time to the sound and character of each syllable. In other words, the syllabary is useful for Cherokee perseverance because it presents meaningful linguistic, historical, and cultural information each time it is used."[46] Just the sheer presence of the Cherokee language in the pages of the *Phoenix* is a constant assertion of Cherokee belonging that itself archives kinship, connection, and endurance, like the Cherokee Nation and Georgia.

Form and Reprinting

Intentional or not, the visual effect of English and the Cherokee language sharing the print on the page echoed the spatial relationship between Georgia and the Cherokee Nation. Sequoyan Cherokee and English can coexist on the same field of print, as should the Cherokee Nation and the state of Georgia. The bilingual nature of the content visually depicted the changing ways Cherokee officials asserted national sovereignty in the late 1820s and early 1830s, some elements of which worked more effectively than others. In the early issues of the *Phoenix*, some pieces were published side by side in both languages (like the constitution), but eventually, the paper moved away from this format. Instead, much of the Cherokee-language content was relegated to pages 2 and 3 of the paper, but this was likely a matter of cost effectiveness and necessity rather than a change of editorial vision.[47] As stated earlier, one of the first things printed in the paper was the Cherokee constitution (including Article III, Section 4, discussed earlier), published on the front page in February and March 1828. If one looks at page 1 of the first issue, one immediately notices the blank space in the Cherokee-language columns (figure 1.1). The syllabary uses fewer characters than English, but the Cherokee appears sparse next to the lengthy English text. Cherokee is a syllabary and not an alphabet, but one could also read its economy on the page as refusing the newspaper norm of colonizing the page by filling up as much printed space as possible.

The boldness of "THE BOUNDARIES" in all caps draws one's eye and emphasizes a sense of distinction between the Cherokee and the English. While the constitution begins with a preamble that echoes that of the U.S. Constitu-

GWY Ꮰ.ᎾᎤᏟ.Ꭰ.

CHEROKEE PHOENIX.

VOL. I.   NEW ECHOTA, THURSDAY FEBRUARY 21, 1828.   NO. 1.

EDITED BY ELIAS BOUDINOTT.

PRINTED WEEKLY BY

ISAAC H. HARRIS,

FOR THE CHEROKEE NATION.

At $2 50 if paid in advance, $3 in six months, or $3 50 if paid at the end of the year.

To subscribers who can read only the Cherokee language the price will be $2 00 in advance, or $2 50 to be paid within the year.

Every subscription will be considered as continued unless subscribers give notice to the contrary before the commencement of a new year.

The Phoenix will be printed on a Super-Royal sheet, with type entirely new procured for the purpose. Any person procuring six subscribers, and becoming responsible for the payment, shall receive a seventh gratis.

Advertisements will be inserted at seventy-five cents per square for the first insertion, and thirty-seven and a half cents for each continuance; longer ones in proportion.

☞ All letters addressed to the Editor, post paid, will receive due attention.

A GOOD CONSCIENCE.

What is there, in all the pomp of the world, the enjoyments of luxury, [illegible] rable to the tranquil spirit of a good conscience...?

CONSTITUTION OF THE CHEROKEE NATION.

Formed by a Convention of Delegates from the several Districts, at New Echota, July 1827.

We, The Representatives of the people of the Cherokee Nation in Convention assembled, in order to establish justice, ensure tranquility, promote our common welfare, and secure to ourselves and our posterity the blessings of liberty; acknowledging with humility and gratitude the goodness of the sovereign Ruler of the Universe, in offering us an opportunity so favorable to the design, and imploring his aid and direction in its accomplishment, do ordain and establish this Constitution for the Government of the Cherokee Nation.

ARTICLE I.

Sec. 1. The Boundaries of this nation, embracing the lands solemnly guarantied and reserved forever to the Cherokee Nation by the Treaties concluded with the United States, are as follows; and shall forever hereafter remain unalterably the same—to wit—Beginning on the North Bank of Tennessee River at the upper part of the Chickasaw old fields; thence along the main channel of said river, including all the islands therein, to the mouth of the Hiwassee river...

ARTICLE II.

Sec. 1. The Power of this Government shall be divided into three distinct departments;—the Legislative, the Executive, and the Judicial.

Sec. 2. No person or persons, belonging to one of these Departments, shall exercise any of the powers properly belonging to either of the others, except in the cases hereinafter expressly directed or permitted.

ARTICLE III.

Sec. 1. The Legislative Power shall be vested in two distinct branches; a Committee, and a Council; each to have a negative on the other, and both to be styled, the General Council of the Cherokee Nation; and the style of their acts and laws shall be, "Resolved by the Committee and Council in General Council convened."

Sec. 2. The Cherokee Nation, as laid off into eight Districts, shall so remain.

Sec. 3. The Committee shall consist of two members from each District, and the Council shall consist of three members from each District, to be chosen by the people for two years; and the elections to be held in every District on the first Monday in August for the year 1828, and every succeeding two years thereafter; and the General Council shall be held once a year, to be convened on the second Monday of October in each year, at New Echota.

tion, unlike the U.S. Constitution, the first article asserts the boundaries of the Nation, Cherokees' immemorial ties to the land, and treaty negotiations with the United States that acknowledged a Cherokee right to their territory.[48] The constitution opens spatially, with an assertion of groundedness and belonging that uses "old" to describe the geographic boundaries, signaling the Cherokees' enduring relationship with the land, and moves almost circularly from a beginning point and back again, reflecting a sense of cohesion and relationality.

The syllabary enables the paper to maintain a sense of stability across its audiences (Cherokee and non-Cherokee) and form (newspaper). However, the unequal distribution between the English and Cherokee content may have had the unfortunate consequence of making the English-language content appear more weighted because of its visual overrepresentation to an audience unable to read Cherokee. The *Phoenix* did not always publish the same content in both languages.[49] Boudinot wanted to publish more material in Cherokee, but the lack of typesetters and printers able to work in both languages posed a major obstacle.[50] While official tribal documents and some Christian prayers are printed in the syllabary (the Lord's Prayer is printed in Cherokee on the fourth page of the first issue) and there are occasionally articles explaining how to read the syllabary, eventually most of the pieces published in Cherokee were correspondence pieces.[51] One can tell this even without a fluent understanding of the language because most of these pieces are found in the running column "Correspondence" and because the visual composition of those pieces follows that of a letter to the editor or other more intimate forms of newspaper prose.

Much like the Cherokees' decision to take their case with the State of Georgia to the U.S. Supreme Court in *Cherokee Nation v. Georgia*, Cherokee participation in both a regional and a U.S. print network made the paper legible outside the Nation. But those legibility-enhancing tactics also threatened to position the Nation *within* the domestic United States through Boudinot's recirculation choices and how he described the paper's relationship to the United States and other U.S.-based newspapers. Part of the problem with circulating among and reprinting from U.S. newspapers is that U.S. content is often not represented as "foreign" news. It regularly appears as "domestic" news, which does not help the argument that the Cherokee Nation is a distinct nation separate from the United States.[52] Like *Cherokee Nation v. Georgia*, the circulation of the paper within state and national U.S. networks was a risky choice and threatened to make it difficult for readers to understand the *Phoenix* (and the Cherokee Nation) as distinctly separate from the

United States, especially when the *Phoenix* followed the same visual cues as U.S. and regional papers.[53]

Notably, the paper's participation in a regional print network signaled a slippage of scale—if the paper read like a typical U.S. paper and actively engaged with regional papers, then what made the *Phoenix* different? What made it distinct from Georgia papers? What made the Cherokee Nation distinct from Georgia? Such engagement with regional papers was necessary if we believe Cherokee insistence that one of the only ways Cherokee leaders learned about Georgia politicians' plans was through reading Georgia newspapers. The supplemental bill submitted to the Supreme Court by the Cherokees' legal team in *Cherokee Nation v. Georgia* included the following: "Your complainants have not had it in their power to procure an authenticated copy of these several laws. Until they can do so, they beg leave to refer to them at present, as they have been published in a newspaper called the Georgia Journal, edited at Milledgeville, the seat of government of the state of Georgia, which newspaper is herewith exhibited; and they pray that they may be considered as part of this bill."[54] However, it came at a cost.

The *Phoenix* was a self-conscious repository of current events in both the Cherokee Nation and Indian Country and an innovative experiment in the politics of circulation. As a result, it serves as an archive containing all of the contradictory mess of its historical moment. It becomes clear from reading every issue of the paper Boudinot edited that he traced where the *Phoenix*'s pieces were reprinted (and how) just as much as the number of physical copies sold.[55] Once the paper began production, issues included substantial reprinting from U.S., British, and European publications. This was common practice for almost all U.S. papers of the era, but one with particular import for the Cherokee Nation because it placed the Nation in conversation with other nations—sometimes literally, as when the *Phoenix* reprinted pieces about the Cherokees from other papers.[56] In his editorials, Boudinot often mentioned where the *Phoenix* was cited as a way of demonstrating strong support for the Cherokee cause. However, these claims often relied on the problematic assumption that *Phoenix* readers could be swayed by what they read in the paper if they were not already Cherokee supporters. In particular, he mentioned overseas support that subtly or not-so-subtly emphasized the *Phoenix* as distinctly of the Cherokee *Nation*, and not the United States, through simple phrases.[57]

As readers with the privilege of historical distance, we also know that Boudinot's perspective on Cherokee anticolonial policy would change dramatically in the early 1830s. Not only was he asked by Principal Chief John

Ross to leave his post as editor when his editorials started promoting Re-
moval, but he was one of the signers of the Treaty of New Echota (1835).
Signed by a group of affluent Cherokee men, including Boudinot's relatives
Major Ridge, John Ridge, and Stand Watie (no Cherokee women signed the
treaty), the treaty arguably marks one of the most devastating moments in
Cherokee history by authorizing the Removal of Cherokees west of the Mississippi. Ross did not sign, and the signers did not have consent from the
Nation to authorize the treaty on their behalf. Many of those who signed personally benefited from the selection of choice lands in Indian Territory, while
far more Cherokees endured the violent Removal known as the Trail of Tears.
It was a betrayal both of the Cherokee ancestral homelands and of the ves-
tiges of community and consensus-driven policy. However, the signers would
emphatically insist that it was the right decision for the Nation at the time
because Removal was inevitable. Either way, the treaty created divisions and
inner conflict that would last for decades.[58]

That Boudinot both edited one of the most important symbols of early
Cherokee nationalism and signed off on arguably the most controversial
treaty in Cherokee history is paradoxical. It is difficult not to read his 1835
decision back on the years he served as the *Phoenix*'s editor (1828–32). However, despite the strong hand he played in the paper's production, it was a *national* newspaper exhibiting the sovereign printscape of an entire *nation*. This
is why Ross asked Boudinot to leave his editorial position when Boudinot
began publishing pieces that did not align with the Nation's anti-Removal
stance. Whatever Boudinot's personal political bents, the *Phoenix* inarguably
raised questions about the efficacy of writing Indians out of territory through
legislation, cultural production, or physical force. The *Phoenix* detailed these
attacks and highlighted the hypocrisy of one democratic republic authorizing
the invasion of another, and demonstrated that print was not an exclusively
(white) colonial technology. At the same time, the newspaper proved a complicated vehicle for asserting Cherokee sovereignty because colonial reading
practices were woven into the print conventions that made the newspaper
legible to a non-Cherokee audience of readers.

Georgia Print Culture and Noncitational Circulation

The *Phoenix* and Georgia newspapers both metonymically gesture toward the
political forms of the Indigenous nation and the state that they respectively represented throughout their coverage of the Cherokee-Georgia sovereignty

debates.[59] Almost all Georgia newspaper coverage in the late 1820s and early 1830s endorses Removal, rejects Cherokee nationalism, and insists on Georgia's total sovereignty over "Cherokee Territory," the term most papers used to describe the Nation. Moreover, the predication of states' rights on enslavement and colonization is inflected in the papers' composition. Despite newspaper editors' political differences—of which there were quite a few—the one thing they could almost all agree on was an anti-Cherokee, anti-Black, pro–Indian Removal stance.

In addition to the content published in these papers, the logic by which they map out such content presents a racial world order spatially rendered across the pages. Discussions of Indians appear in the novelty section as colorful supplemental materials, in editorial opinion pieces, or in official government business and often include materials like letters and notes from legislative sessions. The state's dependence on enslavement and slavery's omnipresence in day-to-day life can be seen in the advertisements published in the weeklies that announce the sale of enslaved people and inform readers of self-emancipated fugitives (usually on page 4 and sometimes the front page). The papers very likely counted enslavers among their subscribers or editors.[60] Indian affairs, most often discussions of the Cherokee and Muscogee but sometimes other Native people as well, were typically printed on pages 2 and 3 of these papers—the standard pages for publishing "domestic" or local news. Indian affairs seldom appear alongside world news pieces, visually affirming the states' rights belief that the Cherokee and Muscogee were subservient to the rule of Georgia and were not, in fact, distinct foreign nations or polities separate from the United States. In both cases, we rarely find the direct voices of Native or Black people.

It is important to note that notices for the sale and surveillance of enslaved and self-emancipating people also appeared in the *Phoenix*. Tiya Miles suggests that the significantly smaller number of these ads than in white papers (eleven in total, three of which were placed by non-Cherokee white people) indicates the *Phoenix*'s ambivalence about enslavement. In general, the *Phoenix* was inconsistent in its messaging, especially in the paper's early years. Boudinot published abolitionist pieces, including the poem "The Slave Ship" in the September 10, 1828, issue. Yet he also published reprints that were explicitly anti-Black, exoticized descriptions of Africa and arguments advocating Liberian emigration (ironic, given Cherokee opposition to their own Removal). But I contend this inconsistence also demonstrates an embrace of the structure of racialization made visually and discursively legible by the racialized newspaper form. You would not, for example, find such ads in *Freedom's Journal*. Their placement highlights not only Cherokee participation in enslavement but also a proximity to whiteness and the white newspaper form.

Two examples from the Georgia papers demonstrate how newspaper production and circulation facilitated the ideological work of states' rights, and both examples were printed in some of the same newspaper issues in 1830: *Cherokee Nation v. Georgia* and David Walker's *Appeal*. I contend that in both cases, Georgia papers attempted to control narratives of Indigenous self-assertion and Black revolution through a practice of noncitation, by which I mean the intentional omission of information to de-escalate the threat both posed to the white supremacist state. While numerous scholars have suggested the *Phoenix* did not directly circulate in Georgia, I argue that this is a misreading of the *Phoenix*'s relationship to a regional print network and the reprinting practices of the day. For example, the front page of the August 26, 1829, issue of the *Phoenix* lists authorized agents for the paper. Out of fifteen, over half of them are Southern, including one in Augusta, Georgia (Capt. William Robertson), as well as one in the Choctaw Nation (Rev. Cyrus Kingsbury).[61] It is true that there is a surprising dearth of *Phoenix* citations in the Georgia press, but since the *Phoenix*'s very existence was a source of ire for many Georgians, by not offering up much space to the *Phoenix* in the pages of their papers, Georgia editors could discount all that the *Phoenix* stood for.[62]

The prevailing belief that there was little Georgia press engagement with the *Phoenix* perpetuates misinterpretation of the false disinterest in Cherokee affairs publicly performed by Georgia politicians, even though we know white Georgians were consumed by an obsessive impulse to resolve their "Indian problem." Likely, many Georgia editors did not officially subscribe to the *Phoenix* but instead read recirculated *Phoenix* articles, which they then often credited to another source. It was ubiquitous to reprint without source citation in 1830s newspapers, but Georgia papers regularly credited other sources, especially for regional news pieces. For example, the October 6, 1832, issue of the *Columbus Enquirer* attributes its reprints from the *Phoenix* to the *Nashville Banner*.[63]

Tracing this politics of (non)citation reveals at least one problem with exclusively relying on subscription records to understand circulation. There is not enough evidence to unequivocally support a (non)citational praxis, making my claim more speculative than definitive, but when one reads complete issues of Georgia newspapers alongside entire issues of the *Phoenix*, certain similarities in content come to the fore. Perhaps editors were not aware when articles they reprinted initially came from the *Phoenix*. Yet I find such an assumption to be inordinately generous and run counter to editors' and politicians' responses to another print cultural flashpoint, the circulation of David Walker's *Appeal*, which I discuss in more detail shortly. Fear of the *Appeal's* circulation led the same Georgians to advocate for increased censorship and surveillance of print circulation.

Black and Native people could not testify in Georgia courts, and their silencing was encoded in print in addition to being formalized in law. One troubling example of censorship involved a Georgia sheriff who attempted to rape and then physically assault two Cherokee women, "Mrs. Oosunaley and Mrs. Foster."[64] When Boudinot reported on the incident in the *Phoenix*, the state charged him with libel and suspended the paper. Tracing the citation of *Phoenix* articles (which Georgia papers sometimes cite but often do not) shows that many editors seem to have obfuscated their awareness of the *Phoenix* to delegitimize Cherokee national sovereignty—an approach echoed by the State of Georgia's unwillingness to respond to the Cherokee Nation's Supreme Court case against it in 1830–31. I want to suggest that a politics of noncitation does not indicate an unawareness of the *Phoenix* or Cherokee print culture, but rather a willful refusal to recirculate it and a belief that Indians could be a paper's content but not the source.[65]

One of the rare exceptions when the *Phoenix* was attributed as a source was following the Supreme Court's decision in *Cherokee Nation v. Georgia*. Cherokees and the *Phoenix* had access to the decision first, and Georgia editors widely reprinted it from the *Phoenix*, even giving credit to the paper in some cases. Most Georgia papers initially interpreted the court's decision as a win for the state, so the citation of the *Phoenix* may have been a somewhat spiteful choice; the Georgia press of the 1830s was certainly not above pettiness. On numerous occasions, Georgia papers would reprint *Phoenix* articles about Removal and add editorials that openly reveled in Cherokee struggles. Editors would also print articles detailing Cherokee desperation with the ensuing assault on their rights and land, along with editorials that spoke back directly to *Phoenix* publications.[66] In addition to a politics of pettiness, performed disinterest, or however we might choose to understand these Georgia papers' approaches to recirculation, the most disturbing iterations of editorial response were those that made veiled threats of violence if Georgians did not get their way.[67] Written under the pseudonym Patrick Henry, an 1830 letter to the editor suggests that anyone unwilling to acknowledge "the sovereign rights of this state" will "be referred to the arbitrament of the God of battle, and the stillness of peace, which reigns over this land, must be broken by the clash of the bayonet."[68]

However, the most infamous example of fearmongering and racial panic was the response to Walker's *Appeal* (1829) that circulated in these same papers. One of the most radical documents published in nineteenth-century America, Walker's pamphlet unequivocally advocated sweeping revolution and immediate global abolition. Walker hoped his pamphlet would circulate throughout the South and nurture in all Black people "a spirit of inquiry and investigation respecting our miseries and wretchedness in this *Republican Land of Liberty!!!!!*"[69] Walker was well versed in the world of print culture circulation, and his choice to use a pamphlet as the primary medium for disseminating his *Appeal* and not a newspaper is an intriguing one. He served as the Boston agent for *Freedom's Journal* and helped drum up financial support for the paper.[70] Perhaps Walker was well aware of the limitations of the newspaper's form I described earlier and how these might hinder his message. As an agent for the *Journal*, he would have a keen sense of the paper's circulation and how subscribers and readers engaged with the content. Moreover, *Freedom's Journal* faced challenges in staying afloat and shut down the same year Walker published the *Appeal*.

With his *Appeal*, Walker engaged in an *insurgent print practice*, meaning he utilized his knowledge of print production and circulation to spread word of his *Appeal* through the text's physical circulation and through the circulation of its content via gossip and other forms of verbal and nonverbal communication.[71] By "insurgent," I mean his ability to disrupt the regulative flows of print culture in Georgia. His approach undermined the white supremacist belief that printed content could be entirely controlled and mediated by those in power.[72] By strategically reaching out to individuals throughout Georgia, Walker demonstrated that not only could Black and Native people become print subjects, but they could also creatively use print in nontraditional ways to challenge white supremacy directly and inspire collective organizing. In the *Appeal*, Walker explicitly excoriates recent Georgia legislation that prohibited enslaved people and free Black people from learning to read or write.[73] If Georgia newspaper editors and politicians imagined they could curtail a substantive Black print culture audience, Walker crushed this racist assumption. His *Appeal* demonstrated print's radical potential to upend enslavement and white supremacy by activating Black revolution. White Southerners quickly worked to prevent its circulation in slaveholding states.[74] Nonetheless, even when new regulations hindered the ability to circulate the *Appeal* via mail, it still traveled informally through secret channels, by word of mouth, and by other means.[75] As with the *Phoenix*, its very existence was perceived as a threat to Georgia's racial regime.

Georgians responded aggressively to the man accused of soliciting copies directly from Walker, newspaper editor Elijah Burritt.[76] Rumors spread about Burritt and his plans for circulating the document. Eventually, he was forced to flee north and abandon his *Stateman and Patriot* newspaper office in Milledgeville.[77] Burritt is mentioned over and over in newspaper coverage, especially in the *Federal Union* (the new name for the *Stateman and Patriot* after Burritt's rivals took over the office), but Walker and his appeal are only gestured toward. Editors occasionally reference "Walker's Pamphlets" or use equally vague verbiage, but there is minimal discussion of the *Appeal's* contents or its writer, at least in the papers I read (figures 1.2 and 1.3). However, this does not mean that Walker was absent for contemporaneous readers or from the cultural imaginary of the moment. If anything, the omission of his name may speak to the infamy of his pamphlet—the papers' readers *already* knew who he was, or at least what he represented.

Nonetheless, the absence of his name and the work's title suggests an attempt to control and contain Walker's intended message "that all coloured men, women and children, every nation, language and tongue under heaven, will try to procure a copy of this Appeal and read it, or get some one to read it to them, for it is designed more particularly for them."[78] We know that Georgia editors were unsuccessful in doing so, but their omissions are not benign. The absence of Walker in the coverage not only shifts the focus away from the source of a radical Black revolutionary treatise and toward white Northerner abolitionist sympathies, but it makes it more challenging to find Walker in the digital archives today, arguably preventing a wider, transtemporal circulation of the *Appeal*.[79] In the case of Walker and his insurgent circulation praxis, the difficulty of tracing where his text traveled and how it was consumed was part of the intent. However, at the time of this writing, if you keyword search using his name in the Georgia Historic Newspapers database, you will not find most of these pieces. The papers' practice of not citing the *Phoenix* and their coverage of Walker's *Appeal* both represent acts of omission that mimic Removal by intentionally leaving voices out of the print record.[80]

The way Georgia papers narrated the scandal demonstrates a collective effort to restage print culture discourse as a conversation among white men of means. Again, Cherokee and Black people could be newspaper content, but their participation in a local and regional print culture not only threatened the white nationalist narrative of belonging but also disrupted the very formulation of the rights-bearing, liberal human subject imagined as the print reader.[81] Newspaper editors helped unify white Georgia men under a states'

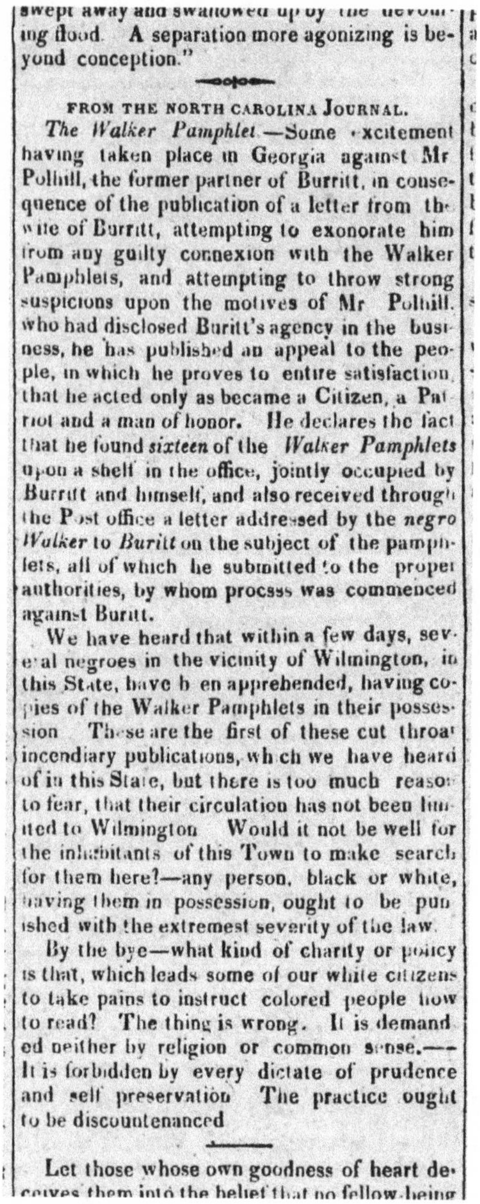

swept away and swallowed up by the devour-
ing flood. A separation more agonizing is beyond conception."

FROM THE NORTH CAROLINA JOURNAL.

The Walker Pamphlet.—Some excitement
having taken place in Georgia against Mr
Polhill, the former partner of Burritt, in consequence of the publication of a letter from the
wife of Burritt, attempting to exonerate him
from any guilty connexion with the Walker
Pamphlets, and attempting to throw strong
suspicions upon the motives of Mr Polhill,
who had disclosed Burritt's agency in the business, he has published an appeal to the people, in which he proves to entire satisfaction,
that he acted only as became a Citizen, a Patriot and a man of honor. He declares the fact
that he found *sixteen* of the *Walker Pamphlets*
upon a shelf in the office, jointly occupied by
Burritt and himself, and also received through
the Post office a letter addressed by the *negro*
Walker to *Buritt* on the subject of the pamphlets, all of which he submitted to the proper
authorities, by whom process was commenced
against Burritt.

We have heard that within a few days, several negroes in the vicinity of Wilmington, in
this State, have been apprehended, having copies of the Walker Pamphlets in their possession These are the first of these cut throat
incendiary publications, which we have heard
of in this State, but there is too much reason
to fear, that their circulation has not been limited to Wilmington Would it not be well for
the inhabitants of this Town to make search
for them here?—any person, black or white,
having them in possession, ought to be punished with the extremest severity of the law.

By the bye—what kind of charity or policy
is that, which leads some of our white citizens
to take pains to instruct colored people how
to read? The thing is wrong. It is demanded neither by religion or common sense.——
It is forbidden by every dictate of prudence
and self preservation The practice ought
to be discountenanced

Let those whose own goodness of heart de-
ceives them into the belief that no fellow-being

FIGURE 1.2 "From the North
Carolina Journal" was one of the
only articles I found in a Georgia
paper that explicitly mentioned
David Walker. Second page,
Federal Union (Milledgeville),
September 11, 1830 (Georgia
Historic Newspapers Archive,
https://gahistoricnewspapers
.galileo.usg.edu/lccn/sn86053071
/1830-09-11/ed-1/seq-2/).

ture of his disease, and the natural frigidity of his constitution, I have been compelled to administer a dose of unusual severity; one which I would never have offered to a patient more easily wrought upon, yet the effects are not likely to be fatal; and it remains with himself to pursue such a regimen, as may prevent an extension of the *mortification.*   A GEORGIAN.

FOR THE FEDERAL UNION.

THE CHEROKEE COUNTRY.

There is no subject which more urgently imposes itself upon the serious consideration of the people of Georgia than the one with which I have headed this communication. That the period has arrived when our relationship with those people residing in this country must assume a new and different character is evidently beyond doubt.— Independent of the just right we have to its possession, there are other reasons of great weight which demand a speedy change. The peculiar condition of the country at this time—presenting the most disgusting scenes of licentiousness, riot, tumult and blood-shed—endangering the peace of that portion of the State which lays contiguous to it—requires of our next Legislature not only prompt but the most vigorous regulations. It is known that the Indians are utterly incapable of preserving the internal quietude even were the right conceded to them—and that it is totally impracticable if not impossible for the General Government to do so is equally certain   This being the unfortunate condition of the country--in whom, it may be enquired, does the right and the ability concentrate, to restore and preserve peace and harmony within its disordered borders.   It is confidently answered that the State of Georgia is that power.   Were she still disposed to forbear pressing her just demands, a due regard for her own peace would forbid it.   Indeed it is a matter of wonder and astonishment that more lives have not been taken, than have by those so eagerly engaged in the pursuit of Gold.   From a knowledge of the human character, we have abundant reason to conclude that if law is not speedily and effectually introduced, spectacles will be exhibited at no distant day at which humanity will sicken and revolt.   It is true that our laws are extended over the country—and it is also true that they are regarded as little as the "idle wind that passes by."   From much observation and mature and deliberate reflection, I have formed the settled opinion that there is no practicable mode of enforcing obedience to our laws without taking immediate possession of the country, and stationing the necessary Judicial officers in it.   To accomplish this effectually, the country must be surveyed and disposed of—and settled by our own citizens who are alone competent to the

---

Apply to   McKENZIE & BENNOCH.
☞ The Georgia Journal and Federal Union, the Athenian, Cabinet, and Washington News, will insert the above once a week, for six weeks, and send their accounts to McKenzie and Bennoch, Augusta.
Sept 11   10

Administrator's Sale.

AGREEABLY to an order of the Inferior Court of Wilkinson county, while sitting for ordinary purposes, will be sold, on the first Tuesday in November next, at the court-house door in Irwinton, Wilkinson county the PLANTATION whereon Brice Paul, late of said county, deceased, resided—containing three hundred acres, more or less.   The same being part of the real estate of said Brice Paul, deceased.   Sold for the benefit of the heirs of said deceased—Terms made known on the day.   JOHN CRUTCHFIELD, *Adm'r.*
Sept 11   10   8t

Administrator's Sale.

UNDER an order of the honorable the Inferior Court of Monroe county, when sitting for ordinary purposes, will be sold, on the first Tuesday in December next, before the court-house door in Forsyth, Monroe county, within the usual hours of sale, two hundred two and a half acres of LAND, being lot No. 14, in the eleventh district said county—said lot of land lies between Cullodens and Ichocunna creek, contains about twenty-five acres cleared and under good fence; the other part well timbered and of good soil.   Sold as the property of Baily Stewart, deceased.   Terms on the day of sale.
                              JOSEPH DAY, *Adm'r.*
September 11   10   9t

FIGURE 1.3 The same issue of the *Federal Union* that published "From the North Carolina Journal" included a pro-Removal letter, "The Cherokee Country," written by "Newton" for the paper. These two pages together provide a sense of the spatial and discursive renderings of Black radicalism and Indigenous self-determination, as well as white supremacist print forms. To the right of "The Cherokee Country" sit multiple advertisements for the sale of land and enslaved people. The article also includes a citation for the *Federal Union*, another Georgia paper, just above the title. Third page, *Federal Union* (Milledgeville), September 11, 1830 (Georgia Historic Newspapers Archive, https://gahistoricnewspapers.galileo.usg.edu/lccn/sn86053071/1830-09-11/ed-1/seq-3/).

rights position that was explicitly anti-Black and anti-Native. In doing so, they created solidarity across otherwise contentious class and political lines. They published editorials and letters to the editor that cohered a consistent message about the necessity of advocating for Georgia in the face of an unfriendly (antislavery) Northern foe. Nonetheless, despite attempts to reinscribe a white Northern other as the real enemy, the omission of Black and Native voices, like those of David Walker, Elias Boudinot, John Ross, and others, is telling. These omissions are as significant as what the papers choose to include. They remind us that they are unapologetically biased publications not to be taken at their word.

The Georgia press's attacks on the Cherokee Nation, the *Phoenix*, and the *Appeal* also challenge prevailing beliefs that education, literacy, and knowledge lead to a greater sense of empathy or understanding. Beth Schweiger incisively argues that in the South, "literacy did not necessarily foster progress and freedom. . . . Most literate slaves remained in chains, most literate women never claimed political equality with men, most literate Native Americans were brutally exiled, and the emancipation of 4 million slaves was ultimately enacted by bullets rather than books."[82] Nonetheless, understanding the spatial and cultural logics of Georgia print culture also helps us better understand why Cherokee leaders may have felt a national paper was necessary. While the paper did not prevent Removal, it did instantiate a relationship between national Indigenous identity and newspapers that endured after the 1830s, and it clearly disrupted U.S. opinions about Native peoples' capabilities to fight for their sovereignty.

The Colonial County Line

Like newspapers, land lotteries and the mapping of county lines played an influential role in shaping a spatial narrative of Removal. Cherokees and other Native peoples of the Southeast were aware that surveys were not benign scientific inquiry projects but in fact politically charged acts of colonization. This recognition is perhaps why as early as 1827, the *Athenian* reports on Native people confiscating compasses from white surveyors near Milledgeville, Georgia.[83] Collectively, land lotteries, county maps, and newspapers crafted a story of state sovereignty that was spatial, ideological, and discursive. For the rest of this chapter, I read the mapping project of state sovereignty. Wilson Lumpkin, whom I will discuss in more depth shortly, declared Georgia law over the Cherokee Nation despite the Supreme Court ruling otherwise and marked out county lines to visually and physically destroy

Cherokee territoriality; one of these, Lumpkin County, was named in his honor. Attending to this violent project of juridico-geographic colonization, including Lumpkin's justifications and the mapping itself, reveals the violence of states' rights logics that crystallized in the decades leading up to the U.S. Civil War. Before analyzing one of the land lottery maps Lumpkin authorized as governor (after he sold Cherokee land and refused to honor Cherokee sovereignty), it is worth reading the justification of his Indian policy as detailed in his writings.

Much like what we find in Georgia newspapers, Lumpkin's writings explicitly evidence the coconstitutive logics of statehood and racialized colonial violence. Attention to Lumpkin allows us to get away from pro-Removal narratives of the era that described genocidal policy in disembodied terms that obscure specific human actors. Moreover, the disembodied "state" is often gendered as female. While this gendering signals the precise connections between colonization, gender, and sexual violence that undergirded logics of land occupation and conquest, such anthropomorphic depictions of the "State of Georgia" animate statehood while obfuscating the (white) men and women who directly and indirectly authorized violent Removal, including Lumpkin.[84]

The phrase *imperium in imperio*, meaning "a state within a state," was used by Georgia politicians in the 1820s–30s to describe what they saw as the "problem" of the Cherokee Nation.[85] This logic was central to pro-Removal arguments that advocated genocidal expulsion of Native peoples west of the Mississippi. Politicians like Lumpkin, one of the most vocal proponents of Removal, first in Congress and later as governor of Georgia, argued that such a political configuration was incommensurate with the U.S. state of Georgia. And if, in fact, the agenda of settler colonialism is to occupy in perpetuity, then he was not wrong. States' rights not only were deployed to support Indian Removal and perpetuate enslavement but were also used by Southern politicians in the early twentieth century to argue against federal antilynching policy and later in the century as a challenge to civil rights; states' rights have always been about Indigenous and Black exclusion. Georgia politicians and newspaper editors' pro-Removal responses to the Cherokee Nation began to crystallize a narrative of states' rights that fueled Removal and became central to state sovereignty narratives elsewhere. Georgia politicians were not the first to assert states' rights in opposition to Indigenous peoples' territorial holdings, but the rhetoric politicians like Lumpkin deployed simultaneously cohered a sense of settler belonging predicated on anti-Blackness and enslavement that gained greater saliency as a regional discourse for the pro-enslaver South in the years leading up to the U.S. Civil War and eventually became the Southern states' driving justification for secession. To put it another way, the debate about whether the U.S. Civil War was a conflict over enslavement or states' rights is moot because the two are fundamentally interconnected.

Concurrent with Georgians' attempts to forcibly Remove the Cherokee from their ancestral homelands was the nullification debate in nearby South Carolina. The enslaver politico-elites of South Carolina, and a handful of other states, felt that the recently passed Tariff Bill of 1828 hurt the cotton industry of the "South," a regional identity that cohered throughout the first decades of the nineteenth century and one that flourished because of Removal and the expansion of chattel enslavement. South Carolina politicians and businessmen refused to honor the tariff, ostensibly "nullifying" its impact in the state, thus ignoring federal law in the name of states' rights. The "nullification crisis" competed with Georgia's Indian policy for coverage in the Georgia papers during this time, and there was debate in Georgia about whether to join the tariff protest.[86] Eventually, Georgia leaders decided against doing so, despite widespread support for South Carolina's cause, because they felt it might further strain Georgia's reputation nationally. Georgia politicians' willingness to turn away as self-interested white squatters invaded Cherokee lands searching for gold was already enflaming criticism from across the United States, especially in Northern newspapers.

The fact that both the tariff debate and Georgia's genocidal Removal policy occurred concomitantly is equally as significant as the strategic choice of powerful politicians to fight the two battles separately. Making one seemingly about industry and the economy (but really about a plantation-based slavocracy) and the other about sovereignty (but also access to gold and land) demonstrates a strategic choice to advocate separately for enslavement and colonialism. To argue for both concomitantly under the banner of states' rights would reveal the necessity of both enslavement and colonization to the perpetuity of South Carolina and Georgia economically *and* ideologically.[87]

Throughout his political career, Lumpkin unapologetically engaged in the ideological work of constructing a cohesive states' rights narrative—and his career was an extensive one that included terms at both the state and federal levels.[88] In addition to his political endeavors, he held several positions related to Indian affairs and was instrumental in Cherokee Removal. While state Indian commissioner, Lumpkin helped establish the Cherokee land lottery, which opened up Cherokee lands for settlement by white people, and, as stated earlier in the chapter, he was part of the negotiations that established the first boundary line between the state of Georgia and the Muscogee and

Cherokee Nations. Lumpkin is well known in the annals of Georgia history for his political service and his explicitly genocidal Indian policy. At the same time, it is important to remember that Lumpkin was an affluent enslaver whose brother, the first chief justice of the Georgia Supreme Court, was "the architect of the state's slave regime."[89] It is for these reasons, in addition to his central role in Cherokee Removal, that I turn to Lumpkin as a representative figure of Georgia states' rights arguments in order to tease out the burgeoning discourse. Specifically, I focus on how he framed Removal and states' rights discursively and spatially, both in his writings and in the forced mapping of Cherokee territory into state counties that he authorized as governor. Lumpkin was adept at navigating the relationships among public print, private correspondence, and state policy—blurring the lines between these when it suited him but affirming physical and ideological boundary lines when it did not.

As states' rights advocates concretized states' rights narratives in the first half of the nineteenth century, they consciously linked enslavement and Indian Removal. In an 1830 speech, the same year as the Indian Removal Act, Lumpkin made the following apologia for Georgia: "Georgia, it is true, has slaves; but she did not make them such; she found them upon her hands when she became a sovereign state. She never has, by her legislation, changed the state of freedom to slavery. If she has ever owned an Indian slave, it has never come to my knowledge; but more than one of the other states of this union have . . . reduced Indians to a state of slavery."[90] The passivity of his claim is staggering, and there is much to unpack, but I want to highlight two things: Lumpkin positions Black and Indigenous people as burdens on the state whose imposition predates statehood, and he describes enslavement as the most abject "state" of being possible. Here we might understand "state" as both metaphysical and political. In Lumpkin's diachronic logic, enslavement precedes statehood; it is past tense, not present; a colonial inheritance, not a structure of violence. Lumpkin invokes "Black fungibility," defined by Tiffany Lethabo King, building on Saidiya Hartman, as "the unfettered use of Black bodies for the self-actualization of the human and for the attendant humanist project of the production and expansion of space."[91] Lumpkin's discussion of enslavement telegraphs a world order that is dependent on enslavement to bring into being the freedom of others, a freedom that excludes Native people as well, but foregrounds the abjection of (Black) enslavement to position colonization as distinct *from* instead of synergic *with* slavery.

In addition, his use of feminine pronouns temporally rewires U.S. settler history by anthropomorphizing Georgia as an innocent (white) woman who becomes burdened with enslavement and Indigenous dispossession upon Georgia's incorporation as a new federated state of the United States; Lumpkin imagines Black and Native people as a postcolonial legacy from Georgia's British colonial past. The invocation of white femininity performs settler innocence and situates white women as rationales *for* rather influential actors *of* U.S. empire-building, although this was far from the case. White women were complicit in *both* the projects of U.S. territorial expansion and the plantation complex.[92] Through an elaborate process of deference, Lumpkin details the racialized and gendered structures of power at play in Georgia through language that simultaneously makes Blackness and Indigeneity present and absent, an ideological Removal that frees whiteness from culpability through his use of metaphor.

Moreover, he argues that Georgia settlers never enslaved Native people or brutalized them in the ways white settlers have in other states. However, in order to make his claim, he reinforces a racialized hierarchy by which he posits Indigenous people as better off than the enslaved (of African descent), at least in Georgia. Later in this passage, Lumpkin suggests that in other states, colonized Indigenous people and enslaved people are treated comparably. Under this rubric, he positions colonization and enslavement as distinct forms of violence that cannot be quantified and compared. Again, he positions enslavement as the most abject state and makes it rhetorically dependent on an anti-Blackness that justifies Georgia's treatment of colonized Native people *and* enslaved Black people. According to that false equivalency, then, Native peoples were treated humanely because they were not enslaved. Unfortunately for Lumpkin's argument, this is historically inaccurate. Throughout the eighteenth century, Georgia colonial law supported the enslavement of *both* Native and Black peoples, and Georgia and South Carolina are the two colonies where Native enslavement was most practiced.[93] In actuality, the enslavement of Cherokees, especially women, fostered the growth of Afro-Cherokee clan members through kinship. By imaging enslavement as something that did not happen to Indigenous people in Georgia, Lumpkin also suggests a division between Blackness and Indigeneity that recenters whiteness through the affirmation of state policy.

When talking about enslavement and colonization, Lumpkin uses passive language, but the arguments for Georgia's rights as a sovereign state are far more active and piercing in tone. States' rights politicians like Charles Eaton Haynes and Lumpkin saw the issue of Removal as a territorial one dating back to the Intercourse Act of 1802, in which Georgia leaders agreed to cede the state's western territorial holdings to the federal government (part of

Georgia's colonial charter), with the understanding that the federal government would eliminate Indigenous title to any and all of the land that remained in Georgia proper.[94] Extinguishing Indigenous title was not a formal part of these discussions, but more importantly, they included no consultation with any Native leaders. By not including Native people in these discussions, Georgians enforced a mapping of colonial space that prioritized the scale of the state in two ways: Georgia leaders consented to ceding territorial holdings specifically so that land could be formally annexed to the United States to establish additional states, and all of this was done with the assumption that, in return, the United States would help white Georgians forcibly displace the entire Indigenous population.

Equally muddled in his writing and speeches is Lumpkin's attempt to outline state sovereignty and why, according to him, the Cherokee Nation has no viable right to their ancestral territories. Most telling is the way Lumpkin's multiple uses of the word "state" trip over each other in his explanation of how he and other Georgia politicians were approaching relations with the Cherokee Nation after the State of Georgia had ostensibly gained control over Muscogee lands by 1827:

> But the state of affairs was far different, in regard to the Cherokees, who still occupied the whole of the northwestern part of Georgia, which is still known as Cherokee, Ga., embracing some five or six millions of acres of the best lands within the limits of the State. This state of things rendered it obvious to all well informed discerning men, that the resources of Georgia could never be extensively developed by a well devised system of internal improvements, and commercial and social intercourse with other portions of the Union, especially the great West, under this portion of the state was settled by an industrious, enlightened, free-hold population—entitled to, and meriting, all the privileges of citizenship.[95]

I quote Lumpkin at length to demonstrate how the Enlightenment rhetoric he employs muddles his attempt to justify white occupation and discredit Cherokee nationalism. The "state of affairs" is not self-explanatory—it is contradictory. To begin with, his description waffles between state markers and Cherokee ones. The first sentence struggles with its geographic descriptions: "northwestern part of Georgia," "Cherokee, Ga." Cherokee County was not established until 1831 under Lumpkin's gubernatorial reign, so the area he describes here is still Cherokee territory. By describing the Nation as "Cherokee, Ga.," Lumpkin attempts to overwrite Cherokee nationalism with state sovereignty; it is a speculative postulation of future geographies.[96] Again, language exposes the contradictions of colonialism in his formulation. His dual use of "state"—a mode of being (i.e., state of affairs or state of things) and a polity (i.e., the state of Georgia)—demonstrates his struggle to justify white settlement. The "state of things" is not as straightforward as Lumpkin seemingly desires—discrediting Indigenous belonging in the name of white colonization proves, at least here, to be a project that necessitates contradiction, even of the term Lumpkin seems most attached to, "state."

Scale as Violence: From Nation to County

In his renouncement of Cherokee sovereignty, Lumpkin fails to mention another driving impetus for the seizure of Cherokee lands: the discovery of gold. After Cherokees found gold in the mountains near Dahlonega, white people began flocking to the Nation to mine, almost exclusively without Cherokee permission.[97] Lumpkin's gubernatorial predecessor George Gilmer, in collaboration with the Georgia legislature, furthered the interests of white intruders by declaring Georgia law over all of the Nation in December 1829 and declaring all Cherokee laws null and void by June 30, 1830. Once Lumpkin took office, he furthered efforts to exert pressure on the Cherokee Nation. He had run on an Indian affairs platform that criticized Gilmer for not doing enough to take over Cherokee lands. Lumpkin's win of the governorship empowered him to push an already aggressive state-driven intimidation policy even further. Again, with the help of the state legislature, he passed a law authorizing the survey of Cherokee lands and encouraged white settlement in the region through a lottery system. As I discuss in more detail shortly, he later established counties from the lottery land, including Cherokee County, in 1831. County formation was an explicit refusal of Cherokee national sovereignty and a watershed moment in state-level disregard of Indigenous sovereignty and Native-U.S. boundary lines (boundary lines he personally helped establish decades earlier). For Lumpkin, surveying was a necessary first step in his ultimate goal: dismantling the Cherokee Nation and forcibly relocating all Cherokees west of the Mississippi.[98] He did not consult the Cherokee Nation on any of his policy decisions, which were a direct violation of Cherokee sovereignty.

Following the survey's completion, Lumpkin declared that the lands were open for white settlement and instituted three land lotteries, two in 1832 and one in 1833, all of which provided eligible white men with either 40 acres for mining gold or 160 acres for farming. The May 4, 1833, issue of the *Phoenix* published the following response to the lotteries: "The legislature of Georgia passed an act dividing the Cherokee Nation into 10 counties, but we ask what has become of our sixteen solemn treaties which guarantee forever to the Cherokees the integrity of their territory? They have been destroyed and put under foot by the same rule that one man would murder another and rob him."[99] Not only were these lands the ancestral homelands of the Cherokee people, but Cherokees still lived in their territory. When Cherokees complained to Georgia and U.S. federal officials, little was done to help extract intruders from the Nation. It was not unusual for these squatters to use force against Cherokees while occupying their lands, and eventually, more and more white settlers began building homes without approval from the Nation.[100] As Cherokees responded by defending themselves and their territory, Georgia papers derided them as savage and violent.[101] According to John Ross, even Hugh Montgomery, the Indian agent charged with extracting intruders from the Nation, had relatives squatting on the land.[102]

Moreover, Lumpkin's survey and lotteries stood in the face of the Supreme Court's decisions in *Cherokee Nation v. Georgia* (1831) and *Worcester v. Georgia* (1832), which collectively found that only the federal government could negotiate with Indian tribes. While Chief Justice John Marshall described Cherokees and other Native peoples as having a "domestic dependent" relationship to the United States that he intentionally painted in vague terms, in the *Worcester v. Georgia* case the court carried this logic further. The court argued that the State of Georgia did not have jurisdiction over the Cherokee Nation because the Nation fell under the federal government's protection, not the state's.[103] Lumpkin was furious with this decision and decided to ignore it. He felt he had support from President Andrew Jackson and therefore was willing to dismiss the court's decision and move forward with the land lotteries.[104]

Like many other official state documents, the land lotteries were printed and bound. The number of names is overwhelming, and the list, when coupled with the orderliness of columns and line-drawn maps, makes Removal legible. The lottery records have an ease and mundanity that paradoxically elevate the violence and trauma they represent. In the 1838 publication of the lotteries, page 66 shows a list of names for the fourth district, second section, of so-called Cherokee County (figure 1.4). The survey is laid out on a grid that stretches across East Branch Swamp and Federal Road, listing plots numerically with little regard for (or interest in) elevation or topographical differences like swamplands, woods, or foothills.[105] Land and ownership are understood mathematically and according to a notion of forced organization

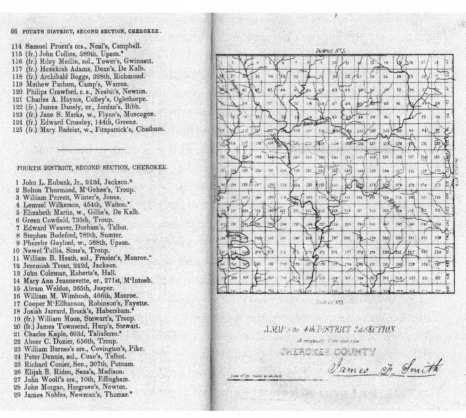

66   FOURTH DISTRICT, SECOND SECTION, CHEROKEE.

114 Samuel Pruett's ors., Neal's, Campbell.
115 (fr.) John Collins, 589th, Upson.*
116 (fr.) Riley Medlin, sol., Tower's, Gwinnett.
117 (fr.) Hezekiah Adams, Dean's, De Kalb.
118 (fr.) Archibald Boggs, 398th, Richmond.
119 Mathew Parham, Camp's, Warren.
120 Philips Crawford, r. s., Nesbit's, Newton.
121 Charles A. Haynie, Colley's, Oglethorpe.
122 (fr.) James Danely, or., Jordan's, Bibb.
123 (fr.) Jane S. Marks, w., Flynn's, Muscogee.
124 (fr.) Edward Crossley, 144th, Greene.
125 (fr.) Mary Badolet, w., Fitzpatrick's, Chatham.

FOURTH DISTRICT, SECOND SECTION, CHEROKEE.

1 John L. Eubank, Jr., 242d, Jackson.*
2 Bolton Thurmond, M'Gehee's, Troup.
3 William Perrett, Winter's, Jones.
4 Lemuel Wilkerson, 454th, Walton.*
5 Elizabeth Martin, w., Gillis's, De Kalb.
6 Green Cowfield, 735th, Troup.
7 Edward Weaver, Durham's, Talbot.
8 Stephen Bodeford, 789th, Sumter.
9 Phoreby Gaylord, w., 588th, Upson.
10 Newel Tullis, Sims's, Troup.
11 William B. Heath, sol., Frasier's, Monroe.*
12 Jeremiah Trout, 242d, Jackson.
13 John Coleman, Roberts's, Hall.
14 Mary Ann Jeannevette, or., 271st, M'Intosh.
15 Abram Weldon, 365th, Jasper.
16 William M. Wimbush, 466th, Monroe.
17 Cooper M'Ellhannon, Robinson's, Fayette.
18 Josiah Jarrard, Brock's, Habersham.*
19 (fr.) William Moon, Stewart's, Troup.
20 (fr.) James Townsend, Harp's, Stewart.
21 Charles Kaple, 603d, Taliaferro.*
22 Abner C. Dozier, 656th, Troup.
23 William Barnes's ors., Covington's, Pike.
24 Peter Dennis, sol., Coxe's, Talbot.
25 Richard Conier, Sen., 307th, Putnam.
26 Elijah B. Riden, Seas's, Madison.
27 John Woolf's ors., 10th, Effingham.
28 John Morgan, Hargrove's, Newton.
29 James Nobles, Newman's, Thomas.*

FIGURE 1.4   James F. Smith, "A Map of the 4th District 2d Section of Originally Cherokee, Now Cherokee County," in *The Cherokee Land Lottery, Containing a Numerical List of the Names of the Fortunate Drawers in Said Lottery, with an Engraved Map of Each District* (New York: Harper and Brothers, 1838). Courtesy of Hargrett Rare Book and Manuscript Library, University of Georgia Libraries.

that runs counter to Cherokee understandings of balance. Here, balance is found through a tidy grid rather than a sense of interrelationality between the land and its human and other-than-human inhabitants. The grid also serves as a spatial precursor to allotment policy, by which the plotting of individual properties was used to try to dismantle Indigenous territorialities and relationships with the land, especially those that ran counter to the capitalist ideal of private property. While these lottery maps are certainly not the first examples of this practice, they foreshadow late nineteenth-century allotment policy and make all the more evident why the Five Tribes in Indian Territory—who had been violently Removed from the Southeast—had such strong reactions to allotment in the 1890s; they had seen it before.

Lumpkin was quite clear that he understood white settlement of Cherokee land to be a necessity in order to secure—through force—settler colonial control of Cherokee territory. As he explains in the lengthy quote excerpted earlier, "The resources of Georgia could never be extensively developed by a well devised system of internal improvements, and commercial and social intercourse with other portions of the Union, especially the great West, until this portion of the state was settled by an industrious, enlightened, freehold population—entitled to, and meriting, all the privileges of citizenship."[106] For Lumpkin, white male occupation is key to Georgia's economic development and necessary for U.S. expansion. He makes the patriarchal white supremacist logic undergirding occupation unapologetically explicit.

This is not to say that there was no such thing as private property in the Nation before the land lotteries. As discussed earlier, there were affluent Cherokees who owned plantations and other large tracts of land and who, as enslavers, actively participated in systems of racial capital, financial accumulation, and exploitation of labor, but they did not do so with the explicit intention of undermining either Cherokee or U.S. sovereignty. And in fact, central to Lumpkin's argument, along with those of most Removal advocates, was the claim that "mixed-blood" Cherokees of wealth and means were forcing the rest of the Nation to resist Removal in order to further their interests. This discourse attempted to delegitimize the Cherokee as a nation by alleging that a small group of outsiders made all political decisions. It posited a disembodied Cherokee collective of savages with no access to tribal governance and little understanding of U.S. politics and culture. While it is true that the consolidation of the Nation did empower a small cadre of Cherokee men of an emerging elite class, an emphasis on blood quantum and assimilation reinscribed racialist notions of Cherokeeness promoted by white people like Lumpkin with the end goal of total elimination, rather than Cherokee-centered notions of identity and belonging. It is essential to interrogate the devastating impact of blood quantum on understandings of Cherokeeness but also be mindful that the same logic has routinely been used to delegitimize the Cherokee as an enduring people capable of governing themselves.

In reading extensively across Georgia newspapers, political documents, and personal writings from this era, it is obvious just how often this notion of a cabal of white and "mixed-blood" men running the Nation was used by white writers to delegitimize Cherokee refusals to leave their homeland. In Lumpkin's case, it was also evidence of an explicit distaste for interracial or intercultural relationships. While it is important to note that the consolidation of the Nation did erode women's long-standing positions of power and benefit men of white ancestry in the Nation, to say that these men made decisions on behalf of the people without any consultation from other Cherokees yet again erases the voices of Afro-Cherokees and Cherokee women. The *Phoenix* reprinted an anti-Removal statement given "by females residing in Salequoyee and Pine Log" that describes Removal west as "highly oppressive, cruel, and unjust." They share the "sentiment of a vast majority of people. The fact is they are not influenced by their leaders—they are actuated by the honest conviction of their hearts."[107] Though the petition was published in the *Phoenix*, it was addressed to the council, demonstrating how Cherokee women used the growth of a print culture discourse to assert their political agency, even as earlier matrilineal protocols lost official influence over formal decision-making.

Returning to the lottery map, its orderly, gridded lines gesture toward Thomas Jefferson's idealized yeoman farmer, whose labors over his individual plot of land feed his family and maintain his physical, spiritual, and political health. In fact, many of the white intruders who forcibly took over Cherokee lands were neither enslavers nor affluent. They were poor people with aspirations for class mobility. However, those who benefited from the lotteries were complicit in perpetuating Georgia's plantation economy and directly aided in the expansion of Georgia's slavocracy.[108] Not all of these new occupiers would gain the kind of economic stability that they hoped for in Georgia, and one of the enduring fables of North Georgia is the claim that there were very few plantations. Instead, the story goes, most farms were family run, making white settlers somehow less complicit in Georgia's slavocracy. But cotton cultivation did facilitate some social mobility for white settlers, and it ensured a state-based economy dependent on enslaved labor that saturated almost all aspects of industry, as well as social and political life.[109]

Perhaps the most discursively significant aspect of the map is the explanation of the county name. The inscription reads, "A MAP of the 4th DISTRICT 2.d. SECTION of originally Cherokee, now CHEROKEE COUNTY."[110] Here, James F. Smith, the book's compiler (whose signature sits below the description), succinctly synthesizes the project of U.S. colonialism, particularly its relation to the state. The Cherokee Nation, listed here only as Cherokee, is no longer legible as a nation—it is a county, the primary territorial subsection of the federated U.S. state. Naming part of the Cherokee Nation "Cherokee County" simultaneously does three things. First, it disregards the status of the Cherokee Nation as foreign to the United States. Second, it attaches the word "Cherokee" to a subset of the state whose autonomy is superseded by state power. Third, it signifies "Cherokee" as subservient to both U.S. and Georgia authority and thus reinforces the argument made by Lumpkin and other Georgians that the State of Georgia had total jurisdiction over the Cherokee Nation. In this brief description of the map, we see the role of state power in perpetuating racialized colonial violence; it is an image of sheer force further promulgated by the hundreds and hundreds of pages of lottery recipients' names that accompany it. Here, and in the Georgia newspapers, printed, textual violence asserts Georgia's colonial rule over Native people. It is not simply the demarcation of boundary lines that enacts long-term Indigenous expulsion, but also the visual and discursive insistence on these surveys, county names, individual deeds, and lottery lists as totalizing spatialities—printscapes of state sovereignty. The visual of the state of Georgia as untarnished by an *imperium in imperio* or any other visual lacunae is the fantasy of U.S. empire—clean wholes without rupture that necessitate Removal.

The visual representation of Georgia's genocidal project perhaps helps illuminate why Lumpkin's distaste for Cherokee leaders, especially John Ross, was matched by his hatred of what he called the "public press of Georgia."[111] The published collection of his writings, *The Removal of the Cherokee Indians from Georgia*, includes a letter he wrote to Colonel William Williamson in 1833 in which he blames the Cherokees' retaliation against the formation of counties and Georgia rule on the state press.[112] This is a peculiar stance to take, given that most Georgia papers heartily endorsed Removal and Lumpkin's gubernatorial reign. There was, in fact, little critique of Removal, at least in the Georgia newspaper records of the 1830s that I read. As I noted earlier, it helped unify white Georgians and repair political schisms rather than exacerbate the already fractured landscape of Georgia politics. Lumpkin's repeated lambasting of the press seems to be misdirected. He is motivated not so much by hostility toward the Georgia press of the 1830s, or even the national U.S. press, as he is by paranoia that the press can serve to work against his goals, as much as it can in favor of them. It is not what the press says, after all, that he calls out, but rather what the "Indians" read in the "unprincipled and lying newspapers" that fuels their resistance to the new counties and Georgia rule.[113] Again, he exhibits a fear of the Indigenous reading subject who does not read according to the mores of the colonial reading praxis. His inability to let the letters speak for themselves betrays an obsessive insistence on controlling the narrative and possible anxiety that it cannot stand on its own without his intervention. This oppressive stranglehold on the historical record echoes Lumpkin's lifelong commitments to oppression and the colonial project of U.S. state sovereignty.

The boundary lines between settler and Indigenous, United States and not United States, are more palimpsestic than suggested by the survey maps. Georgia's assault on the Cherokee Nation in the 1820s and 1830s cohered the narrative of states' rights that continues to dominate states' rights rationales today. Enslavement was central to Georgia's efforts to destroy the Nation and take its land, but Cherokee participation in chattel enslavement also played a critical role in the erosion of matriliny. Georgians felt threatened as wealthy Cherokee plantation enslavers accumulated more wealth than some Southern white enslavers. As Cherokees refused to cede their communal landholdings to the State of Georgia, Georgia politicians saw the Cherokee Nation as an affront to state sovereignty and the seizure of Cherokee territory as a way to expand the white plantation land base. Attending to how the *Phoenix* and regional Georgia newspapers influenced debates about sovereignty and states' rights, we see print's role in shaping physical space and notions of race, as well as the limits of the newspaper-as-form. At the same time, Walker's *Appeal* gestures to the creative potential of insurgent forms of print production and circulation.

"Resurgens"

The seal for the city of Atlanta depicts a phoenix rising from the ashes with the Latin "Resurgens" emblazoned above it. On either side of the phoenix sit two dates, 1847 and 1865, marking pivotal years in Atlanta's emergent role as the capital of Georgia and as a hub of Southern industry. When I lived in Atlanta, I was always unable to shake the affinity I saw between the city seal visible on sewer drains, city flags, and T-shirts and the illustration on the *Cherokee Phoenix* masthead (figures 1.5 and 1.6). The city's seal carries a semiotic trace intended to signal a past resurgence, albeit one that initially celebrated white Confederate endurance. Across the state of Georgia, we repeatedly see these enjambments, contestations, and anomalies that signal the festering legacy of the nineteenth century. For example, Stone Mountain, a sacred site for Muskogean peoples, is also home to the ultimate symbol of states' rights, "Confederate Mount Rushmore," which has become a site of kitsch novelty by the early twenty-first century.[114]

As gentrification has driven up the cost of living in Atlanta and white migrants have begun returning to the city in significant numbers for the first time since the civil rights era, Stone Mountain has shifted from being a white-flight suburb to one that is predominantly Black, another form of Removal that also touches back to the Great Migration(s) of the twentieth century. Disidentifications, resignification, and appropriation dot the landscape just

FIGURE 1.5 Seal of
Atlanta. Courtesy of
Wikimedia Commons,
https://commons
.wikimedia.org/w/index
.php?title=File:Seal_of
_Atlanta.png.

FIGURE 1.6 Closeup of
the *Cherokee Phoenix*
masthead. Courtesy
of the American
Antiquarian Society.

as clearly as North Georgia's ranch houses and pickup trucks. State identity is intertwined with misdirection of anti-Black and anti-Indigenous iconography that gets redeployed to affirm a state sense of self with inarguable ties to white supremacy. What should be a haunting reminder of historical violence becomes resignified iconography of a unified state self—how can one take Stone Mountain seriously with the late twentieth-century techno-garishness of its laser light show, especially given Atlanta's reputation as a Black mecca or "the city too busy to hate," a city previously named Marthasville to honor Lumpkin's daughter? Georgia redeploys these signifiers to denote its boundaries and shore up a sense of colonial autonomy that reinscribes the logic of white supremacy, even when asserting otherwise—not unlike twentieth-century state investment in the Chieftains Trail. Contradiction serves as a stabilizing force, and resignification animates the dangerous and enduring power of states' rights.

CHAPTER TWO

Surveying the Swamp

After the United States acquired East and West Florida in 1822, Congress quickly ordered land surveys of the new territory and established the Georgia-Florida border.[1] Georgia politicians immediately protested, claiming that the boundary line between the state and territory decreased Georgia landholdings. In congressional discussion of the dispute, Representative Richard Wilde described Georgia's position as a matter of "state pride."[2] Even though Florida and Georgia were now part of the same nation, Georgia politicians wanted to maximize the state's land base. It was not until the eve of the Civil War, the moment when both Florida and Georgia ceded from the United States and affirmed a new international boundary (that of the Mason-Dixon Line), that the states' shared border became a site of compromise rather than contestation. Yet, again state sovereignty worked at the behest of a national project of warfare aimed at protecting the same plantation economy that necessitated Indian Removal and enslavement.

As the example of the Florida-Georgia boundary line makes clear, surveys were not apolitical but instead essential to asserting a regime aimed at eradicating other place-based epistemologies—other territorialities—in its wake. As a first step in establishing townships and settlements, surveying often occurred alongside white migration and settler colonialism, and they helped rich enslavers calculate how much land was available for expanding the plantation economy. Surveys and settlement collaboratively fostered white population growth in U.S. territories and were essential for cohering a white supremacist regime.

In Florida, as was the case elsewhere, the settler narrative presented in surveys antagonistically stood in opposition to already-established Indigenous and Maroon territorialities. The heart of the Georgia-Florida boundary line dispute hinged on contradictory claims about the origin of Saint Marys River—disagreements that stemmed from imprecise surveying.[3] During an earlier U.S. survey expedition in 1799, the Okefenokee Swamp proved arduous for white surveyors to navigate and Seminoles refused to help them, so Andrew Ellicott, the surveyor responsible for the project, provided what he felt was an educated guess as to the river's origin. In a 1799 letter to the secretary of state, he complained that "it is with the most sensible mortification I

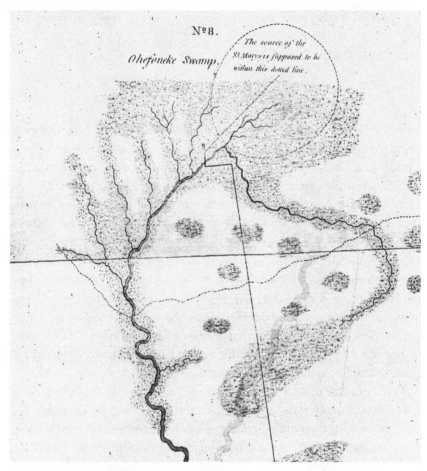

FIGURE 2.1 Andrew Ellicott, insert no. 8, in *The Journal of Andrew Ellicott: Late Commissioner on Behalf of the United States during Part of the Year 1796, the Years 1797, 1798, 1799, and Part of the Year 1800: For Determining the Boundary of the United States and the Possessions of His Catholic Majesty in America* (Philadelphia: William Fry, 1814). Courtesy of the Special and Area Studies Collections, George A. Smathers Libraries, University of Florida.

have ever yet experienced, that I have to inform you of the failure, in part, of our business owing to the hostile disposition of the Indians."[4] Nonetheless, the map he constructed of the Okefenokee Swamp and the Saint Marys River was the official source used to mark the border between Georgia and Spanish Florida and then that between Georgia and Florida Territory (figure 2.1). Despite self-professed failure, Ellicott's mission still had a real, material impact on the U.S. map. It is a reminder of the fiction of colonial borders and the ability of Indigenous people to undermine them. Native and Maroon

communities would continue to actively refuse the violent mapmaking project of surveying Florida throughout the first half of the century.

As in the previous chapter, here I interrogate how the survey and the newspaper, two critical sites for cohering U.S. colonial belonging, inscribed dominant narratives of U.S. state formation. These *sovereign printscapes*, meaning
the production of territoriality through the circulation of print, were influential in the U.S. seizure of Florida but were not always the most effective tools
for colonization. The swampy terrain of Florida, coupled with Indigenous
and Black resistance to U.S. occupation, made surveying difficult, and colonizers would have limited geographic knowledge of the region well into the
nineteenth century. Moreover, due to political disputes, problems with material production, and disease, local newspapers struggled to narrate a sense of
U.S. settler belonging or to cohere a territorial identity.

The limitations of the survey and the newspaper to crystallize a sense of
belonging and autonomy for white settlers in Florida expose the fictive nature of statehood origin stories. To propose statehood, U.S. territorial
residents were typically required to demonstrate to Congress that their communities could (and already did) emulate the structures of U.S. federated
states. Such a process, one that promoted a state-like existence before official
statehood, bolstered the fiction that statehood was something organic and
that happened as a matter of natural course. In Florida, however, white settlers could not agree for decades on whether they wanted statehood (or
whether they wanted one state or multiple).[5] As importantly, Seminoles,
Black Seminoles, and Maroons rejected U.S. occupation with physical force
and, because of the lack of knowledge of Florida's landscape, white settlers
were at an enormous disadvantage.

The larger argument of this chapter is that employing a territorial hermeneutics (i.e., a willingness to denaturalize the geography of the U.S. settler
state) when reading these sovereign printscapes offers a counternarrative
to the one typically told about southeastern Indian Removal, a far murkier
one. During the Second U.S.-Seminole War (1835–42), also called the Florida
War, Osceola became a featured character in U.S. print, embodying the contradictions laid bare by colonization in Florida and by federal Indian Removal
policy. I unpack how contemporaneous white depictions of Osceola attempted to contain the "swampiness" of the conflict in Florida but, much like
the U.S.-Seminole wars, failed to do so.[6] Colonial narratives could not contain Osceola's legacy, and he would continue to serve as a symbol of anti-
imperialist resistance for Indigenous and Black writers. Compounding the
material impact of forty years of expensive and unpopular combat, the United

States was unable to Remove Indigenous and Black communities from Florida entirely. These failures strained the ideology underpinning the stock story of state formation—namely, the genocidal fantasy of the vanishing Indian, Removal, and Black enslavement. In so-called Florida, the land and its inhabitants literally and figuratively worked against white possession.

In contrast to the extensive U.S. print record, there is a dearth of written materials left by Seminoles, Black Seminoles, and Maroons living and fighting in Florida at this time. And for a good reason. In order to evade U.S. capture, Seminoles moved quite regularly through the territory, which they knew exceptionally well. Seminoles, Black Seminoles, and Maroons used their knowledge of the land and their relations with the other-than-human world to evade the gaze of white settlers and the military. Indigenous and Black people found refuge in Florida from the colonial plantation zone and constructed their own autonomous, self-governed communities.

It is clear from treaty language between Seminole leaders and U.S. officials that Seminoles well understood the weaponization of print and writing by the U.S. settler state. Instead of reading non-Seminole and Maroon sources against the grain through predominantly white and U.S.-based print culture, I suggest a different kind of reading practice that attends to the necessary silences and fissures in the printed record as strategic and political choices and not simply lacks of knowledge or access. I contend that the gaps in print knowledge of Seminole, Black Seminole, and Maroon life in this era indicate archives elsewhere and otherwise. They are a critical reminder that writing cannot—and should not—hold every story. I am confident that these stories exist and have been tended to for generations, but as a non-Black and non-Seminole person without direct ties to the communities that call Florida home, they are not my stories to tell, nor do I have direct access to them. Engaging forms of territoriality beyond the state means letting go of the totalizing desire for knowledge accumulation that was also manifested through forms like the survey and the newspaper to work against Black and Native freedom. In holding on to the way Seminoles and others in Florida sabotaged the colonial violence of the survey and print, it is critical to remember that silence tells a story too.[7] Part of engaging a territorial reading praxis that works against the state, especially in studies of print culture, is to read absences and silences not necessarily as spaces to be filled by printed scholarship but sometimes as suggestive of relations, movements, and geographies beyond the printed page (including this one).

The lack of easy access to these accounts as an outsider, I suggest, in fact signals the radical placemaking of Afro-Native communities beyond the state. Through this suggestion, I take seriously Tiffany Lethabo King's description of "Black revolt as performance" when she writes that it "sits both within and outside the bounds of translatability. Sometimes the meaning can be discerned within humanist modes of speech and gestures, and at other times, it is elusive because it speaks outside humanist systems of signification and corporeal protocols."[8] *Because* nineteenth-century stories of Indigenous and Black freedom in Florida seek evasion from the surveillance of enslaver-colonizers, they can be challenging to describe or detail in print, but in this challenge lies their radical potential. Complicating matters was the fact that Seminoles participated in enslavement. While Black Seminoles (a self-identification used to describe Seminole-enslaved people and their Freedpeople descendants) fought alongside Seminole enslavers, their fights for freedom were undoubtedly distinct, and this complexity must be accounted for when we think about Black and Native freedom.[9] Later in this chapter, I read Albery Allson Whitman's epic poem *The Rape of Florida* (1884) as evidencing the power of placemaking outside the state and suggest that the poem opens up ways to imagine the radical potential of Afro-Native community. Through my reading of these texts, I suggest a territorial reading praxis that embraces swampy inbetweenness, silence, and mess in order to attend to harmful chapters of print history in Florida and honor what may have been intentionally kept from the print archive by those targeted as enemies of the state.

It is critical to remember that, despite a dearth of contemporaneous materials, Native and Black people have used print to challenge the dominant Floridian narrative of U.S. occupation after the fact. Many of these accounts think across time, connecting the past, present, and future. They remind us that the temporality of when a story is told (and retold) and the form it takes cannot be prescriptive and may operate outside the conventions of time, space, and narrative that dominate storytelling in the colonial academy. Despite limited use of print in the nineteenth century, in the second half of the twentieth century, the Seminole Tribe of Florida would operate its newspaper, the *Seminole News* (still in circulation today as the *Seminole Tribune*). Betty Mae Tiger Jumper and Alice Osceola established the paper, and both Betty Mae and her son Moses Jumper Jr. would serve as editors.[10] Black and Native writers, including Whitman and Tiger Jumper, provide counternarratives to the dominant one told by the contemporaneous print archive and tell it at some historical distance. Whitman, Tiger Jumper, and others remind us of the territorialities Black and Indigenous peoples continued to nourish elsewhere, forms of marronage obscured from colonial surveillance that refuse the boundaries prescribed by the state. They remind us that stories submerge and surface in various mediums when needed in order to endure, adapt, and best serve their communities.

Territorial Print Culture

Florida's archipelagic affinities with the Caribbean and the continent made it appealing to the United States, just as it had for European colonial powers. Britain had briefly wrested control of Florida from Spain at the start of the nineteenth century, and the U.S. Congress saw the exchange as an opportunity to make the United States' claim to the region, albeit an unsubstantiated one.[11] On January 15, 1811, Congress passed the No-Transfer Resolution, a warning to Spain that if Florida territory "pass[ed] into the hands of any foreign Power," the United States would forcibly secure the territory.[12] In the language of the resolution, Florida is graciously allowed to maintain its identity as a Spanish territory, but Congress suggests that Florida is nonetheless destined to be incorporated into the United States. In the No-Transfer Resolution, the United States is described as distinct from "foreign" powers through proximity—because of the shared border between U.S. states and Florida. It is a statement of pure hubris, but one that set the tone for how the United States would seize Florida.[13] The resolution entirely ignores Indigenous presence, which was a grave error on the part of Congress. It was Indigenous people and not Spain who would prove the most significant military threat to the U.S. seizure of Florida.[14] Throughout the Madison presidency, the U.S. federal government and military systematically exerted pressure on Spanish sovereignty in Florida, arguing that U.S. interventions into the region were necessitated by self-defense, in no small part because Seminoles had an inexplicable antagonism toward the United States.[15] However, while the No-Transfer Resolution imagined Florida would inevitably become U.S. territory, the U.S.-Seminole wars demonstrated the conceit of such an assumption.

The 1821 issues of the *Florida Gazette*, a weekly newspaper published in Saint Augustine (hereafter referenced as St. Augustine), provide one example of what colonial transfer looked like in practice. The paper's run began just days after the U.S. takeover of East Florida. The front page of the July 28, 1821, issue includes a "Historical Sketch of Florida" that details a colonial history of Pensacola from the establishment of a French colony in 1699 to Andrew Jackson's 1818 invasion, forcible possession, and current effort to incorporate Pensacola and the rest of western Florida into the United States. To the right runs a "Notice to Claimants" outlining property disputes negotiated in the Adams-Onís Treaty between the United States and Spain (figure 2.2).[16] Below the notice sits a piece attributed to the *Baltimore Morning Chronicle* celebrating the "liberty of the press" as a "public blessing." A letter to the editors

FLORIDA GAZETTE.

Vol. I. ST. AUGUSTINE, (E. F.) SATURDAY, JULY 28, 1821. No. 3.

THE GAZETTE IS PUBLISHED EVERY SATURDAY EVENING, BY RICHARD W. EDES & CO. AT FIVE DOLLARS PER ANNUM, PAYABLE IN ADVANCE.

No subscription received for a less term than one year, and no paper discontinued until all arrearages are paid, except at the discretion of the Publishers.

Persons wishing their papers discontinued at the expiration of the year will give notice to that effect, otherwise they will be considered as subscribers for another term.

Terms of Advertising.

Advertisements not exceeding fifteen lines, will be charged One Dollar for the *first*, and Fifty Cents for *every subsequent* insertion. Those over fifteen lines, inserted at the same rate. If the length of time is not specified, they will be continued until forbid, and charged accordingly.

All Letters, on business, to the Editors, must be Post-paid.

HISTORICAL SKETCH OF FLORIDA.

(Concluded from last week.)

Pensacola was founded by the French in 1699, and is the capital of West Florida, at the mouth of Escambia and Coeneccup rivers, lat. 30. 15 north, and lon. 87. 14 west. The harbour is said to be spacious and safe; the bar admitting vessels drawing twenty feet water. The entrance into the bay is defended by a small fort on the west end of Rose's island and a battery on the main land nearly opposite. The Governor's palace is a large stone building, ornamented with a tower. Since it has been in possesion of Spain, it has been on the decline. There was formerly a fortification on the sand hills back of the town, but too distant to afford substantial protection to the town or harbour. In 1781, it was taken from the British by a Spanish force, commanded by Don Bernard Galvez, after an obstinate defence. During the siege, a shell bursted open the door of the powder magazine, under the redoubt; which was blown up, and one hundred men killed and wounded. The place was soon after surrendered by capitulation, and remained in possesion of Spain until it was ceded to his Catholic majesty by the treaty of 1783.

In common with the other provinces of Spain in north America; West Florida has been an unprofitable and an expensive burthen to the Spanish government. The civil and military officers and soldiers constitute a majority of the inhabitants; and more than half of the remainder, may justly be compared to the followers of a camp. By the treaty of the 3d of Sept. 1783, East and West Floridas were ceded by Great Britain to Spain.

"Article 5th, His Catholic majesty agrees that the British inhabitants or others who may have been subjects of the King of Great Britain in the said countries, may retire in full security and liberty where they shall think proper, and may sell their estates and remove their effects as well as their persons; the term limited for their emigration being fixed to the space of 18 months—but if from the value of their possessions they shall not be able to dispose of them within the said term; then his Catholic majesty shall grant them a prolongation proportioned to that end." Such as chose to remain in the provinces were secured in all their rights as Spanish subjects.

By the treaty of the 3d of Sept. 1783, between the United States and the King of Great Britain, the line of demarcation between the Floridas and the U. States commences on the Mississippi, in lat. 31 deg. north running due east to the middle of the rivers Apalachicola or Chatahouchie, thence along the middle thro' to its junction with Flint river, thence straight to the head of St. Mary's river, and thence along the middle of the St. Mary's river to the Atlantic ocean. In this treaty, no notice is taken of the proclamation of the King of England of March 2, 1770, by which the northern limits of west Florida were extended to a parallel latitude with the mouth of the Yazoo; which afterwards was made the source of difficulty by the Spanish government, in running the line of demarcation; but the Spanish government ultimately yielded, and the line was run, according to the treaty, in 1783.

By the treaty between France and the U. States dated at Paris on the 30th of April 1803 all the territory mentioned in the 6th article, of the treaty of the 15th of Feb. 1763, between France, Spain and England; was ceded to the United States, as follows.

"Article, 1st. Whereas by the third article of the treaty, concluded at St. Idelfonso, October 1st. 1800, between the First Consul of the French Republic, and His Catholic Majesty, it was agreed as follows: His Catholic Majesty, engages on his part, to cede to the French Republic, six months after the full and entire execution of the conditions and stipulations herein, relative to his Royal Highness, the Duke of Parma, the Colony and Province of Louisiana, with the same extent that it now has in the hands of Spain, and that it had when France possessed it; and such as it should be after the treaties subsequently entered into between Spain and other States. *And Whereas*, in pursuance of the treaty, and particularly of the third article; the French Republic has an incontestable title to the domain and to the possession of the said territory. The First Consul of the French Republic, desiring to give to the United States, a strong proof of his friendship, doth hereby cede to the United States, in the name of the French Republic, forever, and its full sovereignty, the said territory, with all its rights and appurtenances, as fully and in the same manner as have been acquired by the French Republic, in virtue of the above mentioned treaty, concluded with His Catholic Majesty."

Notwithstanding the unequivocal language of right and title, guaranteed by the foregoing article of treaty, the Spanish government refused the surrender of West-Florida. The American government ultimately resorted to military force, and took possession of the Fort at Mobile and the Province.

During the late War, between the United States and Great-Britain, it became an object with the latter, to form an alliance with the Creek and Seminole Indians. To accomplish these purposes, the aid of the Spanish Governor of Pensacola was important; *to* give free access through the Floridas, to British emisaries, to supply the Indians with munitions of war. Under the pretext of a deficiency of military force to preserve neutrality, a British force was permitted to garrison a Spanish fortress at Pensacola.—From this place, Colonel Nicholls enlisted a force, fitted out an expedition against the Fort at Mobile, commanded by Major Lawrence, but was compelled to retire to Pensacola, with a considerable loss of men, and of the Commodore's frigate Hermes.

Major-General Jackson marched into the vicinity of Pensacola, and sent a flag to the Governor, demanding redress for the violation of neutrality, in suffering an expedition to be fitted out from that place against the United States. The flag was fired on, and compelled to return. The situation in which General Jackson was now placed, would not admit of a temporizing policy; he therefore determined to hazard his fame, upon the exercise of his judgment; he demanded of the Spanish Governor, that the different forts, by which the harbour of Pensacola was commanded, should be placed under the protection of the United States, until the Spanish Government should furnish the means of enforcing its neutral rights. This demand not having been complied with, the troops were put in motion, exhibiting evidences of an intention to make the attack upon the western part of the town; while the General, with the main body, entered in an opposite direction, before the garrison was aware of it. They were unexpectedly saluted by a battery in the street, which, after a few vollies, was carried by the bayonet. The Governor appeared with a flag, and offered to surrender the town and forts, unconditionally. The Barancas, which was the most important object of the expedition, remained to be taken possession of, but it was destroyed by the British troops, who suddenly embarked on board of their shipping, and left the bay. The General *returned* from Pensacola, leaving the Spanish Governor well satisfied, that the American troops had not molested the persons or property of the Spanish subjects.

After the conclusion of the war between the United States and Great Britain, some adventurers, who pretended to be subjects and agents of the British government, opened a trade with the Indians through the Floridas, and with the hope of finding their interest in the issue, gave aid and countenance to hostilities, which were carried on by the Creek and Seminole Indians, against the frontiers of Georgia; and several families were murdered. Another army was ordered into the nation, under the command of Gen. Jackson, and the Indians retired into Florida. They were pursued and defeated in several skirmishes; and under the protection of the Spanish government, three of the principal agents, who had joined and aided them in the war, were taken prisoners. These men were tried by a General Court Martial, and two of them, Robert C. Ambrister, and Alexander Arbuthnot, were found guilty—sentenced to suffer death, and were accordingly hanged. John I Arbuthnot, being less criminal, was spared on account of his youth. This measure which policy and justice required, put an end to hostilities, and closed the war.

The preliminaries of a treaty between the United States and Spain, has been the subject of a tedious negociation, and by the latter, a variety of evasive subterfuges were recorted to, for the purpose of producing delay. Finding however, that there was a disposition on the part of the American government, to take forcible possession of the Floridas, as a compensation for a large amount, due by Spain for illegal spoliations committed on the property of citizens of the United States, the Spanish Minister, agreed to a session of the Floridas, as a remuneration, in Feb. 1819. Care had previously been taken by the King of Spain, to lay a plan to replenish his coffers and increase the wealth of some of his favorites, by giving them grants for the whole of the unlocated territory. The American government by this arrangement, would have made itself responsible for the debt due by Spain to the citizens of the United States, and his Catholic Majesty and his favorites, would have pocketed the value of the spoil, out of which these debts were intended to have been paid. Eight months were wasted in Madrid by the American Minister, before the point was yielded by the Spanish Government, and the grants made null and void. The treaty according to the original intent and meaning, finally received the King's sanction, and was ratified by the United States, on the 22d day of February, 1821. A law was immediately after passed by Congress, authorising the President of the United States, to take possession of the Floridas, and establish a territorial government; of which *Major-General Andrew Jackson*, is appointed Governor.

[*Erratum.*—In the contents preceding this Sketch, 6th line from the bottom—for "Boundaries established by treaty, and the Floridas ceded to Great-Britain in 1783"—*read*—Boundaries established by treaty, and the Floridas ceded to *Spain* in 1783.

From the National Intelligencer.

NOTICE TO CLAIMANTS.

Office of the Commissioners, Washington, 14th June, 1821.

The Commissioners, appointed under the 11th article of the Treaty of Amity, Settlement, and Limits, between the United States of America and his Catholic Majesty, concluded at Washington, on the 22d day of February, 1819, *to* ascertain the full amount and validity of the claims mentioned, or referred to, in the said Treaty being organized as a Board, according to the provisions of the Treaty and the act of Congress in that case made and provided have passed the following Orders; of which, all those interested will be pleased to take notice:

"*Ordered*—That all persons having claims under the Treaty of Amity, Settlement, and Limits, between the United States of America and and his Catholic Majesty concluded at Washington on the 22d day of February, 1819, which are to be received by this Commission, do file a memorial of the same with the Secretary of the Board; to the end, that they may be hereafter duly examined, and the validity and amount thereof decided upon, according to the suitable and authentic testimony concerning the same which may be then required. The said memorial must be addressed to this Board; must set forth, particularly and minutely, the various facts and circumstances whence the right to prefer such claim is derived; and must be verified by the *affidavit* of the claimant.

"And, in order that claimants may be informed of what is now considered by the Commission as essential to be averred and established before any such memorial can be received by this Board, it is further—

"*Ordered*, That each claimant shall declare, in his said memorial, for and in behalf of whom the said claim is preferred; and whether the amount thereof, and of every part thereof, if allowed, does now, and, at the time when the said claim arose, did belong solely and absolutely to the said claimant, or to any other, and if any other, what person. And in cases of claims preferred for the benefit of any other than the claimant, the memorial to be exhibited must further set forth, when, why, and by what means, such other has become entitled to the amount or any part of the amount of the said claim. The memorial, required to be exhibited by all claimants, must also set forth, and certainly declare, whether the claimant, as well as any other for whose benefit the claim is preferred, is now, and at the time when the said claim arose was, a citizen of the United States of America—where he is now, and at the time the said claim arose was, domiciliated—and, if any, what change of domiciliation has since taken place. The said memorial must also set forth, whether the claimant, or any other who may have been at any time entitled to the amount claimed, or any part thereof, hath ever received any, and, if any, what sum of money, or other equivalent or indemnification, for the loss or injury sustained, satisfaction for which is therein asked.

"And, that time may be allowed to claimants, to prepare and file the memorials above mentioned; it is further

"*Ordered*, That when this Board shall adjourn to-day, it will adjourn to meet again on the 10th day of September next; at which time it will proceed to decide whether any memorials which may have been filed with the Secretary, in pursuance of the above orders, shall be received for examination.

"*Ordered*, That a copy of these proceedings be published by the Secretary of this Board, in all the public Gazettes in which the laws of the United States are usually printed."

By Order, T. WATKINS,

Secretary to the Commission under the 11th article of the Florida Treaty.

THE PRESS.

There has been much said and sung about the liberty of the press; but that liberty is a blessing or a curse, like every thing belonging to human nature, according to its use. A press that holds a stern, independent, dignified tone; that dares to stand forth the champion of liberty and independence; to frown indignant upon tyranny in every shape; to stand as a sentinel on the watchtower of the constitution, and to sound the alarm on the approach of danger—to volunteer in the service of oppressed and insulted virtue; to bring all the moral force it may command to the assistance of the pulpit; to attack the strong holds of vice and depravity: such a press is indeed, a public blessing.

[*Baltimore Morning Chronicle.*

Messrs. Editors,

Observing in your paper of last week, a "*Caution*," signed *William Robertson*, intending to mislead the public, reflecting, not only against the tribunal which existed in this city during the Spanish authorities, in countenancing illegal measures; whereby he pretends to say his wife is deprived of her brother's estate, but also to injure the character of two gentlemen of the very highest standing whom he had the assurance to name. Lest, from the absence of those gentlemen, the ignorant should credit those base assertions, I come forward *in my own name, and under my own responsibility*, to deny them, and to vindicate if necessary, the integrity of the gentlemen whom he has dared to villify. Mr. Frasier, late of this province, died after executing a will in his own hand writing, which is clothed with all the appearance of sound deliberation and forethought, in which, amongst other legacies, he left to a brother and sister, each one thousand pounds sterling, or the whole to the survivor. The sister, Ann, whilst in Scotland, received the whole amount of two thousand pounds, by the direction of Messrs. Yonge and Kingsly, two of the Executors named in the will. Owing to her alleging to them that the brother was dead, the rest of the property he gave to his own children. Robertson did attempt to proceed at law to set aside that will, and to defeat the intentions of a brother who had acted so liberally towards his sister. I beg leave to inform the public that no such suit is now pending, nor has Robertson exhibited proof to authorize him to appear at any tribunal either as the husband, nor that the person he represents is the bona fide sister of Mr. Frasier named in his will; however, if ever he does, the Executors are ready to establish the propriety of their conduct in the administration of that estate, and to expose the falsehoods which he has propagated against them.

Please have the above published in your next paper, and acknowledge me

Yours respectfully,
J. M. HERNANDEZ.

July 21.

EXCHANGE COFFEE-HOUSE.
Marshall & Ruckman,

RESPECTFULLY inform their friends and the public in general, that they have opened the above establishment opposite the Custom-House, where their bar will be constantly supplied with the best of Malt and Spiritous Liquors.

July 21.

ANN SCHELLING,

RESPECTFULLY informs the gentlemen of St. Augustine, that she has opened an establishment west of the store of Mr. Pablo Sabate, called

THE COTTAGE,

where they may pass their leisure hours in perfect harmony, under the shade of a refreshing grove. Every Sunday, Monday, Wednesday and Friday, green Turtle Soup will be served from 11 to 2 o'clock. Families can be supplied with any quantity by sending early.

July 21.—3t*

DR. C. N. M'COSKNY,

OFFERS his professional services to the citizens of St. Augustine. He may be consulted at any time at the old government house in the square.

July 21.—tf.

SURVEYS, either of city lots, or tracts in the country, will be made with accuracy by the subscriber. Orders left at the Post-Office will be attended to by

GEORGE K. GIBBS.

July 25.—2t

POST OFFICE.

THE Public are informed, that a regular Mail will be continued between this City and St. Mary's—It will leave this, on Thursday mornings, and return the following Monday's. Letters intended to go by Mail, must be left at the Post-Office on Wednesdays.

In future, all Captains of vessels, will be required to deposit all letters brought by them, in this office, except those addressed to Consignees.

D. COPP, *acting Post-Master.*

July 17.—tf

PROPOSALS

WILL be received by the Assistant Commissary of Subsistence, to furnish Fresh Beef to the United States Troops, stationed at Fort St. Marks.

SAMUEL WASHBURN,
Asst. Com'y. Sub.

July 17.—tf.

FOR SALE,

AN excellent BILLIARD TABLE, with Maces, Cues and Balls complete. It is in order for immediate use, and will be sold low if application be made to

THOMAS CAMPBELL,
At Don Fernando Arredondo's Store-House.

July 21.

FIGURE 2.2 Front page, *Florida Gazette* (Saint Augustine), July 28, 1821 (Nineteenth Century U.S. Newspapers, https://link.gale.com/apps/doc/GT3014121719/NCNP?u=ucsandiego&sid=bookmark-NCNP&xid=87a9bc49).

attributed to Joseph Marion Hernández clarifying misconceptions about a local estate dispute sits on the far right of the page. Hernández was a significant figure in the community who initially fought U.S. encroachment into East Florida and St. Augustine but then later became the first Hispanic member of the U.S. Congress, serving as a representative of Florida Territory.[17] Not insignificantly, he was also an enslaver.

The front page of this issue provides an assemblage of pieces that work to position U.S. occupation historically and politically. A direct historical trajectory is drawn between the French establishment of Pensacola and U.S. territorial control. Moreover, including a piece about Pensacola in a St. Augustine paper creates an affinity between the two Floridas. Pensacola was the dominant settlement in West Florida, just as St. Augustine was in East Florida. The sketch concludes with the U.S. seizure of Florida through legal documentation, noting, "A law was immediately passed after by Congress, authorising the President of the United States, to take possession of the Floridas." Many front pages of Florida papers include law and legislative notes, and these were one of the only ways the law materially circulated. The pieces that accompany this history on the front page of the issue detail the economic impact of the regime change, both territorially and locally in St. Augustine. As such, the acquisition of Florida is depicted as a discursive transaction, one mediated and mitigated by (the English) language between two colonial powers. There is almost no mention of the Seminoles, whose economic and political sway dictated commerce as much as that of U.S. and European colonial subjects.[18]

The inclusion of the reprint "The Press" and its prominence on the front page, surrounded by articles about Florida history and the logistics of U.S. seizure, signals the conviction that newspapers play a role in this colonial move, in terms of both their content and their organization. The U.S. acquisition of Florida was a tactical move meant to increase U.S. influence in the Caribbean, and the *Gazette* ideologically and spatially makes visible its participation in formulating the logics of colonial, racialized space in Florida. Running down the far-right column of the front page are advertisements for the post office, the establishment of bars and other local businesses, and surveyors' announcements. Collectively, this assemblage evidences the structural work of incorporation under U.S. settler colonialism. The front-page content obscures Andrew Jackson's unauthorized invasions into Florida that violated international military protocol and obfuscates Indigenous and Black influence in the region. According to the paper, territorial occupation is natural and uncomplicated.

Readers were not oblivious to the ideological work done by newspapers, and in the case of Florida, many of the papers were mouthpieces for the most affluent, plantation owners and other wealthy elites interested in furthering their own political agendas. "Democritus" writes to the paper and expresses concern about journalistic veracity. They describe the sense of anxiety they feel when they read inaccuracies in the press, citing examples from Maryland and Kentucky, and urge the editor only to publish what he can verify to be true because newspapers "exercise a wide influence in this country, and are really engines of vast moral and political power."[19] While Democritus is likely attributing more influence to the press than is due, the writer's "agitation" suggests a *belief* in the power of the press, regardless of the material reality. Published shortly after the U.S. occupation of St. Augustine, the paper makes legible the violence and rupture inherent in U.S. territorial occupation. The structure, order, and temporal organization of the *Gazette* suggest a naturalness of U.S. possession, but there are moments when the tensions of colonization complicate the narrative of a seamless transition.

Significantly, the extent of sickness and death from malaria and other "tropical diseases" in territorial Florida stands in direct contrast to the image of Florida as an Edenic paradise destined for U.S. statehood. It raises questions about white unbelonging.[20] Racist assumptions about Black immunity to diseases like yellow fever and malaria only further fears that Florida is not a space amenable to white bodies.[21] In fact, the *Gazette*'s run as the first U.S. territorial newspaper in St. Augustine was cut short when the publisher-editor, Richard Edes, died of illness. The physical conditions of Florida affected the newspaper's ability to circulate settler propaganda; its inability to continue was a grim reminder of the physical ailments white settlers faced.

As with Georgia newspapers and the *Cherokee Phoenix*, I do not turn to the *Gazette* and other Florida territorial papers as records of historical fact but rather as rhetorical objects whose content and circulation illuminate our understanding of the ideological work done willfully to incorporate territories and people into the United States proper. Like the *Cherokee Phoenix*, issues of the *Gazette* are dual language in 1821. Most advertisements and columns are printed in English, some in Spanish, and a few in both languages. The inclusion of Spanish was not meant to accommodate readers who, until very recently, had been subjects of the Spanish Crown, but rather as a means of asserting the United States' linguistic, political, and geographic authority in the liminal space between treaty negotiations with Spain and the official territorial incorporation of Florida. Most Spanish-language content is city ordinances passed by the new U.S. leadership or instructions for becoming a U.S. citizen. Therefore, bilingualism does not assert the palimpsestic nature of settler colonialism but is imagined as a temporary necessity for supplanting all Spanishness with U.S. domination.[22] At the time, St. Augustine was the oldest continuously colonized settlement under U.S. control. Its U.S. occupation was deeply symbolic, imagined as a transfer of Spanish colonial rule to that of America's Manifest Destiny. President James Monroe would announce his Monroe Doctrine just two years later, explicitly laying out an imagined U.S. influence over the entire hemisphere.[23] However, the doctrine, like early U.S. territorial occupation of Florida, was more discursive than actualized, and it reveals the role of utterance, discourse, and print in instantiating U.S. imperial expansion and influence.

The pages of the *Gazette* evidence the on-the-ground mess of the U.S. transfer of power. Multiple letters to the editor from the subscriber "Americanus" are written (in English) to residents with previous allegiances to Spain. Routinely, Americanus encourages "Spanish inhabitants" who are "free male inhabitants" to accept and embrace U.S. citizenship.[24] Americanus's September 8 editorial is especially illuminating. The letter begins snarkily, addressing Spanish readers as "fellow citizens," even though most of them "have, for the present, declined becoming citizens of the United States." Throughout the rest of the letter, Americanus urges Spanish residents to renounce their allegiance to Spain, so St. Augustine can become unified in the name of prosperity. The argument Americanus makes is an explicitly capitalist one, which makes sense given that the only Spanish inhabitants who could obtain U.S. citizenship were affluent elites. However, Americanus rejects an export model of commerce and advocates "public spirit and industry," which will invariably entice more (white) settlers to move to St. Augustine and increase the city's prosperity. Such an argument posits white U.S. migration, not global trade ties, as central to St. Augustine's economy. U.S. expansion serves as both salve and economic model.

Readers also wrote in with other solutions to the Spanish-U.S. tensions in St. Augustine. In the next issue, dated September 15, "Hymen" responds to Americanus's call for unification by suggesting intermarriage. Invoking the name of the Greek god of marriage, Hymen argues that because "women have an irresistible influence in the arrangement of public, as well as private affairs," it would be beneficial to have "Spanish Ladies and American Gentlemen" wed and "*vice versa.*" Doing so "would, at once, allay all irritation and jealousy that unhappily may have been excited, by a change in the government of the country."[25] To achieve these couplings, Hymen suggests that every husband or wife who has been away from their partner for more than six months immediately divorce that person and remarry someone of the opposite nationality. Hymen's strategy imagines clear, distinct lines between Spanishness and Americanness instead of the fractured colonial, local, and national allegiances actually at play in the community. Moreover, Hymen imagines that the heteronormative practices of U.S. colonialism will invariably ease discord. Like Americanus, who depicts U.S. expansion as an economic model, Hymen imagines sexist, patriarchal kinship networks as key to Manifest Destiny. Heteronormative kinship models and white migration would continue to shape territorial space; however, neither was as collaborative or consensual as Americanus or Hymen depicts. Their writings betray the multiscalar violence (gendered, linguistic, territorial, national) that is an enduring hallmark of U.S. colonial expansion and occupation.

Mapping "the Land of Flowers"

It is important to note that while there was so much effort to forcibly Remove all Indigenous people and enslave all Black people in Florida, statehood was not necessarily the primary goal. Throughout the 1820s–40s, numerous statehood campaigns failed to unify West and East Florida. Statehood was eventually pushed through in 1845 with little fanfare, steamrolled by affluent enslavers driven to increase their plantation wealth. The wars, not statehood, have become the origin story of Florida identity, wars where white intruders actively worked to destroy the communities of Indigenous and Black people.

Florida represented both actual *and* imagined collusions of Indigeneity and Blackness for a mid-nineteenth-century U.S. public. If, as I have argued throughout *Reading Territory*, state ideology is predicated on anti-Black and anti-Indigenous rhetoric, then the very idea of Afro-Native solidarity in Florida imperiled the structural logic necessary to incorporate the territory as a proper state, and we see these fears made manifest through pamphlet and newspaper coverage detailing alleged Afro-Native violence against white colonizers and their property. Much like the Haitian Revolution, such a collaboration threatened to overthrow a colonizing and enslaving ruling class. But unlike Haiti, Florida was just a disputed border away from the United States proper.

In response, the military and U.S. settlers chose to use brutal, physical violence to quell Afro-Native threats through Removal. Specifically, in Florida this meant Removal of all Maroons and Indigenous communities and enslavement of all people of African descent. More broadly, Removal was a multifaceted U.S.

project aimed at stripping Black and Native people from their kinship relations, lifeways, and epistemologies through forms of abjection. However, most telling about the U.S.-Seminole wars is that they never fully achieved their intention. In Moses Jumper Jr.'s poem "Major Dade," the speaker describes the "truth" of the U.S.-Seminole wars as a "black and white" account told from a U.S. perspective. Jumper writes, "Oh yes, it's there in black and white, / And we know who really won the fight!"[26] "Black and white" references the use of print to assert a dominant colonial narrative of U.S. military success that is biased, but one could also read the line as gesturing toward Florida's problematizing of U.S. racial hierarchies. At various points in time, Black, white, Spanish American, and Indigenous people all used print to archive histories of the era—both factually and imaginatively. This poem, written by a Seminole poet in the late twentieth century, challenges the dominant depiction of Major Dade's death as a massacre, as well as the role of print in shaping the historical account:

> In your books you win a great battle, and it
> becomes historical lore.
> The Indian wins and it's a massacre or the
> Heathens have started another Bloody War![27]

The "massacre" of Major Dade became the justification for Seminole Removal. Written almost 150 years after the incident, Jumper's poem challenges the "truth" of the printed colonial archive, both by calling out bias in the hegemonic narrative and by constructing an alternative print archive— Jumper's poem—that refutes the dominant dialectic of Indigenous savagery and white beneficence and insists that "the truth we must never let fade!"[28]

Incorporating Florida into the United States was not a seamless enterprise, but overtaking Florida became of symbolic import and something of an obsession for U.S. presidents and generals, including Andrew Jackson, Zachary Taylor, Winfield Scott, and Thomas Jesup. Florida, its Spanish legacy, and its Native and Black inhabitants represented an ideological threat to the larger U.S. nation just as much as they did a geopolitical one. Moreover, for the presidents and generals just mentioned, all of whom faced losses and embarrassment in the Florida military campaigns, it was likely also personal. Acquiring Florida gave the United States greater access to the Caribbean and control of the southeastern continental seaboard, but it also signified an attempt to eradicate Indigenous sovereignty and prevent Black hemispheric freedom. However, the standard U.S. markers for "reading" race did not work in Florida. Black and Native relations there were complicated, and allegiances did not always map along racial lines. The Seminoles both enslaved people of

African descent and married and accepted people of African descent into their kinship networks and families. Some Black Seminoles lived in their own communities. There were Black and Native interpreters on both sides of the war, sometimes using their power as interpreters to benefit the U.S. government or their own communities rather than the Seminoles in treaty negotiations. Numerous Maroon communities established places of refuge for self-emancipated people that intentionally existed outside any enslaving colonial state, some of which included Africans who continued their own Indigenous cultural and spiritual practices. These Maroon communities were well aware that land surveys and Removal also meant the capture and enslavement of Maroons and the destruction of their communities.

Central to the U.S. colonization of Florida was irreverence for territorial boundaries, be they Spanish, Black, or Indigenous. The First U.S.-Seminole War (1816–18) was the result of Jackson and his troops' complete disregard for international protocol between colonial powers.[29] As a result of the war, the United States gained control over both East and West Florida when John Quincy Adams and Luis de Onís signed the Adams-Onís Treaty on February 22, 1819. At the time of the negotiations, and throughout much of the Second U.S.-Seminole War, the actual geography of Florida (or the Floridas, as they were often called) posed problems for imagining the territory as a cohesive whole, in part because there was still confusion about what Florida actually looked like. The Floridian swamplands, neither land nor water, which soldiers had great difficulty navigating, reflect the categorical ruptures that fueled the wars.

During the first half of the nineteenth century, Florida circulated culturally in the United States as a site of racial, geographic, and political unknowability. If, as Nicholas Blomley suggests, the survey serves to make violence seem orderly and natural, then the absence of a survey necessitated other means of colonial story placemaking. The fact that, at this time, white settlers and U.S. government officials did not even have a clear understanding of the topography indicates the tenuousness of U.S. control.[30] At this time, the United States had only begun the kind of surveying and other colonial projects that were part of making the region accessible and therefore scientifically and culturally colonizable.[31]

Instead, what dominated was a tension between the romantic narrative of Florida as an Edenic paradise and news coverage of the wars that reported the death and disease experienced by soldiers unfamiliar with the environment and climate. In 1836 an anonymous writer wrote the following in *Knickerbocker Magazine*: "EAST FLORIDA, the 'land of flowers'—'sweet Florida'—is the land of fiction, and always has been so. In this sense, it may be the land of poetry, but in sober earnest, it is for the most part a flat, pine barren, full of swamps; and where there are hills, they are sand hills, which frequently fall through, and reveal a pond of water—so that the word *terra firma* has no application to this territory."[32] The mystery surrounding Floridian terrain invited an aesthetic fantasy that was also bogged down with fear and anxiety about the unknown, racially other space.

In her discussion of what she terms the Caribbean "plantation zone," Monique Allewaert describes this tension as one that "confounded Anglo-European efforts to mine American landscapes to produce commodities, to further science, and to fulfill conventional aesthetic categories—ranging from the picturesque to the sublime. Instead of making economic, objective, or aesthetic use of swamplands, Anglo-Europeans were repeatedly sucked into their dense networks."[33] These "dense networks" made a drive for statehood and increased U.S. settlement a tricky process—and one that would test the feasibility of sustaining and expanding an empire. Complementing Allewaert's reading, Michele Currie Navakas argues that while the unknowability of Florida posed a threat to the federalist ideals underpinning the nascent nation-state, demonstrating its limits, there were also arguments that "Florida's fragmentation and dissolution would not dissolve nationhood but, rather, revise it, so that it could accommodate forms of belonging, community, and economy that take shape on shifting ground."[34]

The mid-nineteenth century was also an era of dramatic changes in print production and dissemination, and a thriving U.S. print culture attempted to capture, narrate, and make sense of a project of settler expansion that could not always find the hammock in the swamp, so to speak. Much of the poetry, prose, journalism, and U.S. government documentation written contemporaneously toggles between critique and optimism, often in inconsistent ways that echo the *Knickerbocker Magazine* article.[35] These documents show how a U.S. colonial logic struggled to uphold stereotypes of Indigenous and Black people that would justify the continuation of Removal and enslavement. I do not mean to suggest that these documents are any more trustworthy or viable than the records left by Seminoles, Black Seminoles, and Maroons; if anything, analysis of U.S. accounts shows the disturbing lengths to which writers were willing to go, politically, culturally, and individually, to uphold systems of oppression. The complexities residing in the issues of race and nation were masked, not erased, and served as specters to the narratives, sublimated into the murky landscape of Florida.

The three U.S.-Seminole wars marked the first time the United States conceded large-scale military failure to a print-reading public. This failure was further compounded by the fact that it was not a robust military power that defeated the army but rather seemingly more modest groups of Indigenous, Afro-Indigenous, Maroon, enslaved, and self-emancipated peoples. The ability of these communities to challenge the United States to a costly, multidecade fight for Florida put pressure on the notion that Removal in the Southeast would be a facile process. The Seminoles', Black Seminoles', and Maroons' unrelenting defense of their homelands raised both pragmatic and moral questions about the feasibility of Jacksonian Indian policy and severely put it to the test.

The wars and Afro-Native alliances also threatened the security of slavery and the plantation economy undergirding the U.S. acquisition of Florida. General Jesup infamously described the Second U.S.-Seminole War as "a Negro, not an Indian war," but the less cited second half of his 1837 statement is just as important: "If it be not speedily put down, the South will feel the effects of it on their slave population before the end of the next season."[36] While citations of his statement often focus on his emphasis on Blackness, Jesup connects enslavement and dispossession—namely, that perpetuating white supremacist plantocracy requires Removal. I use "Afro-Native" intentionally here and throughout the rest of the chapter to constellate various subject positions whose communalism challenged U.S. racial and identity categories and signal how the fighting in Florida raised concerns about Black and Native collectives elsewhere. The hyphenated "Afro-Native" demarcates how severely the blurring of Blackness and Indigeneity as anticolonial armed resistance in Florida disrupted the foundations of U.S. settler logic.

Moreover, he alludes to the fear across Florida of a potential Black uprising. By 1837 there were already numerous examples of Seminoles persuading enslaved Black people to run away or revolt against their enslavers. In John Sprague's memoir of his time as an army surgeon in Florida, he discusses white fears of Afro-Native collaboration through a hemispheric legacy of colonization that links U.S. warfare in Florida to a sustained attack on Afro-Native others that exceeds any one colonial power. Sprague argues that even though Native people have resisted the Removal attempts of multiple colonial regimes (France, Spain, England, Spain [again], and now the United States), Florida is militarily valuable and worth fighting for:

> Its position, in a national point of view, should be regarded. It may yet
> be the strong-hold of a powerful foe, who might increase his strength,
> by inducing the blacks from neighboring states to join his standard.
> Twenty-four hours' sail for a steamer, can transport from the island
> of New Providence, W. I., to the coast of Florida, a black force, well

calculated to perfect the work. This done, backed by the will and ability of a powerful nation, may yet make Florida the great field upon which is to be fought the battle of freedom; the settlement of a question upon which hangs the destiny of our country.[37]

Over a decade before Martin R. Delany imagined a pan-national Afro-Native uprising to overthrow white supremacy across the Americas, Sprague describes a similar collective comprising Maroon, Afro-Native, free Black, Native, and enslaved people, along with their allies, whose networks span states, nations, and seas. Such a collective can challenge U.S. Manifest Destiny and the assumption of the totality of white supremacist settler colonialism. Notably, Sprague's vision depicts Florida not just as an extension of the continent but also as part of a larger archipelagic ecosystem that may not be visible on the white colonial map: a territoriality beyond the scope of whiteness.

"Authentic" Narratives

Unlike local newspapers, which attempted to alleviate white fears and naturalize U.S. white settlement, pamphlets circulating during the Second U.S.-Seminole War capitalized on fear by sensationalizing Native and Black destruction of property and violence against white settlers. Two tracts, *An Authentic Narrative of the Seminole War* (1836) and *A Narrative of the Life and Sufferings of Mrs. Jane Johns* (1837), are especially gruesome. Both accounts provide grisly detail, but the fictional tract, *An Authentic Narrative*, was far more popular, perhaps because of the graphic images that accompanied it. The appeal of a macabre visual-textual account of Florida demonstrates the role print culture played in narrating and mapping territorial acquisition. Despite the desire to "read" Florida as an Edenic paradise full of promise for settlement and statehood, Maroons and Native people in Florida offered a double refusal that challenged the romantic notion of an incorporated territory. They refused to be made entirely legible or accessible to a geographically expansive print-reading public and they refused U.S. colonization and enslavement. As such, they were simultaneously present and absent—unwilling to vanish, but also unwilling to be entirely consumable, accessible, and therefore assimilable via the printed page.

Moreover, both pamphlets convey ambivalence about the war. It was not a popular one in the United States, especially after the death of Osceola, who gained celebrity through the pages of the U.S. popular press. Many in the

United States felt the war was a costly, unending, and fruitless endeavor, and they had good reason to feel that way. The conflict of the Second U.S.-Seminole War alone was the most expensive war fought against any tribe, costing more than one year of the entire federal budget.[38] Such losses did not reflect well on U.S. military leadership. Three of the four active major generals who oversaw the war, Edmund Gaines, Winfield Scott, and Thomas Jesup, left with their reputations tarnished. As a result, the combat raised questions about the ethics and efficacy of enslavement and Removal.

An Authentic Narrative offers a sensationalized account of the Second U.S.-Seminole War that imagines horrifying Afro-Native vigilantes wreaking death and destruction across Florida. The pamphlet includes a woodblock print on the title page and a foldout illustration that depicts, in gruesome detail, Afro-Native destruction of white settlement and the murder and torture of white settlers. The tract was republished numerous times, and while each version presented a slightly different narrative—sometimes including more details of the war, sometimes less—all editions detail the story of Mary Godfrey.[39] In the text, Godfrey and her four children flee their home after Afro-Native fighters attack. Her husband leaves to "check the enemy in their murderous career," and so she hides for days in the swamp until she and her children are discovered by a fugitive Maroon, who takes pity on her and her children and helps them escape.[40]

The images that accompany *An Authentic Narrative*, both the title page and the foldout, have received far greater scholarly attention than the pamphlet's textual content, and for a good reason. They are both dramatically violent renderings. However, the images are an assemblage of captivity and rebellion illustrations from previous publications.[41] The title page image (figure 2.3) is from an 1831 woodblock print of Nat Turner's Rebellion (1831), and the foldout illustration is a collage of various prints, including tracts detailing the Black Hawk War (1832), as well as images from the same Nat Turner tract repurposed on the front page (figure 2.4).[42] The repurposing of these images was likely a utilitarian choice, but one that nonetheless shaped readers' perceptions of Florida and Afro-Native collectivity, given the pamphlet's popularity. Because the images were pulled from other materials, there is no unified composition, and instead, what readers get is a fractured pastiche of genre and iconography that reads not unlike a comic book; the Afro-Native collective of Florida exists beyond the borders of 1830s print, revealing the limits of the white imagination to envision Afro-Native warfare against the colonial plantation system.

AN

AUTHENTIC NARRATIVE

OF THE

SEMINOLE WAR;

ITS CAUSE, RISE AND PROGRESS,

AND A MINUTE DETAIL OF THE

HORRID MASSACRES

Of the *Whites*, by the *Indians* and *Negroes*, in Florida,
in the months of December, January and February.

Communicated for the press by a gentleman who has
spent eleven weeks in Florida, near the scene of the Indian depredations, and in a situation to collect every important fact relating thereto.

PROVIDENCE:
Printed for D. F. Blanchard, and others, Publishers.
1836.

FIGURE 2.3 Title page, *An Authentic Narrative of the Seminole War; Its Cause Rise and Progress, and a Minute Detail of the Horrid Massacres of the Whites, by the Indians and Negroes, in Florida, in the Months of December, January and February* (Providence: D. F. Blanchard, 1836). Courtesy of the American Antiquarian Society.

FIGURE 2.4 "Massacre of the Whites by the Indians and Blacks in Florida," in *An Authentic Narrative of the Seminole War: And of the Miraculous Escape of Mrs. Mary Godfrey, and Her Four Female Children* (Providence: D. F. Blanchard, 1836). Courtesy of the Special and Area Studies Collections, George A. Smathers Libraries, University of Florida.

The challenges Afro-Native collectivity posed here echo the challenges they posed to mapmaking. As Tiffany Lethabo King explains, "Black and Indigenous insurrection nibbled at the edges of the White psyche, producing a form of chronic anxiety that provoked nightmares and visions of Black insurrection. In fact, Black movement made some Whites go 'mad.'"[43] The imagery we find in the pamphlet exploits the "maddening" influence of Black movement for white people—"mad" being an expression of anger and disruption of white supremacist reason—by foregrounding fear of violence against settler-enslavers. Afro-Native warfare defies the reading cues of the visual and the textual and the genre conventions of captivity and rebellion narratives. You could not determine one's political or cultural affiliations, or even the languages one was conversant in, by phenotypically reading bodies—a racializing territorial hermeneutics fails. The repurposed iconographic renderings of captivity and rebellion are enmeshed and overlaid without citation, but in some ways they need no citation for the deep cultural ideologies they conjure. In my reading of the illustrations, I de-emphasize the imagery's racial cues and how they encode Indigeneity and Blackness. I do so because the pastiche they produce breaks down these differences and lingers instead on Blackness and Indigeneity's fluid and swampy relationships to the body and the landscape.

Through its visual and textual composition, the title page for *An Authentic Narrative* capitalizes on the horror provoked by warfare for white readers, whether or not they are sympathetic to the Afro-Native cause. James

Cusick, who has carefully traced the provenance of the pamphlet's images, explains that the narrative was written to fit the title page illustration rather than the other way around.[44] The large font "SEMINOLE WAR" gracing the top of the title page looms over the figures as the white mother pleads for her life and the lives of her children. Below the image, the title page assures us of the story's verity, since it was "communicated for the press," although most scholars believe Mary Godfrey was not a real person.[45] By specifying the months of violence, "December, January and February," the title page attempts to place the war in "real time"—that is, Enlightenment space-time marked by the days of the week and the circulation of news in the press—that simultaneously professes its verity while revealing its fabrication. At the same time, the inclusion of specific months without a year fosters a sense of immediacy. The events are not visions of a future uprising but are of the present, placing a white reader even closer to the conflict temporally (if not spatially). As such, Florida Territory is made more familiar through salacious fearmongering and by connecting it to other events that rupture the stability of the settler plantation complex, like Nat Turner's organized uprising.

Since *An Authentic Narrative*'s story of Godfrey was written to comple-ment the picture, there is an inconsistent relationship between text and im-age. The climactic scene detailed on the title page is described far differently in the pamphlet. Also, in the opening pages the author talks about the Black Hawk War in Illinois Territory, an image of which is included in the bottom left corner of the foldout illustration. The connection ties together multiple examples of Indigenous warfare against white settlement and flattens in-stances of Indigenous resistance as interchangeable. The use of Black Hawk here invokes fear that the Indigenous other can never be entirely Removed—physically from the land or psychically from the genocidal work of coloniza-tion in which individual settlers participate. The pamphlet portends that while white settlers and the U.S. government hoped the end of the war marked the end of militarized Indigenous refusals of U.S. colonization and expansion of a federal Removal policy through the United States, the Seminoles chal-lenged that assumption.[46] It also suggests another territoriality, one that is not captured by the map of U.S. states and territories, where Indigenous, Afro-Native, and Black communities continue to affirm their own place-based relationships to the land.

Even in publications capitalizing on war intrigue, especially for a faraway U.S. urban audience, Blackness and Indigeneity do not sit comfortably on a single plane. In the case of the foldout image, the figures are somewhat disproportionate in size, with a lack of continuity in the illustration's depth of field. While seemingly male figures are in the midst of combat, in the foreground, we see an Afro-Native woman who is carrying a baby away from the open arms of a pleading white woman. The image in its totality stages the nightmare fantasy of white occupation in Florida—the Afro-Native destruction of white slavocracy made possible through the theft and colonization of Indigenous lands returned to enact revenge, as well as fears about the absorption of whiteness into Afro-Native kinship systems. Both the white home and the family are destroyed. Physical violence against white settlers, as evidenced by the blood, is represented in the foreground, while sacrifice and cannibalism are suggested in the smoke cloud billowing above dancing figures in the background. The presence of this engraving, which is included as an insert, suggests the appeal of such a gory image, presumably for a white U.S. reader, evoking a tension between spectacle and racial horror. While it conjures the fear that white settlers will have to atone for the originary violences of the modern world order, chattel slavery and settler colonization, it also obfuscates those histories and posits its white figures exclusively as victims.

The images and text of both *An Authentic Narrative* and *A Narrative of the Life and Sufferings of Mrs. Jane Johns* foreground white women's victimhood and invert Removal. White women are the ones forced to leave their homes; homes that seem mostly to be located in the same contested swamplands that Seminoles resisted surveying. Instead of detailing the Removal of Seminoles, Black Seminoles, and Maroons from Florida, the stories depict Afro-Native attacks that force white settlers to flee their homes. In the story of Godfrey, the narrative lingers on the precarity of white women in Florida, not simply as metaphors but as historical actors, operating as enslavers and colonizers. In these stories, white women fend for themselves and their families without the help of white men, most of whom have already been killed.

In both pamphlets, the pivotal moments that determine whether these white women will live or die depend on a complication of racial recognition that informs territorial belonging. In *An Authentic Narrative,* the Maroon who takes pity on Godfrey does so because he thinks of his own enslaved children when he sees hers and fears that God will harm his children if he kills hers. Worried that Seminoles seen in the area might "seek shelter in the swamp in which she was concealed," he aids her and her children in their escape.[47] Brigitte Fielder reads this scene as "illustrat[ing] the complexities of settler colonialist violence and also the relevance of fugitive domestic spaces for forming racialized relations of kinship and power."[48] Here, the space of the swamp, as an Afro-Native territory, provides an opportunity to imagine other forms of kinship and community beyond the plantation system, a system that, as the story suggests, both Godfrey and the man know intimately.[49] By detailing this scene of empathy, however, the narrative also can be read as ameliorating fears about Afro-Native allegiance, even if briefly, and serves to remind the reader that hegemonic racial reading practices break down in the swamp. During the U.S.-Seminole wars, Black fighters aided the U.S. military and fought alongside Seminoles. Seminoles enslaved people of African descent, and some Seminole people were also African-descended. The combat in Florida did not cohere racial taxonomies; it revealed their limitations in distinguishing ally from enemy.

Unlike *An Authentic Narrative, A Narrative of the Life and Sufferings of Mrs. Jane Johns* is verifiably based on a real-life encounter. In it, Johns's father-in-law misidentifies the scalped pregnant woman for an "Indian squaw" and is prepared to shoot her until his companion Mr. Lowther urges him to take pity on the "defenceless woman," at which point they realize she is Johns.[50] Unlike the fictional Godfrey, Johns loses everything to the war—her parents, her husband, her unborn child, and her property. First with her parents and then with her husband, Johns settles on the white frontier, near the Saint Marys River, as an intruder on Seminole lands. Before the assailants killed her husband and left her for dead, "she counted nine: among them was a negro, who joined the Indians in urging Mr. and Mrs. Johns to leave the house, threatening if they did not, it would be immediately set fire to."[51] The narrative details the gory immolation and scalping of Mr. and Mrs. Johns, but the attack did not come without warning. The men's decision not to shoot Jane Johns is presented as an act of fortuitous generosity, but it stands in contrast to Mr. Johns's initial impulse to shoot a Native woman and the use of a charged and highly derogatory term to describe her. The emphasis on Afro-Native brutality directs attention away from the genocide, violence, and trauma of enslaving and colonizing regimes and the repeated invasions into Seminole and Maroon territories that the Johns family engaged in.

As noted earlier, Jane Johns's story did not receive the same attention as *An Authentic Narrative*, arguably because the visuals that anchored *An Authentic Narrative* shore up much, but not all, of the messy signifiers that Johns's story cannot simplify—those of race, gender, victim, and perpetrator. However, all of these images and texts use the figure of the white woman to position a masculinist Afro-Native fighter against a defenseless mother, a move that secures Florida as a U.S. domestic space, not a colonial intrusion.

In most white accounts of the wars, Black and Indigenous women (and children) are mostly absent, and Afro-Native warfare against the United States is depicted as a masculinist affair, consistently embodied by the figure of Osceola, whom I discuss shortly. By positioning the male Afro-Native combatant in contrast to the figure of the white mother who, through her gendered and racialized position, signals white domesticity, Afro-Native kinship and community are foreclosed, another form of discursive Removal. In these pamphlets, we see the limitations of U.S. colonial printscapes to map out (and thus make potentially consumable) the territories of Indigenous and Black freedom. Instead, they illustrate complicated attempts to make sense of a territory that does not follow the normative racial and spatial logics of the United States proper, with little optimism about the future of the war.[52]

The United States entered Florida hoping to efficiently gain territory and Remove Indigenous peoples and Maroon communities but instead sustained four decades of fighting and a failure of its objective that led to a great deal of bitterness and disillusion.[53] Conflict would continue well into the 1850s, years after Florida achieved statehood, as Native people, Black Seminoles, and Maroon communities—groups that had retained a constant relationship to the land and their other-than-human relations despite the numerous European and U.S. power struggles of the late eighteenth and early nineteenth centuries—resisted U.S. encroachment and surveillance. In the 1850s, when U.S. officers attempted to track down the remaining Seminoles, Colonel William S. Harney and a small group of army surveyors provoked Seminole leader Billy Bowlegs (Holatamico/Halpatter-Micco) by sneaking onto his land and destroying his crops, leading Bowlegs to defend himself; the presence of the surveyors is further evidence of the intimate role surveying played in the forced takeover of Florida. Skirmishes continued until 1858, when Bowlegs surrendered, but he only surrendered himself; the Seminoles never surrendered as a people. Thus, fifty years of war ended with no peace treaty, no official surrender, and a failed mission to Remove all Seminoles, Black Seminoles, and Maroons from their homes in Florida.

Osceola and U.S. Print Culture

While *An Authentic Narrative* was popular, it was only one of many publications detailing the combat in Florida. The figure that emerged across almost all accounts of the Second U.S.-Seminole War in the popular press, including *An Authentic Narrative*, was Osceola, who became a main character of sorts in the story of Florida.[54] Due to advancements in print production and circulation in the 1830s, news of the war was accessible to an audience that extended well beyond the circuits of territorial newspapers and other more localized media sources. Newspapers became an important avenue for translating the war for U.S. readers who knew very little about Florida.[55] By 1835 there were newspapers in all six major cities in Florida whose coverage of local events was picked up by the U.S. national press; there were also newspapers published by soldiers fighting in Florida.[56] In addition, the invention of the telegraph and other technological advancements meant that news could be transmitted from greater distances more expeditiously than ever before. In an 1838 letter to her brother, Corinna Brown, living at La Grange in East Florida, commented on the rapidity with which information traveled: "I never send you news of the war because I presume you hear as correctly and quickly as I do by way of newspapers."[57] News from Florida created a sense of connection to the combat as it unfolded. However, like the swamps, the information that was disseminated was not necessarily clear or consistent.[58] By 1840 almost all newspapers were explicit in their political affiliations, and party politics became an intrinsic element of news circulation.[59] Coverage of Florida was not free from such biased reporting, and it was not uncommon for coverage of the Second U.S.-Seminole War to stage the combat as part of a larger ethical battle.

Osceola became a mnemonic for the war and signified attempts to shore up the fracturing, confusion, and chaos that actually surrounded the conflict. He served as a constant "character" gracing the papers' headlines, a stark contrast to the wars' perpetually blurry status, with a rotating list of generals, ever-increasing numbers of troops and volunteers, and a succession of military missteps. He seemed to embody the ideal of the American patriot more than U.S. soldiers or military leaders. Many articles depicted him as a gentleman and an underdog willing to sacrifice everything for his people. His growing mythic status was encouraged by the belief that the military captured him under false pretenses: General Jesup enticed him with promises of peace negotiations if he would meet with Jesup's men, but instead of negotiations, Osceola was arrested. Shortly after that arrest, the Seminole leader fell gravely ill, eventually dying. Afterward, he became a martyr figure of the Seminole cause. This image of Osceola harked back to the revolutionary-era figure of the valiant freedom fighter championing independence and justice.

Osceola was born Redstick Muscogee. The Redsticks had initially challenged leaders in their communities whom they saw as too amenable to the United States, pushing against U.S. assimilation and calling for a return to Muscogee lifeways.[60] They were also opposed to chattel slavery. After Andrew Jackson's Red Stick War (1811–14), Osceola fled to Florida with his mother. His association with the Seminoles was a product of previous U.S. Removal campaigns in so-called Alabama and Georgia. Depending on the context, his alleged racial patrimony either discredited his authenticity or was entirely elided so he could be imagined as a "full-blooded and wild Indian."[61] Some assumed the white trader William Powell, his mother's husband, was also his father. True or not, this assumption reinscribes heteronormative colonial notions of kinship. Because Muskogean kinship is matrilineal, as the son of a Muscogee mother, he was Muscogee. It is true, however, that Osceola spoke and understood at least some English, and throughout a significant part of the war the U.S. military referred to him as Powell and not Osceola.[62] Not until he began to gain national status was he referred to by his Muskogean name.[63] He first gained fame for a theatrical response to the Fort Gibson negotiations. As the story goes, in April 1835, Wiley Thompson read from the materials out loud, and Osceola responded by stabbing the treaty with his knife (there is no official account of this).[64] Osceola and a band of his followers killed Thompson on December 28, 1835, marking one of the first contestations of the Second U.S.-Seminole War.

Throughout the war, depictions of Osceola as a passionate fighter for Seminole sovereignty continued to take hold. M. M. Cohen's account of the war includes what he says was a letter from Osceola to General Duncan Lamont Clinch: "You have guns, and so have we—you have powder and lead, and so have we—your men will fight, and so will ours, till the last drop of the Seminole's blood has moistened the dust of his hunting ground."[65] Finally, in one of the most controversial incidents of the war, General Jesup, ignoring a truce flag, captured several Seminoles, including Osceola, on October 21, 1837.[66] The military sent Osceola to Fort Marion in St. Augustine and then moved him to Fort Moultrie in South Carolina, where his health rapidly deteriorated.[67] He died on January 30, 1838. After his death, Osceola gained greater fame in the United States, partly because of his celebrity during the war and partly because of the unsavory circumstances of his imprisonment.

Osceola was not the only figure or icon who was offered up as representative of an entire Indigenous people. It is a process historian Jean O'Brien (White Earth Nation) describes as "lasting." For O'Brien, in lasting narratives settlers "scripted their 'last' Indians as solitary (and presumably lonely) survivors who somehow managed to maneuver the tricky shoals of English colonialism and find their way into the nineteenth century, only then to succumb to the inevitable process of replacement."[68] While the figure of Osceola does not fit this model precisely—he is not the last Seminole, not even surviving most of the Second U.S.-Seminole War—there is a salient impulse to make him symbolically the last of his kind, the embodiment of a genocidal Removal fantasy. Osceola's untimely death made him an inoculated figure since posthumously he no longer posed a physical threat in Florida. But the Seminole were never entirely Removed from Florida, and, I contend, Osceola was never successfully packaged into a benign "lasting" figure. After he died in 1838, the number of newspaper references to him skyrocketed. Authors continued to publish Osceola literature, including fictionalized biographies, sensationalized adventure tales, poetic odes, and numerous elegies commemorating him and mourning his loss.[69]

As the U.S. literary and print markets created the public Osceola, so too would they strive to define his legacy. George Catlin's bust portrait *Osceola, the Black Drink, a Warrior of Great Distinction* (1838) and his discussion of it in *Letters and Notes on the Manners, Customs, and Condition of the North American Indians* crystallize the contradictory ways in which Osceola figured as *the* symbol of Native resistance at the height of southeastern Indian Removal.[70] In a bizarre moment encompassing the powerful mythos Osceola had come to embody, Dr. Frederick Weedon, who was instructed to keep him alive, called Catlin to Osceola's deathbed.[71] Catlin was not a Seminole, a government officer, or a close friend. He was a portraitist who fashioned himself a chronicler of the U.S. colonial project and what he saw as the extinction of the Indian. Catlin had been fascinated with Osceola's celebrity for some time and wanted to capture his image in the hopes of understanding and capitalizing on the curiosity surrounding him. If Osceola could not be physically contained by the United States, Catlin wanted to ensure that his persona, the construct fashioned for U.S. popular culture, would endure in his absence.

Catlin's observation of Osceola's death is an uncanny moment in an even more uncanny conflict. Many had hoped that the death of Osceola would defuse the Seminole cause. In his observations of Osceola, Catlin describes him as a "gallant fellow, who . . . is grieving with a broken spirit, and ready to die, cursing the white man, no doubt, to the end of his breath."[72] But all other accounts, including that of Weedon, claimed that Osceola was not angered but rather smiling and saying goodbye to his family.[73] The conflict surrounding this pivotal moment in the U.S.-Seminole wars troubles the veracity of Catlin's depiction of Osceola. However, it also illuminates how the U.S. public made sense of and commemorated the wars. Like the conflicting stories of how Osceola looked and felt as he lay dying, representations of the wars presented a disjointed image of Afro-Native refusal of U.S. occupation.

Considering the complicated reality of the wars, one can see why Catlin was so particular about depicting Osceola in a certain way. While Catlin painted multiple portraits of Osceola at the time, I focus here on his most famous portrait. I discuss it at some length, but I chose *not* to include a reprint of it, so as not to reinforce it as the de facto representation of Osceola, for reasons that will become clear shortly. His depiction of Osceola, like his portraits of other famous Native leaders, is two-dimensional and static, attempting to take agency away from the subject of the painting. Furthermore, he aims to portray Osceola as the vanishing hero of a dying race, eliminating any threat posed by him or the conflict he represents to his white viewers. As with many of Catlin's portraits, Osceola, with a look of concern on his face, gazes beyond the viewer into the distance. What Catlin chooses to leave out of his painting is as important as what he presents, if not more so. There is no background, no hint of the Florida territory that Osceola defended.

Fittingly, the only image of Osceola that has remained consistent took shape after he became an icon. It seems that because of his somewhat contradictory past and his previous contact with white America, he was a figure whose history could be reshaped and re-created to project an image of Seminole identity that was more palatable, fitting more cleanly into U.S. stereotypes about Native people. Catlin's portrait embodies an attempt to make the fiction of Osceola a reality. After Osceola's death, Catlin's portrait would become as famous as Osceola had been in life. Canonized in American art, it continues to serve as a representation not only of the man but of the U.S.-Seminole wars as well. U.S.-Seminole wars historian John K. Mahon argues that "this portrait[,] coupled with the flattering things Catlin said of Osceola's character, helped to create the legend."[74] By maintaining such a skewed depiction of the figurehead of the conflict, Catlin and other U.S. artists and writers who took up Osceola as a character in their work often obscured the more complicated issues that Osceola embodied.

Lionizing Osceola and his actions and connecting them to U.S. values and identity is only possible, however, because he no longer serves as a physical threat. Before his death, the popular press portrayed Osceola as a brave but violent man. He was allegedly responsible for the death of the Indian agent Wiley Thompson, which was widely publicized by the press.[75] However, following his death, Osceola was described less as a terrifying villain and more as a tragic antihero.[76] While popular discourse attempted to metonymically consolidate and ameliorate the paradoxes of fighting in Florida by depicting Osceola as a two-dimensional martyr, his complexity as a three-dimensional enemy of the state continued to haunt such attempts.[77]

Misinformation and confusion surrounded both the figure of Osceola and the Second U.S.-Seminole War he came to represent. Fact blended with fiction to create a mythic understanding of both place and people. In the print production and Catlin's painting, there is a politico-poetic elegy for Osceola that produces a nostalgia for something that could still be prevented—the war and Removal efforts did not end with Osceola's death.[78] Instead, the fictional Indian figure stands in for the far more complex Seminole, Black Seminole, and Maroon communities in Florida and obscures the roles of Removal, enslavement, and statehood in Osceola's death. This would continue to be true in white rememberings of the war later in the century and helps explain why Walt Whitman, the self-fashioned poet of U.S. ideological contradiction, would return to an image of Osceola near the end of his life and the end of the century—unable to ignore the violent conquest that had marked the U.S. nineteenth century but desiring freedom from complicity in it.[79]

Twasinta's Afro-Native Printscape

Critically, the Osceola phenomenon also obfuscated Black involvement in the warfare, erasing the very explicit threat to U.S. white supremacy that Afro-Native solidarity posed. We see this most clearly in the contradictions between Catlin's singular portrait of Osceola and *An Authentic Narrative*'s visual and textual assemblages. Importantly, though, the Osceola mythos would sometimes depict him as having a firm allegiance to Maroons, Black Seminoles, and people enslaved by white enslavers, and there is dispute as to whether Osceola's wife was a Black Seminole person. Many historians claim that it was Thompson's enslavement of her that led Osceola to attack him and his troops so viciously. The story of Osceola's wife offers a different version of the gendered dimensions of Florida. We get very little direct access to her and her story, but her possible enslavement in this version serves to explain Osceola's masculine aggression. The dearth of access to her lived experiences, or even fictionalized renderings of them, stands in stark contrast to the details we receive about Mary Godfrey and Jane Johns. She primarily serves as a plot device that furthers Osceola's story, not a historical actor. In addition, this story of Osceola's wife does not address the threat enslavement posed to the disruption of Native and Black homes that it highlights. Osceola's proximity to Blackness elevates the menace he poses to the United States, but it is often abated by emphasizing his narrative as a singular, non-Black male leader. Concomitantly, though, these same iterations produce a powerful counterreading of Osceola in which his legacy signals a fervent waiting for Afro-Native disruption of the white supremacist state; a radical still-becoming. It is important to also note that his legacy in Indian Country has always been quite a distinct one, where he is celebrated not for his tragic death but as emblematic of the necessity to continue fighting for Indigenous decolonial futurity.

Albery Allson Whitman's *The Rape of Florida*, published in 1884 and then republished a year later under the less salacious title *Twasinta's Seminoles*, lingers on this Afro-Native still-becoming. Whitman uses the ambitious rhyme scheme of the Spenserian sonnet in its nine-line stanzas to critique the United States' unjust treatment of Black people and Seminoles during the Second U.S.-Seminole War. Unlike earlier depictions of the war, however, Whitman's does not focus on Osceola's death.[80] Instead, he focuses on the speculative possibilities of Afro-Native marronage, a world-shaping beyond the borders of the United States that queries the radical potential of Afro-Native community beyond the colonial state.

Whitman was one of the most prolific African American poets of the nineteenth century.[81] For a time, he was known as the "Poet Laureate of the Negro Race" or the "Poet Laureate of the Church," and his work regularly appeared in Black periodicals, including perhaps the most well known and well read of these, the *Christian Recorder*.[82] He was a preacher and traveled through most of the territories covered in this book for the African Methodist Episcopal Church, including Florida. *The Rape of Florida* details a romance between Atlassa, a Seminole man, and Ewald, the mixed-race daughter of an unnamed Maroon woman and Palmecho. Palmecho is a landowner of Spanish descent who allows Twasinta, his large Florida estate, to serve as a refuge for Seminoles and exiles (Maroons). *The Rape of Florida* is an epic remapping of Florida that depicts a world of Spanish-Maroon-Indigenous collaboration in opposition to U.S. aggression. While the poem does offer up a counterspatiality, it also reconfigures racial alliances in ways that decenter whiteness and instead turns to Afro-Native coalitional world-building. In many ways, Whitman argues that Black and Native peoples, working outside a U.S. institutional framework, fight for the struggles for freedom and equality more authentically than those white settlers who participate in the project of U.S. empire-building.

Whitman does not center Osceola as his hero, although Osceola does make a guest appearance. Instead, he focuses on communal placemaking in the form of Twasinta, the bucolic home of his Spanish-Native-Black collective. Like the Osceola tales, Whitman's epic ends with tragedy: U.S. troops capture the elderly Palmecho at some point between the First and Second U.S.-Seminole Wars. His daughter Ewald and the young warrior Atlassa organize an effort to free him. Eventually, U.S. troops force Ewald, Atlassa, and the other inhabitants of Twasinta to leave their home and rebuild in Mexico.

While Whitman's masculinist romance flattens out the complexity of Afro-Native solidarity in Florida and reinscribes the Removal of both Black and Native bodies as inevitable, it also posits the kind of Afro-Native world-building that augmented white fears driving Removal, enslavement, and the U.S.-Seminole wars.

Before U.S. occupation, Florida was known as a refuge for Indigenous and Black people fleeing the violence and horrors of colonization and enslavement across the Southeast. There, Maroon communities comprising self-emancipated and free people of African descent could make home outside the enslaver colonial state. According to Seminole scholar Susan A. Miller, territorial struggles established the Seminole as a separate, autonomous people a century before.[83] These Seminole peoples came together, to some extent, to challenge the increased intervention of the United States into Florida. Seminoles and Maroons in the area had an investment in protecting themselves against U.S. intervention to secure their sovereignty and territory. For both Black Seminoles and Maroons, it also meant the potential for enslavement in the United States. For Black Seminoles, enslavement in the United States did not necessarily mean a better or worse form of oppression but a less familiar oppressor potentially farther away from home and family.[84]

Black and Native peoples in Florida experienced U.S. settler violence routinely throughout the opening decades of the nineteenth century, but such violence took its most public form as the U.S.-Seminole wars. While the start date of the First U.S.-Seminole War is contested, General Andrew Jackson's destruction of the Negro Fort in 1816 was undeniably a catalyst.[85] The British had left the fort to Black and Native allies after the Revolutionary War. The fort became a communal refuge for protection under Spanish rule. It became a beacon for Black and Indigenous people escaping warfare, violence, and enslavement across the Southeast and a physical symbol of militarized Afro-Native freedom from slavery and colonization.[86] According to historical accounts, the fort became a flourishing agricultural community where West African, Muskogean, and other Indigenous people shared knowledge of botany, medicine, spirituality, and language. The fort's thriving Afro-Native community represented Black autonomy and successful Black development concomitant with many white settlers' struggles to prosper in Florida, and Jackson's attack on the fort was both strategic and symbolic.[87] While only in operation for a few years, the Negro Fort is a powerful symbol of Afro-Native placemaking, a site of shared marronage in which communities made a home together beyond the piercing gaze of a colonial power.[88]

Whitman's Twasinta is not unlike the Negro Fort, and the poem resists the state-based logic of U.S. geographies and offers a different depiction of territorial belonging. Despite its stilted prose, a reinscription of gendered and racialized tropes, and its reliance on liberal notions of self-making, *The Rape of Florida* provides a sense of radical potential through its formulation of Twasinta. It depicts a counterhistorical narrative critical of settler colonialism and enslavement. The poem's original title feminizes Florida and anthropomorphizes it as an embodied victim of sexual violence, contrasting the violence of U.S. soldiers with the harmony of Twasinta.[89] The revised title, however, centers the space of Afro-Native utopia and describes all inhabitants as "Seminoles," understanding the identity formation as relational in ways that reinscribe kinship rather than race. His Afro-Native world-building outside the purview of U.S. white supremacy indicates Florida's potential to signal things other than totalized white domination, especially for nonwhite people, after the U.S.-Seminole wars, statehood, and the U.S. Civil War. However, Whitman's poem also regurgitates numerous Indian stereotypes in the process.

Such contradiction is not atypical in Whitman's writing. Much of his poetry is patriotic and reifies U.S. exceptionalism; at the same time, it criticizes U.S. territorial expansion and white supremacy. Matt Sandler describes Whitman's work as "an insurrectionary response to the end of Reconstruction" that "rewrites the frontier myth to center the opposition between white rapacity and anticolonial love."[90] The paradoxical nature of Whitman's poetics exposes the challenges of articulating Afro-Native life beyond the United States, but also the necessity of such an effort. In his other work, especially *Not a Man, and Yet a Man* (1877), which details the Black Hawk War, Whitman depicts the masculinist narrative of a Black male protagonist heroically empowering himself and others in a racist world who often finds peace through an affirmed sense of U.S. belonging.[91] While the fact is minimized in Sandler's reading of Whitman, it must be noted that in most of his speculative epic histories, Whitman reproduces stereotypes of Native people, especially that of the vanishing Indian figure.[92] *The Rape of Florida* is slightly different, however. Whitman's hero is a Native man with at least some character development, and Whitman's depiction of Twasinta challenges the American exceptionalist logic of Manifest Destiny that is omnipresent throughout his larger body of work.

In *The Rape of Florida*, Whitman describes a deep alliance between Maroons, or exiles, as he calls them, and Seminoles through a shared love for "their country." He argues that they are all fighting for justice and freedom, and in that, are heroic and worthy of poetic commemoration. He literally and figuratively emphasizes strong bonds between Maroon and Seminole communities in Florida. Against the backdrop of Ewald and Atlassa's love affair, Whitman describes Afro-Native kinship at the grandest scale. He writes,

> Down to the end of time be it proclaimed!
> Up to the skies of fame let it be rung!
> Wherever valor's sacrifice is named,
> *Whenever* plaudits fire the human tongue;
> Or by sweet strings expressed, or mortals sung
> Let it go forth, and let mankind attest,
> That, Seminoles and exiles, old and young,
> Upon the bosom of their country prest;
> By valiant deeds are shrined in ev'ry patriot breast![93]

These lines exude a sense of grandeur. The speaker insists that the Twasinta community is important to all of "mankind" and depicts the community as a shared country. He inverts his use of patriot language, which he typically employs in the service of the United States in his poetry, to describe a "country" that not only is outside the United States but also becomes targeted by it and eventually Removed. In this formulation, Whitman imagines a shared space of marronage that unifies Afro-Native sovereignty.

However, his utopic Twasinta flattens the more complex dynamics on the ground—or in the swamps, if you will. Most critically, he omits the Seminoles' participation in enslavement. Specifics about the actual relationships among the Seminole, Black Seminole, and Maroon communities in Florida have been the subject of much speculation. According to historian Kenneth Wiggins Porter, "As early as 1687, the Spaniards bedeviled rival English settlements by offering freedom and land, in return for military service, to British slaves who fled to them."[94] Susan Miller claims that "in the late eighteenth century groups of such Africans began forming 'maroon communities,' groups of free Africans living together in resistance to slavery. By the end of the century Africans were living near or in Seminole towns as Maroons or slaves."[95] She goes on to say that by the 1830s, "during the Seminoles' war of resistance against the U.S. seizure of our lands in Florida, Africans clearly held at least two political statuses in relation to the Seminoles": Maroon or enslaved person. "Maroon communities appear to have paid a portion of their crops to certain Seminole leaders, but the nature of that relationship is unclear: Were the payments more like rent, taxes, or protection money, for example? Some

Africans were slaves of Seminoles. The status of Seminole slaves was far less onerous than the status of American, Muscogee, or Cherokee slaves."[96] However, as Seminole scholar Kevin Noble Maillard observes, "Freedmen and Seminole view their intertwined history differently, and these understandings emerge in a heated contemporary conflict."[97] Even if enslavement was less "onerous" in Seminole communities than elsewhere, it was nonetheless enslavement. It would also facilitate racially inflected notions of Seminole identity and belonging.

It is critical to remember that one of the reasons Seminole leaders refused Removal was the U.S. government's unwillingness to promise that enslaved people would come with them to Indian Territory rather than be Removed to white enslavers. The Seminole Nation would not abolish slavery until the 1860s. Racialized notions of citizenship would continue to shape the lives of Seminoles—especially for Seminoles of African descent and Seminole-enslaved people who were Removed to Indian Territory, which I discuss in more detail in chapter 4—and led to the Seminole Nation of Oklahoma's Removal of Seminole Freedpeople's membership from the Nation in 2000 (as of the writing of this book, full membership is still suspended). This chapter does not take up the debates surrounding Seminole citizenship and membership in the contemporary moment (Seminole Nation draws a distinction between the two classifications), but highlighting these debates demonstrates the enduring tensions produced by colonialism and enslavement.[98] Interpretations of these relationships, which abide into the twenty-first century, continue to have a far-reaching impact, especially for Black Seminoles. They influence understandings of tribal belonging, which are often intertwined in the friction between tribal sovereignty and federal interference, in part because anti-Blackness is woven into federal Indian policy.[99]

Whatever the specifics of Seminole, Black Seminole, and Maroon communities in the nineteenth century, these Afro-Native collaborations physically posed a severe threat to U.S. troops and ideologically to U.S. constructions of race, raising anxiety about what could occur when Native people and African-descended people collaborated. When Henry Holland visits the "United Nation of Chickasaw and Choctaw Indians" in Martin Delany's *Blake* to propose his plans for Black hemispheric revolution, Chief Culver explains to him the power of Black and Native solidarity: "You see the vine that winds around and holds us together. Don't cut it, but let it grow till bimeby, it git so stout and strong, with many, very many little branches attached, that you can't separate them." Culver goes on to explain, "That what make Indian strong; that what make Indian and black man in Florida hold together."[100] Inarguably, there are numerous examples of Afro-Native allegiances in the border skirmishes, raids, and warfare of the first half of the nineteenth century in Florida. It was also a widely held belief that Seminoles aided and abetted self-emancipating fugitives. In 1834 the territorial governor of Florida, William Pope DuVal, explained to the commissioner of Indian affairs that the first order of business in expelling the Seminoles "must be *the breaking up of the runaway slaves and outlaw Indians.*"[101]

According to Matthew Clavin, "The significant role that self-emancipated fugitives played in the Second U.S.-Seminole War fueled Americans' fear of a massive slave insurrection originating in the Florida territory." Moreover, "the fear of a revolutionary black army from the West Indies landing on Florida's shores was widespread during the Second Seminole War."[102] The conflict in Florida raised questions about the anti-Indigenous and anti-Black logics undergirding Removal and enslavement, particularly given the combat successes of the Seminoles, Black Seminoles, and Maroons. In his memoir from the Second U.S.-Seminole War, M. M. Cohen describes the Black Seminoles and Maroons as the real instigators of revolution: "Their number is said to be upwards of three hundred. They fear being again made slaves, under the American Government; and will omit nothing to increase or keep alive mistrust among the Indians, whom they in fact govern. If it should become necessary to use force with them, it is to be feared the Indians would take their part. It will, however, be necessary to remove from the Floridas, this group of lawless freebooters, among whom the runaway negroes will always find refuge."[103] Cohen expresses great concern about the potential for Black uprising throughout the South and anxiety about the role the Black Seminoles play in the wars, including as translators for the U.S. military; the military could not defeat the Afro-Native combatants without the help of Black translators and scouts, many of whom could speak at least some Mvskoke, English, and Spanish.

The U.S. military used Black scouts strategically to break up Black and Native allegiances in Florida, but it also intentionally placed Black and non-Black Seminole leaders in difficult positions that could fracture relationships along racial lines. Slavery and Removal were used to challenge allegiances between non-Black Seminole tribal leaders and Black and Black Seminole translators. For example, U.S. officials like General Thomas Jesup offered Black Seminole translators freedom if they agreed to persuade Seminoles to emigrate west. Central to U.S. military strategy was the destruction of healthy Afro-Seminole kinship networks. The Seminoles wanted to take Black Seminoles with them to Indian Territory, while Black Seminoles undoubtedly wanted autonomy and freedom in Florida, Indian Territory, or elsewhere. Florida enslavers wanted Black Seminoles handed over to the United States and all Seminoles sent west.[104]

Florida, therefore, existed at the intersection of the two major social issues of the antebellum era, adding deep symbolic weight to the outcome of Removal and the Second U.S.-Seminole War. Albery Whitman touches on this weighty symbolism half a century later. For Whitman, a shared desire for freedom from a system that excludes Black and Native peoples from humanity drives Black and Native collaboration, a point that would have particular salience in the 1880s as Jim Crow became entrenched and the Dawes Act of 1887 authorized the allotment of Native lands, both being policies of Removal intended to control Black and Indigenous movement through space. His poem ends with a rumination on the pressing social questions of late nineteenth-century life and the centrality of anti-Blackness and anti-Indigeneity to U.S. identity. At the end of the poem, Whitman argues that U.S. soldiers fought "for Freedom and for *slavery* too," while the Seminole fought purely for freedom:

> He could not be enslaved—would not enslave
> The meanest exile that his friendship sued.
> Brave for himself, defending others brave,
> The matchless hero of his time he stood,—
> His noble heart with freedom's love imbued,
> The strong apostle of Humanity!
> Mid forests wild and habitations rude,
> He made his bed of glory by the sea;
> The friend of Florida and man, there let him be![105]

The Seminoles did participate in enslavement, making Whitman's account historically inaccurate. But this elision speaks to the ideological potential rather than the material reality of race relations in Florida. Because Florida was such a messy collection of peoples, nations, and power struggles, it made it easy to pick and choose which Florida to feature. In the 1880s the remaining Seminoles in Florida took refuge in the Everglades, cutting off most contact outside their communities except for trade and other necessities. For the most part, the U.S. federal government ignored them and they lived, one might say, "off the map" of official U.S. surveillance.[106]

However, in the poem's conclusion, Whitman reinscribes a totalizing Removal that locates all of his Black, Native, and Spanish characters outside the nascent state boundaries of Florida as they relocate to Mexico. His description of the success of the Twasinta community, even as (double) exiles, offers a contradictory and vexed interpretation of Removal, and one that consolidates Indian Removal and Black emigration outside the United States. It paints an exceptionally optimistic portrait of Removal that rationalizes U.S. interventions into Florida at the same time it excuses them. In the last six stanzas, the narrator deploys tropes of U.S. exceptionalism, as in stanza 49 when he pronounces, "This is a land of free limb and free thought— / Freedom for *all* home-keeping, or abroad."[107] The poem ends by suggesting that the U.S. struggles against "priestcraft" and "tyranny" that led to the forced Removal of Atlassa and Ewald no longer exist. Slavery has been abolished in the United States, and a system of meritocracy has replaced a previous system of racialized violence and inequity. It is an odd pivot at the end of the poem that insists on the temporal gap between the poem's action and the narrator's recitation, but rather than affirm a sense of historical distance, the stanzas raise questions about the parameters of freedom they so emphatically espouse. The narrator is correct that the community we find at Twasinta cannot exist in Florida as a state. An Afro-Native community is an impossibility because it stands in opposition to the structure of statehood; for Florida statehood to exist, Black and Native autonomy cannot. Like Jumper's poetic response to the wars in "Major Dade," Whitman's poem lyrically evokes archival dissonance that questions whether the war ever really ended— politically or ideologically—and more importantly, whether the United States achieved the intended goal.

If the Second U.S.-Seminole War was about breaking up Afro-Native alliances in Florida because of the threat such alliances posed to Florida statehood and to the more extensive logic of U.S. coloniality, then Whitman's poem depicts an Afro-Native territorial alternative. Moreover, he wrests the prevailing U.S.-Seminole wars narrative from the white literati and fashions it as a story of radical Black and Native possibility. He remaps the hegemonic history of the Seminole wars by offering a different territoriality, one that imagines an Afro-Native utopia. While imperfect, Whitman's radical speculations and his emphasis on the power of the poetic to discursively gesture to space beyond the state speak in conversation with twenty-first-century poet-scholars like Alexis Pauline Gumbs, Fred Moten, and Leanne Betasamosake Simpson (Michi Saagiig Nishnaabeg), who imagine the poetic, or what Katherine McKittrick terms the "poetics of landscape," as one way to signal toward—but not capture—the fugitive possibilities of marronage and Afro-Native world-building.[108]

Print Culture and the Seminole Tribe of Florida

Albery Whitman's poetic homage is an emancipatory one in its emphasis, but like other literary accounts, it wields Seminoleness as an aesthetic and symbolic trope rather than an embodied personhood. The assertion has been that because Seminoles did not use print as a tool of combat during the wars with the United States, their voices are absent in the archives, circulating solely as ventriloquized accounts. But this is not entirely true. A strong body of writing produced through U.S.-Seminole talks and treaty negotiations carries the tenor of Seminole voices. These accounts were often filtered through translators, which has led some scholars to question their authenticity, but entirely discrediting them threatens to perpetuate non-Seminole accounts and bequeath a sense of verity to a colonial archive. While I proceed with caution in ascertaining the idea that these accounts are trustworthy (whatever that might mean), it seems equally as important to remember that the letters and records of U.S. military officers, enlisted men, poets, and novelists are also suspect and carry with them their own set of assumptions, objectives, and mediations. I do not say this to equate the two, but merely to challenge the notion that Seminole voices, often filtered through translators, can be discredited while the words of white male U.S. subjects receive far less scrutiny.

As mentioned earlier in this chapter, just because the Seminole people were not proficient in or not committed to engaging in English literacy, print culture, or the circulation of print directly does not mean that they failed to understand the weight that a print archive carried both in negotiating with the U.S. government and in winning support through a broader literate audience—if anything, quite the opposite. On May 17, 1826, in negotiations with Secretary of War James Barbour, Tukose Emathla (also known as John Hicks) allegedly challenged U.S. interest in setting up schools for Seminole children. In his denouncement, as it was transcribed, he reflects on the power of the book. Tukose Emathla begins, "We do not believe the Great Spirit intended we should know how to read & write; for if he had intended this, he would have given us the knowledge as early as he gave it to the white people. Now it is too late; the white people have gained an advantage, we can never recover and it is better for us to remain as we are." He goes on to narrate a story of how the white people obtained control over the book:

> Brother, among our people it is thought that at the time when there were
> but two kinds of people, the red and the white, on the earth, a book was

placed by the Great Spirit in the hands of an old man, blind, and with a long beard, who told the red and the white man, that he who killed the first Deer should receive the book as his reward & he learnt to read it— Both went out to hunt different ways—The white man after going a little way, found a sheep, which being not so wild as the Deer, he easily killed—

He took this sheep to the blind man & told him it was a Deer—The old man believed him and gave him the book and learnt him how to read it—The red man soon after brought in a deer, but he was too late—the white man had got the book. If this cheat had not been practiced, the red man would have been now as the white man is & he as the red man.[109]

In Tukose Emathla's narrative, the book and access to literacy and print are gained through deceit and lies. While the white man ostensibly wins the challenge, he does so at a cost, one that tarnishes the gift he has been given. Though the book and print in the nineteenth century were often reified as arbiters of truth, fact, and legitimacy (even when their readers knew this to be false), Tukose Emathla depicts them as inherently grounded in an act of deceit. In a practice that replicates the expansion of U.S. colonization, the white man defies the rules and takes a shortcut, while the red man goes through the time and labor it takes to hunt an actual deer.

Whether or not Tukose Emathla spoke these words verbatim, they echo sentiments routinely expressed by Seminoles in the decades to come. Resistance to literacy and print continued for almost one hundred years after the conflict in Florida. This was partially a result of life in the Everglades with minimal access to the material means of print production and partially a political move that created and sustained distance from U.S. culture. As they flourished in the Everglades, Seminoles strategically stayed off the colonial map. This disinterest in print raises necessary questions about the role of nineteenth-century print culture studies. Are those who do not participate in a print-driven public positioned outside the purview of such studies, even when print culture directly affected their lived experiences and relationship to power, land, and culture? How might we understand the acts of those who actively resisted interpellation onto the page, if you will?

While treaty discussions, talks, and other forms of formal negotiation dominate the nineteenth-century archive, most of which favored a U.S. perspective, Seminoles, Black Seminoles, and Maroons had their own ways of keeping stories of the wars and the fight to stay in Florida. If they had neither the means nor the desire to participate in print production, literacy, and literature in the nineteenth century, they altered course in the twentieth and twenty-first centuries. In "The Snake Clan Returns to Florida," Betty Mae Tiger Jumper (Pa-ta-kee) tells the story of her great-grandmother's experiences during the Second U.S.-Seminole War as told to her by her grandmother. Tiger Jumper was an influential member of the Seminole Tribe of Florida. As mentioned earlier, she founded the *Seminole News*, the Seminole Tribe of Florida's first tribal newspaper, with Alice Osceola in 1956, and she was the first female leader of any federally recognized tribe.[110] Tiger Jumper was also the first person from her community to graduate from high school. While at a Baptist camp in so-called Oklahoma, she observed a young Native girl reading a comic book. She could not read and did not understand the appeal of the book, but after the girl explained that the book "talks to you," Tiger Jumper was determined to gain English literacy to "unlock the secrets of the talking books" and pursued an education and went on to write several books about Seminole culture and life.[111]

Her family story offers a very different account of the Second U.S.-Seminole War, highlighting her clan, as well as the roles of Seminole women. In this way, Tiger Jumper's account contributes a counter to colonial histories that speaks to Seminole survivance by invoking a narrative that rebukes Removal and gestures toward the matrilineal aspects of Seminole (and Muskogean) culture. After her great-great-grandmother and oldest great-aunt were raped during transport to Indian Territory, her great-grandmother and younger great-aunt escaped. They fled through forests and rivers to find their way home. Eventually, they came upon a camp of Seminoles who knew their father and brothers. Men from the camp reunited them with their family, who had been hiding out in the Everglades. Tiger Jumper explains that because these girls could return, the Snake clan could continue (as kinship was matrilineally determined). She writes, "Because of these brave sisters, the Snake clan did not disappear, but that's why there aren't very many people in our clan. . . . Today there are about forty-five people in the Snake clan. There are mostly boys now, and they cannot carry on their clan to their children. But however small, the Snake clan still continues."[112] In her retelling of Removal, she emphasizes continuity across time and space rather than total rupture, and the role of women and girls in the journey. In Oklahoma—that is, Indian Territory, the site of nineteenth-century Removal—Tiger Jumper gains knowledge and tools she takes back to the community in Florida. Tiger Jumper's movement across Removal routes refuses a linear path of destruction and instead serves to foster adaptation and growth for her community as she travels back and forth. Seminole voices are underrepresented in the paper archives, and those of Seminole women are even more scarce. However, in

Tiger Jumper's story, the clan endures not through combat but through the struggles of two small girls who refused Removal and the matriarch Elders who have kept their story alive. It serves as a reminder of the importance of women in Seminole culture.

In contrast to the settler literature, settler journalism, and the military and governmental records that contain voluminous accounts of how the fight for Florida represented Native insistence on self-determination and undermined U.S. cultural assertions of the ease and necessity of expansion and Florida statehood, Tiger Jumper offers a different, more personal account. In place of masculine figures of iconic proportion, like Osceola, we find two vulnerable girls whose mother and older sister have suffered brutal sexual violence at the hands of U.S. officials while in transit to Indian Territory. Because these girls can survive, the clan continues. In so doing, they represent another form of continued Seminole survivance, one that is grounded in the strength of women and children and the stories they carry. Her family story upends a dominant masculinist voice by foregrounding a matriarchal narrative told by a Seminole woman.

Let Us Alone

The Seminole people, Florida statehood, and the U.S.-Seminole wars raised pressing questions about race, expansion, and Removal for a larger U.S. reading public. For some, the wars raised doubts about the efficacy and ethics of forced Removal of Native peoples, while for others, the Seminoles' unwillingness to leave Florida stood as a direct challenge to U.S. settler empire and expansion. Statehood did not curtail continued warfare, nor did it lead to a population boom, despite U.S. efforts to entice white settlement—and statehood itself was not the result of a sweeping desire by settlers to become a state. Bankers and plantation-owning enslavers who represented the upper crust of Florida society orchestrated statehood to benefit their personal interests and extend their land claims. Nonetheless, Florida was admitted as a slave state in 1845. The new flag, hoisted with the election of the state's first governor, bore the ironic motto "Let us alone," a clear message about Florida political leaders' stance on states' rights, but one that also invoked the stance of Black and Indigenous communities before the wars.[113] Statehood for Florida was not accompanied by great fanfare or pomp, but was instead an unimpressive affair. It was not until Florida seceded in the U.S. Civil War that the state began to cohere a singular sense of identity, bringing together East, West, and middle Florida. Statehood was an anticlimactic resolve, making it seem as if the fighting was, in fact, about something else. A trenchant fight against Black freedom solidified Floridian identity. Understanding this history helps explain how Florida has become animated as a state whose population, politics, and culture sit anomalously in a U.S. national landscape. Moreover, in the twenty-first century, there has been a willful desire on the part of real estate developers to work against the natural character of the land in the name of personal wealth, despite the fact that rising sea levels and climate change threaten Florida's coasts and the infrastructure that crowds them. In actions that echo the past, the Seminole and Miccosukee Tribes have advocated against environmental destruction and degradation, asserting their political, environmental (and in some cases economic) force in Florida to do so.[114]

The fight for Florida statehood was marked by combat and warfare that tested the limits of U.S. expansion and Removal. While the United States attempted to contain, control, and understand the territory through military campaigns and the circulation of the printed page, it did not gain full sovereignty or the final word on the matter. Osceola was initially an English derivation of a Muskogean name, and arguably its translation demonstrated a U.S. settler desire to transform Seminole peoples to suit the needs of U.S. expansion. Since the nineteenth century, it has become a common Seminole surname, and the figure of Osceola (and all he signified) has been reclaimed by Seminoles. With every new Osceola born, Osceolas endure and continue to call Florida home.

CHAPTER THREE

Kansas Bleeds into Cuba

Albery Whitman, the "Poet Laureate of the Negro Race," dedicates the 1890 edition of his epic poem *Twasinta's Seminole* to "Honorable Charles Robinson," an abolitionist hero of the Bleeding Kansas era and the first governor of Kansas.[1] Given that *Twasinta's Seminole* is an epic poem that celebrates Indigenous and Black freedom beyond the white U.S. state, it seems curious that Whitman would choose to dedicate the book to Robinson—a politician and state actor—and not a more radical Kansas symbol of white abolitionist militancy like John Brown. To invoke Robinson is to not quite let go of the belief that statehood promises freedom and Black inclusion and to forget, if even briefly, the lessons of Afro-Native militancy that Whitman puts to verse. Thus, Whitman's homage to Robinson and his celebration of a symbolic "first" in the work of statecraft unwittingly participates in the fantasy of Indigenous and Black disenfranchisement central to state identity. I say this not to critique Whitman directly but rather to highlight the violent and expeditious work of statehood, especially the ways it obscures Black and Indigenous struggle.

As I have argued throughout *Reading Territory*, freedom and liberal inclusion are the false promises of statehood, and they depend on continued violence against Black and Indigenous people, as the case of Kansas demonstrates. Staging Bleeding Kansas as an origin story eclipses the forced Removal of Indigenous peoples from the region and the discursive and geopolitical shift from "Indian Territory" to "Kansas Territory" in the 1850s. Much like narrating Kansas statehood as a struggle over slavery, dedicating *Twasinta* to Robinson symbolically obfuscates Indigenous continuity in the face of colonial genocide. In the 1850s, Kansas Territory became a flashpoint for debates about enslavement and the state (both the federated state and the nation-state). The Kansas-Nebraska Act of 1854 rescinded the earlier Missouri Compromise (1820) and advocated popular sovereignty, leaving the decision of whether a state would legally endorse enslavement up to the majority decision of a territory's voting residents. While supporters of popular sovereignty posited it as an egalitarian response to federal overreach, the impulse reinscribed a racializing colonial world order that firmly reified white supremacy and the belief that white *men* could best determine the geopolitical parameters of a U.S. empire.

The Kansas-Nebraska Act led to extreme unrest in Kansas Territory, now well known as the Bleeding Kansas era, but also revived decades-long debates about Cuban annexation. Immediately after President Franklin Pierce signed the act, he assured the U.S. public that he had no immediate plans to seize control of Cuba, evidencing how the two held a shared space in the public imaginary. According to literary scholar Eric Sundquist, this decision was intended to appease Northerners' anger at the passage of the act, but "in the long run, the conjunction of Kansas and Cuba devastated both the Democratic party and the idea of popular sovereignty; crushed the South's dream of a Caribbean empire; [and] lost a territory destined to be of strategic importance to the United States in later years."[2]

Putting Cuba and Kansas into conversation lays bare the ways statehood, staged as an antiracist, democratic event able to further universal rights and equality, disavowed Black and Indigenous geographies; in this move, metaphors of anticolonial Indigeneity (à la "native" rule in Cuba) and the "free" state paradoxically supplant actual or embodied Indigenous and Black revolution. Looking carefully at statehood movements, like those surrounding Kansas and Cuba, reveals how anti-Blackness and anti-Indigeneity interlock rather than operate on different planes. Critically, at its most democratically aspirational, statehood was imagined to emancipate Black subjects and overwrite Indigenous ones. Such a move positioned Blackness and Indigeneity outside each other and centered whiteness as the necessary core around which all racialized others orbit.

In this chapter, I turn to visual and print culture to unravel some of the ways Kansas and Cuba were made discursively legible and (un)incorporable into the assemblage of U.S. states. Much of the rhetoric bolstering Cuban annexation debates argued for the removal of Spanish colonialism in the name of "native" rule. This rhetoric masked the United States' imperial interests in Cuba and reproduced and countered narratives of U.S.-Indigenous conflict on the continent. Discussion over Kansas's statehood in the 1850s was in direct tension with schemes to annex Cuba. Why did Kansas, formerly part of Indian Territory, become a state while the United States maintained a more unusual relationship with Cuba? Why was Cuba seemingly "read" by the U.S. government and journalistic press as an amendable geopolitical space for the U.S. imperial project? It may be difficult to imagine affinities between Kansas and Cuba in the twenty-first century, but in the mid-nineteenth century the two were understood relationally; each locale signaled distinct ideological challenges to an ever-growing U.S. empire.

Arguably one of the most significant effects of *both* "Bleeding" Kansas and U.S. interventions into Cuban affairs in the 1850s (and during the Spanish-American War at the end of the nineteenth century) was the naturalization of Kansas as "domestic" space and Cuba as "foreign." Moreover, Kansas's inclusion in Indian Territory just years before the sectional debates was critical to how Kansas was read along racial and regional lines. In particular, white men's statehood campaigns, be it in Kansas, Cuba, or elsewhere, furthered the project of U.S. empire by recentering patriarchal white supremacy at the expense of Black and Native world-making and often did so under the banner of abolition or decolonization. What debates about both Kansas and Cuba statehood shared, however, was a belief that the sheer production of a U.S. state could ameliorate the divisiveness of slavery by indigenizing and recentering white masculinity. Paradoxically, efforts in both Cuba and Kansas further laid bare sectional divisions within the United States. Neither the fantasy of an expansive U.S. slavocracy in the Caribbean nor that of an abolitionist Kansas state questioned the genocidal logics of colonization that would continue to perpetuate anti-Blackness and anti-Indigeneity. Moreover, Kansas statehood and abolitionist Free-Soilers' promises of Black civic inclusion did not result in radical Black freedom.

Debates about legalized enslavement recalibrate Kansas as unquestionably domestic to the United States and no longer part of an extra–U.S. "Indian Territory." This move reveals one of the central claims of *Reading Territory*—namely, how statehood and state sovereignty at best demand the subjugation of Indigenous or Black life at the expense of the other, and at worst position Indigenous and Black freedom struggles as oppositional. It is telling that despite the ideological storm that Kansas garnered, over the next century and a half it became a productively white supremacist space, where state power was routinely used to further Indigenous and Black dispossession. Covering an expansive array of sources to challenge the familiar story of statehood that imagines it as an orderly, logical process, I demonstrate that statehood, both in the case of Kansas and in Cuba, was a contradictory, violent one that systematically aimed to shut out all other forms of place-based relations and recenter white male possession. In addition, these statehood debates would continue to inform state formation and the contours of U.S. empire. Some turn-of-the-century Black organizing efforts in Oklahoma and Indian Territories, including a Black statehood campaign I discuss in chapter 4, were direct responses to dissatisfaction with an untenable climate of anti-Black violence in Kansas. If statehood were, in fact, a universally emancipatory project, then the history of Kansas would look much different.

This chapter begins with an analysis of 1850s political cartoons and maps. I read them as an assemblage of *colonial printscapes* that did critical work to indigenize white settler belonging and produce an affinity between Cuba and Kansas. Through a collection of signifiers and signs of civility and savagery, these images expose the iconographic and lexical work necessary for rendering territory as U.S. space. Keeping these printscapes in mind, I turn to the revolutionary imaginings of Martin Delany and John Brown. At the same time Delany was imagining Black hemispheric revolution and leading a colonization expedition through Africa, he was consulting Brown on Brown's plans for a Black state in Kansas Territory. By analyzing Delany's novel *Blake* alongside Brown's statehood proposal, I bring a different dialogue between Cuba and Kansas to the fore, one that is not about expanding U.S. empire, per se, but is about imaging Black freedom outside U.S. empire. However, in formulating their visions for emancipatory territorialities, Delany's and Brown's postulations evidence how U.S.-influenced notions of belonging and sovereignty reinscribe structures of unfreedom for Black and Indigenous people. In the second half of the chapter, I turn to an analysis of how Cuba's essential role in the transatlantic slave trade and the origin story of the "New World" informed debate about Kansas statehood and served to obscure the recent forced Removal of Indigenous communities across so-called Kansas. I end with an analysis of John Brougham's play *Columbus el Filibustero!* (1857), which literally and figuratively stages some of the affective ties that tethered Kansas and Cuba to each other in U.S. expansionist debates.

The Kansas-Cuba Act

Kansas had gained widespread attention in the late 1850s as a lightning rod for slavery debates, but before Kansas's statehood, the region had been part of Indian Territory and home to numerous Native nations, including the regionally powerful Osage Nation. In the 1840s and 1850s, Native peoples in the territory experienced the encroachment of white intruders and the theft of their lands. Federal desires to develop a transcontinental railroad that could link U.S. states and territories on the East and West Coasts incentivized white intrusion into Indian Territory, including onto the lands of the Osage, Shawnee, Kaw, Kickapoo, Delaware, Sac and Fox, Potawatomi, Ottawa, Wyandotte, and Miami. U.S. law enforcement was unwilling to do much to ensure that U.S. citizens did not invade Indigenous communities. While the Kansas-Nebraska Act ostensibly opened up land for white settlement, none of that land was "empty."[3] It was home to over 10,000 Indigenous people who, according to the federal government's own laws, had a right to live there.

Many of the nations had been forcibly Removed from their ancestral homelands very recently, most within the previous twenty years.[4] They had living memory of not only the trauma of Removal but also the ways the United States used surveying, statehood, allotments, and territorial cessions as tactics to steal Indigenous lands.[5] The federal government promised these communities that a move to Indian Territory was their last, but the government's establishment of Kansas Territory abrogated treaty agreements and confirmed decades of suspicion that the United States did not plan to act in good faith and protect the autonomy of Indian Territory.[6] Instead, through forced treaty negotiations demanding land cession in the 1820s through the 1840s to extract even more from Indigenous peoples, federal agents worked diligently to strip as many resources from Native communities as possible. These treaties collectively dismantled the notion of Indian Territory as a geopolity organized under sovereign Indigenous rule. Tribal leaders fought to defend their peoples, territories, and lifeways as best they could, but the aggression of federal and squatter invasion created a relentless series of challenges that attacked both the structural and the intimate contours of Indigenous lifeways.

By 1854 when Congress passed the Kansas-Nebraska Act, Indigenous land titles were ignored, even though they were never legally terminated. Osage scholar Robert Warrior writes of the opening of Kansas Territory,

> In spite of the fact that not a single inch of Kansas Territory was open to settlement when it was created in 1854 and all of the Native groups there had treaties guaranteeing secure boundaries for their homelands, squatters had already moved freely into Native lands, and the United States government failed to police its own citizens. The idea of squatter sovereignty, linked as it was with the Jeffersonian ideal of yeomanry, populism, and Manifest Destiny, was much stronger than any concept of the rights the aboriginal inhabitants, like the Osages or the emigrant tribes like the Shawnee, Kickapoo, or Sac and Fox, held through negotiated agreements with the United States.[7]

Warrior makes clear that assertions of popular sovereignty reentrenched a violent regime of extraction and genocide. While popular sovereignty arguments posited a slightly broader radius of white male inclusion, they did so by affirming the exclusion of all others, especially Indigenous people. The debate over popular sovereignty for U.S. citizens was just as much about Indigenous sovereignty as it was about the reach of the U.S. federal government—popular sovereignty *was* squatter sovereignty. Before 1854, only about 800 settlers occupied Kansas Territory, but after the Nebraska Act, hundreds began to descend on the territories of its Indigenous caretakers through brazen land grabs.

It is important to remember that despite U.S. efforts to strip Native people of their titles and forcibly Remove them south, not all Native people complied; the terra nullius fantasy of genocidal erasure that fueled the forced Removal of the Cherokees and the Seminoles was no more successful in Kansas than it had been in so-called Georgia or Florida. Large numbers of Osages did not move south to the significantly shrunken Indian Territory until the 1870s, well after the United States had rescinded the promises the federal government made to them for their contribution to Union efforts during the U.S. Civil War. Debate in the 1860s about whether to move to Indian Territory and live communally or stay in Kansas, accept U.S. citizenship, and live on individual allotments of land led to a division of the people into two distinct nations.[8] The Bleeding Kansas debate—and the repositioning of Kansas as a territory caught between North and South, legal enslavement and abolition—simultaneously ignored Indigenous geopolities altogether. Such colonial amnesia is all the more confounding when one realizes that many of the locations significant to slavery debates of the 1850s were also sites of colonial violence and control that, in many cases, still functioned as such.[9] For example, the Shawnee Indian Mission still operated as a manual training school for Shawnee and other Indigenous youths when the proslavery "bogus laws" were first passed there.

Supplanting Indigenous territoriality with settler possession was a discursive project aided by print. A map included in the March 17, 1855, issue of the *Kansas Free State* newspaper serves as a powerful visual reminder that Kansas was Indian Territory (figures 3.1 and 3.2).[10] In the upper right-hand corner of the front page sits a "Map of Eastern Kansas" detailing tribal spaces. The paper explains that the map was engraved by the commissioner of Indian affairs for the *Kansas Tribune*. Both the map and the explanatory text appear to be reprinted from that paper. However, such context is misleading. The map is almost identical to an 1853 map intentionally drafted to make it appear as if Indigenous people only occupied the eastern corner of Indian Country, leaving the rest of the territory empty and open for settlement. This widely circulated 1853 map and its omission of legal settlement boundaries encouraged white invasions of Native land and all but attempted to cartographically erase Indigenous nations as a step in physically doing so.[11] As such, it is a *colonial printscape* that maps white fantasy, not Indigenous reality.

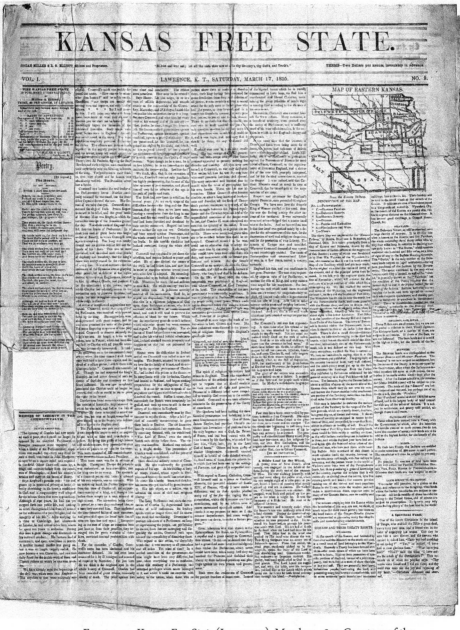

FIGURE 3.1 Front page, *Kansas Free State* (Lawrence), March 17, 1855. Courtesy of the American Antiquarian Society.

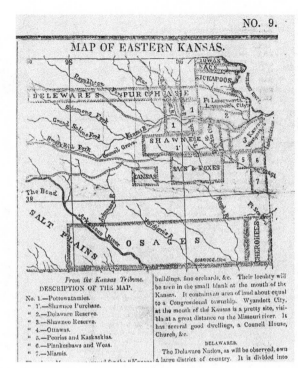

FIGURE 3.2 Closeup of "Map of Eastern Kansas." Front page, *Kansas Free State* (Lawrence), March 17, 1855. Courtesy of the American Antiquarian Society.

The map's function as an advertisement, not explication, is evident even without this context. It details the wealth waiting to be accumulated by white colonizers through the rendering of solid black borders, and the visual and discursive cues directing its reader. The verity of the map is suspect at best as a work of colonial propaganda. In addition, the story it tells paradoxically challenges a narrative of Bleeding Kansas that attempts to read along a north-south axis. Instead, the map privileges proximity to the east through the title, and the tribal boundaries and rivers blur the gridded, state-based rendering of space. Despite cartographic efforts to contain Indian Territory, it squirms beyond the confines of a colonizing printscape. Some tribal holdings appear squared off, but others challenge the grid and curve the edges back. Fort Leavenworth (built without tribal consent on Indigenous land) and Lawrence City both appear, but they are blurred by the tribal names that surround them.[12]

Compare this with *Reynolds's Political Map of the United States*, meant to visually and geographically render the tensions around slavery in the United States (figure 3.3). There is a great deal to unpack in this image as well, but I want to focus on the map's rendering of the Mason-Dixon Line running through the middle of the left side. Appearing on the same plane,

FIGURE 3.3 William C. Reynolds and J. C. Jones, *Reynolds's Political Map of the United States, Designed to Exhibit the Comparative Area of the Free and Slave States, and the Territory Open to Slavery or Freedom by the Repeal of the Missouri Compromise* (New York: Wm. C. Reynolds and J. C. Jones, 1856). Map. Courtesy of the Library of Congress Geography and Map Division (https://loc.gov/item/2003627003/).

demarcated as white space, is the "Indian" of Indian Territory. Through their absence of color and their placement at the center of the image, the Kansas and Indian Territories draw the viewer's attention. Kansas is inked with the same gray tones as "British America," but "Indian" sits, absent color, at an intersection between territories and proslavery states. As indicated by its title, Kansas is clearly meant to be the center of the image, but "Indian" hovers directly below it. While the project of Kansas statehood willfully attempted to ignore Indigenous presence, the center-justified "Indian" on the map serves as a reminder that Indigenous dispossession and enslavement are part of the same throughline, despite deliberate efforts to disentangle the two.

While debate in the popular press raged over the importance of the "people's" voice in deciding Kansas's future, this debate hinged on the systemic squatting of predominantly white intruders; "people" did not include Indigenous people. To invoke the "cacophony" of colonial relations described in the work of Chickasaw scholar Jodi Byrd, the claim for democratic decision-making in concert with the ethos of U.S. constitutionalism is consistent, but discordant, built on the unacknowledged presence of Indigenous people. Byrd challenges the reading of American empire as that which "replicate[s] itself through a detachable and remappable 'frontier' or 'wilderness,'" and she instead argues as an additive that U.S. empire "does so through the reproduction of Indianness that exists alongside racializing discourses that slip through the thresholds of whiteness and blackness, inclusion and exclusion, internal and external, that are the necessary conditions of settler colonial sovereignty."[13] For her, the figure of the Indian is the original enemy of the settler colonial state, for whom truth and reconciliation cannot be and are never offered.

As disturbing as the colonial erasure of Indian Territory was the deployment of "Indianness" to mitigate the Kansas statehood conflict, perhaps best evidenced by John Brown's redface. As he was raiding Border Ruffian settlements in Kansas, Brown donned the persona of Osawatomie Brown, "playing Indian" as he burned down settlements and attacked, and sometimes gruesomely killed, proslavery squatters.[14] Philip J. Deloria (Standing Rock Sioux) understands Indian performances like Brown's as asserting white male belonging, and he argues that "Indianness provided impetus and precondition for the creative assembling of an ultimately unassemblable American identity."[15] As white settlers, regardless of their ethical and political positionings, fought in Kansas, they assembled a messy knot of signifiers that deployed "Indianness" at different times as a form of belonging or savagery. Both distanced whiteness from the violence in Kansas. Behaving like an Indian or accusing others of behaving like Indians was a way to articulate vehement political and ideological disagreements that allowed whiteness to come to the fore or recede to the background with fluidity as needed.

In J. L. Magee's 1856 political lithograph *Liberty, the Fair Maid of Kansas in the Hands of the "Border Ruffians,"* we see this figure of the Indian at play, as Magee offers a satirical critique of voting malfeasance in Kansas Territory (figure 3.4). In the lithograph's foreground, Kansas is adorned in the stars-and-stripes shawl and cap used in numerous nineteenth-century Lady Liberty and Columbia depictions. She pleads with Democratic leaders William L.

FIGURE 3.4 J. L. Magee, *Liberty, the Fair Maid of Kansas in the Hands of the "Border Ruffians,"* 1856. Lithograph. Courtesy of the American Antiquarian Society.

Marcy, James Buchanan, Franklin Pierce, Lewis Cass, and Stephen Douglas to "spare me, gentlemen, spare me." They are described as "border ruffians," lawless men wreaking havoc on the territorial frontier. This derogation references the number of Missourians and others who allegedly fled into Kansas to swing the vote so Kansas would enter the United States as a proslavery state. On May 4, 1855, the Garrisonian newspaper the *Liberator* published a series of resolves submitted to the House of Representatives addressing this voting fraud. One of these, the second resolve, "call[ed] upon the President of the United States to take instant and effectual measures for sustaining in Kansas the sovereignty of the people against the violence and invasion of mobs from Missouri."[16] The article's description of the Missouri invaders could also be applied to the settler squatters who infiltrated Indigenous lands in the territory before the passage of the act. The rhetoric of invasion, sovereignty, and land rights folds in on itself and gets deployed in multiple ways to describe competing views of the same political questions. The narrative of expansion embraced by Manifest Destiny, then, also serves to critique internal debates among white U.S. settler-citizens.

In Magee's illustration, the Democratic leaders all don weapons and gleefully grin as they violently maim and murder. Douglas is scalping a man, holding his hair and flesh up seemingly with triumph. In the background, the

violence is reinforced with scenes of men, women, and children being tor-
tured and murdered. While scalping was by no means an exclusively Native
practice in combat, it served as shorthand for "Indian savagery" in the nineteenth century. By depicting the Democratic leaders as "savage" participants
in the physical combat, Magee suggests that their proslavery rhetoric in Congress was as damaging as the actions of the vigilantes on the ground, making
them complicit in the bloodshed. Their savageness is contrasted with the vulnerable femininity of Kansas, as she pleads to them as "gentlemen" to stop the
violence; the masculinized terror they depict stands in contrast to the feminized liberty of Kansas.

The gendering of the image invokes the erasure of lived Native presence in
the territory through this contrast between Democratic politicians and Kansas. The anthropomorphic maiden references the notion of virgin land—that
is, land untainted by "man." Not only does her depiction as the "fair" white
maiden of liberty, defenseless against the bloodthirsty Democrats, invoke the
stereotypes of defenselessness and purity associated with femininity, but her
whiteness colors the land in a way that ignores Blackness and Indigeneity, especially Black and Native women. In this gendered and racialized narrative
of terra nullius, Native peoples are written out and written over in a critique of
mismanagement, violence, and federal, state-sanctioned corruption.[17]

In a second political cartoon in 1856 by Magee, *Forcing Slavery down the
Throat of a Freesoiler*, one observes a similar critique of Kansas corruption. In
this image, however, Magee also makes explicit the relationship between the
fight for Kansas and the debates over Cuba (figure 3.5). Buchanan and Cass
stand on the Democratic platform pulling back the hair of a Free-Soiler, while
Douglas and Pierce force-feed a Black male figure down his throat. The
Democratic platform they stand on bears the inscriptions "General America,
Cuba, and Kansas." Unlike *Liberty*, this image focuses on how southern and
western territorial expansions further exacerbate the lightning-rod issue of
the day, slavery. While Kyla Wazana Tompkins demonstrates that the consumption of Black bodies in the nineteenth century was often an attempt to
shore up the stability of the white (male) body, here the consumption is non-
consensual, as proslavery politicians "force" the white figure to consume
Black flesh. The image signals a fractious political climate in which cannibalism of the Black male figure is the result of political manipulation and evidence of the violent divisiveness of the cultural moment.[18]

We can think of these lithographs as companion pieces. When paired, they
engage the complex relationships among slavery, race, Indigeneity, and popular sovereignty that deeply marked the 1850s. Notions of savagery and civility

FIGURE 3.5 J. L. Magee, *Forcing Slavery down the Throat of a Freesoiler*, 1856. Lithograph. Courtesy of the American Antiquarian Society.

are mobilized as a particular trope that runs in contrast to the values of liberty and freedom ostensibly espoused in the founding of the imperial nation-state. As Sylvia Wynter reminds us, the savage Black or Native Other is a necessary antithetical to liberal Enlightenment "Man," the "rational self," by representing all that he is not.[19] Although savagery denotes something contrary to the espoused U.S. sociopolitical values, in Magee's lithographs it is redeployed to bodies other than those of the Indian while also invoking the figure of the Indian and the initial and continuing injustice of colonialism. The issues of race, enslavement, and Removal are coconstitutive and, as evidenced by the example of Kansas (and, as this chapter will argue later, Cuba), often materialized both in geopolitical flashpoints and in the bodily collisions of the intimately local and the day-to-day. "Filibusterism" is most commonly associated with the private military operations (white) men in the nineteenth century organized to invade other countries, primarily in Latin America, in an effort to force political change, often in the name of U.S. expansion or their own grandiose desires for power.[20] However, the term "filibuster" was also deployed to describe insurgencies in Kansas.[21]

By marking the Democratic platform with the word "Cuba," Magee demonstrates the space Cuba held in the national consciousness. In text almost as large as "Kansas," it serves less as a specter than as an additional cultural touchstone whose name carries a deep symbolic weight. As Cuban historian Louis A. Pérez Jr. argues, the United States and Cuba each captured the attention of the other's cultural imagination through circuits of print, economy, migration, and geographic proximity in the nineteenth century.[22] In the United States, "Cuba entered the North American imagination as the 'tropics,' which is to say, as the opposite of what the United States was, specifically, what it was not."[23] There was a wealth of news coverage, literature, and travel narratives committed to publishing Cuban politics and Cuban life. To travel to Cuba was to travel "less to a place than to a time, to a past in which to pursue undistracted pleasure, in which to linger delighted with the promise of recuperation and rejuvenation."[24] Partly due to its status as a colony and partly due to its proximity to Spanishness, Cuba carried with it a mythic, antiquated aura. This view of Cuba reproduced the U.S. imperial narrative of progress—the notion of the white, male, modern constitutional republic that steps into the present, offering liberation, technology, and free-market capitalism to the less advanced colony. Matthew Pratt Guterl offers a slightly different reading of the interwovenness of Cuba and U.S. culture and economy in the nineteenth century. To Guterl, Cuba's significance can also be read as futurity and possibility, with Cuba imagined as an extension of U.S. empire and, more specifically, an extension of U.S. Southern slavocracy for wealthy Southerners and supporters of enslavement.[25]

"The Vine That Winds around and Holds Us Together"

In contrast to the fantasies of Cuba as both future territory and Old World past is Martin R. Delany's speculative tale of Afro-Native revolution, *Blake; or, The Huts of America: A Tale of the Mississippi Valley, the Southern United States, and Cuba.* Written in 1858–59 and published between 1859 and 1862, *Blake* follows Henry Blake, the "lost boy of Cuba," as he escapes enslavement and travels throughout the United States, Indian Territory, Canada, Cuba, and Africa to drum up support to overthrow the colonial plantation system. Delany published part 1 of the novel serially in the *Anglo-African Magazine* in 1859.[26] A few years later, upon Delany's return from Africa, he published the novel in its entirety in the *Weekly Anglo-African* (1861–62), a newspaper run by Thomas Hamilton, who also edited the *Anglo-African Magazine.* However, because there are no known surviving copies of the May 1862 issues, the novel's ending remains speculative for twenty-first-century readers. Both the *Weekly Anglo-African* and the *Anglo-African Magazine* catered to an educated audience critical

of anti-Blackness and enslavement, publishing some of the leading Black intellectuals of the era, including Mary Ann Shadd Cary, Francis Ellen Watkins
Harper, and James McCune Smith. Derrick Spires describes the *Anglo-African
Magazine* as catering to "readers with critical judgment by which to see around
the corners of systems that maintained white supremacy, who were familiar
with not just the literary and historical world the *Anglo-African* drew on but
also the underlying political principles subtending Hamilton's editorial practices."[27] The magazine cultivated a dynamic reading praxis through its "sheer
diversity, its openness to arguments that intrude on and interrupt each other:
the monthly bursts at the seams with contending discourses, philosophies,
and political sensibilities."[28] Therefore, we must understand the serialized
Blake as already part of a polyvocal *Black sovereign printscape* committed to
imagining the contours of Black geographies made possible through print.

   Blake bends colonial time and space to highlight anticolonial networks of
oppressed people. While Henry Blake travels great distances, in most of the
places he visits, he finds collective awareness of the injustice of the modern
capitalist state and its contingency on the exploitation of particular bodies.
The same awareness could likely be attributed to Delany's *Anglo-African* readers, as suggested by a section of the blurb accompanying the initial run of
chapters 28–30. Of the novel, it says, "It not only shows the combined political and commercial interests that unite the North and South, but gives in
the most familiar manner the formidable understanding among the slaves
throughout the United States and Cuba."[29] While filibusters like Narciso
López touted U.S. republicanism to justify his missions into Cuba, Delany's
characters are often deeply critical of U.S. liberal democracy, keenly aware
that it hinges on an economic system of inequality that is inherently anti-
Black. Instead, Delany postulates a global Black community beyond the limitations of the United States, Cuba, and other settler-enslaver regimes. Many
scholars, including Katy Chiles, Marlene Daut, Andy Doolen, Judith Madera,
and Ifeoma Kiddoe Nwankwo, have all theorized how and why Cuba is
so prominent in Delany's formulation of Black transnationalism (or what
Nwankwo terms "Black cosmopolitanism"), especially in the second part of
Blake. I build on the work of these scholars by connecting part 2's emphasis
on Cuba as the critical site for organizing Black revolution to Henry's conversations with Mr. Culver, the Chickasaw-Choctaw chief he meets in chapter 20
of part 1.[30] Read collectively, these sections of the novel demonstrate the possibilities *and* the challenges of imagining Black and Native revolution, figured
both through Indigenous complicity in chattel enslavement and an erasure of
Taínos and other Indigenous peoples in Cuba.

In the first part of the novel, Delany describes Henry's encounters with post-Removal Choctaws and Chickasaws in Indian Territory. The conversation directly takes up the question of Black-Native solidarity. Unlike Albery Whitman, who in *Twasinta's Seminole* chooses to omit Seminole enslavement of African-descended people in a narrative about an Afro-Native utopic community, Delany foregrounds Indigenous complicity in chattel enslavement. When Henry arrives, Dr. Donald, a white man married into the Nation, tries to shut down Henry and Mr. Culver's conversation about enslavement. His interjections upset Mr. Culver's nephew, Josephus Braser, who complains that Dr. Donald "assumes so much authority" and will "make the Indians slaves just now, then negroes will have no friends."[31] Mr. Culver sends Dr. Donald away, and once Dr. Donald leaves, Henry and Mr. Culver speak frankly about enslavement, armed resistance, and coalition in a scene that condenses the charged messiness of Black and Native revolutionary possibility and its limitations.

In the scene, Henry presses Mr. Culver, "the intelligent old chief of the United Nation," to explain why Native people participate in enslavement. The old chief explains to him that Native enslavers are different from white ones, arguing the "Indian work side by side with black man, eat with him, drink with him, rest with him and both lay down in shade together; white man wont even let you talk! In our Nation Indian and black all marry together. Indian like black man very much, only he dont fight 'nough."[32] Importantly, Mr. Culver mentions white men's unwillingness to listen to Native and Black people just a few paragraphs after Dr. Donald is excused for trying to shut down the conversation. Most importantly, though, he also gestures toward a Black-Native intimacy forged through physical proximity, be it through labor, meal sharing, or kinship.

Unfortunately, the distinction Mr. Culver draws is not true of Choctaw and Chickasaw enslavers in the 1850s. As Barbara Krauthamer demonstrates, by the 1820s, elite Choctaw and Chickasaw enslavers embraced notions of Black inferiority and associated Blackness with enslavement.[33] This is something Delany likely observed or experienced, having visited the Chickasaw Nation himself. Mr. Culver's explanation, then, is more fantasy than reality, especially given his status in the Nation as a leader who owns two plantations. However, Josephus's earlier comment hangs over those of Mr. Culver: "Make the Indians slaves just now, then negroes will have no friends." His comment is a reminder of a racial world order that positions Native and Black people as distinctly separate and enslavement as the ultimate form of abjection. Josephus's comment suggests that while some Native nations participate in enslavement, they are still a necessary alternative to white supremacy, both as distinct nations and as nations comprising nonwhite people.

The two men continue to discuss enslavement and revolution, and Henry asserts that if Black people had their own country like Native peoples, they would fight to protect it. He tells the chief that, unlike Indians, native Africans kept white people out of their continent, in an attempt to debunk Mr. Culver's assertion about Black peoples' capacity to engage in warfare. This is, again, another moment that is more fictional than factual: white colonization in Africa instantiated the transatlantic slave trade, and colonization of the Americas did not occur simply because Native people could not defend themselves. The argument that colonization occurs because Native people are not skilled fighters was a prevalent anti-Indigenous rationalization of settler colonialism, one used to justify Removal and other genocidal U.S. Indian policies. Delany's characters push directly into painful racialization rhetoric in these two short pages, tugging at the tensions forged via stereotypes about Black and Native people. At the same time, Mr. Culver and Henry's discussion signals Indigeneity as a point of connection. Henry reminds Mr. Culver that Africa, like the Americas, was invaded by European colonizers. While Blake misrepresents the history of African colonization, his point remains and is a reminder that the Dutch invasion of western Africa in 1441 foreshadowed the events of 1492.[34]

One important question lingers: How might the conversation differ if Henry sought out a Choctaw or Chickasaw person with less tribal authority? An Afro-Choctaw or Afro-Chickasaw person? An enslaved woman? Enslaved people in the Choctaw Nation received news of Liberian emigration and protested their own enslavement through publications like *Frederick Douglass' Paper, Douglass' Monthly,* and the *Liberia Herald.*[35] Mr. Culver represents economic affluence and is also a figurehead of political authority in ways that are distinct from most other characters in the story. In a novel that foregrounds those most oppressed by structures of enslavement, colonization, and capitalism, the character of Mr. Culver stands as something of an anomaly. Featuring an elite enslaver who speaks in semidialect perhaps reveals the limits of Delany's ability to imagine an Indigenous interlocutor. While Mr. Culver represents Indigenous survivance, Removal, and anticolonialism, his authority to speak entrenches the ethos of singular male authority, whose means and political power register both in his nation and, to a certain extent, in the United States. The centering of Mr. Culver in a novel about revolution repeats romanticized tropes of the wizened elderly Indian chief.

In this moment of attempted coalition-building, chattel enslavement hovers over every statement. In the mess of these tensions, Henry asks Mr. Culver if he would support a Black revolution, despite his prejudices and his enslavement of Black people. In offering his support, Mr. Culver references Florida as an example of the power of Black-Native alliances:

> "The squaws of the great men among the Indians in Florida were black women, and the squaws of the black men were Indian women. You see the vine that winds around and holds us together. Don't cut it, but let it grow till bimeby, it git so stout and strong, with many, very many little branches attached, that you can't separate them. I now reach to you the pipe of peace and hold out the olive-branch of hope! Go on young man, go on. If you want white man to love you, you must fight im!" concluded the intelligent old Choctaw.[36]

Mr. Culver argues that the relationship between Black and Native peoples is more than solidarity; it is symbiotic, communal, and familial. His metaphor reinscribes a patriarchal, heteronormative notion of kinship, but it also foregrounds women as forging Afro-Native kinship bonds. For Mr. Culver, Floridian Afro-Native resistance is an example of what can occur when Black and Native peoples align. Joined together as sovereign equals, Maroon and Native communities collectively thrive. The vines that grow around them serve as a reminder of their responsibilities to the other-than-human world and signal the naturalness of such a union. As such, Mr. Culver posits a relationality and understanding of what it means to be human that is different from that of white Enlightenment humanism, what Sylvia Wynter terms "Man." Moreover, as one of the more quietly radical voices in the novel, Mr. Culver asserts the necessity of such an uprising, without which whites will not "love" Black people and will perpetuate a racist system of oppression. It is not amorous love that the chief seems to describe but rather the collective necessity to exert power and engage in physical rebellion to elicit change. Despite Henry's suggestion that Native people did not fight white people successfully enough to stave off colonization, Mr. Culver's call to arms is one of the most direct in the novel, perhaps suggesting that it requires Black and Native people to make peace with each other in order to harmoniously fight to overthrow the white supremacist state.[37]

It is curious that Delany has Mr. Culver detail Seminole and Maroon solidarity in Florida but does not have Henry visit the Seminole Nation in Indian Territory (near the "United Nation" of Choctaws and Chickasaws) or Seminoles in Florida. Instead, Henry spends time with the Choctaw-Chickasaw Nation and visits a Maroon community in the Great Dismal Swamp.[38] As a result, Afro-Native revolution is always set slightly to the side, just out of view in the novel. Nonetheless, by foregrounding the Chickasaws and Choctaws in Indian Territory, Henry highlights an additional Black and Native shared experience, forced Removal on the Trail of Tears and forced Removal from Africa to the Americas. Byrd's notion of transit as to "be in motion" and "to be made to move" is helpful here in understanding Removal and movement as shared experiences of Black and Native people whose mobility is made necessary and impossible by the settler plantation system.[39] Movement, especially one's autonomy over movement and the ability to resist movement, is a central trope of the novel. Henry's travels are catalyzed by the sale of his wife Maggie to an enslaver in Cuba (he emancipates himself to search for her), and throughout the first half of the novel he helps other self-emancipated people flee north to Canada. Henry's ability to move freely and evade capture is critical to creating a coalition of oppressed people.

Sean Gerrity reads the novel's Great Dismal Swamp scene as exemplary of a marronage ethos that frames the entire novel. Gerrity argues for "marronage as a constellation of resistance flight and freedom-seeking practices in African American literature."[40] He suggests that, in light of Sylviane Diouf's careful study of U.S. marronage and Neil Roberts's theorization of marronage as freedom through flight, we can begin to expand and complicate understandings of marronage in the U.S. context.[41] *Blake* shows us how marronage upsets white supremacy by refusing the structures and logics that hold it in place. Marronage does not seek inclusion in the liberal nation-state project. Instead, it seeks freedom elsewhere. When Henry leaves the Nation and enters Arkansas, the "roughest" Southern state, Aunt Rachel and Uncle Jerry welcome him. They can anticipate his arrival because of a network of Black communities that cross the United States and Indian Territory.[42] As Aunt Rachel explains, "Some of de black folks, da all'as gwine back and for'ard, and da larn heap f'om dem up dar; an'da make 'ase an' tell us."[43] Henry's movements outside the colonial gaze are aided, and in fact dependent on, infrastructures of travel, information systems, and land-based epistemologies operating alongside the enslaver-colonizer map, sketching out a territoriality that is not dialectical (inside/outside) but multiform and palimpsestic.

While the plot of part 1 of the novel takes place in a post–Fugitive Slave Act United States (1850), part 2 takes up the 1840s uprisings organized across Cuba by enslaved Black people and free people of color preceding the La

Escalera years. The 1840s rebellions signaled as a rallying cry for anticolonial revolution and provoked white anxieties about the possibility of Cuba becoming a second Haiti.[44] While one could read this chronology as an assertion of the Old Worldness, or pastness, of Cuba in contradiction to the modernity of the United States, Delany's collapsing of time seems to do something else entirely. It allows him to construct affinities through disruption of the colonial world order rather than through a shared presence in capitalist time and space.

Delany's creative use of historical fact means Henry can reunite with his cousin Gabriel de la Concepción Valdés, or Placido. Delany based his character Placido on the Cuban poet Plácido, who was executed for his alleged involvement in the Conspiración de la Escalera.[45] In the novel, Delany's Placido does not die as a victim of governmental retaliation, as was the case for the historical figure Plácido.[46] Instead, he is beaten to death by U.S. businessmen on his way to a U.S.-run bookstore in Havana. Placido's poetry serves as an inspiration for Henry when he reads it in a New Orleans paper, and it is in this space of reading that Placido meets his demise.[47] Delany highlights networks of peoples and print between the United States and Cuba to demonstrate how such hemispheric exchanges are not exclusively the parlance of white U.S. or Creole and Latin American filibusters but also can be used toward radical ends for trans-American Black coalition-building.

These print networks, and those of the communication networks he details in Arkansas, construct a Black nationalist printscape. Instead of the white possessive forms of the survey and the periodical that attempt to make Blackness visible and controllable, *Blake* presents alternative renderings of both that characters utilize for their own mobility and to share and adapt Black geographies that operate within, outside, and against the United States and Cuba. Placido's prominence in part 2 also suggests a meta-commentary on reading across authors, texts, and genres, given *Blake*'s initial publication in the *Anglo-African Magazine* (and later in the *Weekly Anglo-African*). The novel, published in serialized installments alongside other essays, fiction, and poetry, some of which also write about Cuba and Haiti, interpellates *Anglo-African* readers into these printscapes, implicating us in the questions of control, power, and freedom that these publications bring to the fore.

Perhaps more radical than Delany's analysis of print circuits, though, are the Black-Native alliances he returns to in part 2. Near the end of the novel, as Blake and his allies listen to a plaintive ballad in the drawing room of his home, the narrator ruminates on the necessity of colonial resistance: "Their justification of the issue made was on the fundamental basis of original priority, claiming that the western world had been originally peopled and possessed by the Indians—a colored race—and a part of the continent in Central America by a pure Black race. This they urged gave them an indisputable right with every admixture of blood, to an equal, if not, superior claim to an inheritance of the Western Hemisphere."[48] Delany's narrator reiterates the claim Delany makes in "The Condition, Elevation, and Destiny of the Colored People of the United States" that there is a Black community in Central America comprising Africans who discovered the Americas separately from Christopher Columbus. Therefore, he rationalizes colonial resistance through a counter-narrative to the first contact narrative. Blake simultaneously acknowledges Indigenous peoples' originary relationship to the land and also "indigenizes" Black people on the island. His argument is that because both Indigenous and Black people are figured as people of color—or at the least, not white—they have a stronger natural affinity for one another. However, he does so by subtly suggesting hierarchies between Blackness and Indigeneity. We might also return to the scene between Mr. Culver and Henry in part 1, where the novel suggests a similar intimacy between Black and Native people in the Americas. One way of reading this passage is to understand Delany as locating Black people as, to some extent, autochthonous to the Americas and the rightful inheritors of Indigenous land. We might also read this passage as another moment in the novel when Delany attempts to imagine points of connection between Black and Native people that resist the colonial-racial machinations politically distancing Black and Indigenous people from one another. The paradoxical messiness of this passage exemplifies the limits of nineteenth-century prose to narrate Black and Native revolution, which slips beyond the reach of the printed English language.

Chapter 58 of *Blake* takes place on Gala Day in Havana. As part of the celebration, we witness the "sport of the chase," where trainers demonstrate bloodhounds' adeptness at catching fugitive self-emancipated people.[49] Occasionally, the enslaved person is "caught and badly lacerated, which produces terror in the black spectators, the object designed by the custom."[50] The bloodhounds' performance serves as a public display of the plantation regime's violence and control. The scene unites all spectators of the "African race" in their horror at the spectacle, and it also cuts across racial differences of Blackness, Indigeneity, Asianness, freedom, enslavement, and servitude.[51] The hounds who participate in the "sport of the chase" see no difference in enslaved or free bodies when poised to attack—they are only trained to pursue bodies at the instruction of their trainers.

The hounds do not strike fear in the audience as they usually do; instead, "masses of the Negroes, mulattoes, and quadroons, Indians and even Chinamen" segregate themselves from the white spectators, carrying on conversations of their own and showing little interest in the entertainment at hand. They "could be seen together, to all appearance absorbed in conversation on matters disconnected entirely from the occasion of the day."[52] While Creole spectators watch the hounds with interest, an assemblage of Black people, people of color, and Indigenous people talk among themselves, seemingly about Henry's plans for an uprising. The action occurs off-stage, so to speak, and we, the readers, are not privy to their conversation. This collective of Cubans who should be fearful of the bloodhounds and what they symbolize—violence against Black, Indigenous, and of-color people who attempt to disrupt the plantation complex—pays little attention to the spectacle and evidence none of the fear it is meant to engender. A note is included, either by Delany or by the publisher, indicating that the Indians referred to are Yucatánian Mayans forcibly shipped to Cuba as enslaved people to quell discord and uprising in the region. However, in addition to being "homeland to the descendants of the indigenous Arawak Taíno peoples," for "over the half millennia after contact," Cuba was also an important haven and point of trade for "indigenous peoples as diverse as the Yucatec Maya of Mexico, the Calusa, Timuca, Creek, and Seminole of Florida, and those of the Apache and Puebloan cultures of the northern provinces of New Spain."[53] While Delany acknowledges the presence of Indigenous communities in Cuba, they are displaced Indigenous peoples brought to the island to bolster the Cuban economy.[54] The Indigenous-Black-Asian collaboration Delany describes is negotiated through a mobility produced by the global reach of colonial economies, what Lisa Lowe terms the "intimacies of four continents."[55]

Starting in 1847, the number of Chinese workers, derogatorily called "los culíes chinos" or "coolies," increased dramatically in Cuba, primarily at the behest of plantation owners who demanded more labor.[56] While the dominant scholarly trend has been to understand this migration as the product of a waning in African slave labor, Asian diasporas scholar Lisa Yun argues that in fact the numbers of Africans forcibly brought to Cuba increased. Yun reads both forms of racialized labor as "concomitant and coproductive."[57] As such, we can understand the addition of large numbers of Chinese workers not as supplementing one oppressed group of peoples with an exploited other but rather as indicating the rapid growth of the sugar industry and its racialized labor regimes. The addition of a significant new population complicated

hierarchies of race, class, and, invariably, gender, as most of the Chinese laborers transported were male. While there were deep-rooted stereotypes
about Blackness, stereotypes of Asianness took hold as well. But, in a move
that made the malleability of racial categories palpable, Chinese and Chinese
Cubans were understood for a time as "white."[58] The fact that we witness
Chinese participants in this Gala Day cabal suggests that despite attempts to
position Asianness in opposition to Blackness, the individuals in this collective decide to align with others positioned as outsiders in a white supremacist
regime through labor and racialization.

The gala scene complicates Henry's plans for revolution as it widens the
scope of who counts among his coconspirators. Like white U.S. nationals and
Cuban Creoles who forged an affinity for one another (through whiteness) in
their writing, Delany offers a similar alliance among nonwhite racialized
people. Nonetheless, readers are left to draw their own conclusions about
Blake's revolution and Cuba's fate. As I mentioned earlier, whether Delany
finished the novel is still unknown, since, as of the writing of this book, there
are no known copies of the 1852 issues of the *Weekly Anglo-African* that would
have included the final chapters. We are left with possibility and potential but
no concrete understanding of what such a change would look like for Delany.
Whatever the case, we are not privy to the whispers of Delany's cabal. As with
the unfinished ending of the novel, we are left to speculate, and the omission
raises questions about the relationship between periodical print culture and
liberal humanist notions of freedom and emancipation. Is it possible to share
plans for the disruption of a colonial plantation social order on the page? Or
does such an act demonstrate the limitations of print and writing for emancipatory futures? From the 1860s through the 1890s multiple wars would over-
come Cuba, but none like that foreseen by Delany. While Cubans abolished
slavery and recruited Black soldiers for the rebel armies, "native" rule would
not result in an ideal egalitarian republic.[59] Understandings of identity, race,
and power would continue to affect the daily lives of Cubans in disparate
ways, and the ideal of a racialized rebellion was replaced in the work of revo-
lutionaries like José Martí with a raceless, utopic Cuba Libre.[60]

The second-to-last paragraph of the Gala Day chapter provides some
sense of what such a revolution might look like, but the description is more
embodied than structural. The participants in the Gala Day cabal envision
their path forward as "dark and gloomy" with the occasional "outbursting of a
concealed flame deeply hidden in their breast." They move toward the "Star
of Hope," which "encourage[s] them onward."[61] The description is hazy and
invokes an interiority driven by a celestial calling. It does not reference

specific geographic locations or political trajectories. Instead, the Star of Hope suggests a process of movement, a "slow but steady march" that is not about rushing into battle but a deliberate path forward, what Judith Madera describes as "embodiments of transit."[62] In this scene, to imagine futures otherwise requires a Fanonian decolonization of the mind that necessitates an entirely different cosmological perspective. It also demands an unwillingness to settle on nationalist structures of belonging that are predicated on Enlightenment notions of the human, freedom, and liberty from which "Negroes, mulattoes, and quadroons, Indians and even Chinamen" are excluded. The Star of Hope gestures to a scale of time-space that is vast and affective. It exists beyond the terrestrial (and print) and outside the current world order—it is otherworldly—but can be witnessed by all who look up to the heavens.[63]

Liberia and Kansas

While Delany's novel is critical of state apparatuses in *Blake,* his political work in the 1850s revealed a more complex relationship to colonization, statecraft, and belonging, especially his work with the Niger Valley Exploring Party and his involvement with infamous abolitionist John Brown's statehood plans.[64] In Frank [Frances] A. Rollin's biography of Delany (commissioned by him), Rollin narrates Delany's involvement with Brown. As described in the biography, Delany consulted Brown on Brown's statehood proposal around 1858, although his involvement was limited because Delany was busy planning the logistics for Liberian emigration. Delany claims Brown wanted to make Kansas, not Canada, the destination of the Underground Railroad, naming his proposed state the Subterranean Pass Way: "instead of passing off the slave to Canada, to send him to Kansas, and there test, on the soil of the United States territory, whether or not the right to freedom would be maintained where no municipal power had authorized."[65]

Delany helped Brown organize a convention in Chatham, Ontario, bringing together Brown, "his son Owen, eleven or twelve of his Kansas followers, all young white men, enthusiastic and able, and probably sixty to seventy colored men."[66] Delany also agreed to serve as president of the "permanent organization of the Subterranean Pass Way" with Isaac Shadd, although his own emigration plans to Africa meant he could only be cursorily involved in Brown's organizing.[67] Importantly, though, participants at the convention decided U.S. statehood was not an option because "according to American jurisprudence, negroes having no rights respected by white men, consequently could have no right to petition and none to sovereignty."[68] Instead, there was the proposal to form "an independent community": "To obviate this, and avoid the charge against them as lawless and unorganized, existing without government, it was proposed that an independent community be established within and under the government of the United States, but without the state sovereignty of the compact, similar to the Cherokee nation of Indians, or the Mormons."[69] Delany's biography suggests it was an edited copy of this proposed constitution that Governor Henry A. Wise found on Brown's person when he took Brown into custody after the Harpers Ferry raid.[70] Delany expresses surprise at Brown's turn to the revolutionary tactics seen at Harpers Ferry. He claims he knew nothing of Brown's change in plans from statehood to overthrow of the government.

I want to return to Delany's comment about the Cherokee Nation. We receive this information sideways, filtered through Delany's memory of earlier events as retold to Rollin, who then retells them through biography, so I am not especially interested in whether everything Rollin details can be verified. As in *Blake*, we learn of these plans secondhand and at a distance, and it is hearsay at best by the time it reaches us. Instead, I am interested in thinking through the Cherokee Nation as an exemplar of how to get around the problem statehood posed for Black freedom. In this narrative, the Cherokee Nation, as a symbol of political autonomy, erases Osage, Shawnee, Kaw, Kickapoo, Delaware, Sac and Fox, Potawatomi, Ottawa, Wyandotte, and Miami presence.[71] Indigeneity serves as a referent that displaces actual Indigenous life when taken up metaphorically. Delany's symbolic use of the Nation is also not attentive to historical reality. Cherokees had displaced Osages when forcibly Removed west, and some Cherokees still participated in enslavement in the 1850s. While it is clear statehood is untenable for Black world-making in Brown's and Delany's formulations, the only model proposed upholds the foundations of settler colonialism and ignores Indigenous specificity. The Cherokee Nation, because of the Trail of Tears and the Nation's Supreme Court cases, is operationalized metaphorically. However, the use of Cherokee-as-metaphor fails to acknowledge the actual complex sovereignties and spatialities at play between the Cherokees, the Osage, and Kansas Territory. It bears reiterating that Brown himself participated in similar work by donning the persona of an Indian warrior from Osawatomie, a free-state emigration community that combined the names of two Indigenous nations, Osage and Potawatomi, in the act of indigenizing white belonging that disturbingly stole both names and land in a fight for freedom.

It is curious that Delany details this slippage between metaphor and materiality, given the imaginative interest in Black and Native solidarity he depicts in *Blake*. Things get even murkier when Delany explains that he was unable to aid Brown's efforts substantively because he was busy making plans to travel to Yoruba territory.[72] I want to resist a clean sorting of the messiness in Delany's reminiscences and instead observe the ways Yorubaland and Indian Territory are both displaced by the expansion of U.S. ideologies of citizenship and subjectivity, even when both are imagined outside or in opposition to the United States proper. As Shona Jackson saliently reminds us, "There is *always* a 'native' to contend with, both in territories where there is a visible presence and in others where there is not: either as something that has been left behind (premodern and hence essential to understanding and articulating modernity, especially in regional historiography) or something that one is moving toward and that must be realized as modern throughout race—that is, the production of new natives."[73] The activism and writings of Albery Whitman, Delany, and Brown (via Delany) all expose how state-based rights make it impossible to understand Black and Indigenous freedom in tandem. Native and Black male leaders in Indian Territory faced similar challenges decades later when their communities turned to statehood as a means of securing self-determination and freedom. In addition, we cannot forget that in the 1850s, white squatters and vigilantes exploited the federal government's and the press's preoccupation with the feuds over slavery in Kansas to steal Indigenous peoples' land without repudiation, acts Maile Arvin terms "possession through whiteness," which secured white belonging in Kansas but not the end of anti-Black violence.[74]

Like Delany and Whitman, Osage writer John Joseph Mathews retells the story of the era in a way that reveals this tension. Of the 1850s in Kansas, he writes, "It had been explained to the Little Ones in some manner that the Heavy Eyebrows were fighting over *Nika-Sabe*, but there were so few of *Nika-Sabe* there on the prairie to fight over. The abstractions were too much for the Little Ones, and they couldn't see any reason for these wild, unthinking men murdering each other, burning houses and whole communities, and shouting themselves into uncontrollable emotionalism."[75] In Mathews's incisive prose, he notes the disconnect between ideology and physical presence driving white people (Heavy Eyebrows) to incite violence. However, his narrator is unable to understand that while there may be a reasonably small Black (Nika-Sabe) population in the territory, the affinities between them and the Osage (the Little Ones) are nonetheless present and will have a profound influence on their future (and already do) in Kansas Territory, as well as in Indian and Oklahoma Territories. One can read the passage in various ways—as commentary on the fervor surrounding squatters' convictions about enslavement, a critique of the ways slavery debates recentered white masculinity in Kansas, or a hundred-years-later reflection informed by decades of Jim Crowism and an anti-Blackness that minimized abolitionist refusals of enslavement. What is evident in the passage, however, is that Heavy Eyebrows are the ones who bring "wildness" and murder with them, not the stability and civility that statehood allegedly promised.

Mathews, like Brown, Delany, Whitman, and Magee, frames statehood as a masculinist enterprise, and a glaring omission in these texts and images—as well as in this chapter—is Black and Native women's responses to land grabs and militarized disputes in Kansas Territory. There is great need for scholarship that explores how women, especially Indigenous and Black women, experienced social and political change in Kansas.[76] Statehood may seem like a reparative geopolitical model, especially for men whose gender suggests a greater possibility of inclusion in a political formation that upholds patriarchy. However, the U.S. logic of state sovereignty is also white supremacist at its core and about upholding white male propertied subjectivity, fracturing the terms of universal male suffrage and who constitutes a liberal "male" subject. The experiences and narratives of women, who are situated outside imagined civic inclusion in the state in the 1850s, not only cast light on the patriarchal white supremacy of the state but also suggest other forms of community and civic life. In noting the masculinist overtones of *Blake*, for example, Maria Windell argues that Black mothers and daughters in the novel develop a "revolutionary sentimentalism" that is critical to Henry's planned revolt, even though Delany does not foreground them in the novel. Windell contends that "family relations are central to the moments that most closely approach revolt." Like Windell, Aisha Finch posits capacious understandings of nineteenth-century Cuban revolution and revolt that foreground women's often underacknowledged contributions.[77] Kai Pyle's (Métis and Sault St. Marie Nishnaabe) exciting and important work showcases the lives of Two-Spirit, trans, and queer Anishinaabe people, including a nineteenth-century trans Prairie Potawatomi woman.[78]

While Frances Ellen Watkins Harper's short story "Chit Chat, or, Fancy Sketches" (1859) is not specifically about Kansas Territory, it does grapple with some of these questions from the perspective of a Northern Black woman narrator who is deeply skeptical that migration and settlement lead to greater prosperity and freedom for Black people. In the story, published in the same *Anglo-African Magazine* issue as coverage of Brown's trial, a group of educated, middle-class urban African Americans debate emigration and self-determination. Our narrator, who identifies herself as a country girl of simple means, rejects emigration as a path to freedom. She argues for the importance of distinguishing imitation from "apishness." According to her, imitation is "simply a copying or making patterns," while apishness is "servile imitation or abject mimicking" that often leads "us to copy the vices and follies of others."[79] For her, apishness includes investments in capitalist accumulation or, in the case of emigration, participating in the theft and occupation of Indigenous lands. She is critical of the possessive logics that undergird the belief in land as property.

The narrator criticizes another character as well, a "dreaming scholar," for placing too much emphasis on books and intellect that can abstract material problems.[80] Instead, she suggests that one finds freedom through a balance between spirit, mind, and body and communion with the other-than-human world. She expresses an embodied, sensorial experience of radical freedom that echoes Delany's Star of Hope, but one that is more affinitive than sublime, invoking a relationality not unlike that theorized by twenty-first-century Indigenous and Black feminists like Leanne Betasamosake Simpson, Alexis Pauline Gumbs, and adrienne maree brown. Harper's story disrupts how capitalism, U.S. liberalism, and urbanization encourage forms of accumulation that do little to aid Black freedom. Her story is deeply critical of settlement and all but rejects the false promises of Black inclusion in U.S. empire-building, especially for free Black women, whose civic rights statehood did little to further.[81] Published in a magazine that also included chapters of *Blake* and a variety of essays about Kansas, Haiti, and Cuba, Harper's short story materially and politically interjects the voices of Black women as a challenge to masculinist projects of revolt like those of Brown or filibusters like Narciso López, whom I discuss shortly.

Filibusterism and the "Universal Yankee Nation"

By the 1850s, the United States and Cuba were politically, culturally, and economically imbricated. A significant portion of the Cuban economy in the 1850s was dependent on trade with the United States, and by the mid-nineteenth century, the United States was the biggest importer of Cuban sugar. Sugar exportation to the United States would drive an expansion of the market (and the enslavement of more people) and produce a Cuban dependence on U.S.-imported goods. Travel between the United States and Cuba rose alongside economic codependency. As economic and cultural ties between the island and the continent strengthened, tens of thousands of Cubans came to the United States for business, education, or travel, or as permanent residents, while many others came as exiles from what Finch terms the "devastating re-pression" of La Escalera (1840s–1860s). La Escalera emerged in 1844 in re-sponse to organized Black freedom struggles across the island, including those enslaved, those free, and those living in rural plantations and the urban spaces of cities. The threat this ostensibly posed to the white plantation re-gime was used to rationalize an era of violence, strict surveillance, and height-ened governmental oversight, especially over enslaved people and free people of color in Cuba.[82]

Across racial lines, Cubans immigrated to the United States to escape the La Escalera regime's heightened control over daily life, but race and slavery were significant factors in the decisions of particular Cuban populations to leave. Many Black Cubans fled because of elevated persecution, torture, and the killing of both free people of color and enslaved Black Cubans, itself a form of forced Removal.[83] Meanwhile, some Creoles left out of fear of Black revolution, and others were banished. Strict censorship guidelines, mainly as applied to dissidents and free people of color, made it easier for some exiles to write critically about Cuba from the United States. It is these struggles that undergird Henry's return to Cuba in *Blake*. *Blake* features not only Plácido, believed to be one of the revolt conspirators during La Escalera, but also Nar-ciso López, the well-known filibuster who organized multiple campaigns to overthrow the Cuban government.

U.S. interest in Cuba began long before the 1850s, however. Thomas Jef-ferson was the first president to express interest in acquiring Cuba. In 1823 he famously said of the island, "I candidly confess, that I have ever looked on Cuba as the most interesting addition which could ever be made to our sys-tem of states."[84] A robust effort was not made, however, because Spain was unwilling to sell and the United States feared British retaliation if Cuba were forcibly taken. After a trip to Cuba that instilled in John O'Sullivan, editor of the *United States Magazine and Democratic Review*, a belief in the necessity of Cuban annexation, he began lobbying the Polk administration to try, yet again, to purchase Cuba.[85] The following year, in 1848, he returned to speak with the president, this time bringing the western Illinois senator Stephen Douglas with him. There were rumors later in 1848 about alleged plans for a Creole uprising on the island, so the Polk administration kept its distance. In July, conspiracy plans were confirmed, and López, a Venezuela-born Spanish paramilitary soldier, was named one of the leaders of the planned uprising. López then fled Cuba for New York City. There he organized Junta Cubano, a group of filibusters who planned to return to Cuba to agitate widespread rebellion. Junta Cubano would come to count among its rank-and-file members and attempted recruits Douglas, Cirilo Villaverde, and John C. Calhoun.[86] The informal means of U.S. occupation imagined by López were intertwined with those of official U.S. state actors. These men's occupation fantasies reveal how liberal individualism benefited the expanding colonial state.

In 1851 after a failed invasion of Cuba, López planned his second and final mission. He led one set of troops while Colonel William Crittenden led another. As in the first invasion, the filibusters were quickly outnumbered by the Spanish. However, this time, they were unable to escape, and many were executed, including López and Crittenden. López's execution was widely publicized, with mixed responses. Some saw the means of execution as excessively cruel and indicative of Spanish brutality. A journalist for the *Christian Advocate and Journal* wrote, "The barbarous policy pursued by the authorities of the Island toward the prisoners, must have a fatal reaction."[87] Others linked the expedition's failure to more extensive critiques of aggressive annexation. The *New York Observer and Chronicle* had this to say: "It would be well if our countrymen could be patient. Ripe fruit falls into the hand. When Cuba wishes to be annexed, Cuba will come. . . . We do not *need* Cuba, nor Canada, nor the Sandwich Islands, nor Ireland, nor England; but if any or all of them wish at any time to take part with us, 'the universal Yankee nation' has arms to embrace them all. But we would not *give the life of one decent man* for the sake of annexing the whole."[88] Yet others saw López's efforts as valiant and reflective of U.S. revolutionary origins. The Boston-based *Gleason's Pictorial Drawing-Room Companion* said of López, "Had he succeeded in liberating Cuba, [he] would have been declared a second Washington."[89]

Given the magazine's ties to the expeditions, it is perhaps little surprise that the *United States Magazine and Democratic Review* offered a provocative rationale for the overthrow of Spanish rule: "The inhabitants of Cuba have no constitutional rights; no voice or influence in making their own laws, or choosing their own officers; and in addition to these deprivations, by far the larger portion of them, the Creoles, natives of the island, are excluded from all the high offices, and considered as an inferior race by what are called 'The old Spaniards.'"[90] Like other pro-filibustering rhetoric, the article references those rights ostensibly granted by the U.S. Constitution (to white men of means) but also ties those rights to the "natives of the island," Creoles. In so doing, the article asserts that their rights to rule are tied to their relationship to the land as indigenous inhabitants, unlike those of Spaniards. While this logic echoes similar critiques launched by British colonists in continental North America, both arguments function under a logic of indigenizing whiteness while erasing actual Indigenous peoples.

As discussed earlier with the example of Brown's redface performances, similar moves to indigenize white patriarchal possession occurred concomitantly in the newly established Kansas Territory. Again, the Kansas-Nebraska Act establishing Kansas escalated interests in Cuban annexation and statehood. According to historian Charles H. Brown, many affluent Southern enslavers were less preoccupied with the impact of the Kansas-Nebraska Act on Kansas Territory and more invested in the ways it might affect Cuban statehood. Alexander H. Stephens, who later served as vice president of the Confederacy, responded to the act with the following: "The measure upon which the Nebraska principle will be tested is that of the acquisition of Cuba."[91]

Cuban statehood was not solely the desire of Southern enslavers, however. Because of the economic relationship between the United States and Cuba, many affluent Northerners were equally interested in conquering the island. Nonetheless, Cuba came with a discrete set of ideological problems that made it a complicated territorial conquest for a spectrum of white supremacist expansionist schemes. Following abolition in the British colonies, it was the largest Caribbean participant in the transatlantic slave trade, and it had a non-Anglo majority population. I close this chapter with an analysis of John Brougham's play *Columbus el Filibustero!*, which stages some of the ways Cuba falls in and out of U.S. discourses of territorial expansion and enslavement through a reimagining of Columbus's discovery of America that is deeply informed by 1850s U.S. politics. Brougham's comedic take on Columbus evidences how Kansas and Cuba as signifiers operationalize each other under U.S. enslaver colonization.

Columbus el Filibustero!

In 1857, a year after some of the most violent clashes in Kansas, Brougham debuted his energetically titled play *Columbus el Filibustero! A New and Audaciously Original Historico-plagiaristic, Anti-national, Pre-patriotic, and Comic Confusion of Circumstances, Running through Two Acts and Four Centuries* at the Burton Theatre in New York City. A satirical account of Columbus's voyage to the New World, the play (with Brougham performing the role of Columbus) enacted the moment of first contact. But in the play, Columbus does not arrive in the Caribbean. Instead, he lands in New York City, and there he encounters a nineteenth-century urban U.S. landscape. When he returns to King Ferdinand's court in Spain, he brings along a motley consortium of New World representatives, including all the U.S. states—and a very teary Miss Kansas Territory. While the play revels in absurdity, as evidenced by its humorous (and lengthy) title, it also evokes the geopolitical climate of U.S. culture in 1857, a year marked by financial panic, filibusterism, the *Dred Scott* decision, and the continuing Third U.S.-Seminole War, all of which exacerbated visceral political schisms concerning slavery and the material and symbolic roles of territoriality in U.S. policy, ideology, and culture.

Brougham was part of an emerging cadre of playwrights in the 1840s and 1850s who wrote and performed a brand of popular theater intended to capture quintessentially "American" subjects, often through melodrama or burlesque. Like his fellow Irishman Dion Boucicault, Brougham immigrated to the United States from London in the mid-nineteenth century and became one of the most prolific and popular dramatists of the U.S. stage. Many of Brougham's works were satires that recited racist and gendered stereotypes for comedic relief, occasionally swapping Native and Black characters for one another, as evidenced by his rewrite of *Metamora; or, The Last of the Wampanoags* (1829) as *Met-a-mora; or, The Last of the Pollywogs* (1847).

Burlesques like Brougham's performed some of the most contentious current events of the day for a more economically diverse audience of theatergoers in New York City, in Philadelphia, and along the Eastern Seaboard than ever before in the United States.[92] In the case of *Columbus el Filibustero!*, Brougham anachronistically stages a first-contact narrative in 1850s New York City. What he obscures in his play is as telling as what he includes. Brougham's New World origin story explicitly addresses internal geopolitical turmoil in the United States while omitting a Caribbean provenance. His first-contact narrative privileges an "antenational" moment but also anticipates U.S. imperial nationhood. The historical collision of the two positions the United States as a hemispheric nexus. The elision of Cuba, visited by Columbus on his first voyage, is particularly telling, given public interest in the island in the 1850s. As one magazine proclaimed in 1856, "At the present time, there is a great and remarkable degree of interest throughout the whole country in regard to every thing connected with the Island of Cuba."[93] The newly elected James Buchanan had gained recognition just three years earlier for the secretly drafted Ostend Manifesto, which outlined plans to buy Cuba from Spain, and as president Buchanan showed his continued interest in annexation.[94] As one Southern newspaper alleged, before the election Buchanan had informed "some friends at Wheatland, that if he was elected, and could see the Slavery question at rest, and *Cuba annexed*, he would willingly die."[95]

Whether this is true is less important than the sentiment it expressed: there was a reading audience with vested interests in Cuban annexation.

While U.S.-led efforts to annex, seize, or liberate Cuba operated under a different vision of Cuba's future from that of nationals like the writer and revolutionary José Martí, efforts to remove Spanish rule, despite their political impetus, typically employed a repeated trope: the erasure of precontact Indigenous presence on the island and the supplanting of Spanish colonialism with "native" rule. Shona Jackson's rereading of Antonio Benítez-Rojo's "repeating island" proves helpful here. In her study of Guyanese Creole identity, Jackson argues that Indigeneity is an intrinsic, though underarticulated, element of Benítez-Rojo's theoretical framework. For Jackson, the factual assertion of a "repetition of indigenous disappearance" or the narrative of terra nullius as the rhetorical infrastructure buttressing the settler contract is essential to postmodern Caribbean ontologies.[96] Additionally enmeshed, particularly in the case of Cuba, were repeated U.S. interferences into the internal affairs and economy of the island. As Jackson convincingly demonstrates, Indigeneity served as a useful rhetorical tool in the project of postcolonial nation-building throughout the Americas. By invoking an Indigenous past, postcolonial nations articulated a distinction from their colonial predecessors. Indigeneity also informed the narrative tactics of U.S. imperial expansion that justified paracolonial intervention into other nations. As the story often goes, the United States must free the Americas from colonial or dictatorial oppressors and usher in democracy.

Like many nineteenth-century U.S. origin story retellings, Brougham's melds the Columbus contact narrative with that of Puritan New England.[97] As Elise Bartosik-Vélez argues, "When the story of empire in the Americas has sought a protagonist, it has often found one in Columbus."[98] Loose links were made between first contact, British colonial settlement, and U.S. nation-building that collapsed time and space in ways that tethered the settler colonial nation to a hemispheric network of European colonialisms, depicting the United States as always already an outcome of contact, but also a polity with a deep history and long-standing presence in the Americas.

I return to one of this chapter's framing questions: Why *not* Cuba? Despite continued U.S. political and cultural interests spanning the entirety of the nineteenth century—and stretching into the twenty-first—the United States' relationship to the island did not replicate the pattern of annexation and territorial governance that had marked many prior conquests. Cuba's continued prominence as a hemispheric symbol of enslavement, the racial constitution of its population, and the oceanic distance between the island and the United States proved insurmountable challenges to the repeated narrative of U.S.

expansion dominating the majority of nineteenth-century territorial ventures.[99] However, the nuanced relationship the United States would continue to foster with Cuba served as a template for strategic interventions into other previously Spanish territories, as the colonizing United States extended its political and cultural interests beyond the continent and into the Caribbean, into the Pacific, and across the globe.[100]

Cuba is an absent presence in Brougham's play—spectrally hovering over the figure of Christopher Columbus, not only because Columbus landed in Cuba but also because Brougham depicts Columbus as a filibuster. As mentioned earlier in the chapter, "filibusterism" was the popular mid-nineteenth-century term used to describe excursions into Latin America to seize land and peoples, ostensibly from oppressive, tyrannical governments. While many of these filibusters were white male U.S. nationals (most famously William Walker), numerous Cuban exiles participated in filibusterism as well.[101] Narciso López's filibustering excursions gained the rapt attention of an antebellum reading public in the United States, as narratives of the exploits and adventures of filibusters swept through the pages of newspapers, magazines, and literary texts.[102]

While there were aspects of the founding constitutional principles of the U.S. nation-state that many filibusters valued, not all of these exiled Cubans had a strong vested interest in the United States proper. As literary scholar Rodrigo Lazo argues, many of these individuals challenged the notion that the filibustering era was entirely based on a desire to spread the expanse and ideology of U.S. empire. For many, collaboration with U.S.-driven plots was strategic and nuanced, rather than wholesale consumption of U.S. jingoism, and spoke not only to imperial expansionism but also to a "protonationalist" Cuban impulse.[103] Like their U.S. counterparts, Cuban filibusteros, to use Lazo's term, also utilized the popularity and widespread circulation of the popular press to spread their messages. There was even a newspaper established in 1853 that took *El Filibustero* as its name and "highlight[ed] the anticolonial dimensions of the Cuban filibustering efforts . . . to emphasize that the island's inhabitants had a right to govern themselves."[104]

Brougham's play premiered in New York City, which was not only a hub for numerous Spanish-language Cuban papers, including *El Filibustero*, but also home to one of the most prominent Cuban exile communities in the United States.[105] Whether in jest or not, the choice to cross-pollinate the narrative of first contact and the prevailing social debates of the day makes a double move. First, it highlights a desire to establish the United States as having a deep history in the Americas. It is, after all, an urban (seemingly white or white-aligned) population that greets Columbus and his sailors upon their landing, not an Indigenous one. He is welcomed by a barrage of party-politicking "committee men" who immediately start fighting over who can get Columbus to run for a smattering of elected offices. One observer holds a sign reading "Columbus for President," and another "Liberty for ever."[106] This last slogan pokes fun at the political climate of the 1850s, calling into question the vitality of U.S. foundational values, such as liberty and democracy. Second, this humorous critique reveals an equally discordant mashup: the settler nation and Indigenous peoples of the Americas. In the play, it is the modern nation-state that is indigenous to the Americas. As a result, the narrative goes beyond another often-repeated teleology of U.S. origin stories—the false belief that Native peoples stepped aside in deference to U.S. empire—and omits Indigenous autochthony almost entirely.

The return to Ferdinand's court in Spain stages a new world order as Columbus displays his discoveries from the New (York) World. Upon returning to King Ferdinand, Columbus declares,

> Our filibustering scheme I've carried through,
> The country's safe, and now belongs to you.
> Bye and by, perhaps, when they've experience bought,
> They may return us the same blow we taught.[107]

This farcical turn literally and figuratively stages the United States as a priori sovereign. It also subtly justifies filibustering efforts in Cuba, if not U.S.-sanctioned occupation, and reorganizes relations between the United States and Spanish America as sovereign-to-sovereign in order to indigenize U.S. belonging in the Americas. The U.S. procession is represented by a menagerie of caricatures, including P. T. Barnum, a glass ballot box, and an assemblage of Black and Native figures, as well as "beautiful young ladies" representing the states and a crying, bloody-nosed Miss Kansas following on their heels and desperately wanting inclusion in the Union. The Black figures, described as "Ethiopians" and carrying quintessentially U.S. Southern alcoholic drinks, telegraph enslavement and the Black transatlantic. They precede King Powhattan, Pocahontas, and John Smith, three characters who embody the Jamestown narrative and thus British continental contact rather than Spanish Caribbean and Latin American colonization. These figures stand in the background, a paltry gesture toward a precontact Indigenous world. Finally, the "Almighty Dollar [appears], in regal robes, and promiscuously attended."[108] While the dollar is a clear indictment of capitalist greed, it also self-referentially gestures back to Queen Isabella's performance of the min-strel tune "Lucy Neal" sung a moment before the scene opens in anticipation of the procession.

The semiotic chorus stand silent after they have assembled, mere spectral witnesses in the background of the play's main action: the bloody-nosed cry-ing fit of Miss Kansas as she laments her exclusion from the other states.[109] By centering Miss Kansas's tantrum (and Bleeding Kansas) at the play's climax, Brougham makes clear the play is not meant to challenge the projects of U.S. empire and Manifest Destiny substantively. Columbia (also part of the group) calms Miss Kansas, and "harmony is restored."[110] Columbia reassures the king and queen that she has another "unruly babe in 'arms,' / Miss Utah, but we soon shall soon cure her ills."[111] Along with Pocahontas (whose pres-ence links Native women's bodies and conquest), the states, Kansas, and Utah reinscribe gendered notions of colonization.[112] Miss Kansas's woes are relieved not by freeing the Ethiopians, King Powhattan, or Pocahontas of their duties in the party but instead through the comfort ministered by Co-lumbia, a feminization of the Columbus figure who serves as both father and mother of New World colonization. Statehood ameliorates the discomfort of territorial babes—and, at least in the play, pleases the King of Spain. The play's humor does not challenge the genocidal project of colonization; it sim-ply makes a joke at its expense.

Together these figures signify slavery, colonization, and the capitalist mar-ket that served as driving forces in the U.S. imperial project, but Brougham uses anti-Blackness and anti-Indigeneity to frame the satire. To put it another way, he pokes fun at both the United States and Spain through Indigenous and Black caricature. As Kyla Wazana Tompkins demonstrates, antebellum renderings of the Black body as food, or, in the case of the play, through drink, signal "the violent intimacies" of the plantation economy in the United States and the Caribbean.[113] Moreover, she argues that "eating is central to the performative production of raced and gendered bodies in the nineteenth century."[114] Eating and minstrelsy both attempt to consume Black bodies to demonstrate the impermeability and security of the white body. The Black and Indigenous figures stand as sexual, embodied offerings of hospitality. The unnamed Ethiopians, Powhattan, and Pocahontas enter before the U.S. states and territories to proffer a teleology of the New World that imagines statehood as the culmination of hundreds of years of history. In this formu-lation, states become animated as they take on subjectivity and person-hood. The play ends with a celebration of U.S. expansion, as characters sing

"Hail, Columbia." At the same time, Columbus takes his place among a "selection from American celebrities."[115] Brougham's play recasts a history of the New World that authorizes U.S. expansion throughout the Americas as an indigenous response to European colonization, and Columbus is placed among American celebrities because they predate him in Brougham's play; the United States becomes the Indian fighting off colonial rule.

However, as Tompkins reminds us, eating tropes also threaten to upset the autonomy of the white consuming body, what she terms "racial indigestion." *Columbus el Filibustero!* reinscribes Blackness and Indigeneity as working at the behest of the U.S. nation-state symbolically, via minstrelsy or the Pocahontas myth, in ways that obscure the genocidal legacy of the Americas as well as radical Black and Indigenous rejection of the U.S. colonial project. While the states and territories follow the Black and Indigenous figures and take center stage, the Ethiopians and Pocahontas still stand as reminders of the genocidal legacies of slavery and colonization, both of which inform the codependent relationship between the United States and Cuba and the ways slavery and Indigeneity framed the mid-nineteenth-century Cuban annexation debates. Miss Kansas theatrically takes center stage and Columbus finds his place among a pantheon of U.S. icons, but the Ethiopians, Powhattan, and Pocahontas still spectrally look on, reminders of the narrative elements obscured in the tableau.

"Filibusterism," when denoting white men's rogue insurgencies into Kansas and Cuba (and through Latin America), reveals the interconnectedness of state-making, enslavement, and Indigenous dispossession. It is important to note that when the term "filibuster" was first taken up in the U.S. Congress, it was used by enslavers like John C. Calhoun to provide Southern politicians disproportionate influence in Congress. Historically politicians have routinely deployed the filibuster to reinforce racist policies and limit citizens' rights. In both cases, as a political tactic and as a rogue insurgency, the filibuster becomes weaponized to amplify the political influence of a minoritarian view. Its genealogies trace back to white male exceptionalism that typically secures white male possessiveness at home and abroad. Given its history, it should come as no surprise that the filibuster has become the hallmark strategy of politicians when they fear a threat of decreased political influence or greater enfranchisement for historically marginalized communities in the twenty-first century. Therefore, the description of Christopher Columbus as "el Filibustero" in Brougham's play situates the explorer within proslavery discourse and the interrelated narratives of 1850s U.S.-based land grabs on the continent and in Latin America.

Conclusion

After the fact, populist violence in Kansas was narrated as a precursor to the sectionalist fighting of the U.S. Civil War. The centrality of Indian Territory and Indigenous rights to land in Kansas all but falls out of the narrative. Indigenous peoples are forcibly Removed (again) through statehood, be it that of a U.S. state or some other formulation of settler community. Staging Bleeding Kansas entirely in racialized terms recalibrates the fight for statehood as a fight for racial inclusion. Cuba becomes the exterior other, and Kansas is always already interior on a map that narrates statehood as rules, order, and consistency. In other words, Kansas became a state because it made sense that it would, while Cuba did not. The passive past-tense production of Kansas forecloses other worlds (Kansas simply "became" a state).

What the Cuba-Kansas debates demonstrate is how Indigenous dispossession and anti-Blackness shape projects of U.S. expansion—namely (and paradoxically), by both redefining and cohering understandings of race and Indigeneity as visible, spatial, and knowable but distinct from one another. Indigeneity marks land and people as outside a priori capitalism and modern time, while racialization marks subjects caught in the nets of modernity. Because Cuba was part of a plantation economy–based industrial world order, symbiotically enmeshed with the U.S. economy, it was not like Kansas. Kansas, as Indian Territory, facilitated a terra nullius fantasy. While this line of reasoning may seem obvious, it shouldn't be. The notion that this equation is logical reveals the naturalized narrative of U.S. state-making and the stretch of U.S. empire as having a cogent logic. Instead, as evidenced time and again, the genocidal project of U.S. expansion was erratic, illogical, and often violent. As the United States incorporated (unincorporated) territory following the Spanish-American War, formerly Spanish occupied extracontinental territories' proximity to Blackness raised questions about their viability as states. It is telling that both Hawaiʻi and Alaska, currently the only two noncontinental state occupations, were vigorously narrated as "Indian Territories" proximate to whiteness in U.S. literature, political cartoons, and the press before statehood.[116]

Cuba's proximity to Blackness and Spanishness, especially the specter of Black revolution and growing independence movements across the Caribbean and Latin America that it invoked, meant that it was not "read" along pure white lines. This proximity is not why Cuba *did not* become a state, but racializing spatial discourse crafted an after-the-fact narrative about why Cuba *was not* viable. That is the work of statehood and states' rights. Statehood profoundly

influenced racial formation in the United States by spatializing racial taxonomies, especially Blackness, what Katherine McKittrick terms the "racial-sexual
terrain" of geography.[117] The origin story of Kansas centers antislavery heroism
almost exclusively in the hands of white men. The story omits the project of
genocidal whiteness, which was imagined to supersede and remove Indigeneity
as a way to indigenize white propertied belonging. White men become the sav-
iors able to emancipate enslaved Black people in an expansionist fantasy that
declares white virtue through statehood, foreclosing Black liberation and Indigenous belonging in its wake. It also stands in tension with twenty-first-century
Kansas politicians who were at the vanguard of a rise in voter restriction policies aimed at disenfranchising voters of color, especially poor and working-class
voters, and eroding participatory democracy. When Kansas bleeds, the anthropomorphized territory or state takes shape as a (white) subject of U.S. empire.

CHAPTER FOUR

Sequoyah and the Stakes of Statehood

Statehood fueled Indigenous dispossession throughout the nineteenth century, so why did Native leaders of Indian Territory organize the large-scale Sequoyah statehood campaign in 1905? The efforts of Five Tribes leaders to pursue statehood indicated their awareness of just how powerful the scale of the state was for securing rights, but in the end, the campaign's failure also revealed the empty promises of such a pursuit.[1] Instead of forming the State of Sequoyah, the United States violated its own protocols for dissolving Indigenous lands when forcibly admitting Indian Territory as the eastern half of the state of Oklahoma in 1907 without discussion. In previous chapters, I emphasize how states' rights rhetoric on statehood, especially as narrated through print and visual culture, asserts a spatial and political dominance that secures Indigenous dispossession and anti-Black exclusion. However, in this chapter, I turn to moments when Native communities and Black communities organized their own statehood campaigns, with special attention to the largest and most successful of these, the State of Sequoyah movement. The campaigns opened up moments of dynamic spatial possibility and creativity but also affirmed racialized Black and Native divisions in the territory that secured white statehood.

The Sequoyah movement, and other fin de siècle Indian Territory statehood movements, transpired in a thriving world of print. It serves as just one example of how print shaped different forms of territoriality—be it Indigenous sovereignty, the vitality of "All-Black towns," or U.S. statehood. The Indian Territory print culture I discuss circulated allotment records, emigration advertisements, maps, constitutional proposals, and literature—sometimes all in a single issue of the same newspaper. It visually and discursively reveals competing desires for the territory's future. By approaching Indian Territory print culture with a "territorial hermeneutic," by which I mean a reading praxis attentive to geographies that do not map cleanly onto U.S.-prescribed borders and places, we can resist reading Oklahoma statehood as a foregone conclusion. Instead, other articulations of territoriality and belonging come into play, especially those imagining Black and Indigenous spatialities. Decentering Oklahoma also helps remind us that, following the *McGirt v. Oklahoma* (2019) decision I discuss in the introduction (and will return to in the conclusion), the State of Oklahoma was unsuccessful in fully colonizing Indian Territory. Despite white settlers' best efforts to write (and print) a different story, Indian Territory never stopped being Indian land.

I focus particular attention on the 1905 State of Sequoyah movement, organized by leaders of the Five Tribes (Cherokee, Chickasaw, Choctaw, Muscogee [Creek], and Seminole) because it is a unique example of a large-scale, pan-tribal response to settler colonialism that attempted to weaponize both the geopolitical scale *and* the discursive form of the state. However, statehood prioritized a desire for U.S. hegemonic incorporation, and it did so (at least on the surface) by furthering already-present divisions between Native and Black communities. When Oklahoma became a state in 1907, the founding documents immediately worked to dismantle tribal governance, disenfranchise Black residents, and consolidate white property-owning power. These Removals are the printed ground on which the white supremacy of state identity stands. If midcentury Florida signified the possibility of Afro-Native alliances, then Indian Territory statehood campaigns in the early 1900s narrated something more divisive. Sequoyah never became a state, but its inevitable failure demonstrates the white supremacy inherent in statehood and the futility of organizing for Indigenous and Black freedom *through* the state. Letting go of state belonging, as well as the reading practices that accompany it, is critical to imaging Black and Native territories of freedom.

Indian Territory print culture had a more profound influence on place and belonging, especially Indigenous and Black endurance, than Sequoyah or any other statehood campaign.[2] Papers themselves imagined space differently from a U.S.-based publication *because* they were produced in Indian Territory. Many of these papers, especially those addressed to Black and Native readers, emphasized cohesion across their content that asserted a stable local world. They did so with the understanding that this world was constantly under attack from outside pressures; newspaper pieces were less about situating the local in the global and more about asserting the global necessity of maintaining the local. As *sovereign printscapes*, newspapers mapped the contours of Indigenous and Black geographies of civic, political, and cultural life *outside* the hardened (though porous) boundaries of U.S. empire. They were venues to assert sovereignty and political autonomy over a physical land base. These papers did not simply imagine what Black or Indigenous space might look like; they provided their readers news *from* these spaces.

This chapter begins with further elaboration on the contours and complexity of Indian Territory print culture that make it a critical site for print culture studies. I then analyze how newspaper land sale listings made visible the spatial violence of allotment. Throughout *Reading Territory*, I have traced the use of the newspaper and the survey to affirm white possession. Allotment evidenced how the two worked in tandem to restructure the geopolitical terrain of Indian Territory and reorient Black and Native land-based relationships. Next, I show how Black and Native print culture in Indian Territory shaped community, took up questions of statehood, and asserted self-determination through the form of the newspaper. I end with an analysis of Indian Territory statehood movements, with an emphasis on the State of Sequoyah, to show how these movements utilized print to map space and imagine distinct forms of political belonging. I argue that the papers, and the geopolities they asserted, demonstrate printscapes of sovereignty, meaning the narration and construction of place through visual and discursive elements.

The dominant narrative of Oklahoma's origin story imagines a romanticized incorporation of Oklahoma and Indian Territories into the United States proper, embodied most famously in the musical *Oklahoma!*[3] But this is a post-statehood mythos that flattens the past, and it is a story whose fiction is belied by the material print archive. Statehood was hotly debated in Oklahoma and Indian Territories, and while it seemed inevitable after the Oklahoma Organic Act of 1890, the form that statehood would take was less definitive. Much of the mess of statehood debates was staged on the pages of territorial newspapers and magazines, especially debates about whether Indian Territory and Oklahoma Territory would enter the United States as one state or two (figure 4.1). Many publications filled their pages with rhetorically charged editorials, and when read in conversation with one another, the dissonance of the moment is palpable. Land allotment, institutionalized Jim Crow policies, and personal and corporate greed (especially that of railroad and oil tycoons) made the disparities and inequity shaping the political landscape visible. This period in Indian Territory print culture illuminates not only the historical era but also our own contemporary moment by pointing out how Native nations in Indian Territory—including the Five Tribes, the Delaware (Lenape) and the Eastern Shawnee, Miami, Modoc, Ottawa, Peoria, Quapaw, Seneca-Cayuga, and Wyandotte—continue to assert their political and cultural force, and their reservation boundaries, in the region. One might say that *print runs* had as profound an impact on the geopolitical changes at the turn of the century as the more famous *land runs* that continue to dominate the official cultural memory of Indian Territory.[4]

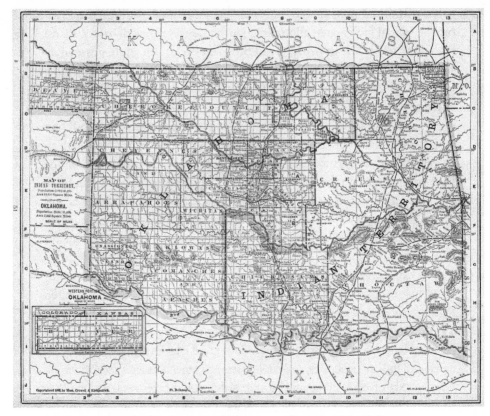

FIGURE 4.1 Map of Indian Territory Oklahoma, 1892 (OK-Docs Map Collection, Oklahoma Digital Map Collection, https://dc.library.okstate.edu/digital/collection /OKMaps/id/3672/rec/5). Courtesy of Oklahoma State University Library.

Severalty and Seriality

Despite the rich body of work published at this time, especially by Native and Black writers, Indian Territory print culture represents an understudied archive. I argue this is partly because thorough study requires some knowledge of the region's highly complex nineteenth-century legacy in order to understand the richness and depth of 1890s and early 1900s print. Conjointly, because many writers published almost exclusively in local newspapers and magazines, their work has gone undernoticed. Few of them ever published full-length books or works in other conventional literary forms, and many published anonymously or under pseudonyms. While digitization has increased accessibility for twenty-first-century readers, some papers are still neither digitized nor easily accessible. Authoritarian colonial claims to print production and circulation have produced an intellectual lacuna that cannot imagine Native editors or newspaper subscribers and therefore overlooks the vital role periodicals played in the lives of many people living in the territory.[5] Change occurred at a rapid clip during this era, and newspapers provided an essential means for readers to keep up with and make sense of it. Papers were crucial for disseminating information about local affairs, and for some territorial residents, they were the primary source of news. Newspapers were sometimes the only reading material available, especially for rural subscribers—and much of Indian Territory was rural.[6]

It is important to remember that print had deep Indigenous roots in the space. Periodicals and print ephemera began to be circulated in Native nations in Indian Territory in the 1830s, mostly disseminating information about tribal affairs and as school or church newsletters and pamphlets. The Five Tribes ran robust school systems that had a disproportionate impact on print production because of their use of tribally specific print materials. This included material printed in English but also in their languages. In 1835, shortly after Cherokee Removal, one of the first things Rev. Samuel A. Worcester established was a printing press at Union Mission. The first publication on the press was a book printed by Rev. John Fleming in the Mvskoke language, *Istutsi in Naktsoku*, or *The Child's Book*.[7] Not all early publications were published by Native authors and editors, as evidenced by the examples of Worcester and Fleming. However, most materials *were* published on behalf of a Native nation or were intended for Native readership, and publishers had to obtain the nation's approval for circulation and publication.

Newspapers were produced, circulated, and consumed in Native space. I want to emphasize this point. While there is much debate about the provenance of print, its affiliations, its intentions, and the identity of authors and editors in Indian Territory before statehood in 1907, all of these discussions happened in Native spaces and produced a print culture tied to them.[8] To dismiss the significance of print's Indigenous geopolitical ontologies threatens to reproduce the same logic used to erode Native sovereignty and fuel a single statehood movement—that Native nations were unable to manage and control their lands or the people inhabiting them. Nonetheless, the stakes were great for all participants and often were deeply politicized along racial and national lines.

While print was initially dominated by official publications of the tribal governments, by the 1880s and 1890s it had become a sophisticated and diverse media that represented a staggering array of opinions and beliefs about the current status and future fate of the territory and its inhabitants. Editors and contributors used papers to articulate different futures, formulate geopolitical imaginaries, and debate current affairs while calling on the multiple scales of subjectivity that Indian Territory editors, authors, and readers experienced: members of specific Native nations fighting to maintain tribal autonomy and political strength; members of townships or other local communities, including Black towns; members of a territory that understood itself as a network of various Native nations that still maintained civic and judicial agency. Authors published in both English and Native languages, and a number of newspapers, including the *Cherokee Advocate* and the *Choctaw Intelligencer*, printed dual-language issues that included pages in Cherokee or Choctaw and English. However, most of the papers—at least those that survive in the physical archive—were predominantly printed in English.[9] As both Craig Womack (Muscogee Nation) and Daniel Heath Justice (Cherokee Nation) persuasively argue, English not only was incorporated into Indigenous discourses but became a lingua franca for speaking trans-Indigenously.[10]

By the end of the century, territorial newspapers functioned like political tracts in many ways, and editorial opinions and articles served an evidentiary function in congressional debates about the status of Indian Territory, sometimes carrying more weight than the petitions and claims of tribal leaders and delegates.[11] While some publications continued to make arguments beneficial to the tribes, others represented the interests of white settlers, Black townships, or specific political parties, ethnic groups, or businesses—many under the pretense of being nonpartisan, unbiased news sources; parsing out the political bents of territorial newspapers, therefore, becomes an incredibly difficult task.[12] Many non-Native residents established newspapers and magazines as recruitment tools to entice settlers to the region or advocate for the opening of Native land, as well as to launch critiques against tribal rule (non-Native settlers technically had no voice in tribal government and had no control over the tribally run school systems, but they paid taxes on any business ventures in the nations). White settlers, in particular, turned to newspapers to argue against Indigenous sovereignty and in favor of settler statehood, as they had in Georgia, Florida, and Kansas.

David L. Payne's newspaper, the *Oklahoma War-Chief* (also called the *Oklahoma Chief*), demonstrates especially saliently the vital role newspapers played in the theft of Native land. Payne, the founder of the Boomers, felt Indian Territory should be available for homesteading, with or without federal approval.[13] Throughout the 1880s, Payne and the Boomers staged occupations by squatting on Native land, and Payne used his paper to disseminate his pro-colonization philosophy. His need to circulate his politics in print was so strong that he routinely printed the weekly while on the lam from federal marshals or while establishing new encampments; the weekly was rarely published from the same location twice. Grace Ernestine Ray observes of one issue, "[It] was printed on brown wrapping paper, and was smeared with grease. Whether it had been printed on some paper in which the bacon and other camp supplies had been wrapped, or whether it was stained with grease after being printed, is a matter for speculation. But the result was a newspaper that was scarcely legible. The two inside pages were blank, indicating either that there were other shop difficulties besides shortage of paper or that the camp was forced to move before the entire edition had been printed."[14] Her description suggests an urgency in Payne's publishing method. While the reason for his sloppy printing is uncertain, the drive to publish was strong enough that he and his fellow Boomers were willing to do so by any means, which says much about the impulse to print and the symbolic power associated with newspaper circulation. After Oklahoma's statehood, Payne would be commemorated by the creation of Payne County, where I grew up, further demonstrating how county borders and naming serve white settler histories of state belonging.

Understanding a paper's provenance continued to be necessary because the context in which the paper was produced reflected how it shaped perceptions about what was actually going on in the territory for readers outside the region. For example, if a paper was assumed to be Native run, even if this was an inaccurate assumption, it was often presumed to speak for an entire tribe. The notion that Native people could disagree or speak individually challenged prevailing colonial assumptions about Native identity. Perhaps most famously, Elias C. Boudinot (Elias Boudinot's son), whose 1879 article in the *Chicago Sun-Times* roused interest in opening Indian Territory land to the railroads, established the *Indian Progress* under the auspices that it was an official source of Native opinion in the territory, "owned, edited, and printed by Indians."[15] However, it did *not* speak for a collective; it was a venue for Boudinot's personal interests. His previous stint as editor of the *Cherokee Advocate*, the long-standing official newspaper of the Cherokee Nation, contributed to the confusion about the *Progress*'s backing and support. Those familiar with Boudinot believed that the publication was "calculated to convince Congress that the tribes themselves were advocating territorial government," meaning greater U.S. intervention in tribal affairs, and intended as a way to line Boudinot's pockets (he had business ties to the railroads).[16] Boudinot was able to deploy a sense of the collective as a front for personal gain. While the paper was not an official statement of the Cherokee Nation, it was perceived as such outside the territory; one Indian spoke for all Indians, especially if what they were saying worked to benefit white business interests.

In addition, Black residents in the territories used print to advertise emerging Black communities, including "All-Black towns," to potential African American immigrants. Newspapers lent a sense of stature and stability to Black communities and offered Black perspectives on news and current events. Like white newspapers, they often advocated for increased U.S. control of Indian Territory and the erosion of tribal governance. Unlike white editors, however, Black editors were bolstered by a desire for freedom from anti-Black racism, both in the United States and in Indian Territory. While white settler justifications were about *extending* existing spaces of white belonging, the Black press argued for *creating* spaces of Black freedom.

The number of newspapers published rose dramatically in the 1890s. In the Cherokee Nation, more than fifty newspapers were established (and became defunct) between 1890 and 1900; many of them published by non-Natives writing in favor of allotment.[17] While most of the non-Native press called for an increased occupation of Native land and the end of Native control over the territory, it is important to reiterate that there was a long history of Native production and circulation in the region and all of the region's print culture was in some way still deeply rooted in tribal protocols and practices. The *Indian Chieftain* (Vinita), under the operation of its white editor D. M. Marrs, would consistently emphasize the paper's number of Cherokee readers and its commitment to Cherokee issues through editorials, letters to the editor, coverage of Cherokee tribal affairs, and the publication of Cherokee writers.[18] Many papers operated in Native nations whose governments dictated all national commerce. That is to say, there was an actual and symbolic power of Native sovereignty exerted on the fields of print—a form of printscape sovereignty.

Indian Territory periodicals, especially those aimed at Black or Native audiences, often fostered a sense of collective cohesiveness that stood in contrast to the individualizing, singular quality of allotment or the organizing structure of a typical U.S. newspaper. They elicited calls to action, particular mappings of place and history, a sense of connection between contemporaneous readers and previous generations, the confluence of storytelling practices (both Black and Native) with current events, and new media technologies. That being said, the unification and cohesion of territorial public opinion that many papers also presented were more performative than actual. Some believed that textual consensus countered claims that the territory was lawless and chaotic by providing a different portrait of territorial life—one that could be legible to non-Native readers through the familiarity of the newspaper. In the next section, I show the powerful role settler print played in making allotment geographically legible, by closely reading a 1905 list of lot sales in the *Muskogee Phoenix*, one of the most popular newspapers in Indian Territory.

The Justified Margins of Allotment

On the surface, allotment was meant to create equal landholdings for all members of a tribe (every tribal member received an individual plot), but at its core, it was about breaking communal ties and asserting race-based citizenship. Allotment enabled the U.S. federal government to erode Native autonomy in Indian Territory as it had in Oklahoma Territory.[19] However, unlike Oklahoma Territory, Indian Territory was an unincorporated territory that continued to operate under tribal governance in the late nineteenth century. The Five Tribes were initially exempt from the Dawes Severalty Act (1887), but the Curtis Act of 1898 demanded they construct tribal rolls and allocate land through individual title to members of each tribe.[20] The Dawes Commission argued that allotment would create better equity of land use and train Native people how to be property-owning liberal subjects.[21] There is no question that there were economic inequities in the territory, but the commission's efforts did little to promote a more egalitarian economic system, and in fact, many Dawes officials personally profited from the allotment process.[22]

Allotment's objective was to plot, graph, and account for people and space in an orderly way that allowed seemingly more accurate surveillance by the United States than previously available. In addition, it was an attempt to force Native people to think of themselves as individuals, as U.S. citizens, rather than as members of a collective. It was a deeply spatial shift that can be viscerally felt when one looks at newspapers' rendering of the allotment process. The May 23, 1905, issue of the *Muskogee Phoenix*, one of the most popular newspapers of the era, includes a list of allotted land for sale. As a printscape, it demonstrates how allotment imagined a spatial orderliness that echoed U.S. print conventions but also renders visible the affective intensity of allotment's chaotic disruptiveness (figure 4.2).[23]

On the page, we see a visual echo of the new spatial arrangement allotment introduced. Newsprint, with its columns and rows, is as orderly as the ideal formulation of allotment, which generates a great deal of its authority from our tendency to accept and naturalize the logic of the right-justified newspaper column, a confining frame that holds and (re)orders information much as allotment itself seeks to hold and (re)order Native conceptions of

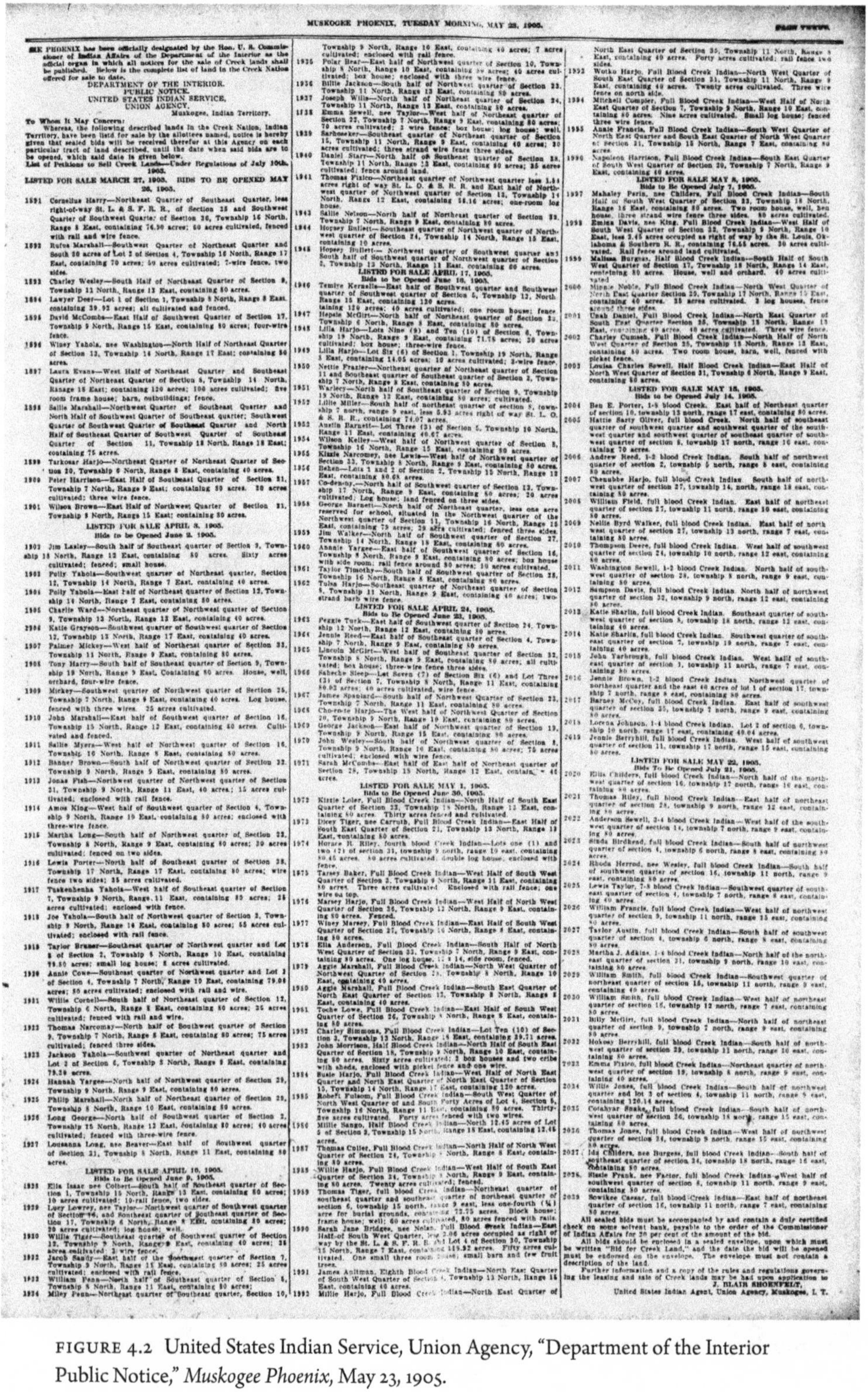

MUSKOGEE PHOENIX, TUESDAY MORNING, MAY 23, 1905.

THE PHOENIX has been officially designated by the Hon. U. S. Commissioner of Indian Affairs of the Department of the Interior as the official organ in which all notices for the sale of Creek lands shall be published. Below is the complete list of land in the Creek Nation offered for sale to date.

DEPARTMENT OF THE INTERIOR.
PUBLIC NOTICE.
UNITED STATES INDIAN SERVICE,
UNION AGENCY,
Muskogee, Indian Territory.

To Whom It May Concern:
Whereas, the following described lands in the Creek Nation, Indian Territory, have been listed for sale by the allottees named, notice is hereby given that sealed bids will be received therefor at this Agency on each particular tract of land described, until the date when said bids are to be opened, which said date is given below.

FIGURE 4.2 United States Indian Service, Union Agency, "Department of the Interior Public Notice," *Muskogee Phoenix*, May 23, 1905.

space.[24] Each entry lists an available plot and includes an item number, as well as the personal information of the original allottee, including full name and blood quantum. Tiny print and the sheer number of plots for sale make it almost impossible to distinguish one from the other, producing a daunting and overwhelming sense of both modularity and excess in this Whitmanesque catalog of names, places, and descriptions. Visually, this looks more like a late eighteenth- or early nineteenth-century newspaper than a twentieth-century one; there is minimal white space here, and print fills the page much as allotment attempted to fill the land.

Order, in fact, veers toward claustrophobic overload due to the sheer volume of information quantified here, in a print form that was meant not just to fix and store data (like tribal rolls) but to make it available to readers. This chaotic quality was, in fact, a reality for many people during allotment. Five Tribes leaders did all they could to make the commission's work more challenging at various points in the process, including withholding previous census records and other relevant documents; they were well aware that allotment was not the benevolent restructuring project that federal agents claimed.[25] The material effect of print, like that of allotment or statehood conversations, was deeply spatial. While railroads and the Dawes Commission surveys might have attempted to turn Indian Territory into a linear, graphable space that flattened power and networks of communication, the reality on the ground was simply different. The ostensibly pragmatic methods of the Dawes Commission were disorganized and poorly planned, bringing more corruption and disarray to the territory than had previously existed. Allotment, dramatic shifts in tribal and territorial boundaries, and the influx of non-Native settlers created a climate of disruption and chaos. However, while allotment aimed to create racially divided categories of individuals, it also revealed the far more complex ways people understood themselves and their communities, as well as the ways they resisted race-based logics.

While newspapers rendered the violence of allotment—the colonial land survey in its ultimate form—periodicals also tracked the changing geography, political structures, and regulation in the territory. They not only materially demonstrated the effect of allotment by including advertisements for land sale, but they also served as a space to track the workings of the Dawes Commission and engage in debate about the effects of the commission's work. It was newspapers that revealed the corruption and scandal within the allotment processes.[26] Contemporaneous U.S. news coverage (and sensational fiction) often depicted Indian Territory as a lawless place dominated by outlaws, crime, and corruption—a stereotype many territorial journalists vehemently discredited—and alleged that statehood was necessary because tribes were not adequately governing the territory. In fact, the influx of settlers and the chaos and corruption brought in by the Dawes Commission created the most unrest. The ever-increasing number of white settlers, backed by Congress, fervently pushed for statehood. Non-Native settlers wanted greater say in territorial affairs and did not like living under the authority of Native nations that dictated much of territorial life—statehood became the "solution" to the problem of Native control. As statehood became seemingly inevitable, discord became palpable in the diverse spectrum of statehood arguments that emerged in newspaper coverage. Native nations, political factions, and racial and ethnic communities all organized their own statehood proposals. Some imagined separate statehood for Oklahoma Territory and Indian Territory; some lobbied for admitting the two territories—often termed the Twin Territories—as a single state. Collectively these movements palpably demonstrated the shared belief that statehood would bestow power to the victorious party, as whoever gained control of statehood planning would shape the new state's economic and political landscape.

Removal Territory

By the end of the nineteenth century, Indian Territory was a space profoundly shaped by Removal, as the relocation zone for forcibly Removed Native people from across the entire continent and Black migrants fleeing anti-Black violence in the U.S. South. Removal also whittled away at the landholdings and displaced Native nations with previous ties to the region, including the Apache, Osage, Pawnee, Quapaw, Caddo, Wichita, Kiowa, and Comanche. I understand "Removal" capaciously throughout this chapter, and the entirety of *Reading Territory*, to gesture to more than Indian Removal; "Removal" attends to Indigeneity and Blackness paradoxically as both fixed in place and moveable, malleable, and transferrable under race-based settler colonialism. "Removal" signals the threat that Indigenous and Black freedom (of movement) poses to the racial settler state. I also use the term to attend to how enslavement forcibly Removed Africans from their homelands and their own land-based epistemologies and how Jim Crowism and anti-Black violence left many Black people with little choice but to flee the South following the U.S. Civil War. Understood this way, Removal demands that we address the double Removal that enslaved and formerly enslaved people of African descent experienced. And again, it reminds us to understand Black immigration to Indian Territory at the end of the century as related to the forced Removal of

Indigenous people throughout the nineteenth century. In both cases a white supremacist regime of violence made life untenable for Black and Native people, especially in the U.S. South. Removal bears witness to the role of forced movement in shaping Black and Native intimacies and antagonisms.

By "Removal," I mean not only the forced Removal from land, across both Africa and Turtle Island, but also the intentional work of separating peoples from themselves and their ways of being. By "land," I do not mean a colonial notion of physical terrain that can be occupied as property—I mean the other-than-human world that includes language, lifeways, culture, and understandings of how to be in good relation to our other-than-human relatives. To Remove people is to try to genocidally sever ties that Indigenous peoples (of Africa and the Americas) have nourished since time immemorial that make them who they are as peoples. In the nineteenth and early twentieth centuries, Indian Territory, as a space of Removal, also became a space of Native and Black possibility. To fully understand the impetus for an Indian statehood movement, one must deal with the Gordian knot of federal policy that had continually disrupted the stability of Indian Territory for almost a century. Understanding some of these contours allows us to appreciate the sophistication and nuance of Indian Territory print culture and why Native and Black communities might organize around statehood to protect the future of their communities.

In 1825 "Indian Territory" defined the entire region west of the Mississippi, and the area served as a home for many Native nations forcibly Removed from their lands by the United States. However, throughout the century, the federal government routinely eroded Indian Territorial landholding in order to "make room" for white settlement via statehood. From the mid-1850s through the 1880s, "Indian Territory" described the region south of Kansas and north of Texas, but the boundaries were shrunk again when the western half of Indian Territory was formally opened for non-Native settlement as Oklahoma Territory in 1899. The Five Tribes had the most extensive landholdings and the most political influence in Indian Territory during those decades, in no small part because of the wealth and power they gained through their participation in chattel slavery both before and after Removal from their ancestral homelands in the East.

The U.S. Civil War had a significant impact on Indian Territory. All five nations signed treaties with the Confederacy. The war revived decades-long intratribal schisms, and while the Choctaws and Chickasaws overwhelmingly supported the Confederacy, citizens of the Cherokee, Muscogee, and Seminole Nations were far more divided (the majority of Cherokee soldiers fought for the Union).[27] The Fives Tribes' allegiances to the Confederacy complicate the story typically told about the U.S. Civil War. The dominant Confederacy argument for succession furthered enslavement under the banner of states' rights, but the Five Tribes' allegiances aimed to *combat* statehood and protect Indigenous sovereignty, including the right to enslave people. Following the war, the federal government demanded the tribes sign peace treaties with the commissioner of Indian affairs to rebroker political relationships with the United States. Known as the treaties of 1866 or the Reconstruction Treaties, these negotiations fundamentally reshaped geopolitics and race relations in Indian Territory.[28] There were four "general provisions" in the treaties: (1) give railroads access through the territory; (2) establish a territorial government, including an intertribal council, monitored by the United States; (3) abolish slavery and recognize Freedpeople as tribal citizens (people formerly enslaved by the Five Tribes); and (4) cede "surplus" lands to other Removed tribes and to Freedpeople as reparations.[29] The first two stipulations of the treaties enabled the U.S. federal government and railroad magnates to finally gain the economic and political access to Indian Territory they had sought for decades.[30] The last two stipulations would prove the most influential for Freedpeople and Native people already living in Indian Territory.

Following the treaties, Freedpeople were able to work their own farms and build their own communities, and as a result, many Freedpeople became economically more secure than their African American counterparts in the U.S. Reconstruction South. However, the U.S. federal government also weaponized the treaty provisions to shrink Indigenous landholdings and intervene in tribal affairs more directly. For some Native people, the 1866 treaties were a clear violation of Native sovereignty because they denied Native nations the right to determine who their citizens were. This association between enslavement and sovereignty continued to position Freedpeople's belonging and Indigenous self-determination as politically at odds.[31] While enslavement was abolished and Freedpeople had *some* of the same rights as Native people in Indian Territory, they did not have *all* of the same rights; racism, exclusion, and anti-Blackness undeniably persisted.[32] Except for the Seminoles, the Five Tribes governments actively worked to either exclude Freedpeople, through policies like school segregation, or Remove them from tribal lands entirely.[33] Interpersonal relationships tell different stories and reveal how people made kin and community in ways that challenged racialist divisions, but far less often was this the case structurally. Structurally, anti-Black racism became increasingly entrenched.

The impact of allotment on identity, gender, kinship, tribal sovereignty, geography, and politics was unparalleled, and allotment resulted in massive land losses. It changed the relationship between the United States and Native nations, as well as the relationship between Native nations and their citizens. Additionally, decisions about who qualified for official enrollment on the Dawes lists raised questions about blood quantum, citizenship, and inclusion that ran contrary to more traditional understandings of kinship and community. It racialized "Nativeness" on a scale previously unprecedented. Freedpeople were placed on separate rolls, and typically anyone who identified as both Afro-Native and a Freedperson or Freedperson descendant was placed on the "Freedmen's rolls."[34]

Some Freedpeople used their allotments to nurture the growth of Black communities. It is critical to remember that the thriving neighborhood of Greenwood in Tulsa was first established by Cherokee Freedpeople who used their landholdings to build a vibrant community.[35] By 1921, in a city that became increasingly segregated along racial and class lines, white resentment at the prosperity of Greenwood led to a full-scale assault that was orchestrated and endorsed by some of the most influential white politicians and businessmen in the state. In all of these historical examples (the treaties of 1866, allotment, the Tulsa Race Massacre), we see how the white state (be it the nation-state or the State of Oklahoma) weaponized the painful interwoven histories of Black and Native life to cleave divisions across communities further. As a result, white propertied power is recentered as that which is most capable of maintaining rights and order. Or, in the case of Indian Territory, statehood.

"Specialty of Local and Territory News"

As a Muscogee (Creek) editor-writer and one of the territory's most well-known residents, Alexander Posey embodied turn-of-the-century print culture ethos in Indian Territory. An analysis of a 1902 issue of the *Indian Journal*, edited by Posey, shows that Native periodicals performed a particular model of acculturation and "progress"—a version of modernity that stood in contrast to the allegations of Indian Territory backwardness undergirding allotment and colonization. In doing so, many of these territorial magazines and newspapers generated a sense of autonomy and stability and argued implicitly (and sometimes explicitly) against excessive external intervention. Additionally, analysis of the *Journal* reveals Native-run newspapers' political roles. They typically asserted a visual and rhetorical argument for Indian Territory as a progressive space in order to challenge external arguments about the territory's lawlessness and incivility—arguments used to delegitimize tribal control and political self-determination. To see the Native space tribal leaders, editors, and writers constructed requires that we as readers understand the territory as connected to but distinct from the United States proper. Indian Territory housed numerous Indigenous nations with political and economic authority in the region throughout the nineteenth century, and most tribal leaders, editors, and writers understood themselves as negotiating this multivalent position.[36]

Daniel Littlefield Jr. and James Parins have argued that despite stereotypical assumptions that Native people were isolated, writers in Indian Territory were well versed in U.S. literary and print trends.[37] An emphasis on the local in Indian Territory print was a choice. These writers and editors were as committed to addressing readers there as they were to a broader U.S. audience, if not more so in most cases. To embrace the mappings of Native space produced by Native writers and editors, they used writing to create a sense of community within the space of the territory, not simply as a way to "speak back" to U.S. empire. Writing was, after all, not merely a defensive tool wielded in diplomacy with the United States. It was also a tool Native people used to speak to one another, both in the present and to future generations.[38] Attention to what circulated in Indian Territory newspapers reveals how Native writers expressed themselves, especially to a Native public. Moreover, the print record demonstrates the mundanity of colonialism—the quotidian, buzzing acts of violence that shaped peoples' lived experiences as much as sweeping political declarations and congressional acts.

The Muscogee-run *Indian Journal*, one of the most widely read newspapers in Indian Territory in the early 1900s, was self-professedly more territory-centric than other newspapers; it rarely covered news outside Oklahoma and Indian Territories.[39] In May 1876 the *Journal* was established in Muskogee, a railroad hub in the Muscogee (Creek) Nation, and the Creek national government initially subsidized it. Muskogee was chosen as the paper's initial locale so that Creeks could "fight the railroads and their lobbyists at Washington and elsewhere in efforts to break down and nullify rights of the people guaranteed them by law."[40] The treaties of 1866 demanded the Five Tribes allow railroads to build through their territories, but the interests of the railroads stood in stark opposition to those of the Native nations, and their construction brought with them non-Native settlers and non-Native development.[41] At the same time, the railroads brought greater access to U.S. print culture and enabled Indian Territory periodicals to reach a wider audience. While the paper was established within the Creek Nation, it drew a far broader readership. I analyze an issue of the paper to demonstrate how Indian Territory newspapers, especially those with Native editors, contributors, and sizable numbers of Native readers, crafted printscapes that differed from those of standard white U.S. publications of the same era.

The July 25, 1902, issue offers a model of how this functioned. It was published early in Posey's time as editor and the same year Pleasant Porter began his campaign for an Indian Territory state. On the cover page, one sees a large advertisement for a mercantile company highlighting its hardware inventory. The ad invokes the increased infrastructure and commercial development that accompanied settlement and allotment (figure 4.3). Directly below the advertisement is a special letter to the *Journal* from the Creek Council titled "Following Preamble and Resolutions Appealing to the President for the Protection of the Creeks against Lawless Land Grabbers Submitted to Council by Chief Porter Yesterday." The advertisement for the hardware store is oddly juxtaposed to a formal resolution to President Theodore Roosevelt, making tensions about land in the territory palpable on the front page. At the same time, the coupling of advertising and governance creates a space that reveals the political economy of the moment, in which the front page functions both commercially and communally.[42] The end of the Creek Council's piece indicates that Chief Porter will submit the resolution to Roosevelt, but printing it beforehand in a newspaper with a strong Creek readership combines more "traditional" forms of tribal discussion and politics with the medium of the printed circular. There is a tension, however, between Porter's message about preserving Creek property rights and the advertisement that hovers above.

The second page of the paper, like the first, offers an odd melding of advertisements that allude to tribal politics and includes Creek writer Charles Gibson's running column "Rifle Shots."[43] An advertisement for Grayson's Grocery stretches across the top of the page while Gibson's piece sits below it. "Rifle Shots" is sandwiched between advertisements for dentists, lawyers, and other professionals on the left and advertisements for banks and the Saint Louis stockyard on the right. Grayson's Grocery offers the following in its ad, which one could read as an allusion to the contemporaneous metaphor of Mr. Oklahoma and Miss Indian Territory used to describe joint statehood for the two territories: "The young man loves the young lady. That's his business. The young lady loves the young man. That's her business. Pretty soon they'll be married and wanting all kinds of Fancy and Staple Groceries. **That's my**

j c wallace

THE INDIAN JOURNAL.

TWENTY-SEVENTH YEAR. EUFAULA, IND. TER., FRIDAY, JULY 25, 1902. NUMBER 30

CREEK COUNCIL.

Following Preamble and Resolutions Appealing to the President for the Protection of the Creeks Against Lawless Land Grabbers Submitted to Council by Chief Porter Yesterday.

Special to the Journal.

Whereas the Muskogee people, after tedious and trying years of doubt, debate and anxiety, yielded at last to the importunities of the representatives of the government, and confidently relying on their solemn and oft-repeated promises and assurances that if they will abandon their system of holding their lands in common for that of individual ownership under separate deeds to each citizen, then they would be protected by the government in the undisturbed possession and use thereof for an indefinite period; and desiring to aid and facilitate the work of the government in the settlement of the landed and other important interests of the nation, they have, in good faith, selected and are still selecting their lands in severalty, and

Whereas, in pursuance of the promises and agreements of the government, the Commission to the Five Civilized Tribes has issued to each of about 13000 Creek citizens certificates descriptive of the lands selected by each as his prospective individual allotment for which he will finally receive a deed, and

Whereas, in consequence of this determined policy of the government involving a change from collective to individual ownership of land in the Muskogee nation, and the issuance of the certificates above mentioned, our nation has become infested and over-run with non-citizen residents and others arriving from the adjoining states who have gone into the business of securing from the ignorant and very needy of the Creek people, written obligations based on the certificates they hold, in which they engage to sell their allotments and surrender their deeds therefor as soon as these are issued by the chief to the citizen, at a price in many cases so far below the real value of such lands as to be tantamount to simple acts of robbery of the ignorant and needy, and

Whereas it is elsewhere currently remarked, and now by this body believed, that these land companies plying their unrestricted vocation among our people, will by fraud and dishonest dealings soon make homeless paupers of a large number of the citizenship of the Muskogee nation unless some preventive measure is by the proper authorities adopted to protect our people against the lawless methods practiced by the land buyers, and

Whereas the transactions of the land buyers with our citizens, include though they be, are, in the opinion of this body, in glaring disregard of the plain provisions of the act of congress approved March 1-t 1901, thus placing the actors in the attitude of persons conspiring to prevent the operation of this law of congress specially enacted to effectuate its promises to the Creeks, and

Whereas the authority and government of the Muskogee nation have been abolished by the United States, leaving us in times of great public peril such as we believe now confronts our people, with no refuge save an appeal to the power of the president of the United States for needed protection; and having an abiding faith and confidence in the will and purpose of the president and his advisers to extend full protection and justice to the Creek people in fulfilment of the promises of his agents; and since he cannot apply remedial measures unless apprised of our dangers and fears as we see them, therefore

Be it resolved by the national council of the Muskogee nation in extraordinary session assembled at Okmulgee, in the Muskogee nation that, his excellency the President of the United States be and he is hereby informed that it is the opinion of this body that a formidable and rapidly growing number of citizens of the neighboring states, now resident in the Muskogee nation, have, in various towns therein, organized themselves into business companies, and taking advantage of the poverty and need, their ignorance of values and the law against the transfer of Indian land title, of many of the citizens of the Muskogee nation, are engaged in the buying and leasing from them at ruinously low prices, of the prospective allotments of land that are to be deeded to them in accordance with descriptions in certificates of allotment given them by the commission to the Five Civilized Tribes which is destructive of the welfare of many of our people, and, if not arrested, must at no distant day result in rendering homeless paupers of the ignorant poor of the citizenship of our nation. It is the further opinion of the council that the

Continued on page 4.

FIGURE 4.3 Front page, *Indian Journal* (Eufaula), July 25, 1902.

business."[44] W. C. Grayson was a friend of Posey's and a well-known Creek citizen actively involved in the allotment process; he had been on the Creek Nation's committee that approved allotment. However, Grayson was also considered "antiprogress" by many in the Nation and supported Porter's decision not to sign thousands of Creek allotment deeds in Muskogee until the United States consented to a supplemental agreement discouraging the sale of "excess" lands to non-Creeks.[45] The allusion to the heteronormative marriage trope of the two territories offers a humorous endorsement of joint statehood that alludes to the profit of "my business," meaning that of Grayson. The use of the first person places Grayson directly into the pages of the paper, connecting his own economic prosperity to the economic advantages ferried in by statehood. Moreover, the advertisement draws a correlative between reproduction, sexual intimacy, and kinship and economic prosperity, highlighting the ways intimacy and heteronormativity were dexterously collapsed into statehood, even in the most quotidian of places.

Below Grayson's advertisement sits the first of Gibson's two "Rifle Shots" pieces for July 25. "More about the Spokogees" uses the case of the Spokogees to share a pre-Removal Creek history of land use. Gibson says that while the Spokogees could be viewed as "pullbacks," a problematic term used in this era to denote Native people committed to older ways and traditions, they understood that General McIntosh's negotiations with the U.S. government did not benefit the Creeks. And "so it was that Gen. McIntosh and one other was killed for having signed a treaty with the U.S. government ceding Alabama cont[r]ary to the law and will of the Creek people." Gibson ends the piece with the assertion that "what we have written is no guess work but a plain statement of facts." While Gibson's piece self-identifies as a history lesson on pre-Removal Creek politics, its allusion to the contemporary moment is no guesswork either—the case of the Spokogees echoes many of the same concerns facing the 1902 negotiations between the U.S. federal government and the Creek Nation.[46]

The year 1902 was also when Chitto Harjo and the Snakes regrouped to combat the work of the Dawes Commission.[47] The Snakes, also known as the "Crazy" Snakes, were a collective of Muscogee (Creeks) who rejected all U.S. interference. They refused to participate in allotment and sometimes used direct action to thwart the work of the field officers, "pulling up the measuring stakes and cornerstones that were necessary for the surveyors."[48] They were often tagged with the derogatory term "pullback" that Gibson uses for the Spokogees. Gibson's use of the term suggests a potential connection between the Spokogees of the past and the 1902 "traditionals," Snakes, and Snake sympathizers.[49] One can read between the lines in Gibson's piece and see a commentary on the debate in the Creek Nation about Porter's decision and the Snakes' organizing efforts; fighting against the erosion of Creek land-holdings had a long tribal history and was an imperative of Creek law. Gibson uses long-standing forms of Muscogee metaphor and allusion to stage a fairly radical commentary by framing it as a story of history and tradition that posits itself as "folksy" rather than political. Whether or not they were intentionally placed side by side in the newspaper's layout, Grayson's advertisement and Gibson's story narrate two competing notions of territorial identity and Creekness. Coupled together, they display a sense of multiple scales of readership and present a progress narrative actively engaged in the capitalist projects of modernity and state-making alongside skepticism about the Nation's political direction. Together, they reflect the diversity of Creek opinions, co-existing together, sometimes in tension, on the same territorial landscape of the newspaper page.

The newspaper's third, fourth, and fifth pages cover a vast array of local and territorial news and announcements that create a sense of intimacy, referring to individuals in the community with familiarity. "Bower," for example, "is still doing business at the same old stand." Here Posey includes news from other newspapers, notably the *Holdenville Times'* praise of "Charlie" Gibson and Alex Posey. These pages are also peppered with advertisements from banks, railroads, and land sales—again reflecting the current moment in Eufaula and the Creek Nation. A full-page advertisement takes up the fifth page of the *Journal* (figure 4.4). It is an advertisement for advertisers, full of open space and varied font size and style. It draws the reader's eye first to the newspaper's title, as well as its subscription numbers. The eye is then drawn to the ad's assertion of its intended or assumed audience through its "Specialty of Local and Territory News." If allotment produced a dizzying sense of atomization and excess, then a paper like the *Indian Journal* countered that with a sense of cohesion and communalism. Not only does this solicitation assert its dedication to the territory, but it also emphasizes "the people," a reading public. Instead of individual listings, the *Journal* surrounds its advertisement with one thin border, encompassing all the print on the page. Indeed, it looks less like an advertisement than a title page—an ornate calling card for the people of Indian Territory writ large. The last two pages of the newspaper continue to offer local and territorial news, as well as "The Cruise of the Good Vrouw," excerpted "from a diary by one of the crew," a short narrative piece anonymously penned by Posey.[50] Under Posey's editorship from 1902 to 1904, the *Journal* and its advertisements, essays, and news pieces offer readers both

FIGURE 4.4
Advertisement, *Indian Journal* (Eufaula), July 25, 1902.

then and now a sense of the political and cultural moment. Posey also used the pages of the *Journal* to advocate for the work of other Native literary writers in the territory.[51] Given the *Journal*'s popularity, Posey's praise of other writers helped showcase the rich output of Native literary production by authors who were often multigenre writers themselves involved in tribal politics or Indian Territory journalism.

Notably, Posey's curatorial work as editor echoed his work as a writer. His Fus Fixico letters satirized the era for territorial readers, including the State of Sequoyah movement, and his decision to publish the letters in various Indian Territory papers, crossing national lines (some published in "Creek" papers, others in "Cherokee," etc.), underscores a unified Indian Territory community. Likewise, the *Journal* "make[s] a specialty of local and territory news," and its emphasis on community and cohesion functions as a political response to allotment debates, which were grounded in questions about the strength and futurity of the Creek Nation. The Nation, like the paper, is communally affiliated, even if contentious, and balances a deep sense of Creek identity and nationalism with an awareness of broader territorial discussions and modern forms of capital, technology, and print. The paper both performs and coheres to a typographical and geospatial sense of the tribal and the territorial.

A Poetic State

In addition to being a well-known writer and editor, Posey served as secretary for the State of Sequoyah convention. His appointment, along with the proposed state name, gestures to the synthesis of print, literature, and politics in Indian Territory, what we might understand as a *political poetics*.[52] The state name was an homage to one of the most beloved Cherokee figures of the nineteenth century, Sequoyah. Sequoyah and his daughter Ayoka are credited with creating the Cherokee syllabary in the 1820s, an innovative technology that, within a few years, transformed the Cherokee into a literate, print-reading, and print-circulating nation.[53] As I discuss in chapter 1, they developed the syllabary while living near what would become Cherokee lands (and Indian Territory) following Removal. They then brought the syllabary back to the National Council, where it was approved as the official language of the Nation. Soon, a majority of Cherokees could read or write in Sequoyan Cherokee. Therefore, the syllabary connected writing and literacy to tribal endurance and continuity across geographies of Removal and survivance for Native people.

Sequoyah symbolically resonated with Cherokee and non-Cherokee Native people alike; poets wrote sonnets in honor of him, many of them echoing the poetic tradition of praising mythological or heroic figures. The use of classical allusion and traditional meter and rhyme—typical of much nineteenth-century poetry—asserted the poet's skill and Sequoyah's importance in Western civilization by demonstrating an awareness of common English-language poetic tropes and revealing an author's versatility with language and content. Additionally, a number of Sequoyah poems share a celestial invocation of his timelessness. He transcends nations, time, and space, much like heavenly bodies or constellations. Sequoyah becomes symbolic of Native survivance, with the ability to endure long after the era of U.S. colonization—through print and its conventions, which are understood as culturally fungible and translatable.

Cherokee lawyer and poet DeWitt Clinton Duncan, who wrote under the pen name Too-Qua-Stee, published a "Sequoyah poem" in the *Vinita Weekly Chieftain* (previously the *Indian Chieftain*) in 1904 that invoked the most common nineteenth-century tropes of the genre.[54] In the first line of the poem, Too-Qua-Stee describes Sequoyah as an anomaly, more than a man: "Great man? Or wondrous, should I say?" He goes into an extended conceit comparing Sequoyah to a planet, describing him as a "flaming orb" that shot from the earth into the sky as it "launched," "hurled," and "rose and shone," "eclipsing constellations in its flight." Sequoyah's genius is like a star shining down from the heavens that can be seen by all below, "a Sun gone out—the universe its tomb." Therefore, Sequoyah and his creation of the syllabary are imbued with a legendary status that surpasses material understandings of time and space. As such, he embodies the endurance of the Cherokee people.

This stretching of time is representative of Sequoyah poems written decades earlier by Cherokee poets Joshua Ross in 1856 and David J. Brown in 1879. Brown's rendition invokes a similarly celestial Sequoyah who shines down on the world, a "giant of thy age" who is "in history a living page."[55] Brown's Sequoyah is a visionary seer, like an Old Testament figure, who understands better than others what is needed for the futurity of the Cherokee Nation. Ross's poem "Sequoyah" (signed with the pen name "The Wanderer") depicts a similar Sequoyah. Unlike Too-Qua-Stee's Sequoyah, who shines down from the heavens, Ross's is deeply rooted in the earth. In Ross's poem, Sequoyah is not remembered as a name on a tombstone but honored through language. He is someone who can see the future—that is, who can "read the writing on the wall"; his legacy will live on eternally through the use of language that will endure well beyond U.S. empire's attack on the Cherokee, "when the Nation fades away / Before the mighty Saxon sway."[56]

An early poem, written by the same Posey who edited the *Indian Journal*, puts forward a similar image of Sequoyah. Some of Posey's earliest success is attributed to his poem "Ode to Sequoyah," published in Ora V. Eddleman's monthly periodical *Twin Territories: The Indian Magazine* in April 1899. After its initial printing, the poem recirculated through several territorial and U.S. publications.[57] Posey's ode was initially accompanied by a brief introductory paragraph that paradoxically introduces the author as both exceptional and typical, alleging that most "Indians" are "anything but poetical" and offering a sense of the odds, "about one in ten thousand."[58] However, the introduction asserts that the poet's education and intelligence are quite common, noting "there are thousands of educated Indians in the territory—many of them graduates from famous institutions of learning, but they do not deal in

poetry."[59] In doing so it argues for the poem as a unique, erudite piece of literature, but without claiming that its allusions or adeptness with language
would be lost on a well-educated Native territorial audience.

The blurb ends by saying that one cannot read this poem without acknowledging the sophistication of life in Indian Territory. This introductory
remark was most likely written by Eddleman or one of the other editors of
Twin Territories and not Posey. In a statement Posey made to the *Philadelphia
Press* in 1900, he argued, "If they could be translated into English without los-
ing their characteristic flavor and beauty, many of the Indian songs and
poems would rank among the greatest poetic productions of the time....
The Indian talks in poetry; poetry is his vernacular, not necessarily the stilted
poetry of books, but the free and expressive untrammeled poetry of nature."[60]
Posey simultaneously critiques the poetic limits of the English language and
refutes the notion of the Native poet as an anomaly; instead, he argues that
Native understandings of poetry are as good as, if not *better* than, those of
white people.

Posey's poem lauds Sequoyah, and like the proposed Sequoyah state map
I discuss later on, it performatively demonstrates a mastery of Western conventions and forms. It begins,

> The names of Waitie and Boudinot—
> The valiant warrior and gifted sage—
> And other Cherokees, may be forgot,
> But thy name shall descend to every age;
> The mysteries enshrouding Cadmus' name
> Cannot obscure thy claim to fame.[61]

Here, Posey praises Sequoyah by comparing him not only to Cherokee leaders like Stand Watie and Elias Boudinot but also to Cadmus, the prince who
introduced the Greek alphabet. Sequoyah's greater claim to posterity is explicitly linked to the endurance of written language and storytelling, through
the comparison to Cadmus but in other ways as well. The second stanza
reads,

> The people's language cannot perish—nay!
> When from the face of this great continent
> Inevitable doom hath swept away
> The last memorial—the last fragment
> Of tribes, some scholar learned shall pore
> Upon thy letters, seeking ancient lore.

In this formulation, written language and the oral stories told about Sequoyah's creation ensure his immortality, as well as that of the Cherokee people. Posey suggests that memorials—we could interpret these as material markers or as written memorials (a genre Cherokees routinely used to lobby the U.S. government)—may fade and "the last fragment / of tribes" may be "swept away," yet "the people's language cannot perish." Even in the face of colonialism, settlement, and allotment, the people will endure, if not physically, then lyrically through the language that forecasts its own futurity.

However, the poem's ending is slightly more ambiguous, as Posey closes by alluding to Sequoyah's biographical disappearance and uncertain fate. He writes,

> By cloud-capped summits in the boundless west,
> Or mighty river rolling to the sea,
> Where'er thy footsteps led thee on that quest,
> Unknown, rest thee, illustrious Cherokee![62]

Concluding as it does by questioning Sequoyah's whereabouts, this stanza seems to tilt the poem toward elegy—and mourning—and, with it, toward the well-known settler trope of the vanishing Indian, here Sequoyah himself, whose final resting place is unknown. At the most basic level, these lines simply ask whether Sequoyah, wherever he died, is at peace. But this poem is not an elegy, and it ends with an exclamation mark. It is emphatically titled and framed as an ode, a celebration of survival rather than an act of grieving, and Posey is almost certainly asking a broader question that depends not on Sequoyah's disappearance so much as it does on his people's endurance: Posey may not be asking whether Sequoyah is literally at rest but rather hopes Sequoyah can rest easy with Native responses to the moment of cultural and political upheaval Posey is writing from. In this way, the poem reaches both backward and forward from the ground it stood on in 1902. Sequoyah ascends at the poem's end as a founding father watching over the present crisis; a figure pressed into the service of a nationalism so deep and long-standing that it rivals European modernity, whose constituent nation-states were, in this period, hard at work inventing similarly primordial pasts for themselves.

Posey's ode was the most well known, but it was certainly not the only poem dedicated to Sequoyah. Like other Sequoyah poems, many of which circulated in territorial periodicals, Posey's ode emphasizes Sequoyah's achievements as eternal, but this is seemingly in tension with the material form of the publication—an ephemeral magazine. The magazine's performance of Native power complicates its additional function as a site of everyday circulation for communal dialogue and discourse. As a marker of Native cultural potency, the periodical (like Sequoyah) speaks to its contemporary and future readers. While the actual text of the poem may not continue to circulate among the same number of individuals today as it did in the nineteenth or early twentieth century, it contributes to a long legacy of Native endurance.

Moreover, it challenges the dominant U.S. narrative of the era, which depicted Native nations as unable to wield control over space and people. Print culture geared toward Native readers and Native interests in Indian Territory challenged (and continues to challenge) the notion that print was the exclusive tool of U.S. imperialism in the nineteenth century, just as the State of Sequoyah challenged the idea that only the United States could produce a functioning and recognizable state of the union. Therefore, Sequoyah and his legacy gesture toward an understanding of Indigenous subjectivity deeply invested in the power of print to cohere a nation's people and to archive for future generations the nuance of a particular historical moment.

The Black Territorial Press

Like Native publications in Indian Territory, Black papers often used their pages to assert geopolitically sovereign printscapes to multiple readerships. Most consistently, they argued for the necessity of sovereign Black space. There is no doubt that some papers deployed anti-Indigenous rhetoric in doing so (there was ample anti-Black content in tribally run papers as well). However, they did not simply reinscribe settler colonial narratives of occupation and property—the geopolitical and cultural work we find in their pages is far messier and more complex. In some cases, Black towns participated in and benefited from the structural attempts to destroy Native nations, but I want to reiterate that Black participation in Indigenous dispossession was distinctly different from that of white participation. Black and Native people were Removed from the U.S. South throughout the nineteenth century through violent force—more pointedly, violent force that served to sustain and entrench white supremacy. Anti-Blackness and anti-Indigeneity converged in Indian Territory at this time, and part of the work of resisting the divisiveness between Black and Native people enflamed by white possession is to seek out points of commonality in addition to points of discord.

Black territorial newspapers were part of a thriving Black print culture in Indian Territory. In a June 8, 1905, article in the *Muskogee Cimeter*, a Black paper published out of Muskogee, Indian Territory, by William Henry Twine, proudly declared that "four colored printing offices in Muskogee kept busy is evidence of a live commercial activity amongst our people. It's a big thing for a town of 17,000, but it is a fact."[63] Historian Jimmie Franklin estimates that there were "more than seventy" Black papers published in the territories before 1920, although many of them were short-lived, most likely due to the financial burden of maintaining a newspaper.[64] Due to anti-Black economic disparities, Black editors often had far fewer resources than their Native and white counterparts.

Like many contemporaneous white publications in Indian Territory, Black newspapers often included advertisements for local businesses. They consciously served as recruitment tools to entice migrants, but they also operated holistically in ways more akin to Native newspapers by utilizing an assemblage of articles, advertisements, and images to argue for the viability and success of Black-dominant spaces, what I term "sovereign printscapes." Like Black papers in the United States, Black Indian Territory papers were venues to challenge anti-Black racism and report racial violence, which was often downplayed by non-Black publications in the territories. As such, they posited notions of citizenship and belonging that emulated what Derrick R. Spires describes as the "practice of citizenship" evoked in early African American print culture. According to Spires, this practice fosters "civic ethos and protocols of recognition and justice that call on audiences to think about their relation to citizens and others as one of mutual responsibility, responsiveness, and active engagement."[65] Much like those who worked on *Freedom's Journal* and the *Anglo-African Magazine*, discussed in earlier chapters, the editors of and contributors to Black Indian Territory papers utilized the periodical form and its content to challenge anti-Blackness in Indian Territory, arguing for full inclusion of the Black citizen-subject but also organizing Black spatialities that could not be limited by national borders. These papers operated as spaces of Black political and intellectual debate and insisted on the complexity of Black life. They also invoked the long nineteenth-century tradition of utilizing newspapers to promote immigration and autonomous Black communities, such as Mary Ann Shadd Cary's *Provincial Freeman* or the twentieth-century *Chicago Defender* (founded in 1905).

These territorial papers are clearly in conversation with the much longer Black print culture traditions that Spires details, but they distinctly engage in such theorizing in "All-Black" towns operating in Indian Territory, outside the United States proper, and represent some of the most affluent Black communities anywhere in North America at this time. Moreover, they complicate studies of Black print culture as they imagined and asserted Black sovereignty in Native nations with robust print culture traditions. Black editors, especially those in Black towns, used their papers to assert forms of Black sovereignty that evoked *both* the well-established U.S. Black press and Native papers like the *Cherokee Phoenix,* whose pages affirmed place-based sovereignty. Black Indian Territory papers imagined Black political and social autonomy free from external interference, albeit often combined with skepticism of Indigenous sovereignty. While such autonomy often envisioned U.S. sovereignty as on the horizon, it utilized *printscape sovereignty* to imagine Black life both within and beyond the state. We must remember that many of these papers were established in towns and communities whose economic origins are connected to Freedpeople's landholdings and that counted Freedpeople and other Afro-Native people among their numbers. Therefore, these papers are part of Indigenous placemaking in Indian Territory and not entirely distinct from official tribal publications; they are an intrinsic subgenre of Indian Territory print and blur the lines between Black and Native.

Papers like the *Boley Progress* circulated throughout the United States and understood their audiences as both territorial and U.S. readers. The *Progress,* published out of Boley, Indian Territory, circulated across the United States as a symbol of Black economic and political prosperity.[66] Boley, initially created from the allotment of a Freedgirl, was the "largest predominantly-Black town in North America at the turn of the century."[67] Throughout 1905, the first year of the *Boley Progress's* run, every front page included an advertisement for the community titled "Come to Boley" (figure 4.5). The ad describes Boley's rapid development and prosperity hyperbolically, noting, "Nothing like her ever happened before. Nothing like her will ever happen again."[68] Boley is described in gendered and sexualized terms as a "buxom young giantess" whose origin story echoes the narrative of the land runs that opened Indian Territory to non-Native settlement in the 1890s: "The whole of Boley, in which but a few short months ago almost the only fire scent was that raised from the Indian tepee or hunting camp, is now curling from hundreds of chimneys of the residents, and the busy hours of business mark the onward march of civilization."[69] The rest of the front page includes various articles that also advertise the economic possibility and amenities Boley residents enjoy. Unlike a broadside or a single one-page advertisement, the newspaper constructs a more nuanced and textured narrative of place incorporating culture, politics, ideology, and progressive advocacy of respectability, capitalist investment, and education. In this way, it combined the "practice of citizenship" described by Spires with the place-based approach of Native newspapers in the territory.

THE BOLEY PROGRESS.

"All Men Up--Not Some Men Down."

VOL. I.　　　　　BOLEY, INDIAN TERRITORY, THURSDAY, JULY 13, 1905.　　　　　NO. 19.

Come to Boley

The Story of Boley. The story of the glory of Boley has been told and told again. But it loses nothing in the telling; and unless for some particular reason one is interested in the progress of the city, he is apt to miss connection with the record of its wonderful prosperity; for the story of yesterday is soon old, and that of today is quickly changed into a back number. In her onward march of prosperity, so wonderful, the changes so numerous, the only way to remain in touch with them is to keep one eye continuously on her record of activity. Not even the Boley of today would recognize the Boley of a year ago, in spite of the short space of time.

Boley Stands Apart. Nothing like her ever happened before. Nothing like her will ever happen again. The birth of this town reads like a fairy story, and her marvelous development has the effect of intensifying the likeness to the results that were produced through the agency of Aladdin's lamp.

Boley never wore swaddling cloths. She had no period of childhood. For her there was no baby food. Instead, at the signal for the opening of the town, she may be said to have leaped at one bound to the adult age; a buxom young giantess, with a harvest hand's appetite and the capacity of a genius for accomplishing things. Boley surprised the country from center to circumference when she was born. Since then, more quietly, but none the less effectively, she has continued on her way, demolishing all known records and astonishing the world by the push and activity of her people and the variety of her resources.

A wooded hill and valley has been transformed into a wonderfully short space of time into one of the most progressive of all the new towns along the Fort Smith and Western R. R. This statement is a broad one, but if can be made good. The whole of Boley, in which but a few short months ago almost the only fire scent was that raised from the Indian tepee or hunting camp, is now curling from hundreds of chimneys of the residents, and the busy hours of business mark the onward march of civilization.

Ready Access to Markets

The part of the territory in which Boley is situated has not heretofore had a recognition of its merits because of inadequate railroad facilities. This defect has been remedied by the construction of the Fort Smith and Western railroad, and from now on there will be a rapid development of the territory tapped, which will undoubtedly place it in the front rank in production and civic development.

What the Country is Like. The country which surrounds Boley, for the most part, consists of rolling prairie. There is considerable timber land of heavy growth. Practically every square mile of the district is tillable. Very little of the land is so cut up or so rough as to be unavailable for farming. Corn, wheat, potatoes, cotton, alfalfa, apples, peaches, grapes and all kinds of berries can be successfully cultivated. There is not a crop produced in the temperate zone which will not thrive in this district, and in the case of many of them the returns are unsurpassed in quarter.

These lands can be bought or leased at reasonable prices. The time to secure them is now. They will make a priceless heritage for your children and a veritable paradise for you in your old age. Come and see.

MARLIN

When They Fly Fast
The Marlin 12 Gauge REPEATING SHOTGUN

Is the all-around favorite. It is made for both black and smokeless powders and to take heavy loads. It has one-third less parts than any other repeater, and handles very fast. Marlin Breechbolt that shuts out rain and water and keeps the shells dry. It a great wet-weather gun. It has Marlin accuracy, buoyancy and reliability. Our foremost Book has hundreds of good Marlin stories, sent with Catalogue for 3 stamps postage.

MARLIN FIRE ARMS CO., 42 Willow St., New Haven, Ct.

Advertise in THE PROGRESS.

The Boley Progress

O. H. BRADLEY, Editor.

Entered as Second-Class matter at the post Office at Boley Ind. Territory.

Published every Thursday at Boley, Creek Nation, Indian Territory.

All letters and communications should be addressed to the Boley Progress, Boley, I. T.

SUBSCRIPTION RATES
One Year $1.00
Six months .... .50
Three months .... .25
Single Copy .... .05

Advertising rates made known on application to the office.

Boley is the garden spot of the southwest. Its natural advantages can not be surpassed.

Grasp the opportunity while it presents itself, as time moves on your chances to secure a home in this great country lessen.

Your children's children will call you blessed if you take advantage of this wonderful opportunity and secure for them a home in this land of liberty.

Come and get a home now while it is in your reach. Then it matters not what happens it does not lessen the productiveness of your soil; and with the land yours you are always sure of a place to stay and a plenty to eat.

We know of no place in the Indian Territory where so much of the essentials of health exist as in Boley. For here you have not only the most productive soil for the growth of all kinds of fruits and vegetables, but a water most excellent which can be found any where from 18 to 25 feet, which is clear and soft and free from all injurious mineral matters but contains many medicinal properties. Boley is the garden spot of the B. T. when its natural resources are taken in consideration.

Boley is located in one of the finest sections in the United States, and the more you see of the surrounding country the more you think so. There are more inducements here for the colored homeseeker than in any place in this whole country. (1) Absolute and unrestrained exercise of all public privileges. (2) A liberal education for your children. (3) A productive soil. (4) Good water and healthy climate. Don't take our word for this, but come and we will show you all of this and even more.

A Negro Town.

The fact that a negro, taken to Lahoma by a contractor, was run out of town before sunset, recalls the fact that there is a town in the western part of the Indian Territory, near the Lincoln county line called Boley, and if there is a white man in it or near it he is blacked up or stays under cover. It is purely a colored town composed of highly colored people with various posted to warn white men not to let the sun set on them in Boley, and this is part of that wonderful, rich intelligence and productive country that the politician wants to take in this great state of Oklahoma and Boley is a credit to some of that "wonderful country."
—Kansas City Journal.

The above article appeared in Kansas City Journal. It is as false as can be as far as Boley is concerned. There are many white people who live near Boley, it is their post office, trading point and railroad station. They come to town whenever...

---

they feel like it, night or day, often they have to come for a doctor or some other necessity. Every day in the year, except Sunday, there is a drummer (white) soliciting the patronage of our merchants. There is not a week but that some white person enjoys the hospitality of our hotel. The citizens of Boley are, to say the least are civilized and we will treat any one with respect who respects himself, be he white or black. While no white people live in the town, yet they are treated as any other citizen as far as their public privileges are concerned. "And Boley is a credit to some of this 'wonderful country'."

NOTICE!

All who are indebted to this paper will please settle at once. A blue mark after your name signifies that your subscription has expired.

WESTERN NEGRO PRESS ASSOCIATION.

To the Press:—

Pursuant to the regular appointment under the Provisions of the Constitution, the Western Negro Press Association of the United States of America is hereby called to convene at Muskogee, I. T., in its Ninth Annual Session, Wednesday, Thursday and Friday September 20th, 21st and 22nd, 1905.

All proprietors, editors, managers and correspondents west of Mississippi River are eligible to membership in said association and are urged to be present.

We cordially extend an invitation to the members of the fraternity and the friends of the newspapers in general throughout the country, to meet with us at Muskogee to consider those questions so vital to the welfare of the race in the United States of America.

We also extend and expect all ministers and college professors, business men and professional men and women to join in this coming meeting.

Recent development shows the need of action on the part of the intelligent and thoughtful members of the race and the Press with the aid of the Pulpit must undoubtedly take the lead. The official program that will be published later will be up to the usual high standard.

We would again urge upon every paper and its entire staff to make this meeting a personal matter in order to secure a large and enthusiastic gathering.

James Wadkins,

Builder, Contractor and Bill Maker

No bohgoldin, but work guaranteed. If you are contemplating to build, I will figure your bill and do your work. All matters in this line of business solicited. It will pay you to see me before you let your contract. Boley, I. T.

Chas. Brown,

GENERAL CONTRACTOR and BUILDER

My work in Boley speaks for itself, so if you have any building to do

See Me Before Contracting with Others.

FIGURE 4.5　Front page, *Boley Progress*, July 13, 1905.

The *Muskogee Cimeter* pointedly discussed race relations in Oklahoma and Indian Territories, often warning readers of anti-Black violence and providing information about where Black people could safely travel. There were clear distinctions between papers from Black towns like the *Boley Progress*, aimed at potential settlers outside the territory, and papers catering to Black readers in larger multiracial cities and townships, like the *Cimeter*. As the largest settlement in Indian Territory, Muskogee was the nexus of statehood campaigns, and Black Muskogee papers published extensive coverage of the 1905 statehood debates. Papers like the weekly *Cimeter* provide a sense of how Black leaders in Indian Territory negotiated anti-Blackness in statehood campaigns and strategized responses that they felt would best serve their communities.

Black newspaper production and circulation asserted participation in the public sphere and a sense of economic stability, and many publications highlighted the accomplishments of residents as an expression of racial pride and Black progress.[70] The *Cimeter* regularly printed images of local and U.S. Black leaders, especially on its front pages. Including these images was an effort to circulate proof of Black progress and respectability, both through the images' content and through the publication's financial means to publish them. Moreover, the images provided tangible specificity to Black respectability. Few other territorial papers of any kind that I found published as many photographs—most of them did not publish any. Printing photographs was not cheap, and their inclusion was additional evidence of a publication's economic prosperity. These photographs not only assert Black belonging in the territory—they assert Black *prosperity*. In this way, they utilize the sovereign printscape logic of the tribally run press to insist on Black spatial sovereignty in Indian Territory.

Black Statehood

Tiya Miles and Sharon Holland observe in their introduction to *Crossing Waters, Crossing Worlds* that "by the late nineteenth century and early twentieth century, many African Americans had come to see the Western lands called Indian Territory as a refuge in America, and more as a potential *black space* that would function metaphorically and emotionally as a substitute for the longed-for African homeland."[71] The allure of settling in Indian Territory for many African American migrants was the possibility of greater economic and political autonomy—a spatial imaginary where Black people could build their own communities and dictate their own cultural, social, and political lives. In this way, migration to the territory was not unlike other Black nationalist efforts, such as Garveyism or Martin Delany's Niger Valley Exploring Party, mentioned in the previous chapter. In fact, Kendra T. Fields argues that we should understand Indian Territory and Africa as "part of a continuum of flight" that shaped Black responses to the failures of Reconstruction in the U.S. South and the Jim Crow policies that followed.[72] Essential to the narrative of Indian Territory's utopic possibility was the circulation of newspapers and pamphlets encouraging Black people to migrate to the territories, promising prosperity and autonomy and the possibility of forming a Black state. As such, Black communities, like Native communities, utilized print circulation and newspapers to further their interests in political recognition, developing a distinct Black territorial print culture. As importantly, Black towns, often run entirely by Black civic and political leaders and composed almost exclusively of Black residents, asserted a form of Black sovereignty that insisted on autonomous Black place.

Edward McCabe, who became one of the most vocal Black leaders in the territories, moved near Guthrie, Oklahoma Territory, following the 1889 land run and established Langston City.[73] Shortly after, he organized the first Black daily newspaper in Oklahoma Territory, the *Herald*. McCabe believed that a sizable Black population in Oklahoma Territory could ensure a strong political voice and possibly gain the necessary momentum to dissuade white settlement. He was active in Kansas Republican politics before moving to the territory and used his prior experience to lobby for a Black state. While the character Belton Piedmont in Sutton E. Griggs's contemporaneous *Imperium in Imperio* (1899) argues Black freedom is only possible by creating a state *outside* the United States, McCabe advocated for freedom through statehood. Throughout the 1890s, McCabe led a movement proposing a Black state that would purportedly free African Americans from the burden of racial oppression in the U.S. South and across the Midwest and West but would also formally organize and protect Black self-determination.[74] However, McCabe's statehood proposals participated in the colonial usurpation of Native land for non-Native community-building and the belief that Native nations must be eliminated in order to create new communities.

McCabe and others circulated advertisements across the United States encouraging migration to Oklahoma Territory.[75] However, his plans for Black statehood never achieved fruition. The *Indian Chieftain's* response to McCabe's plan, intentionally or not, struck at the movement's central challenge: palpable anti-Black racism in Oklahoma and Indian Territories. A piece from March 6, 1890, curtly commented, "There is an attempt by the negroes throughout the U.S. to make Oklahoma a negro state, occupied and governed by negro people. It seems a hard joke on the Oklahomaists to get the land from the Indians and then have the negroes take it away from them."[76] White settlers, or "Oklahomaists," were not only unwilling to entertain the notion of a Black state—they saw such organizing as a threat to their own visions for the region and reacted with hostility and violence.[77]

In his study of Black Oklahomans, Arthur Tolson includes a lengthy series of excerpts from local newspapers in the early 1900s that reveal explicit racial violence. One of the more extensive excerpts pulled from the *Oklahoma Guide*, the first recorded African American newspaper in Oklahoma Territory, describes a 1902 incident in Lawton, Oklahoma Territory:

> Senator Stevens wired Governor Ferguson tonight that the town of Lawton, Comanche County, was in the throes of a race war and asked the executive to have troops in readiness to be sent there. When the Kiowa country was opened to settlement a large colony of negroes were located there. . . . The feeling against the negroes has been tense for weeks. It culminated in several street fights between blacks and whites. Information which came to the governor from Lawton says the whites are in arms and threaten to drive every negro out of Lawton before sunrise, before Monday morning.[78]

The incident, as detailed here, bears a haunting resemblance to the 1921 Tulsa Massacre less than twenty years later. Here, we see the explicit anti-Black assumption that Black community-building posed a threat to whiteness. The residents faced double Removal, first from Southern states and then from Lawton, presumably due to structural anti-Black violence in both cases. As would be the case in Tulsa, white settlers would follow through on the threat of militarization. The rest of the twentieth century would show that very rarely did institutional power, be it under territorial or state government, actively protect the lives of Black Oklahomans.

McCabe and others felt that organizing towards structural support for Black residents in the territories was a necessity. Black towns provided one point of refuge and protection, which was why a sense of Black sovereignty in those communities was so essential. Once statehood seemed less feasible, McCabe's vision of Black separatism shifted to developing Black towns and a Black voice in territorial Republican politics. However, most Black towns were established in Democratic Indian Territory and not in Oklahoma (figure 4.6). Quite a few were initially established by Freedpeople who constructed collective spaces together after 1866 in order to pool resources and

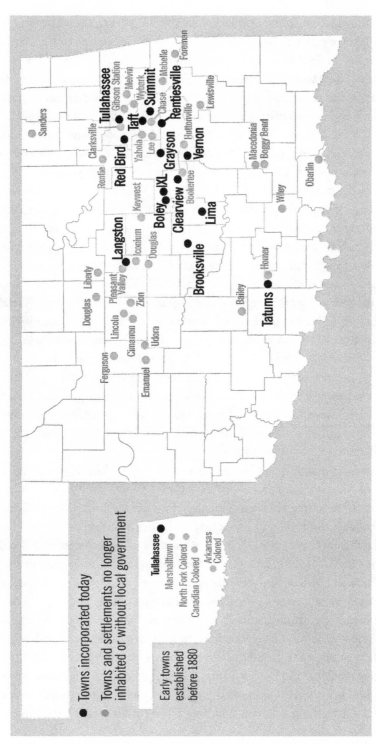

FIGURE 4.6 *All-Black Towns of Oklahoma*. Map. Created by the Oklahoma Historical Society.

protect one another from anti-Black violence.[79] However, the settlement of Indian Territory Black towns was also made possible because of the Dawes Commission's efforts to wrest large communal tracts of land from Native nations in an effort to weaken their political power in the region and to invite non-Native colonization.[80] Incentivized migration was another way to position Black and Native people against one another under a late nineteenth-century colonial regime invested in their sustained oppression. Land runs, settlement, and allotment amplified tensions between Native people, Afro-Native communities, Freedpeople, and African American settlers. In the case of the Muscogee (Creek) Nation, David Chang argues that allotment and a sense of impending statehood disrupted "the basis of nonracial Creek national political life." He writes, "Calls for black political organization in preparation for statehood suggest that the political ground had shifted under the strain of allotment politics. Some black Creeks were turning toward political action based on race rather than nation."[81] This was in no small way due to the redrawing of the territories along racial, not national, lines. Racial logics prioritized the individualized racial body over that of the sociopolitical collective. While lawmakers, U.S. government officials, and social reformers argued statehood was an effort to civilize Indians, much like allotment, it worked to break down Indigenous kinship structures and biologically taxonomize individuals via blood quantum. Critically, it also fueled racialized divisions that polarized Black and Native communities and recentered whiteness as a mediating force—greasing the wheels of white supremacist statehood.

A systemic practice of U.S. Indian policy that continually positioned people of African descent and non-Black Native people against one another fueled racial tensions. This was evidenced, for example, by the Dawes Commission's decision to list all Freedpeople's blood quantum as zero on the official tribal rolls, even though many of these same people were also listed as being "Indian by blood," asserting the false logic that one could not be both Black and Indian. The various operations of the Dawes Commission and federal Indian policy vigilantly worked to remap Indian Territory along legible race lines, rather than as a collective of Black and Native geopolitics.[82] Tribal governments were complicit in such racialization, as demonstrated by attempts to minimize Freedpeople's claims. One of the most damaging results of the Dawes Commission's rolls was the attempt to make Native identity something marked on the body and visible to an outside observer—something that could be "read." And it *was* read. Returning to the list of land sales published in the *Muskogee Phoenix*, one observes that a person's blood quantum is included in most records.[83]

While tracing lineage was also critical, many Dawes classifications, especially for Afro-Native people, were based on what commission employees "felt" was the person's race or blood quantum. These racial assessments were often informed by a person's physical appearance, and Blackness was almost always used to delegitimize a person's "authenticity" as Native. Therefore, how race operated in Indian Territory demonstrates a palimpsestic legacy of enslavement, colonization, and power that disrupts dialectic models of oppression and kinship that often relied on Black-white and Native-white binaries and did not account for a multiethnic, multinational, and multiracial Indian Territory reality; the categories of Freedperson, Afro-Native, and African American get collapsed while Indigeneity becomes identified as fractious via blood quantum.[84] These tensions were often staged as political party disputes, especially in the early years of the twentieth century, but went beyond dominant Democrat-Republican divisions. They were attached to ideologies of race, nation, and empire in straightforward ways that were particular to Oklahoma and Indian Territories, and these particularities played out in periodical coverage of both the State of Sequoyah movement and Oklahoma statehood. The gendered, animated renderings of Mr. Oklahoma and Miss Indian Territory, which I discuss in more detail shortly, obscured the influence of Black voters and all but erased Black placemaking in the territories. They positioned Indigeneity as something absorbable into white patriarchal structures. But, as evident from the rise of miscegenation laws in the United States *and* across Indian Territory, the same was not true of Blackness or the "buxom young" Boley, who is excluded from the animation of territorial subjectivity.[85]

Constituting a Sequoyah Printscape

While the proposed state was named for a beloved Cherokee innovator, the strongest advocate for Sequoyah and the first to lobby on behalf of the movement was principal chief of the Muscogee (Creek) Nation, Pleasant Porter. Porter was one of the most well-known Native leaders in fin de siècle Indian Territory. He came from an affluent plantation-owning family and was often referred to as "General," in reference to his service in the Confederate army during the Civil War.[86] Angie Debo argues Porter was "the greatest chief of the constitutional period," but he was also a controversial figure. Some critics, including Alex Posey and Charles Gibson, were concerned that his affluence made it impossible for him to advocate on behalf of all Creeks in the Nation and not just the upper crust.[87] Some saw him as too progressive and assimilationist, willing to compromise with the United States on matters of Creek affairs when he should refuse concession. Others viewed him as too unrelenting and stubborn in his policy negotiations. Nonetheless, Porter became the visible leader of both the State of Sequoyah movement and the Five Tribes' refusal to relinquish tribal governance.

In the years before 1905, Porter tried multiple times to organize an Indian Territory statehood convention. He saw statehood as inevitable and felt that the best way to maintain political influence and autonomy was for tribal leaders to organize for their own. While Porter's 1902 and 1903 statehood efforts fizzled, he had more success in 1905 after residents from both Oklahoma and Indian Territories held a single-statehood convention on July 12, 1905, in Oklahoma City, Oklahoma Territory. Convention attendees drafted proposals for joint statehood, also called single statehood, and planned to lobby for Oklahoma and Indian Territories to enter the United States as a unified state.[88] Fearing that joint statehood would further dilute tribal sovereignty, Porter and other tribal leaders drafted their own proposal for separate statehood.[89] It became clear to the Five Tribes' leaders that fighting the dissolution of tribal governance required them to work collectively and to gain support from non-Native people in Indian Territory.

Understanding why tribal leaders were opposed to joint statehood necessitates some familiarity with the acute cultural and political divisions between the two territories. Between 1890 and 1907, the population of Oklahoma Territory increased from 60,417 to 722,441, primarily white intruders who had little interest in upholding Indigenous ways.[90] Many of them came as part of the land runs or land rushes, dramatic spectacles of settler occupation in which non-Native people would rush to stake their claim to a plot of land.[91] The first run in 1889 helped establish Oklahoma Territory, and land runs became the iconic image of the state of Oklahoma.[92] Land openings in Oklahoma meant increased settler influence and decreased Native control in that territory, but Indian Territory was still politically and economically dominated by the Five Tribes. Unlike most other U.S. territories (including Oklahoma), Indian Territory was not organized under a territorial governance structure operated by the United States, and the Five Tribes held civic and political control of their respective nations. They wielded enormous power, sometimes to the detriment of other tribes, but they used their power to maintain Native control over the territory.

The political divide was as contentious a division as that between Native and non-Native territorial control; most Five Tribes members were Democrats, and if Indian Territory became a state, it would likely enter the United States as a Democratic one. The start of the twentieth century saw several congressional bills proposing statehood, and these, coupled with President Theodore Roosevelt's repeated endorsements for joint statehood, made clear that statehood of some form was all but ensured.[93] However, because the population of Oklahoma Territory was larger, joint statehood would result in a state with more Republican leanings.[94] This political party rift meant that there were external interests at play. With a Republican majority in Congress and a Republican president facing a reelection campaign, there was federal incentive for a joint statehood proposal that ensured Republicans' dominance in the next election.

The tensions between the two territories were consolidated in Mr. Oklahoma and Miss Indian Territory, a shorthand for these territorial differences. As Kerry Wynn explains in her discussion of the conceit, it not only depicted joint statehood as consensual but also implied that "the nationalizing and gendering of the wedding participants was necessary to achieve the simultaneous recognition and erasure of indigenous sovereignty, as it was necessary to communicate the power relationship that the organizers expected to see in the new state."[95] The trope invoked a racialized and gendered dialectic, that of the pioneering cowboy and the young Indian maiden, meant to reference histories of intermarriage between Native women and white men in the Five Tribes as a metaphor for political union. Beth Piatote (Niimiiipuu) terms such a move "entangled consent," to describe "the structure of settler-national laws that sought to transfer property and cultural rights from indigenous polities into the settler-national domestic under the rubric of consent and love."[96] The Mr.-Miss trope also gestured to the ongoing epidemic of white men swindling Native women and girls out of their allotments in both territories through coercion, sexual and physical violence, and sometimes murder.[97] In this anthropomorphism of territory, we see the animating work of statehood that, in this case, narrates place as person, harking back to the invocation of Osceola as a figurehead of the U.S.-Seminole wars and Florida. One of the most public celebrations of Oklahoma statehood was a performance of Mr. Oklahoma and Miss Indian Territory's wedding—the metaphorical becoming embodied in racialized and gendered terms.

Women's bodies were central to narratives of geopolitical control and consensual colonialism—a Native woman's place was in a heteronormative marriage, not in a self-sustaining Indian Territory. However, gendered distinctions between the two territories were deployed by the press to launch critiques and further the conceit. Cover illustrations for *Sturm's Statehood Magazine*'s September and October 1905 issues explicitly depict statehood tensions through Mr. Oklahoma and Miss Indian Territory illustrations. While the September issue shows an Uncle Sam figure consecrating their union, the October issue depicts a seemingly disinterested Miss Indian Territory dismissively glancing over her shoulder at Mr. Oklahoma while asking, "Do you think I want to be tied to that?" (figure 4.7). As the political power of the non-Native population increased in Oklahoma, interest in the territories' future grew. Would they "wed," or would they continue to function as two autonomous geopolitical bodies?

This gendering of Indian Territory as feminine perhaps helps to explain the choice to call the state Sequoyah. The iconic figurehead of Cherokee literacy, Sequoyah symbolizes Cherokee nationalism, adaptability via literacy, and the innovation to harness a vital tool of U.S. settler colonialist projects, written language, in the interest of Native survivance.[98] The name is a strategic political choice that aligns the State of Sequoyah with a particular notion of cultural advancement and textual production. It suggests a knowing sense of control over print media and the discourses it circulated—and a masculine representation of the territory. Sequoyah projects an image of Indian Territory that challenges feminine tropes of Miss Indian Territory and asserts a sense of patriarchal control. However, it obfuscates women's role in territorial print culture and politics, much like the erasure of Ayoka in dominant narratives of the syllabary's production. It foregrounds a story of singular male genius and makes evident that statehood is seen as a patriarchal affair. Even for a matrilineal tribe like the Cherokee Nation, a singular male figure like that of Sequoyah was seen as the most viable option for assimilation into the state.

On August 21, 1905, delegates representing twenty-six districts in the territory met at the Hinton Theatre in Muskogee to draft a constitution for the proposed State of Sequoyah. According to Cherokee historian Julie Reed, the delegates and alternates represented a racial, tribal, and linguistic diversity of Indigenous participants (albeit one entirely composed of men).[99] Representatives from all Five Tribes drafted the convention call in a meeting: General Pleasant Porter from the Muscogee (Creek) Nation, Chief W. C. Rogers from the Cherokee Nation, Governor Green McCurtain from the Choctaw Nation, Governor John Brown from the Seminole Nation, and William H. Murray, who stood in as representative for Governor Douglas Johnson from the Chickasaw Nation.[100]

FIGURE 4.7 Front cover, *Sturm's Statehood Magazine* (Tulsa), October 1905.

Based on the print record, the Sequoyah movement was initially met with some skepticism, despite widespread opposition to joint statehood with Oklahoma. For some, the question was not whether to advocate for Sequoyah but whether to advocate for statehood at all. Many, like the Cherokee lawyer, poet, and essayist Too-Qua-Stee, understood any form of statehood as a violation of the Five Tribes' Removal agreements.[101] For others, there was concern that the United States would never allow an Indian Territory state separate from Oklahoma. They saw lobbying for one as a wasted effort that could sour Oklahoma–Indian Territory affairs if and when Congress called for joint statehood. The *Indian Chieftain,* a newspaper published out of Vinita, Indian Territory, offered scathing opinion pieces criticizing Porter and other Sequoyah leaders.[102] Groups like the Cherokee Keetowah Society and the Snakes vehemently opposed allotment and any form of statehood.[103] Despite efforts by pro-joint-statehood newspapers to deter voters, the Sequoyah proposal received a majority of votes in the territory, although turnout was arguably modest.[104]

The State of Sequoyah map, drafted by delegates at the 1905 convention, is legible to colonial literacies but grounded in Indigenous spatialities (figure 4.8). It works on multiple registers as it simultaneously demonstrates technological advancement and more long-standing values of communalism. On the one hand, it "reads" along familiar county lines and borders like typical U.S. state maps. The land is gridded into squares of fairly similar shape and size and offers a sense of its proximity to other U.S. states and territories. On the other, the map reinforces tribal boundaries. The counties look like those on any other U.S. map, but many of them invoke specific tribal relationships, districts, and national boundaries through their names. The similarly sized county lines also reflect long-standing tribal borders, and these tribal holdings are reinforced through the county names. For example, Byrd County and McCurtain County are named for Chickasaw and Choctaw tribal leaders. Names also credit key leaders of U.S. Indian Affairs, such as Tams Bixby and Charles Curtis.[105] The map visually archives its own historical moment and the political processes driving the Sequoyah movement.

While the map includes the names of Black towns, it obscures a clear sense of Black people's and Freedpeople's spatialities, and as best I can tell, none of the counties are named for prominent Black leaders, although some were named for white officials. Furthermore, tribes like the Quapaw and Delaware (Lenape) are relegated to county names much as was done in the shift from Cherokee Nation to Cherokee County in 1830s Georgia, reflecting the politi-

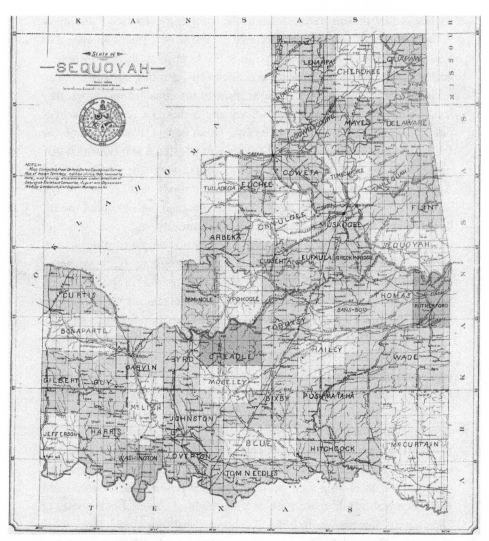

FIGURE 4.8 *Map of the Proposed State of Sequoyah, circa 1905* (ITMAP.0034, Oklahoma Historical Society Map Collection, Oklahoma Historical Society, www.okhistory.org /publications/enc/viewer?entry=SE021&id=260980#page/0/mode/1up).

cal disputes between the Delaware and the Cherokee. That being said, cartographically, the map registers tribal borders but also elicits a sense of cohesion across the Five Tribes, the Delaware, Eastern Shawnee, Miami, Modoc, Ottawa, Peoria, Quapaw, Seneca-Cayuga, and Wyandotte. If allotment was an attempt to atomize and taxonomize land to disrupt a sense of tribal cohesion intentionally, then the Sequoyah map operated as a way to preserve specific configurations of relationality.

The Sequoyah constitution is an equally complicated artifact. It outlined a voting policy that was quite progressive for the state, perhaps an appeal to President Roosevelt's Progressive politics. For example, it included women's voting rights along with those of all U.S. citizens, granting citizenship to an unusually large population.[106] Despite some of the constitution's progressivism, it was also unequivocally anti-Black and included a segregated school policy. Since the treaties of 1866, the Five Tribes had established schools for Freedpeople, but almost always, these were segregated institutions that garnered fewer resources and support than schools serving other Native youths. Again, schooling became a pressure point. Questions about what children learned, where they learned, and whom they learned with gestured toward broader ideological questions about race, community, and access. The Sequoyah constitution ensured that school segregation would continue in perpetuity. Segregationist language sent a clear message to Black territorial residents—anti-Black racism would be structurally codified in Sequoyah. The constitution's language made clear that Sequoyah organizers were willing to leverage the implicit anti-Blackness of U.S. state formation to their own ends.

Charles N. Haskell and William H. Murray later claimed credit for much of the constitution's language, and there was some frustration that they used coercive tactics to frame it to suit their political interests as Democratic segregationists. Unfortunately, the meeting minutes from the convention did not survive, so we can only speculate about much of the content of the discussion, including the map and constitution. While Murray and Haskell had ties to Native nations, they were affluent white men in the territory with personal interests in maintaining the status quo—namely, protecting their financial holdings and increasing their personal political power. Their involvement with Sequoyah would make both of them highly influential in the state of Oklahoma. They helped draft the Oklahoma constitution, and both served as governor (Haskell the first; Murray the ninth). Like their Dixiecrat counterparts, Haskell and Murray used their power as governors to structurally secure Jim Crow and segregation in Oklahoma.

African Americans, Freedpeople, and Afro-Native people were not unified on the issue of statehood in 1905, but the segregationist language of the Sequoyah constitution helped tip the scales. There was widespread distrust of the Democratic party politics backing the State of Sequoyah, as well as the explicit segregationist leanings of some key Native members, particularly Cherokee lawyer Robert L. Owen, who was a vocal proponent of segregated schools. Initially, most African American leaders were stalwart members of the Republican Party. They supported joint statehood in the hopes that Republican gains would mean more robust Black representation and resistance to segregationist policies, but as Black representatives became increasingly excluded from single-statehood conventions, concerns grew that statehood would not include Black Republicans in the policymaking.

The *Muskogee Cimeter* wrote of Owen and separate state supporters, "The double staters will never go on record as favoring universal suffrage. The democratic prohibition part of the outfit are strictly against the Negro as a voter. This was shown in Robt. L. Owen's address to the So. McAlester pow wow when he rang in the old Chestnut of mixed schools if we should have single statehood."[107] The Republican Party only held a slim majority in Oklahoma Territory and needed the Black vote in order to stand in more vigorous opposition to the State of Sequoyah separate statehood movement. However, as Black press coverage from 1905 makes clear, attempts to garner the Black vote from both parties were done halfheartedly, if not begrudgingly. Like Native citizens living in Indian Territory in 1905, Black residents understood that how they engaged in the statehood debates would materially affect their lives and the lives of future generations. Both single and separate staters made clear: race would play a central role in shaping the new polity.

The October 26, 1905, issue of the *Muskogee Cimeter* indicts the Sequoyah movement's hypocritical desire for Black support while including segregationist language in the proposed state constitution. The entire issue is representative of the complex space Black editors and community leaders found themselves in during this time period, in which they strategically maneuvered to determine whether aligning with the Sequoyah movement (mostly organized by Native leaders) or the single-statehood movement (mostly organized by white Republicans) would prove most beneficial for Black people in the territories.

The cartoon at the bottom of the front page depicts a white male figure and a racialized Black figure with a disproportionately large open mouth, with the words "Ring Master and His Slave" above them (figure 4.9). The image, along with its caption, scathingly critiques the alleged circus that is Sequoyah, especially the "double staters" (those who wanted separate statehood for Indian Territory) demanding Black support for the movement.[108] The Black figure's wide-open mouth echoes J. L. Magee's *Forcing Slavery down the Throat of a Freesoiler* (1856), discussed in chapter 3, but instead of depicting racial consumption via eating, the *Cimeter* image portrays a speech act. The Sequoyah movement, represented by a white male figure with a cane, demands that the "great black spell-binder," the figure he refers to as

The Muskogee Cimeter.

Vol 7   Muskogee, I.T., Thursday, October 26, 1905.   No 3

Climbing to Success.

Dear readers:

Through thrift, economy and perseverence we have established an independent job printing department that merits distinction among others.

Ten months ago when we announced to the public that type and material had been installed to do first-class work we had the least anticipation that before the close of the year this outfit would be so nearly paid for, but but the owner is congratulated by the results of his assiduous attention to business, assisted by EFFICIENT business manager, Mr. E. D. Nickens.

There have been times when prospects were gloomy and it seemed that failure was certain, obstacles were strewn along the path of success from divers sources; but we kept sawing wood, faithfully filling our promises, striving to please our customers with SUPERIOR work and using the BEST material regardless to cost.

The literature printed for the Rising Sun Insurance Company, the offices of Secretary of O. B. A. and Grand Master of Odd Fellows, and the office of Grand K. of R. and S., K. of P's serve as fitting models of the class of work we do; these gentlemen are ever proud to exhibit to those who are ready to place an order for printing and are anxious to know who can do it best.

It is as essential that your stationery have a neat appearance as it is that your office and personal appearance. We do your printing with a guarantee of satisfaction.

To those of you who are trying to do business without patronizing the printer, we say, you are making a vast mistake and in the city of Muskogee where competiton is so great you can not keep pace with your competitors; therefore, we advise you to let us assist you. Deeming we have said enough and made sufficient references to engage your attention

We are yours.
Cimeter Job Printing Departm't
F. QUALLS, Proprietor

"Indian" Thomas of Muskogee, does not deserve the support of a single Indian Territory republican. When Mr. Thomas lived "down in Egypt," state of Illinois, he was a rock-ribbed democrat, and at heart is still a democrat, at least the company he is keeping so indic't s. He is so new to republicanism that he does not appreciate the fact that the names of republican candidates are placed on republican tickets thrugh the action of legally constituted conventions, in which republicans preside and participate. In a political sense there was not a respectable republican in Muskogee's no-state convention Mr. Thomas finds himself out of joint and out of harmony with the republican organization,and not only that, he is in direct opposition to the expressed wishes and hopes of President Roosevelt in reference to the state local situation.—Vinita Republican.

Press Notes
And Comments.

The session of American Bankers' association which was was held in this city during the past three days, came to a close on Friday evening, Oct. 13, with a brilliant banquet at the New Williard Hotel. It is the opinioe of these financiers that this session was one of the most successful in the history of the association. One of the pleasant features sf this convention, as concerns the colored people, is the membership of John Mitchell, Jr., who is president of a creditable and very successful banking institution in Richmond, Virginia. Mr. Mitchell participated in all the functions, social and otherwise, enjoyed by the members of the association wile in the capital city.—Topeka Plaindealer.

RING MASTER AND HIS SLAVE.

Speak slave lest I smite you

Humph

The great black spell-binder is here represented at a meeting of the double staters where the colored contingent are supposed to deliver the goods. The luricating oil and the oil of joy having run low it has become necessary for the ring master to resort to extreme measures, and at this stage of the game the lash is resorted to. The kink-bee was called up and told to orate, which he is doing to the best of his ability. The noise and soupderation was there, dud in thick gutteral tones the spell-binder is saying:

"Cum up of thuse fur de greatest depopulation un de comperssation un de finite composerbility ob de dubble state, doan you see, huh?"

The declaration of Independence made by Senator Rayner cannot be read without a thrill of pride that the high official life of the nation include some men capable of such a challenge as this Maryland Senator delivered to his colleague:

You have declared in your convention and through your committee that any man who will not sell his birthright and support this amendment shall be driven, like an outcast and a pariah, from the democratic ranks. I accept this challenge, and to show you how little a threat and menace of this sort affects men who cannot be scourged like quarry slaves to their dungeons, let me also now declare that if there is to be any political emulation in Maryland you report to your master of ceremonies that if by sacrificing myself I can save the people of this state from bondage and captivity which it is proposed to impose upon them, then I shall cheerfully submit myself as an offering for this purpose, and I shall proceed to the place of torment with a spirit of exultation and with a smile of triumph.

In itself this declaration has a touch of grandiloquence, but the subject justifies the fervo.-Kansas City Star.

Bishop Turner's Reply to Mayor of Carrollton, Mo.

Bishop Turner reponded to the gentleman in a few sarcastic remarks, which seemed to have wings of flame attached, for this man cringed rs the lash of the tongue fell. Bishop Turner said he was surpised to find a presiding officer of a city so ignorant of the Negroe's progress in this country, and said that the Negro was not seeking social equality with the white race, and called the attention of the congregation by saying: "If there are any here seeking social equality with the whites let them stand up." None arose

(Continued on last page)

FIGURE 4.9 Front page, *Muskogee Cimeter*, October 26, 1905.

"slave," speak. The caption below the image translates what the Black figure says, from gibberish to dialect meant to endorse separate statehood.

The depiction's invocation of minstrelsy tropes unequivocally castigates the explicit anti-Blackness of the Sequoyah constitution and the ongoing statehood debates. One can also read it as accusing Black supporters of Sequoyah of simply working at the bidding of white (and Native) people. The fourth page of the paper reinforces the front-page cartoon in multiple brief editorials where William Henry Twine, the paper's editor, makes his views more explicit. One of these reads, "The Negro contingent of the Sequoyah outfit have about given up the fight, the oil of joy as well as the lubricating fluid has been exhausted and the fellows refused to enthuse."[109] In another, Twine suggests that the Sequoyah movement, depicted by the white male "Ring Master" figure in the front-page cartoon, is simply the scheme of a few wealthy white businessmen manipulating Native leaders.[110]

The description of the Black figure as a "spell-binder," an accomplished orator, leads us to believe that the spell-binder has been forced to perform a caricature of himself in speech for the audience, and his actual skills and accomplishments are not only unwanted but punishable (the whip). The cartoon's text and image invoke legacies of anti-Black racism, enslavement, and minstrelsy and do so in the pages of a Black-run paper that is an embodiment of Black print expression, suggesting the naïve hubris of requesting Black support for the movement. In stark contrast to the cartoon sits F. Qualls's likeness, printed at the top of the front page. Qualls is the paper's printer, and his image looms large over the text and the cartoon that sit below him. His letter, written in direct address to readers, suggests they send print jobs to the *Cimeter* office and boasts about his expertise and talent. The inclusion of his photograph speaks both to the skills of Qualls and the print office and to the financial stability of paper (again, printing photographs was not necessarily easy or cheap). But as importantly, it asserts Black belonging in Indian Territory. Including his likeness provides specificity, "a face," to Black Muskogee. In the photograph he does not look directly at the reader but just past us, with body language that exudes a sense of confidence and self-assuredness. The entirety of the rest of the newspaper—it is a large document at eight pages (the average territorial newspaper was four)—serves to discredit any notion that Black voters are simply pawns. Whether it is true or not, the paper performs a cohesiveness of Black community. As a Black *sovereign printscape*, it celebrates Black life in ways that often explicitly reject white supremacist discourse.[111]

The front-page cartoon, Twine's consistent critiques of the Sequoyah campaign's anti-Blackness, and sustained efforts by Black leaders to advocate for the Black community in all statehood campaigns evidence the strained relations between Black and Native people in Indian Territory that had been fomenting long before the start of the twentieth century. Black leaders like Twine were unwilling to witness the ways anti-Blackness was shaping statehood proposals passively. The formatting of Twine's paper and the ways in which each issue collectively works to craft a singular narrative of Black belonging, including by dexterously speaking to multiple readers (Black residents, Black readers in the United States, and non-Black readers), echo the conventions of Indian Territory print that had developed from tribal papers throughout the nineteenth century, as well as a long history of Black print culture in the United States, but in distinctly Black territorial terms. Unlike the *Boley Progress*, which operated in a Black town, the *Cimeter* was printed in Muskogee (Creek Nation), the urban nexus of Indian Territory and home base to the Dawes Commission and State of Sequoyah organizing. One can imagine how the circulation of the paper's Sequoyah commentary, through its cartoon and editorials, inflected the ongoing statehood debates as the paper materially circulated on the streets of Muskogee and elsewhere. By placing these critiques in the sovereign printscape of a Black paper, the *Cimeter* insists on Black belonging on Black terms (in this case, the printed page) in Indian Territory.

After Sequoyah

In the end, the Sequoyah movement did not succeed in creating an Indian Territory state. To little response, the memorial, constitution, and voting results were presented to President Theodore Roosevelt and Congress in December 1905 and January 1906. In the same congressional session that established the Enabling Act (also known as the Hamilton Bill), authorizing Oklahoma statehood, Congress also passed the Five Tribes Act, which ended the official tribal enrollment proceedings of the Dawes Commission, took school control away from the tribes, and established greater U.S. oversight of tribal leaders and tribal affairs.[112] Within the two years following the movement, the federal government "declared the nations non-existent" in violation of its own laws and the state of Oklahoma was formed in 1907. However, it is imperative that we remember the territory was never legally ceded by Native tribes in Indian Territory, and those reservation borders (borders demarcated in the 1866 treaties) were reacknowledged by the federal government and the State of Oklahoma in 2020.[113]

Turn-of-the-century Indian Territory print culture and the State of Sequoyah movement fracture the dominant notion that allotment cast such a large shadow over the era that Native communities had little recourse. While allotment policy left an unquestionably devastating legacy, it was met with multifaceted resistance that was often worked out materially and typographically on the printed page. Moreover, the often understudied print culture of Black towns and communities reveals an era, albeit brief, in which Black editors and politicians collectively grappled with the idea that Black land-based sovereignty might be possible within (or without) the United States. The State of Sequoyah and the Black statehood movements confirmed very clearly the incommensurability between statehood and Indigenous and Black freedom. None of the campaigns could have achieved fruition because statehood is predicated on the endurance of state violence against and control of Black and Native people. Moreover, it should come as little surprise that the formalization of Jim Crow policies and the drastic erosion of Native self-governance were two of the very first steps in initiating Oklahoma as a state. While Black and Native communities would challenge the new state government's racist investments, they would also endure great material, cultural, bodily, and psychic losses.

One of the most vocal critiques of the United States during the last three decades of the nineteenth century was Too-Qua-Stee, whose "Sequoyah" poem I discussed earlier in the chapter. While humorous at times, Too-Qua-Stee's poetry and political essays explicitly and aggressively critiqued U.S. imperialism and the erosion of Native control over Indian Territory. He was a lawyer and educator for the Cherokee Nation by trade, but he regularly wrote editorial pieces and poetry, which he published in territorial newspapers.[114] His writings are both tribally and territorially specific in their intended audience, but the scale at which he writes about land and power struggles is more expansive. He compares U.S. interventions in China to attempts to eat up the "delicious morsel" of the "Cherokee republic" in his 1900 piece "IMPERIALISM: Abandonment of the Monroe Doctrine," while also explicitly linking enslavement, anti-Blackness, sexism, and treaty erosion to the same U.S. imperialist machine.[115] Too-Qua-Stee sees multiscaled connections in the stretch of U.S. influence, understanding that what happens in the territories is linked to U.S. interests overseas. While his writings were committed to upholding self-governance for the Cherokee people and other

Native nations in the territories, he also understood that what Native people experienced was directly linked to a much more expansive network of power, capital, and peoples.

Too-Qua-Stee wrote few pieces about the 1905 statehood discussions. By then, he was in his seventies and nearing the end of his life. However, in the few writings where he does discuss statehood, he halfheartedly advocates separate statehood for Indian Territory as the best option for maintaining Native political strength in the region. Too-Qua-Stee had radical views on U.S.-Cherokee relations and denounced anything that seemed to him a concession—statehood unquestionably was. In the poem "Indian Territory at World's Fair," he mentions what he feels will be the future of Indian Territory if statehood proves inevitable.[116] At the 1904 Saint Louis World's Fair, Indian Territory was given a building separate from Oklahoma Territory's, physically manifesting their distinction from each other. The title of Too-Qua-Stee's poem plays on "world's" as a contraction—the world is fair—in addition to referencing this particular event. The poem acerbically depicts Indian Territory as a grieving mother who must put on a good face and show her assets and skills to the world. While she has lost her firstborns, she must pull herself together for her living children. The last stanza of the poem imagines the futurity of Indian Territory statehood and the loss of its own firstborns—its Native inhabitants:[117]

> Ah! grandest glories wait upon thy torch,
> When thou becom'st a state, or something such,
> ('Thout Oklahoma's parasitic clutch,)
>   Thou'lt dwelt sublime in an unwonted sphere;
> Installed a member of that mighty group,
> The banner of thy pride may never droop.
> Say, mother, wilt thou then disdain to stoop.
>   And give thy buried race a tear?[118]

The poem does not advocate statehood with Oklahoma and its "parasitic clutch." However, the speaker asks whether separate statehood would, in fact, be enough to maintain Native self-determination. While there might be some pride in becoming a state and being "installed a member of that mighty group," the line sarcastically hints that such an honor may not benefit its Native inhabitants. This speculative poem looks to a statehood future with great pessimism and concern; Too-Qua-Stee saw a bleak future if things continued on their current trajectory.

In the poem, Too-Qua-Stee invokes the feminization of Indian Territory that the State of Sequoyah movement renounced. His invocation of a matriarchal figure mourning the loss of her deceased children stands in contrast to the young, virginal Miss Indian Territory. The mother in his poem invokes images of Selu, corn mother of all Cherokee people, who sacrificed herself so that the people might live, rather than Sequoyah. She invokes the matriliny of Cherokee communities that predated contact, reminding us of women's power and the necessity of sacrifice for future generations. Too-Qua-Stee's depiction of Indian Territory as a mourning mother who experiences great loss with statehood serves as a counter to the State of Sequoyah. He hauntingly foreshadows the outcome of statehood and reminds his readers, at least Cherokee readers, of the importance of thinking in terms of community that are Cherokee specific and not dictated by the state.

The State of Sequoyah movement marked a critical moment in Indian Territory, but it has faded out of dominant narratives of the era. In some respects, this is not surprising since the movement was unable to achieve fruition, but it nonetheless has important lessons to teach. For one, Sequoyah demonstrates the incommensurability between state power and Indigenous sovereignty. It is not a particularly revolutionary or dramatic example of Indigenous resistance to settler colonialism, and Stacy L. Leeds (Cherokee Nation) has argued that Native nations would actually have had less autonomy under the Sequoyah constitution than they did under the 1907 Oklahoma one.[119] Concomitantly, it tactically positioned Indigenous authority in opposition to Blackness—explicitly at the expense of Black inclusion—in ways that strengthened white politicians and their anti-Indigenous and anti-Black policies. While Sequoyah does not offer an altruistic moment in which aesthetics, print, and politics cohered in one ideal, it does serve as an invaluable case study of states' rights and statehood. At the turn of the twentieth century, Black and Native communities got as close as they ever would to achieving statehood. However, the failures of those efforts are lessons in the inability of statehood to contain Indigenous and Black freedom and the necessity of Black and Native collectivity for imagining alternative spaces in other ways.

One finds in Indian Territory at the start of the twentieth century a crystallization of violent conflicts that both marred and defined nineteenth-century America, most palpably enslavement, Indigenous dispossession, extractive capitalism, and U.S. expansion. The new state's first legislative act was to legalize segregation, firmly situating Oklahoma along the color line with its new state borders.[120] The confluence of these inherently violent imperial projects in fin de siècle statehood debates demonstrates how painfully intertwined and coconstitutive they were—and that such histories of oppression very clearly continued to inform how different racial and ethnic groups interacted with one another and what they imagined for a shared future. It is only when we attempt to keep all of these struggles in play that the stakes of statehood become palpable. The exigent pressure for statehood opened up a new geopolitical scale on which to negotiate struggles for recognition. However, statehood is inherently incommensurate with Indigenous and Black life because it depends on their abjection, and thus Oklahoma made shared freedom for Indigenous and Black people impossible. While the statehood campaigns reveal the anti-Black and anti-Native logics of state formation that often position Blackness and Indigeneity in competition, the use of print circulation and production established strong communication networks that continued to nourish rich literary communities of Black and Native writers. By turning to the robust print trails left by Black and Native people who grappled with statehood at this time, not only can we better understand their challenges, but we can better refuse the interpellation of the state and continue to collectively seek community through other means.

Conclusion
Unmaking the State

Two of the most successful cable TV shows in 2019, *Live PD* and *Watchmen*, centered on Tulsa. While *Watchman* depicts a techno-futuristic world grappling with the United States' violent white supremacist legacy, the A&E reality show *Live PD* follows police officers as they patrol a handful of cities, including Tulsa, making arrests in "real time."[1] At first glance, the two shows seem to share little in common besides location—they tell very different stories about race, policing, and U.S. history—however, both contribute to the development of Tulsa as a cultural flashpoint entering the third decade of the twenty-first century, and they foreground policing as a way to tame the chaotic geopolitical histories Tulsa conjures forth.

In 2020, as *Watchmen* won eleven Emmy Awards, *Live PD* went on hiatus amid Black Lives Matter uprisings. The City of Tulsa decided to part ways with *Live PD* after repeated accusations of Tulsa police violence and criticism that the show encouraged overpolicing; the show was becoming bad PR.[2] As the city neared the hundred-year anniversary of the Tulsa Race Massacre, community activists also demanded the city finally address the massacre and its legacy in meaningful ways. Local unrest grew tenser when the Republican Party decided to hold its national convention in Tulsa around Juneteenth that summer, a calculated afront to anti-racist organizing in the city. A place that rarely receives much attention had suddenly become a synecdoche for broader national introspection.[3]

To complicate matters further, a few weeks later, in July 2020, the U.S. Supreme Court ruling in *McGirt v. Oklahoma* affirmed the Muscogee Nation's reservation boundaries and found that the United States had an obligation to uphold its treaties with Native nations. The ruling made it one of the most significant court cases for Indian Country in decades. This meant that the State of Oklahoma must recognize most of so-called eastern Oklahoma as Indian Territory, including Tulsa. The ruling affirmed what leaders of Indian Territory knew in the years leading up to 1907, that the federal government never abolished their reservations even under its own legal protocols.

I end this book by grappling with this maelstrom of events and how Tulsa's cultural moment might encourage us to think collectively about speculative futures beyond the state. There is something inherently contradictory about the current fascination with Tulsa. One reason the city became a cultural flashpoint at a moment of national crisis is that its legacy simultaneously shorthands anti-Black violence, Indigenous dispossession, and environmental extraction (*McGirt* raises questions about oil and natural resource rights), as well as Indigenous self-determination and Black economic affluence. At the same time, the histories it attempts to cohere are too messy to be cleanly sutured together. This mess is necessary, which is why I decided not to streamline the political and cultural events of 2019–20 I just narrated. The affective confusion brought forward by Black and Native dissent provides a necessary discomfort to state-centric storytelling. Seemingly inchoate, these events are intrinsically knotted together. By putting these television shows in conversation with the *McGirt* decision, we see how cultural narratives and legal discourses of the twenty-first century weaponize law enforcement to affirm states' rights and to criminalize Black and Indigenous freedom, almost always by imagining Blackness and Indigeneity separately from each other.

The *McGirt* decision has stirred up paranoia about white and non-Indigenous belonging in what was eastern Oklahoma and, as this book goes to press, tribal nations are grappling with the U.S. Supreme Court's ruling in *Oklahoma v. Castro-Huerta* (2022), a follow-up case to *McGirt* and to the 2019–20 moment I just detailed. In June 2022, the majority of the court ruled in favor of the aggressive attacks launched by Governor Kevin Stitt, Oklahoma politicians, the oil and natural gas industry, and other private industries against *McGirt*. In *Castro-Huerta*, the court ruled that states have the right to prosecute in certain cases where non-Native people commit crimes against Native people, defying centuries of precedent, including the court's determination in *Worcester v. Georgia* (1832), that states do not have authority over tribal nations. The majority opinion, written by Justice Brett Kavanaugh, states, "this Court has long held that Indian country is part of a State and not separate from it."[4] As I have painstakingly shown throughout *Reading Territory*, this is not the case. In his scathing critique of the majority opinion, Justice Neil Gorsuch reiterates as much: "After the Cherokee's exile to what became Oklahoma, the federal government promised the Tribe that it would remain forever free from interference by state authorities. Only the Tribe or the federal government could punish crimes by or against tribal members on tribal lands. At various points in its history, Oklahoma has chafed at this limitation.... Where our predecessors refused to participate in one State's unlawful power grab at the expense of the Cherokee, today's Court accedes to another's."[5]

The Court delivered their *Castro-Huerta* decision near the completion of this book, and the impact it will have on Native people and Native nations is still unclear. It is highly unlikely *Castro-Huerta* will be the last case this Supreme Court hears that is intended to erode Native sovereignty.[6] The erosion of Native sovereignty has become a key interest for politicians, lawyers, and businessmen on the far right. Throughout this book I have aimed to provide historical context to help us understand how and why these contestations between states and tribal nations continue, so we can better challenge the legacies of violence they uphold, but here I want to reflect on how we might do so in real time. Therefore, I am less interested in thinking about how the *Castro-Huerta* decision *contracts* recognized Indigenous sovereignty and more interested in thinking about how *McGirt* potentially *expands* relational possibilities.

What is telling in both *McGirt* and *Castro* is the emphasis on policing and public safety. The argument made by Stitt and other opponents to *McGirt* has been that Native nations are not equipped to enact robust law enforcement at the scale necessary for their reservation boundaries. In response, Native nations have had to prove they are capable of maintaining law and order. This puts Native nations in a complicated position in which recognition of sovereignty is aligned with participation in the carceral state. Emphasis on policing and surveillance of Indigeneity stands to reaffirm the existing contours of criminalization and belonging already at play, in which Blackness and Indigeneity are invariably crimes against the white supremacy of Oklahoma statehood. Emphasizing that *McGirt* exclusively affects Native people on Native land is telling and clarifies the centrality of policing and the criminal justice system to maintaining settler colonialism. Since the nineteenth century, Indian Territory (including the Muscogee Nation) has been cast as lawless and settler encroachment rationalized as necessary for creating order.

As a result of *McGirt*, the State of Oklahoma had to cede its jurisdiction over cases involving Native people to the tribes and the federal government. A year earlier, the court heard a very similar case, *Carpenter v. Murphy*. However, the court was deadlocked in that decision. Justice Neil Gorsuch was recused from voting because he ruled on the case at the Tenth Circuit.[7] Two-Spirit Cherokee journalist Rebecca Nagle's podcast *This Land* (2019) garnered a fair amount of publicity for raising awareness about the stakes of reaffirming the Muscogee Nation (and the Five Tribes) reservation boundaries, in part by contextualizing it in the history of Indian Territory. While *This Land* and other coverage of both *McGirt* and *Murphy* delve deeply into the cases' significance for Indigenous sovereignty, Blackness and Indian Territory's legacies of enslavement play a vital role as well.[8]

The erosion of state borders rarely occurs in a concrete, material sense in the continental forty-eight. The solidity of state boundaries is a cornerstone of U.S. settler colonialism that anchors the continued occupation of Indigenous lands but also justifies paracolonial and imperial interests outside official U.S. territories—military bases and other forms of U.S. occupation are often seen as temporary or contingent in contrast to states like Oklahoma, despite the fact that there are military and territorial occupations currently longer standing than some statehoods. If states' rights and state identity are central to settler colonialism and what Saidiya Hartman terms the "afterlife of slavery," then the erosion of state maps opens up a potential for radical decolonial spatialities.[9]

As I have argued throughout *Reading Territory*, both anti-Blackness and anti-Indigeneity are central to the logic of states' rights in the United States, and it is on this point that Black and Native solidarity has great untapped potentiality. The state of Oklahoma was forged out of anti-Black and anti-Indigenous policy—both are knitted into the very fabric of the state's foundational documents. However, if tribal nations affected by *McGirt*, especially the Five Tribes, do not account for the legacy of anti-Blackness essential to the treaties of 1866, allotment, and tribal citizenship, then the tribes' ability to make life more livable for Native people as we continue to work toward decolonial freedom is limited; one freedom is not possible without the other.

Black and Indigenous people are the most killed and most incarcerated people in the United States, not including the number of African-descended and Indigenous migrants detained at the southern U.S. border.[10] Furthermore, Oklahoma is repeatedly a world leader in incarceration, especially of women, and it incarcerates more people per capita than any other state and more than any democracy on earth.[11] Incarceration itself is another form of violent Removal from the liberal public sphere, and Oklahoma's own unlawful existence is continually justified through criminalization of tribal sovereignty, as well as the relentless entrenchment of anti-Blackness. Therefore, it should come as little surprise that in a moment when the federated state must concede some of its power to Indigenous nations, law enforcement becomes the genre through which Native nations can assert their sovereignty.

Lawyers, including Sarah Deer (Muscogee Nation), argue that that greater tribal jurisdiction enables Native nations to do more to protect women and prosecute violence against them and finally address the continuing crisis of missing and murdered Indigenous women across Turtle Island, including in Indian Territory.[12] Based on jurisdictional slippages and perceptions of Indigenous women as either disposable or invisible, most violent crimes against Indigenous women are never prosecuted. Deer's contention stands in contrast to Governor Stitt's unrelenting argument that *McGirt* makes Oklahoma less safe. Mired in these debates is the misogynistic formulation of Native (and Black) women as threats to the state's security. They exist outside the imagined liberal subject of the patriarchal white state unworthy of safety. The tension between state safety and the safety of Native women is pronounced. While Miss Indian Territory was someone to be protected through statehood, actual Native and Black women in the territory seem less so.

All-Black Towns Are Indian Territory

Oklahoma statehood forcibly brought together Indian and Oklahoma Territories as an explicit effort to erode tribal authority in the region. As I have argued throughout *Reading Territory*, states' rights have historically been used to authorize disenfranchisement and violence against Black and Indigenous people but have also staged an oppositional relationship between them. This oppositionality not only obscures Afro-Indigeneity in all forms but also imagines Black and Indigenous rights as in conflict in an effort to obscure the reality that the liberal notion of rights is dependent on Black and Indigenous exclusion in the first place. Such oppositionality is a form of Removal. To push back, it is critical to understand the *Murphy*, *McGirt*, and *Castro-Huerta* cases as part of an interwoven landscape sculpted both by the violent, colonial state of Oklahoma and by Indigenous and Black people's refusal of it.[13] For this reason, it is especially important to include the *Murphy* case in my discussion, because the *Murphy* case illuminates some of these connections.

Patrick Murphy, his girlfriend Patsy Jacobs, and the man Murphy murdered, George Jacobs, were all residents of Vernon. Murphy is a Muscogee citizen, and the murder occurred within the boundaries of the Muscogee Nation but included in the Nation are the town of Vernon and the legacies of Black town sovereignty it conjures forth. In the *Murphy* case, the Muscogee Nation's council argued that because Vernon falls within the Nation's reservation boundaries and because both Murphy and Jacobs were Native, the State of Oklahoma had no jurisdiction over the case. To my knowledge, there was little discussion of Vernon, specifically, even though Vernon is one of the few Black towns still in existence (see figure 4.6).[14] The murder occurred in the countryside near a rural road, but Patrick Murphy, Patsy Jacobs, and George

Jacobs all called Vernon home. Vernon was not established until 1911, years after Oklahoma statehood, and thus not one of the "All-Black towns" I describe in chapter 4. However, it is part of a genealogy of Black civic life and communalism that has deep roots in Indian Territory, albeit complicated ones, that were often aided by the federal government's theft of Native land and attacks on tribal sovereignty. Moreover, according to the Muscogee Nation's legal team, it is understood as part of the Nation and part of Indian Territory.

It is critical to hold on to these details from the *Murphy* case because they bring forward Afro-Native legacies that must be accounted for if we are committed to understanding the intimacies of Black and Native life in Indian Territory. The same treaties of 1866 discussed in chapter 4 played a critical role in the *Murphy* case because the reservation borders the lawyers were asking the court to uphold were the same boundaries demarcated in the Muscogee Nation's Reconstruction Treaty of 1866. Again, this was the same treaty that demanded the Nation abolish slavery and provide the formerly enslaved with reparations and full tribal citizenship. The map that takes hold post-*McGirt* is one shaped by enslavement, civil war, and Black sovereignty. Therefore, I want to reiterate the limits of *McGirt*'s emphasis on law enforcement and territorial alterities and urge us to think in nonlegal, abolitionist ways that learn from the lessons of the nineteenth century and might instead open a shared space of Indigenous and Black freedom in Indian Territory. I want to be very clear that I am not suggesting that Native nations should not take the opportunities made possible by *McGirt* to expand their ability to care for their people. Rather, I urge us to continue to think carefully about why law enforcement is central to *McGirt*. *McGirt* is a necessary and strategic tactic—an unquestionable win for Native nations—but it is not a decolonizing solution.

The tension between Indigenous dispossession, Indigenous complicity in enslavement and anti-Blackness, and Black homesteading on Indigenous lands shapes the Oklahoma terrain politically, culturally, and affectively. If states' rights and state identity are central to the genocidal project of settler colonialism and enslavement, what Tiffany Lethabo King terms "conquest," then the erosion of state maps opens up a potential for radical decolonial spatialities and different modes of citizenship and belonging.[15] However, such a project is only possible if Black freedom is an essential component of the Five Tribes' territorial claims. Following the *McGirt* ruling, Freedpeople's descendants and their advocates have expressed the necessity of bringing the Black Lives Matter movement to Indian Territory, arguing that Freedpeople and Afro-Native people must be included in housing and other subsidized federal funding for Native nations (including additional funds allocated by the federal government during the COVID-19 pandemic). To think about Indigenous and Black freedom on the same plane continues to prove challenging, in no small part because of the extreme threat to white settler possession that such a project poses. Derrick Spires argues that citizenship is "not a thing determined by who one is but rather by what one does."[16] If so, then how the Five Tribes decide to take up *McGirt* is as culturally and ideologically imperative as the rights it arguably reinstates, even though all of this is mitigated in the realm of policing and law enforcement, which has been a means of containing and controlling—that is, Removing—Black and Native peoples.

The post-*McGirt* moment opens up an opportunity to affirm the intimacies of Black and Native history and life in Indian Territory. As of the writing of this book, Freedpeople only have full citizenship rights in one of the Five Tribes, Cherokee Nation. At an online event honoring Cherokee Freedpeoples' history in early 2022, Principal Chief Chuck Hoskin Jr. insisted that honoring treaties means honoring the treaties the tribes made with Freedpeople in 1866. If these treaties were recognized and all Freedpeople were granted full citizenship, then, as I understand *McGirt*, they would also fall under tribal jurisdiction.[17] This does not mean that people who self-identify as or are read as Black will receive better treatment under federal and tribal jurisdiction than they currently do from the state, but full citizenship rights would enable Freedpeople to have far greater influence over official tribal affairs and policies. I acknowledge that in a book that is critical of the state, there is some irony to my insistence on the power of national inclusion. As J. Kēhaulani Kauanui demonstrates, juridical models of sovereignty can never be the end goal for decolonization because those models are "inextricably linked to the ongoing pulverization of Indigenous worldviews and lifeways."[18] However, statist sovereignty (in this case the nation) also serves as an influential tactic for combating unrelenting settler colonial attacks on Indigeneity because of its legibility under international law, albeit one that must always be understood as a provisional strategy and not an end goal. Inclusion on its own does not ensure healing of the wounds of centuries of trauma, but it does recognize the long history of the state-as-Removal, by affirming the interconnectedness of Black and Native life and honoring the commitments made between Black and Native people in Indian Territory. Full citizenship is a critical way to shift the ground toward Black and Native territorialities and away from the white supremacist state. As I have argued throughout *Reading Territory*, these affinities pose the greatest threat to the colonial state, which perhaps helps explain why in *McGirt, Live PD,* and *Watchmen,* we see allusion to an enduring preoccupation with policing Indian Territory.

Watchmen's Telescape

For many, *Watchmen* cohered the popularity of the comic book superhero with the Black Lives Matter movement and calls to defund police. The HBO miniseries won critical acclaim for its sharp critique of the ways anti-Blackness is woven into the fabric of US political, social, and cultural life. It also raised broader awareness of the Tulsa Race Massacre. The Tulsa Massacre of 1921, arguably the most violent act of white terrorism in twentieth-century America, occurred less than a decade and a half after Oklahoma statehood was forced on Indian Territory residents. Starting on May 31, 1921, white assailants staged an assault on Greenwood, the city's thriving Black community, in one of the most violent incidents of civil unrest in U.S. history. After the massacre, there was a systematic attempt to erase all traces of its occurrence, and the City of Tulsa, the State of Oklahoma, and the federal government did almost nothing to address the travesty until the late twentieth century, in no small part due to local and state government officials' complicity in the incident.

What is not contextualized in the history that *Watchmen* compellingly narrates, however, is that Tulsa is and was part of the Muscogee and Cherokee Nations. Most accounts of the Tulsa Massacre depict it as white-on-Black violence in a biracial city, failing to recognize Tulsa's origins as a Muscogee town stolen from the Muscogee Nation by the State of Oklahoma. As vitally, it also omits Greenwood's origins as a Cherokee Freedpeople community made possible by the treaties of 1866. This essential fact about Greenwood reminds us of its consequential origins and its important place in Indian Territory. The common historical account also fails to acknowledge that booms in Tulsa's oil industry not only produced racial tensions between Black and white people but also fueled the large-scale exploitation of Native communities across the region, including the "Osage murders" and systemic physical and sexual violence against Black and Native women and children. The machinations of settler statecraft continue to systematically obfuscate the interconnections between anti-Black racism and anti-Indigenous violence and corruption in Oklahoma. Native people, and Indian Territory, are all but absent in *Watchmen*; the absence of Indigeneity on the show is even more glaring, given Tulsa's substantial Native film community.[19]

On the other hand, *Live PD* routinely depicts Tulsa police officers arresting Native residents, who code as Native through surname, clothing, neighborhood, self-identification, or phenotype for those familiar with Indian Country. *Live PD* evidences what Heidi Kiiwetinepinesiik Stark (Turtle Mountain Ojibwe) terms "Indigenous criminality," meaning "the imposition of colonial law, facilitated by casting Indigenous men and women as savage peoples in need of civilization and composing Indigenous lands as lawless spaces absent legal order, made it possible for the United States and Canada to shift and expand the boundaries of both settler law and the nation itself by judicially proclaiming their own criminal behaviors as lawful."[20] Every time we witness police encounters with Native Tulsans on the show, it reaffirms the state of Oklahoma's sovereignty through a voyeuristic spectacle of enforcement.

Episode 1 of *Watchmen* opens with a law enforcement scene as well. We find ourselves watching a silent film in medias res. In it, the legendary "Black Marshal," Bass Reeves, protects a white-presenting town in Oklahoma Territory from a corrupt white sheriff.[21] Before the scene ends and it pans away, the camera zooms in on Reeves's badge, letting us know he is a "Deputy U.S. Marshal, Oklahoma Territory."[22] This opening shot sets the scene for the rest of the miniseries, which develops a genealogy of Black (super)heroes who follow in Reeves's footsteps. The real Reeves was formerly enslaved in Arkansas and Texas and then became one of the most successful and effective U.S. marshals of the late nineteenth century, but *Watchmen's* representation of him takes some historical license. I do not take issue with historical inaccuracies in fictional narratives, but I want to linger on this historical rewrite because, I argue, it is a missed opportunity to reflect on Black-Native intimacies.

Reeves was a marshal in Indian Territory, not Oklahoma, in the final decades of the nineteenth century, and as I demonstrate in chapter 4, there were significant differences between the two. One can assume the showrunners resituate Reeves in Oklahoma Territory because it makes him more geographically locatable for a viewing audience who most likely is not well versed in Indian Territory history. However, this choice does two things by erasing Indian Territory from its speculative history. First, it naturalizes statehood (Oklahoma Territory invariably becomes the state of Oklahoma). Second, it removes Indigeneity from the narrative, crafting a simpler racial arithmetic of place.

Art T. Burton, who wrote the definitive biography on Reeves, argues that Indian Territory provided a unique venue for Black law enforcement because a significant portion of marshals were formerly enslaved Black men, many of them Five Tribes Freedpeople, and some of whom also identified as Afro-Native. As a result, most Black marshals already understood Native languages and cultural norms, enabling them to move through communities effectively and efficiently—and most people in Indian Territory preferred them to white marshals.[23] The Reeves mythology is complicated. On the one hand, he patrolled Indian Territory on behalf of the U.S. federal government and was complicit in policing, which, as a construct, was developed in the United States specifically to control and contain Black and Indigenous people. On the other, Reeves and the other Black marshals represent a method of policing that included the punishment of white criminals intruding on Black and Native land. Reeves is a figure enmeshed in structures of U.S. settler colonialism but one who also represents, albeit messily, retribution for white vigilantism and violence against Black and Native people. He is not an abolitionist figure who stands outside the law but rather one situated complexly within it. By Removing (intentionally capitalized) this extremely significant element from Reeves's history, *Watchmen* constructs a world, one we might describe as a *telescape*, not unlike nineteenth-century printscapes, in which territorial history is whitewashed. This rewrite, along with the omission of Black-Native intimacies that made Greenwood possible, maps out a white supremacist world divorced from its Indigenous past. To embrace the messy Black and Native world that Tulsa, Greenwood, and Reeves ushered forward would be to refuse the racialized reading and viewing practices of dominant U.S. state narratives. While Reeves's legacy and the *McGirt* ruling continue to imbricate Black and Native people in Removal's policing and surveillance systems, they also both open up moments in which we can at least imagine Indigenous and Black freedom.

Alterritories

It is easy to critique *Watchmen*'s double erasure of Indigeneity, both through Native absence in the Tulsa landscape and through the show's filming in Georgia, the ancestral homelands of Muscogee and Cherokee people before Removal, but lingering too long on where the show falls short distracts from something arguably more necessary—looking for alliances instead of gaps. Policing, surveillance, and management of Black and Native bodies circulate in both the real and imagined narratives of Indian Territory (and Tulsa). The centering of law enforcement and crime management continues to nurture white supremacy in ways that keep decolonization and Black and Indigenous freedom from fruition. Instead of resting on problematics that accompany moments when Black and Native creators attempt to render Black-Native intimacies on the page or on screen, we might reckon with how they signal the violent regimes that still make Black and Native people unfree and gesture us toward efforts that work collectively toward freedom nonetheless. Returning to Sylvia Wynter's contention that Black and Native territories of freedom are untenable in our current world order (but still shimmer through), these messy renderings serve to remind us of the revolutionary potential they gesture toward—and that the work continues.[24]

In contrast to *Watchmen*, the Afro steampunk comic *Bitter Root* does attempt to situate 1920s Tulsa in Indian Territory. In issue 7 of the comic, Dr. Walter Sylvester loses his wife while living in Boley. Two years later, he loses his children during the Tulsa Massacre. He is rescued outside Tulsa by two monster hunters: Iris, who is Afro-Cherokee, and Bernice, who is Black and from Harlem. Standing over him, they see what they believe to be a *jinoo* (called a *hanîsse'ono* by Iris), a monster that crosses over from the spirit realm to feed off of human hatred, racism, and sorrow. Iris and Bernice take Walter back to Iris's community, "Northern Oklahoma, Between Osage Nation and Cherokee Nation."[25] Upon reflection, they realize the monster is not a *jinoo* but something more powerful and sinister. In the scene, Iris and Bernice share their collective knowledge of medicine and the spirit world to determine how to combat the creature. Eventually, in later issues, they return to New York to collaborate with other people of color who possess their own ancestral knowledge of spiritual realms and build a demonological oral archive of sorts. The comic's depiction of Iris is full of cultural inaccuracy (including some cringey iconography), but, again, I am less concerned with accuracy than possibility. In the friendship between Iris and Bernice, we witness a collaboration dependent on their respective kinship networks and a 1920s map that foregrounds Black and Indigenous community (Boley, Tulsa, Osage Nation, Cherokee Nation, Harlem, and others) as networked. Critically, Iris lives between two nations. She and her family operate outside the nation(-state), living in the slippage and gaps in between. As monster hunters, both Iris and Bernice move through space with an awareness that other worlds exist and other worlds are possible—the colonial map limits neither of them in these other spaces. What links them and their network is a root system that is familial, medicinal, and geographic and invisible to the gaze of white supremacy, even in its most monstrous forms. Their efforts are not unlike those of Black and Indigenous feminist, queer, and Two-Spirit science fiction writers and poets, including Billy-Ray Belcourt, Dionne Brand, adrienne maree brown, Alexis Pauline Gumbs, Cherie Dimaline, Robyn Maynard, and Leanne Betasamosake Simpson, who do not necessarily prescribe the contours of Indigenous and Black freedom in their writing but prepare themselves for its arrival, doing the work of loving and caring community-building as we move toward a collective elsewhere. Through Iris and Bernice's friendship, we get glimpses beyond the state, and, importantly, these moments are staged not in a future-future but in a futuristic past that demands we contend with life across both time and space.

Much of *Reading Territory* has been about highlighting the violent racist settler regime inculcated by states' rights discourse, with less attention to what Indigenous and Black freedom looks like beyond the state. Print and other forms of unembodied cultural expression, such as television, remind us that we are still living in unfree times. They routinely remind us of their limitations in getting us free, but open space to imagine ways to do so. I say this not as a pessimist but as an optimist who sees Black and Native print archives as one form of "showing the work" of freedom struggles. The "problems" we may find in current efforts to represent Black-Native affinities do the critical work of reminding us of the challenges in registering such freedom visually or discursively under the current post-Enlightenment humanist regime that often depicts Indigeneity and Blackness in caricatured, flat relief.[26] As a result, these print and cinematic stories demand that we also commit to turning beyond the printed page or the computer screen to freedom-searching that takes us elsewhere, toward more embodied, metaphysical encounters with each other and the more-than-human world.

Notes

A Note on Terminology

1. Leanne Betasamosake Simpson, *As We Have Always Done*, 25. Grounded normativity is a concept that Simpson adapts from Glen Coulthard (Yellowknives Dene First Nation).

2. Justice, *Why Indigenous Literatures Matter*, 6.

3. Justice, 6.

Introduction

1. "Governor Stitt Delivers 2021 State of the State Address," press release, February 1, 2021, https://oklahoma.gov/governor/newsroom/newsroom/2021/february/governor-stitt -delivers-2021-state-of-the-state-address.html.

2. In using "Indian Territory," I am also thinking of Jodi Byrd's theorization of the Indian figure and Indianness. Byrd writes, "American empire does not replicate itself through a detachable and remappable 'frontier' or 'wilderness.' Rather, I am arguing as an additive here, it does so through the reproduction of Indianness that exists alongside racializing discourses that slip through the thresholds of whiteness and blackness, inclusion and exclusion, internal and external, that are the necessary conditions of settler colonial sovereignty." Byrd, *Transit of Empire*, 27.

3. Moreton-Robinson, *White Possessive*.

4. Wynter, "1492."

5. I am grateful to Brigitte Fielder for suggesting the term "printscape."

6. Castronovo, *Propaganda 1776*, 9. My use of "printscape" is also influenced by Mark J. Noonan's insistence on the term's "dynamic possibilities." Noonan, "Printscape," 9.

7. Castronovo, *Propaganda 1776*, 9.

8. See Barker, "For Whom Sovereignty Matters," 17–24; and Kauanui, *Paradoxes of Hawaiian Sovereignty*, 21–30.

9. In this approach, I am also reminded of Katherine McKittrick's and Sara Ahmed's respective work on the politics of citation—in particular, McKittrick's cautioning against citation practices that become too "easy" and thus do not read carefully the work of Black women and her emphasis on how bibliographies and notes can disrupt a single-author narrative and instead "reference, source, and cite" and risk "unknowing ourselves." McKittrick, *Dear Science*, 16–18; Ahmed, *Living a Feminist Life*, 14–16.

10. King, *Black Shoals*, 13.

11. Saranillio, *Unsustainable Empire*, xiii. Here, I am especially thinking of Aileen Moreton-Robinson's suggestion that Michel Foucault's notion of biopower is helpful for understanding how whiteness and colonization produce "disciplinary knowledges and regulatory mechanisms" in the biopolitical state by foreclosing Indigenous sovereignty. She asks, "How does biopower work to produce whiteness as an invisible norm, and does it

function as a tactic and strategy of race war?" In the United States, statehood is one of the ways it does so. Moreton-Robinson, *White Possessive*, 129, 130.

12. Alyosha Goldstein reminds us in his discussion of U.S. colonialism, "The United States encompasses a historically variable and uneven constellation of state and local governments, indigenous nations, unincorporated territories, free association commonwealths, protectorates, federally-administered public lands, military bases, export processing zones, *colonias*, and anomalies such as the District of Columbia that do not comprehensively delineate an inside and outside of the nation-state." Goldstein, "Introduction," 1. Additionally, Bethel Saler's study of statehood in the "old Northwest" painstakingly recounts how U.S. territorial acquisition, empire, and colonization built on prior European practices of North American colonization but also developed spatial relations that differed from European models for controlling lands and people. Saler also reminds us how much of this state-making work was cultural work. Saler, *Settlers' Empire*, 249.

13. Typically, a territory must be considered "advanced" enough for Congress to consider a statehood proposal. Advancement is based on a triumvirate of increased population, increased governance, and systematized land use. Typically, once more than 5,000 settlers were in a territory, the federal government appointed a territorial governor, secretary, and judges. Once the population increased, land was actively divided into private holdings and put to agricultural and economic use; the residents could elect territorial representatives and, ideally, draft a state constitution.

14. For a discussion of the Insular Cases and their impact on U.S. definitions of territory, see Burnett and Marshall, *Foreign in a Domestic Sense*.

15. See Kirsten Silva Gruesz's keyword for "America" in the 2007 *Keywords for American Cultural Studies* edition. Gruesz, "America."

16. Beer, *To Make a Nation*; Coleman, *American Revolution*; LaCroix, *Ideological Origins*.

17. Chen, *Animacies*, 9.

18. Chen, 10.

19. Some tribal schools operating in Indian Territory at that time, such as the Cherokee male and female seminaries, were considered as educationally rigorous by Western standards as elite preparatory schools on the U.S. East Coast.

20. Saranillio, *Unsustainable Empire*, 199.

21. Lowe, *Intimacies of Four Continents*.

22. Saldaña-Portillo, *Indian Given*.

23. Here I am also thinking about Tuck and Yang's discussion of the settler "move to innocence." Tuck and Yang, "Decolonization Is Not," 3.

24. Bill HB 2497, 87th Legislature, Texas Legislature Online, accessed August 1, 2021, https://capitol.texas.gov/BillLookup/Text.aspx?LegSess=87R&Bill=HB2497.

25. Scott, *Seeing like a State*, 2.

26. Catherine Beecher, preface to Stowe, *First Geography for Children*, 3.

27. Beecher, 4. Martha Schoolman offers a brief but engaged reading of Stowe and Beecher's 1833 *Primary Geography for Children*. In a footnote, Schoolman explains the differences between the 1833 and the 1855 geographies and why the two should not be conflated. Schoolman, *Abolitionist Geographies*, 134–37, 214.

28. In *The Republic in Print*, Trish Loughran argues that Stowe develops two principles that serve as a throughline in Stowe's other works, "a sense of relational orientation (North, South, East, and West) that nevertheless places New England at the center" and "the desire to make a 'map' of the world that places her reader's body and home at the center." Loughran, *Republic in Print*, 385.

29. Stowe, *First Geography for Children*, 89.

30. The full entry for Texas reads, "You see the large State of Texas on the south, directly west of Louisiana. Its first settlers from the United States were chiefly slaveholders; and it has thus become one of the slave states. This state was the cause of a war between Mexico and the United States. It was formerly a part of Mexico but is now annexed to our country. This one state is larger than the whole of both the New England and the Middle States. You may remember this state as the one that caused a war." Stowe, *First Geography for Children*, 88–89.

31. For further discussion of the relationship between geography and U.S. nation formation, see Brückner, *Geography Revolution*; Hsu, *Geography and the Production*; Schulten, *Mapping the Nation*; and Stoler, *Haunted by Empire*.

32. Moreton-Robinson, *White Possessive*, xii. See also Cedric J. Robinson's discussion of racial capitalism in *Black Marxism*.

33. Moreton-Robinson, *White Possessive*, xxiv, xxiii.

34. Moreton-Robinson actively engages Harris in *The White Possessive* as well. Harris, "Whiteness as Property," 1725.

35. Wynter, "1492."

36. Sharon P. Holland and Miles, "Afro-Native Realities," 525.

37. Holland and Miles, 524–25.

38. Byrd, *Transit of Empire*, xvii.

39. "Object of property" is Cheryl Harris's way to distinguish Blackness as a form of property that is available for others' ownership from whiteness as a form of property meant to exclude and as the only credible form of property rights. Harris, "Whiteness as Property," 1716.

40. Justin Leroy succinctly reminds us, "Empire has functioned by making its victims both Indian and black." Leroy, "Black History," 6.

41. Arvin, *Possessing Polynesians*, 55.

42. This is what Hortense Spillers terms an "American grammar" of the New World. Spillers, "Mama's Baby, Papa's Maybe."

43. While the debates go back much further, in 2006, then–principal chief Chad Smith, through a constitutional convention, amended the Cherokee Nation's constitution to only allow citizenship to descendants by lineal descent in an effort to exclude ancestors of the Cherokee Freedpeople listed on the Dawes Rolls from citizenship. The Smith-led constitutional change sparked controversy both within and outside Cherokee Nation about the limits of tribal sovereignty and the efficacy of using tribal rolls to determine citizenship. In 2017 a U.S. District Court (and not a tribal court) ruled in favor of Cherokee Freedpeople, and Cherokee Nation agreed not to appeal the decision and instead reinstate Freedpeoples' citizenship. In 2021 Secretary of the Interior Deb Haaland (Laguna Pueblo) approved the new Cherokee Nation constitution. See Sturm, *Blood Politics*, chap. 7; Byrd, *Transit of Empire*, chap. 4.

44. King, *Black Shoals*, x.

45. King, xi.

46. King, 13.

47. See Brooks, "'This Indian World,'" 5; and Carretta, *Phillis Wheatley*, 45–46, 159–60.

48. Jeffers, "Lost Letter #4: Samson Occom, Mohegan, to Susanna Wheatley, Boston" and "Lost Letter #5: Susanna Wheatley, Boston, to Samson Occom, Mohegan," in *Age of Phillis*, 54–55.

49. Here I am also thinking of Jean M. O'Brien's important point that in the eighteenth century, Native and Black people had intermarried for decades and Native communities' "failure to comply with non-Indian ideas about Indian phenotype strained the credence for their Indianness in New England minds." O'Brien, *Firsting and Lasting*, xxi.

50. Amber Starks (@MelaninMvskoke), Twitter post, April 30, 2021, https://twitter.com /MelaninMvskoke/status/1388368138236956679.

51. My understanding growing up was that Tulsa officials and supporters of the riots physically cut out all coverage of the massacre in the newspaper archive, so there would be no paper trail. If true, this is another example of the power of printscapes to shape the stories we tell about history and place.

52. Nineteenth-century U.S. concepts of territory were indebted to earlier European understandings of the term that were codified in the Peace of Westphalia in 1648. Stuart Elden argues that starting in the Middle Ages, the notion of territory became "a central prerequisite for the establishment of the modern state" in Europe. Elden, *Birth of Territory*, 322. Elden traces the origins of territory as a European political concept to show that "territory," when attached to the modern nation-state, is a "bundle of political technologies" that are always historically produced. Elden, *Terror and Territory*, xxvi. For further discussion of the United States, territory, and the law, see Burnett and Marshall, *Foreign in a Domestic Sense*; Goldstein, "Introduction"; and Raustiala, *Does the Constitution?*

53. Kevin Bruyneel pushes away from a binary model of U.S.-Indigenous jurisdictions that reinforces a notion of firm, enforced boundaries. His notion of the third space of sovereignty as a "refusal of the imperial binary" understands "American boundaries as active locations for the expression of forms of sovereignty and political identity that do not conform to the seemingly unambiguous binary choices set out by the liberal democratic settler-state." Bruyneel is skeptical of the ability to disrupt U.S. colonial occupation by simply trying to erase or change boundaries. Instead, he aims to "refuse" that binary in its entirety. However, his account omits the cultural, aesthetic, and literary components to border production—and border refusal. Bruyneel, *Third Space of Sovereignty*, 21, 6.

54. Laleh Khalili describes the relationship between the law and territory as work of "imagined jurisdictions." She explains, "Laws convey not just a set of rulings but also imaginaries of territories as jurisdictions, the contours of rule (how the law gets implemented), and the subjects of the law—who is the population to whom the law applies, whom the law interpellates (the police's 'Hey, you there' of Althusser), who is punished (or spared or ignored or excluded), who can sidestep the law, who is the law." Khalili, *Time in the Shadows*, 99.

55. Wynter, "How We Mistook," 274.

56. Barker, "Territory as Analytic," 20–21.

57. Goeman, *Mark My Words*, 34.

58. Kauanui details how the Hawaiian Kingdom's adoption of Western governance enacted a form of "colonial biopolitics" that destroys Indigenous lifeways in *Paradoxes of Hawaiian Sovereignty*.

59. McKittrick, *Demonic Grounds*, 2.

60. My spatial thinking has been influenced by the critical and cultural geography work of many intellectuals, but especially Mary Pat Brady, David Harvey, Doreen Massey, and Edward Soja.

61. Work by Pasifika artists and scholars has provided a rich terrain in which to think through Indigenous-centered understandings of territory beyond the state. Chamoru poet Craig Santos Perez's Unincorporated Territory poetry series challenges U.S. notions of territory and dismantles them by centering Indigenous ways of being in relation to land and water. Perez has suggested a spatial heuristic along similar lines to visualize the Pacific world. For Perez, "terripelago" is a way to understand "territoriality as it conjoins land and sea, islands and continents." Perez, "Transterritorial Currents," 620. Perez's essay begins with a description of his own experience learning the U.S. map as a child growing up on Guåhan. It echoes the logics of Stowe's geography discussed earlier: "'Growing up on the Pacific Island of Guåhan (Guam), I learned American history and geography. To memorize the states and capitals, I studied a political map in which the continental United States was represented as a large island against a blue background. On the bottom left corner of the map, Alaska appeared as an island off California, and Hawaii appeared as a group of islands off the southern coast of Texas. America was not a continent; America was an 'imperial archipelago.'" Perez, "Transterritorial Currents," 619–22.

62. Amber Starks (@MelaninMvskoke), Twitter post, June 14, 2021, https://twitter.com /MelaninMvskoke/status/1404505225918959618.

63. Justice, *Our Fire Survives*, 37.

64. One version of Ellison's book of essays *Going to the Territory* includes this inscription. John Callahan also mentions this quote in his edited collection of Ellison's essays. Callahan, introduction to *Collected Essays of Ralph Ellison*, xviii.

65. Intertwined with notions of U.S. territory and territorial expansion, particularly in the first half of the nineteenth century, was the notion of Indian Country, a term used to demarcate as many different spatial relations and sovereignties as the word "territory." By the middle of the century, however, there were efforts to consolidate the terminology as both Indigenous peoples and the U.S. government attempted to map and quantify spatial sovereignties in the face of U.S. expansion.

66. Synonymous with Indian Territory was the "boundary line," an imagined border dividing Indigenous lands from U.S. lands. The 1795 Treaty of Greenville was ostensibly an attempt by the U.S. government to demarcate Indigenous lands from the United States, but in actuality, the treaty made it even more challenging to distinguish national borders, especially between Indigenous nations. As such, the treaty set a precedent of contradiction and confusion rather than one of clear distinction and deference to Indigenous sovereignty and treaty agreements. For further discussion of the treaty, see Saler, *Settlers' Empire*, 60–82. The 1834 modifications to the Indian Intercourse Act legally defined "Indian country," which was also termed "Indian Territory," as all lands west of the Mississippi that were not yet part of a state (Missouri or Louisiana) or an incorporated U.S. territory (Arkansas). See

"Trade and Intercourse Act, July 22, 1790" and "Trade and Intercourse Act, June 30, 1834," in Prucha, *Documents of United States*, 14–15, 63–68.

Chapter One

1. Georgia Department of Economic Development, "Chieftains Trail," Explore Georgia, accessed August 31, 2021, www.exploregeorgia.org/cartersville/general/historic-sites-trails -tours/chieftains-trail. As of August 2021, the website for the Chieftains Trail no longer seemed to be functional. The previous website address was www.chieftainstrail.com.

2. I have found earlier records that do include an apostrophe (Chieftain's), but as of the writing of this chapter, the official websites do not include an apostrophe in Chieftains Trail or Chieftains Museum/Major Ridge Home. In addition to the Explore Georgia web-site, see the Chieftains Museum/Major Ridge homepage, accessed September 7, 2021, https://chieftainsmuseum.org/.

3. In *The House on Diamond Hill*, Tiya Miles also writes about the State of Georgia's and residents' attachments to these Chieftains Trail sites, especially the Vann House. Miles, *House on Diamond Hill*, xi–xv, 1–26, 187–97. For more on commemoration of the Trail of Tears and Cherokee Removal history in the Southeast, see Denson, *Monuments to Absence*.

4. The Miles quote continues, "While black slavery conjures feelings of guilt, defensive-ness, and even denial among many white southerners . . . Indian Removal can be viewed as a point of connection between martyred southern whites and ousted southern Indians." Miles, *House on Diamond Hill*, 15.

5. This was at least the case, as best I could tell, when I last visited in 2017.

6. I struggle with what terms to use when describing Indian Removal and the Trail of Tears. None seem to capture the magnitude of the trauma adequately. I continue to use the term "Removal" for reasons detailed in the book's introduction. To briefly summarize, I understand "Removal" as indicating more than the forced migration of Indigenous people; it is also a way to account for the settler plantation's world-breaking and world-making ef-forts to (re)move Indigenous people at will across Africa and the Americas. "Removal" is suggestive of attempts to destroy the Indigenous cosmologies, languages, and lifeways of African-descended and Native people in the Americas through genocide and enslavement, and it also accounts for the entanglements of Black and Indigenous oppression.

7. Jean M. O'Brien defines this process as "firsting." O'Brien, *Firsting and Lasting*, xii. While her focus is on local histories of New England, her contention that "local histories claim Indian places as their own by constructing origin stories that cast Indians as prefatory to what they assert as their own authentic histories and institutions" saliently describes the Chieftains Trail sites as well. O'Brien, *Firsting and Lasting*, xxiii.

8. See Denson, *Monuments to Absence*, chap. 4.

9. In doing so, it participates in what Meredith McGill terms a "culture of reprinting." McGill, *American Literature*.

10. Beth Barton Schweiger writes that by the 1840s, "print was a commonplace in the rural South." Schweiger, *Literate South*, 1. She discusses Southern print and literacy num-bers in the book's introduction, "The Presence of Print," in *Literate South*, 18–21. However, Schweiger's study only attends to the literacy of free Black people and enslaved people briefly. Keri Leigh Merritt is skeptical of the claim about overall Southern literacy rates that

Schweiger makes in her article "The Literate South: Reading before Emancipation." Merritt contends that such a claim almost entirely ignores enslaved and free Black people, but she does agree with Schweiger that the Southern white elite fostered a thriving print culture. Merritt, *Masterless Men*, 151. For more on enslaved people's literacy, see Williams, *Self-Taught*.

11. While papers often spatially separated Blackness and Indigeneity, at times, they also revealed moments of convergence, primarily through advertisements and editorials. For instance, Tiya Miles demonstrates how advertisements provided traces of Black and Native community through mention of enslaved people's self-emancipation journeys to Native nations or through suggestions of Afro-Native intermarriage and kinship. Miles, *Ties That Bind*, 29. Miles includes a few examples of advertisements that specifically mention the Cherokee Nation. Jack Forbes, whom Miles mentions in her discussion of advertisements, explains that the terms "mustee" and "mulatto" were used to describe Native people in eighteenth-century newspapers and did not always indicate African ancestry. Forbes, *Africans and Native Americans*, 207–9.

12. The first issue of *Freedom's Journal* was published in New York on March 16, 1827, and the first issue of the *Phoenix* was published on February 21, 1828. For further discussion of *Freedom's Journal*, see McHenry, *Forgotten Readers*, 84–140; and Bacon, *Freedom's Journal*.

13. McHenry, *Forgotten Readers*, 87.

14. For analysis of the Black nationalism of *Freedom's Journal*, see Asukile, "All-Embracing Black Nationalist."

15. The newspaper also became an appealing medium for anticolonial resistance projects elsewhere, used by Kanaka Maoli in Hawai'i, Mexicans, and Cuban and other exiles and migrants from Spanish America. For Hawaiian newspapers, see Silva, *Aloha Betrayed*; and Silva, *Power of the Steel-Tipped*. For Latinx and Spanish American print culture, see Coronado, *World Not to Come*; Gruesz, *Ambassadors of Culture*; and Lazo, *Writing to Cuba*.

16. These are most of the papers published in Georgia at some point during the first three decades of the nineteenth century. However, given just how many papers went boom and bust quickly, consolidated, or changed names, it is difficult to provide a definitive list. There are sixteen in total: *Athenian* (later the *Southern Banner*), *Augusta Chronicle*, *Augusta Herald*, *Columbus Enquirer*, *Federal Union*, *Georgian*, *Georgia Constitutionalist*, *Georgia Courier*, *Georgia Journal*, *Georgia Statesman*, *Macon Telegraph*, *Mirror of the Times*, *Southron*, *Southern Recorder*, *Southern Sentinel*, and *Times and State's Rights Advocate*.

17. "To the Public," *Cherokee Phoenix* (New Echota), February 21, 1829.

18. The initial boundary line was negotiated in the Treaty of Hopewell (1785). The Hopewell negotiations were among the first acts taken up by the newly formed U.S. federal government.

19. The 1791 Treaty of Holston, part of Secretary of War Henry Knox's civilization approach, was especially significant for Cherokee assertions of self-determination and autonomy in the nineteenth century. The treaty authorized yet another boundary line—on that point it was not exceptional—as well as yet another repeatedly broken promise that the United States would stop white intruders from invading Cherokee territory. However, the treaty also established a "civilizing" project. Ostensibly, the Cherokees agreed to be under the care of the federal government as they learned to "become herdsmen and cultivators." Cherokees were already adept farmers, but most agricultural work was the responsibility of

Cherokee women, not Cherokee men. Therefore, the federal government's civilization program was less about agrarianism and more about compulsorily embracing a system of gendered (and racialized) labor that would prove to reshape Cherokee families and communities profoundly. Kappler, *Indian Affairs*.

20. Daniel Heath Justice also explains that Removal began to "haunt" the Cherokee long before the eighteenth and nineteenth centuries, noting the trope of forced migration found in numerous Cherokee stories. Justice, *Our Fire Survives*, 48–53.

21. I use the term "Cherokee elites" throughout to describe the small cadre of wealthy Cherokee men who gained disproportionate influence and power in the Nation through their involvement with the government and their success as enslaver businessmen and politicians. Most of them attended U.S. universities for secondary education, were multilingual, and were familiar with U.S. upper-class society.

22. In 1817 the National Council also established the National Committee, and over time, the committee would go on to have more and more control of official national affairs. While the National Council was more representative of Cherokee life, the committee was composed of a more homogeneous group of elite male Cherokee enslavers educated in U.S. schools and raised in mixed Cherokee and white families who believed in protecting personal wealth. See Miles, *Ties That Bind*, 104–5.

23. In the late eighteenth and early nineteenth centuries, Cherokee elites centralized Cherokee governance by creating a three-body national government and establishing a constitution. For a discussion of the centralization of Cherokee government, see Sturm, "Blood, Culture, and Race: Cherokee Politics and Identity in the Eighteenth Century," in *Blood Politics*, 27–51; and Perdue and Green, "Civilizing the Cherokees," in *Cherokee Nation*, 20–41.

24. See Perdue, *Cherokee Women*. Cherokees found ways to continue matriarchal forms of governance and communitarianism, but the centralization of governance invariably affected Cherokee women.

25. The April 24, 1828, issue of the *Cherokee Phoenix* quotes a U.S. agent as saying, "The subject of your having formed a Constitution and Constitutional Government, has Raised a Considerable Clamour particularly in the adjoining States." "Communication to the Chiefs of the Cherokee Nation 16 April 1828," *Cherokee Phoenix*, April 24, 1828. Charles Haynes, who was a Georgia senator at the time, made this argument before the U.S. House in an 1838 speech advocating complete Removal:

> I will now add, that the very last of all the old States, as she was the last one planted on this continent, to extend her jurisdiction over the Indians, was Georgia. Various acts of legislation, it is true, were adopted by her some forty or fifty years ago, in relation to the Indians; but she deferred the whole and entire exercise of her sovereignty over them until within the last ten years.
>
> The occasion was this: In the summer of 1827 a council of delegates of the Cherokee nation assembled, and adopted, and promulgated, a formal Constitution, setting up a permanent, independent, sovereignty, embracing some four or five millions of acres of territory, within the limits of Georgia. Notwithstanding the proceedings of this convention were known to the Governor and Legislature of Georgia, at its meeting in November, 1827, even then, Georgia forbore to interfere with this pretended Cherokee sovereignty. (Haynes, *Speech of Mr. Haynes*, 5)

26. "Constitution of the Cherokee Nation," *Cherokee Phoenix*, February 12, 1828.

27. Celia E. Naylor argues that anti-Black legal structures were formalized as Cherokee nationalism cohered. Naylor, *African Cherokees*, 13. The anti-Blackness embraced in the constitution would continue to be a prominent aspect of formal Cherokee notions of race and belonging well into the twenty-first century, as I discuss in the book's introduction.

28. The majority of Cherokees, however, did not embrace participation in enslavement. Miles writes, "Out of the 16,542 Cherokees in the Nation in 1835, only 7.4 percent owned slaves, and the majority of these slaveowners lived in mixed-race, white-Cherokee families. These census numbers are an indication of the widening economic gap between Cherokee planters and small farmers and of most Cherokees' separation from and rejection of slavery." Miles, *Ties That Bind*, 124.

29. For further reading, see Julie Reed, "Taking Care of Our Own, 1800–1829," in *Serving the Nation*, 22–59.

30. Daniel Heath Justice was generous enough to share this when offering feedback on an earlier draft of this chapter.

31. As Julie Reed explains, "Membership in a Cherokee clan made a person a Cherokee, so clan identity provided a national identity." Reed, *Serving the Nation*, 7.

32. Perdue, "Defining Community," in *Cherokee Women*, 41–59.

33. There were some exceptions, but very few. See Miles, *Ties That Bind*, 114–28.

34. Two years earlier, the council had approved funds to start a paper, and from then until 1828, when the first issue of the *Cherokee Phoenix* appeared, Principal Chief Ross, Boudinot, and others worked to procure the needed equipment for a printing office at New Echota, the recently established capital of the Cherokee Nation. The Cherokee Nation had to take a loan from the American Board of Commissioners for Foreign Nations (ABCFM) in 1827 to get enough money to buy the press and materials. The ABCFM was already an active presence in the Nation. Samuel Worcester, an ABCFM minister, would later be an important figure in the Nation's fight for sovereignty and the plaintiff in *Worcester v. Georgia* (1832). For further discussion of the resources needed to start the paper and logistical information about the print shop and materials, see Brannon, *Cherokee Phoenix*.

35. The ABCFM cast the initial Sequoyan type in Boston on behalf of the Nation and shipped it to New Echota. Parins, *Literacy and Intellectual Life*, 52.

36. Parins, 55–57. The material requirements for printing a weekly paper added extra hurdles (consistent access to ink and paper), some of which Boudinot openly discussed in the pages of the paper.

37. The August 26, 1829, issue includes the following in Boudinot's "New Echota" column:

> Our readers will perceive from the articles we insert in our paper under the head of Indians, that an interest is creating in the public mind in regard to the rights of the aborigines. We hope this interest will increase until public opinion shall decide either for or against us. We wish to know what the United States thinks of us—whether they are willing to sacrifice us to the cupidity of some of our white brethren—whether they will sustain the doctrine of Secretary Eaton, and say that the guarantee *for ever* solemnly given by the United States to us, is not sufficient to protect us in our rights, and the only alternative is for us to remove across the Mississippi. (Editorial, *Cherokee Phoenix*, August 26, 1829)

38. Trish Loughran has persuasively argued that the networked national print culture that cohered in the mid-nineteenth century revealed the fractious nature of the United States rather than its unification. Building on her claim, I argue that the production and circulation of a nationalist Indigenous paper further problematized the fantasy of U.S. cohesion, to which the aspiration of complete settler control (even of print) was central. Loughran, *Republic in Print*.

39. Ross, *Papers of Chief John Ross*, 141. Ross's message is also printed in the October 22, 1828, issue of the *Phoenix*.

40. Kirsten Silva Gruesz discusses some of the challenges that editors faced when publishing bilingual papers in New Orleans and New York. The challenge was significant enough that many of them did not publish bilingually for very long (this was the case for *La Patria*), and many of these papers published content in Spanish and English on separate pages rather than side by side. She explains that "although many Spanish papers initially evolved out of sections in established English ones," *La Patria* was the first paper to do the reverse. She goes on to explain that "this bilingual experiment envisions facing-page translations as an instrument of painless assimilation; yet in this case the assimilation is to be mutual." Gruesz, "The Mouth of a New Empire: New Orleans in the Transamerican Print Trade," in *Ambassadors of Culture*, 118, 119.

41. While it is clear that the paper did cater to affluent Cherokees and Cherokees literate in English or Sequoyan (written) Cherokee, this does not mean those were the only Cherokees who engaged the paper's content. Cherokee-only speakers also paid a significantly reduced price for the paper. Very likely, quite a few Cherokees who did not understand English or were not literate in either English or Cherokee had the paper read to them—a common practice in the early nineteenth century—or learned about the paper's content via word of mouth. There were invariably many ways the paper and its content circulated in the Nation.

42. Both Justice and Parins discuss the various ways Cherokees used the syllabary to communicate. Justice, *Our Fire Survives*, 80–81; Parins, *Literacy and Intellectual Life*, 35–37. Much like the *Phoenix* and the creation of a republican government, the syllabary has garnered both glowing praise and pointed critique. However, to think of the syllabary in either-or terms—as either assimilationist or nationalist—is to engage in a limited colonial dialectic rather than thinking about the complexity *within* Cherokee culture, and it thus reinforces the kinds of binaries that Cherokee scholars like Justice speak against. Instead, as Justice proposes, I prefer to think in Cherokee terms of balance, endurance, and adaptation. Justice, *Our Fire Survives*, 27–42.

43. Missionaries, with the help of Cherokee students at mission schools, attempted to develop alphabetic versions of written Cherokee but none of them with much success. I am particularly thinking of David Butrick and David Brown's collaboration on their Cherokee spelling book published just before Sequoyah and Ayoka completed the syllabary. Butrick was one of the founders of the Brainerd Mission, established in the Cherokee Nation by the ABCFM, and Brown was a Cherokee preacher and brother of the famed Catherine Brown. See Butrick and Brown, *Tsvlvki sqclvclv*. Parins also talks about Butrick and Brown's work on an alphabet in *Literacy and Intellectual Life*, 29–31.

44. Ellen Cushman explains that Sequoyah's interest in signing his name to his silver work catalyzed his interest in written language. Cushman, *Cherokee Syllabary*, 27.

45. The year of Sequoyah's birth is debated among scholars, but he was likely born in the 1770s. Anderson, "Sequoyah."

46. Cushman, *Cherokee Syllabary*, 66.

47. In the May 6, 1828, issue, Boudinot includes the following explanation of why there is not more Cherokee content:

> Since the commencement of our labors, we have not been able to insert as much Cherokee matter, as might have been expected, and desired. It may be necessary to state, that we have devoted a good portion of our time to that part of our business, and that if any of our Cherokee readers think we have slighted them, we can assure them that it has not been through neglect, or for want of attention. Those who know any thing of the duties devolving upon us, will acknowledge that we have a heavy task, & unless relieved by *Cherokee correspondents*, a greater amount of Cherokee matter cannot be reasonably expected. We hope those of our correspondents, who take a lively interest in the diffusion of intelligence in their mother language, will lend us aid in this department, and by far the most arduous part, of our labors. ("To the Cherokee Correspondents," *Cherokee Phoenix*, May 6, 1828)

48. Perdue and Green also discuss the constitution's emphasis on establishing boundaries in *Cherokee Nation*, 40–41.

49. According to Brannon, "The original intent was to print each article in both English and Cherokee, but the printers did not know Cherokee well, so the translations were difficult to produce. Generally, one-fifth of the four-page newspaper was printed in Cherokee, with most Cherokee text appearing on pages one and three." Brannon, *Cherokee Phoenix*, x. Also see Cullen Joe Holland, "Cherokee Indian Newspapers," 41–49.

50. See Parins, *Literacy and Intellectual Life*, 57.

51. According to Holland, Worcester would have been the person who translated the prayer for the newspaper. Cullen Joe Holland, "Cherokee Indian Newspapers," 122.

52. As one example, I am thinking of the emergence of the "Foreign" column in the April 22, 1829, issue.

53. The lawyer for the Cherokee Nation, William Wirt, argued that even though the Cherokee were a foreign nation, they felt compelled to take their case to the U.S. Supreme Court, which is only tasked with hearing domestic cases, because the Nation was unable to find recourse elsewhere, especially from Congress. *Cherokee Nation v. Georgia*, 5 Pet. 1, 5–6 (1831).

54. Richard Peters, *Case of the Cherokee*, 36.

55. Frank Brannon speculates the following about the paper's actual circulation:

> We do not know the number of newspapers printed for each weekly edition, but we do have some information to make an estimate. One source tells us that Boudinot *intended* to print 200 copies for the Cherokee Nation, and by mid-1828, we understand that the *Phoenix* had up to 40 paid subscriptions in the United States. In addition, Boudinot's proud father-in-law Benjamin Gold states in 1829 that the *Phoenix* was exchanged with approximately 100 other newspapers, a common practice in this era. From this, we arrive at an estimate of 200 to 400 newspapers per issue. This estimate is regarding the early years of the newspaper and less applicable to the last years of the *Phoenix* as conditions in New Echota worsened politically. This estimate is also dependent upon

the availability of ink and paper for a particular week's issue. (Brannon, *Cherokee Phoenix*, 29)

56. Evidencing this circuitous matrix of print networks is an April 1830 reprinted excerpt from a Vermont paper commenting on a London piece. The article, as reprinted in the *Phoenix*, reads, "The following remarks, from the London Missionary Register for February, will show how the Indian Question is regarded by the wise and good in Europe. The reader will notice the inaccuracy of calling these Indians 'subjects' of the United States.—*Vt. Chron.*" This piece reveals a constellation of print circulation in Christian missionary, U.S., and British print networks, many of which overlap and repurpose one another. Moreover, it demonstrates the temporal speed of reprinting: the *Phoenix* publishes in April a piece seemingly (although not necessarily) from February of the same year "North American Indians," *Cherokee Phoenix*, April 21, 1830.

57. For example, the May 8, 1830, issue included an article titled "English Opinions on the Indian Question," and an August 26, 1829, article solicited external feedback: "We wish to know what the people of the United States think of us. Editorial, *Cherokee Phoenix*, August 26, 1829; "English Opinions on the Indian Question," *Cherokee Phoenix*, May 8, 1830.

58. After settling in Indian Territory, a number of the signers were killed, including Boudinot, and these executions were justified as part of older Cherokee models of retributive justice. Cherokee women played an essential role in determining justice for a victim under these long-standing models. The women from a victim's family and clan made collective decisions about appropriate punishments for acts of wrongdoing. See Julie Reed, *Serving the Nation*, 8–11.

59. The papers also help fill important gaps in the political archive. Unfortunately, official records of the Georgia legislature were not kept at this time, making it challenging to capture an in-depth sense of the legislature's discussions. However, local newspapers frequently reported on the activities of the general assembly. While they are not official documents per se, they offer at least some sense of how newspaper editors perceived the general assembly's work and often include meeting summaries or letters from representatives that provide some texture and nuance.

60. Miles, *Ties That Bind*, 75.

61. "Agents for the Cherokee Phoenix," *Cherokee Phoenix*, August 26, 1829. For a discussion of the paper's agencies, see Griffith and Talmadge, *Georgia Journalism*, 3; and Parins, *Literacy and Intellectual Life*, 56.

62. In his study of the *Phoenix*, Parins suggests that Boudinot, Ross, and others suspected the paper would likely escalate the already tense situation with Georgia. He writes, "Although it may be difficult to gauge the effectiveness of the *Cherokee Phoenix*, one incident suggests that by the end of its first year, it had become an irritant to the state of Georgia." Parins, *Literacy and Intellectual Life*, 59.

63. "The Cherokees," *Columbus Enquirer*, October 6, 1832, Georgia Historic Newspapers, https://gahistoricnewspapers.galileo.usg.edu/lccn/sn82014931/1832-10-06/ed-1/seq-2/.

64. After Governor John Forsyth declared Cherokee Nation part of Georgia when in office in the late 1820s, the Georgia Guard were instructed to assault any Cherokee women who did not comply with his policy, evidence that sexual assault of Indigenous women is knitted into the work of state sovereignty. "Sufferings of Cherokee Ladies," *Cherokee Phoenix*, July 27, 1832; Miles, *Ties That Bind*, 133.

65. As an article reprinted from the *Richmond Enquirer* in the *Southern Recorder* notes, it was one thing for Indians to have land; it was another for them to organize a government and a press. "The Indians," *Southern Recorder* (Milledgeville), June 20, 1829, Georgia Historic Newspapers, https://gahistoricanewspapers.galileo.usg.edu/lccn/sn82016415/.

66. The *Southern Recorder* reprinted a piece from the *Phoenix* and, taking up a question posed in the article, offered this response: "Commenting on the above, the Phoenix remarks— 'What will the Cherokees do? Will they go to Nashville and add another treaty to the long list to be violated? No. The great question, are treaties with Indians worth any thing, must first be settled. They are determined to stay until they receive a satisfactory answer; but the government must not suppose they agree to come under the laws of the States. The Council will meet at this place on Monday—we will not therefore anticipate the reply which will probably be given.'" Editorial, *Southern Recorder*, July 24, 1830, Georgia Historic Newspapers, https://gahistoricnewspapers.galileo.usg.edu/lccn/sn82016415/1830-07-24/ed-1/seq-2/.

67. Several papers also indicted what they perceived as a questionable alliance between the "Northern" press and the Cherokee Nation. Some articles suggested that Cherokees manipulated the white Northern press's sympathies, and others alleged that Northern sentiment was harming the Cherokee Nation. The February 11, 1832, issue of the *Columbus Enquirer* suggests that "*Elias Boudinot* and *John Ridge* are *begging* our northern Brethren for money to relieve Cherokee embarrassment and to enable them to pay their Counsel.—This is pressing *the figure a little too far*; could they not be content with *sympathy—good wishes—* praise of the Red men and the abuse of the Georgians?" Editorial, *Columbus Enquirer*, February 11, 1832, Georgia Historic Newspapers, https://gahistoricnewspapers.galileo.usg.edu /lccn/sn82014931/1832-02-11/ed-1/seq-3.

68. "To the Editors of the Journal," *Georgia Journal* (Milledgeville), September 4, 1830, Georgia Historic Newspapers, https://gahistoricnewspapers.galileo.usg.edu/lccn/sn82014251/1830 -09-04/ed-1/seq-3/.

69. Walker, *David Walker's Appeal*, 5.

70. Hinks, introduction to *David Walker's Appeal*, xxiv. He was also influential in one of the first Black political organizations in the United States, the Massachusetts General Colored Association.

71. For the *Appeal*'s circulation, see Hinks, *To Awaken*, 116–72. For Walker's typography, see Dinius, "'Look!! Look!!!" For citizenship and recognition, see Nyong'o, "Race, Reenactment"; and Rogers, "David Walker."

72. Here I am thinking of Saidiya Hartman's reference to insurgency in her analysis of "stealing away" as a praxis of disruption: "These practices also created possibilities within the space of domination, transgress the policed space of subordination through unlicensed travel and collective assembly across the privatized lines of plantation households, and disrupt boundaries between the public and private in the articulation of insurgent claims that make need the medium of politics." Hartman, *Scenes of Subjection*, 69–70.

73. Walker, *David Walker's Appeal*, 56.

74. Anxieties about a future in which Native and Black people might take the South back were implicitly expressed in papers' content but sometimes were expressed quite explicitly as well. One *Georgia Journal* editorial criticized white Northerners, claiming they would not "be satisfied until they can witness the flames of our dwellings, the destruction of our fields, and the bleeding corpses of the white inhabitants of the South, mangled by Indian or

African barbarity." "Cherokee Indians—N. York—," *Georgia Journal*, January 16, 1830, Georgia Historic Newspapers, https://gahistoricnewspapers.galileo.usg.edu/lccn/sn82014251 /1830-01-16/ed-1/seq-2/. Walker exploits these fears in his pamphlet. He rhetorically asks his audience why white people have not enslaved Native people and provides the following response: "They know well that the Aborigines of this country, or (Indians) would tear them from the earth. The Indians would not rest day or night, they would be up all times of night, cutting their cruel throats." Walker, *David Walker's Appeal*, 65. In a note to this passage, he also reminds his reader that "people of color" outnumber white people in Georgia and South Carolina, suggesting they might be able to overtake white settlers easily. For further discussion of the *Appeal's* circulation in Georgia, see Crocket, "David Walker's *Appeal.*"

75. The *Phoenix* also ran a piece about Walker. It was a reprint from the *New York Journal of Commerce* that attributed much of the *Appeal's* popularity to the Southern white press's reaction, especially the one out of Milledgeville. "Walker's Pamphlet in the South," *Cherokee Phoenix*, April 21, 1830. Additionally, Peter P. Hinks recounts the recollections of one man who claimed that Samuel Worcester and Dr. Elizur Butler were "imprisoned in 1829 or 1830 for having one of Walker's pamphlets, as well as for admitting some colored children into their Indian school." Hinks, *To Awaken*, 127.

76. McNair, "Elijah Burritt Affair," 449.

77. Glenn M. McNair challenges the prevailing belief that Burritt was forced to flee because of enslavers' fears of insurrection. Instead, he argues that the case made against Burritt was personal and was more about rival newspaper editors appropriating his equipment for their political agenda, but I would suggest that we can read the Burritt scandal as both personal and structural. This was the case for much of what the papers printed and how they framed their political messages—as both intimate and grand in scale. The violence of Removal and enslavement operated at a quotidian level, much like the newspaper columns and advertisements of a weekly newspaper. McNair, "Elijah Burritt Affair," 450.

78. Walker, *David Walker's Appeal*, 2.

79. McNair, "Elijah Burritt Affair," 473.

80. While Black and Native voices are almost entirely absent in the Georgia papers, there was an insistence on counting Black and Native residents in the 1830 census. When explaining the importance of counting Indians and Black people to increase Georgia's influence in the federal government, a *Georgia Journal* editorial (reprinted in the *Athenian* on April 27, 1830) also suggests that all Cherokees would be subjects of Georgia soon enough: "We have noticed the subject, because the interest of the Southern States demands that their influence should be felt in the federal councils, physically as well as morally. . . . It is, therefore, all important, that the marshal or his assistants should be careful in taking this enumeration, not only of the white and black inhabitants; but of all the Indians residing in Georgia, because they will be, when the enumeration commences, inhabitants of this state, entitled, as all other citizens are, to the privileges, except as to evidence and subject to the restraints and requirements of all its laws." "Census of 1830," *Athenian* (Athens), April 27, 1830, Georgia Historic Newspapers, https://gahistoricnewspapers.galileo.usg.edu/lccn/sn85027027/1830 -04-27/ed-1/seq-3/.

81. Here I am thinking in particular of what Sylvia Wynter describes as "ethnoculturally coded narrated history," a "history in whose now purely secular terms we are all led to imag-

ine ourselves as Man, as purely biological and economic beings. The *history* of Man, there-fore narrated and existentially lived as if it were the *history-for* the human itself." She describes this history as one "in which the idea of humanism, of its de-godding of our modes of self-inscription first erupts, where Man and its human Others—that is, Indians, Negroes, Natives—are first invented." David Scott, "Re-enchantment of Humanism," 198.

82. Schweiger, "Literate South," 342.

83. Editorial, *Athenian*, January 26, 1827, Georgia Historic Newspapers, https://gahistoricnewspapers.galileo.usg.edu/lccn/sn85027027/1827-01-26/ed-1/seq-2/.

84. In her work, Sarah Deer elaborates on the correlations between violence against In-digenous women and colonization. See Deer, *Beginning and End*.

85. Both Jeremiah Evarts in his William Penn essays and Wirt in his argument before the Supreme Court in *Cherokee Nation v. Georgia* remark on the optics of colonial geography as a particularly vexing problem for Georgians, and both note its aesthetic rather than pragmatic leanings. But pro-Removal advocates also used similar language in their arguments. In a committee report submitted to Congress on behalf of the Georgia General Assembly, the com-mittee described white Georgians' desire for Cherokee land in the following way: "It was an object of peculiar interest to Georgia, to acquire a speedy possession of her Cherokee lands. Too long had the government delayed to liquidate the Indian possession. She had become justly jealous of her rights, and her people had become impatient of the restraints imposed by the delay of the Federal Government to fulfill her treaty obligations." Georgia General Assembly, *Report of the Committee*, 4.

86. The Georgia newspaper network collectively staged discussion and debate about the two issues perceived as *the* states' rights issues of the era for Georgians: the Tariff of 1828 controversy that catalyzed the South Carolina nullification crisis, and Indian Removal. Some papers covered one more than the other, potentially giving us some insight into distinc-tions among readers. Papers that were published in northern Georgia, especially in areas witnessing large numbers of white migrants flocking to the state to squat on Cherokee land and illegally mine for gold, published more on Indian affairs and more polemical editorials about the necessity of Removal, while papers that served an audience that included en-slaver gentry focused more heavily on the tariff debates. For an example of this, one can compare the *Athenian* and the *Georgia Courier* (Augusta).

87. Newspaper opinion pieces regularly commented on this strategy. As one example, an editorial by "Caroliniensis" alleges that despite Georgia newspaper editors' attempts to distance Georgians from the South Carolina nullification debate, "we of the south shall be all Roman citizens together, and the bravest shall lead—Georgia has pledged herself to State rights. Her colours are nailed to the mast, and when they go down, the *ship must go with them*." Carolini-ensis, editorial, *Constitutionalist* (Augusta), May 25, 1830, Georgia Historic Newspapers, https://gahistoricnewspapers.galileo.usg.edu/lccn/sn84025807/1830-05-25/ed-1/seq-1/.

88. He was elected to the Georgia House of Representatives in 1804 and served as a U.S. senator from 1827 to 1831 (and again from 1837 to 1841). He was elected governor of Georgia in 1831 and held office until 1835.

89. Lumpkin's brother Joseph had a heavy hand in shaping Georgia's enslavement laws during the nineteenth century. According to Jennison, "He was the architect of the state's slave regime, having authored the opinions in more than half of the sixty most important cases related to those issues during his twenty-one years on the bench." Jennison, *Cultivating*

Race, 289. For further discussion of Joseph Lumpkin's influence on enslavement laws in Georgia, see Jennison, chap. 8. Wilson Lumpkin's role as an enslaver is a biographical fact rarely included in encyclopedia entries, on historical markers, or in scholarship. Almost no state-centric encyclopedia or database that I searched explicitly makes this clear. According to the 1830 census, however, he enslaved nineteen people. "1830 United States Federal Census," Walton, Georgia, s.v. "Wilson Lumpkin," accessed August 16, 2021, Ancestry.com. The omission reveals as much as it aims to conceal, reinforcing racialized colonialism's obfuscation of the connection between enslavement and settler colonialism under which it operates.

90. Lumpkin, *Removal of the Cherokee*, 71. Charles Easton Haynes, in his remarks to the U.S. House of Representatives on June 27, 1836, describes Georgia in the anthropomorphized, feminized way I detailed earlier, but he also makes clear a connection between enslavement, race, and colonialism that echoes the Lumpkin quote. Haynes says,

> The Cherokee drove her to the alternative of surrendering forever to a hostile and foreign Government a portion of her own territory, or extending her jurisdiction over it. In this extremity she adopted the course sanctioned by the example of all the original States of the Union. She determined to govern her own territory, and the people upon it, in her own way. Whatever of seeming severity may be found in her legislation on this subject, is the consequence of Cherokee defiance of her lawful authority, sanctioned and encouraged here and elsewhere, by those whose sympathies are a thousand times stronger toward the Indian and African race, than for the white man of the south, especially if he be a citizen of Georgia—by men who have but one short step to take, to be found brandishing the tomahawk and scalping knife in the ranks of the Indian. (Haynes, "Remarks of Mr. Haynes", 15–16)

91. King, *Black Shoals*, 24. See also Hartman, *Scenes of Subjection*, chap. 4; and Wynter's theorization of "Man," Indigeneity, and Blackness in "1492."

92. See Fielder, *Relative Races*; Glymph, *Out of the House*; Jones-Rogers, *They Were Her Property*; Kaplan, "Manifest Domesticity," in *The Anarchy of Empire*, 23–50; and Limerick, "Empire of Innocence," in *Legacy of Conquest*, 35–54.

93. According to Deborah Rosen, other legal categories were more common in the other British colonies, but Native enslavement was most pervasive in Georgia and South Carolina and throughout the South: "For example, in the preamble to a 1755 statute, the Georgia legislature noted the fact that 'in his Majesty's Plantations in American Slavery has been introduced and Allowed the people commonly called Negroes, Indians, Mulatoes, and Mestizos have been deemed Absolute Slaves.'" Rosen, *American Indians*, 10–11.

94. Haynes, *Speech of Mr. Haynes*. Supporters of the Cherokee cause like Robert Campbell of Savannah, Jeremiah Evarts, or William Wirt also yoke the compact of 1802 discussions to the Georgia-Cherokee sovereignty disputes, although they have an almost antithetical reading to that of Hynes and Lumpkin. Robert Campbell, "Memorial to the Honourable President and Members of the Senate of the State of Georgia," *Cherokee Phoenix*, April 29, 1829; Evarts, "Essay 20," in *Cherokee Removal*, 153–61; Cherokee Nation v. Georgia, 5 Pet. 1 (1831).

95. Lumpkin, *Removal of the Cherokee*, 42.

96. In response to the Cherokee constitution, the Georgia General Assembly began passing legislation to seize control of Cherokee territory, but the federal government and

the Cherokee Nation challenged these attempts. Lumpkin seems to be projecting a future Georgia onto the past of 1827, a colonial rewriting of history.

97. Present-day Dahlonega is part of Lumpkin County—yet another example of how Georgia's violent history folds into county names and state maps. It is also a popular tourist destination that celebrates its gold mining past.

98. For a discussion of the Gilmer-Lumpkin gubernatorial race, see Jennison, *Cultivating Race*, 285–89.

99. "Progress of the Georgia Laws," *Cherokee Phoenix*, May 4, 1833.

100. Miles succinctly describes Georgia politicians' total disregard for Cherokee sovereignty:

> After the discovery of gold in Cherokee territory, the governor of Georgia, already incensed at the Cherokee adoption of a constitution, made the unprecedented move of extending Georgia's legal jurisdiction over the Cherokee Nation and annulling all Cherokee laws. As far as Georgia was concerned, the Cherokee government no longer existed, and Cherokee people were subject to the mandates of the southern state. This action would be challenged and legally overturned by the United States Supreme Court in 1832, but in the meantime, Georgia politicians enforced the takeover with military might. Cherokee country was now occupied territory, patrolled by officers of the Georgia militia and peopled by an influx of white settlers and gold seekers. (Miles, *Ties That Bind*, 132)

101. An issue of the *Athenian* details a secondhand account of Cherokees turning out white intruders from Vann's Valley. It describes the Cherokees as "savages" and "barbarians" who chose a stormy day to turn out women and children. The Cherokees claim it is their land, but Georgians claim jurisdiction since the cession of Creek lands to the state. The article unapologetically expresses comfort in the violent suppression of Cherokees: "We regret that the mob who accompanied the party in pursuit, could not be rest[r]ained from inflicting more summary punishment upon the barbarians—we regret that it was not let for the laws of the state to take their silent but sure course in bringing them to justice." "Indian Depredations," *Athenian*, February 23, 1830, Georgia Historic Newspapers, https://gahistoricnewspapers.galileo.usg.edu/lccn/sn85027027/1830-02-23/ed-1/seq-2/.

102. Ross says the following in a letter to Secretary of War Lewis Cass:

> Yet strange as it may seem to be, but it is nevertheless true, that these complaints have not been made to cease by any effectual order from the Department to the agent (Hugh Montgomery). However, when we reflect and see that the agent (Colo. Montgomery) has himself countenanced and permitted his own son-in-law John Hardwick to reside in the nation and to cultivate Cherokee lands in the vicinity of the agency, regardless of the remonstrances of our Genl. Council, it is a circumstance not so much to be wondered at, that he should indulge other intruders who have only followed the example of his own son-in-law. (Ross, *Papers of Chief John Ross*, 266)

103. Marshall was a staunch Federalist and continually at odds with President Jackson and the states' rights agenda of the Democratic Party. Marshall and Jackson's tension was well known in the 1830s. For further discussion of the Marshall trilogy, see Barker, "For Whom Sovereignty Matters"; and Norgren, *Cherokee Cases*.

104. However, in *Removal of the Cherokee*, Lumpkin critiques Jackson for occasionally *not* being pro-Removal enough. Lumpkin, *Removal of the Cherokee*, 194–95.

105. Federal Road was built starting in 1810 by Georgians, Tennesseans, and Cherokees as a toll road running through the Nation. James Vann lobbied to have the road run through Cherokee Nation and close to his plantation and businesses to increase his wealth. Miles, *House on Diamond Hill*, 60–62. It aided travel, transportation of goods, and a broad postal network. However, it also facilitated greater access to the Nation for non-Cherokees, initially an influx of white squatters and later the Georgia Guard.

106. Lumpkin, *Removal of the Cherokee*, 42.

107. "To the Committee and Council," *Cherokee Phoenix*, November 12, 1831.

108. An influx of white migrants in the first decades of the nineteenth century reshaped the political and economic terrain of Georgia; as less affluent white people came to Georgia, many of them to dig for gold or invade Cherokee lands without consent, the affluent, established class of elite white Georgia men lost an oligarchical hold on state politics. Politicians were forced to pay greater attention to the interests of the growing numbers of white migrants if they wanted to maintain their positions. Lumpkin's appeal among this new migrant class of white workers is one of the reasons he beat Gilmer in the 1831 gubernatorial election. Jennison, *Cultivating Race*, 210–13.

109. Jennison, 225–26.

110. Smith, "A Map of the 4th District," in *Cherokee Land Lottery*.

111. Lumpkin, *Removal of the Cherokee*, 184.

112. He writes, "The insolence and irregularity of the Indians may be traced first, to the imprudence of the Legislature in abolishing the guard; and, secondly, to the unprincipled and lying newspapers and demagogues of our own State." Lumpkin, *Removal of the Cherokee*, 218.

113. Lumpkin's writing, collected in *Removal of the Cherokee*, also betrays anxieties about the historical record and his ability to control his legacy. Almost a decade and a half after the forced Removal of Cherokees from their homelands, Lumpkin still complains that the press promulgated a false understanding of Removal and tarnished his reputation, while insisting that his commitment to Removal was a just cause. He writes, "I continue to see, up to the present day (May 1st, 1852), newspaper articles, letter writers, periodicals, and religious magazines filled with articles calculated, if not designed, to falsify all the truths of historic facts in relation to Cherokee history—more especially, everything connected with the actings and doings of Georgia, in connection with these Indians." Lumpkin, *Removal of the Cherokee*, 186. Lumpkin imagines his book, a collection of earlier speeches and writings as well as autobiographical reflections, to refute popular histories that depict the state of Georgia (as well as him) disparagingly for the unspeakable treatment of the Cherokees (and Creeks). Nonetheless, even these refutations express anxiety about his ability to control the print record. In a brief reflection Lumpkin includes at the end of volume 1 of *Removal of the Cherokee*, he argues that reading the letters he is reprinting in their entirety "as I have arranged them" leads any "sensible reader" to see that Lumpkin's actions as governor were not only laudable but also beneficial to the Cherokees. Lumpkin, 368–69.

114. The annual Native American Festival and Pow Wow, one of the largest powwows in Georgia, is held at Stone Mountain Park.

Chapter Two

1. At the time, the Floridas were also referred to as East and West Florida.

2. "Georgia & Florida Boundary Line," *Georgia Journal* (Milledgeville), February 4, 1828, Georgia Historic Newspapers, https://gahistoricnewspapers.galileo.usg.edu/lccn/sn82014251 /1828-02-04/ed-1/seq-2/.

3. The disputes about the Florida-Georgia boundary had an even more extensive history going back to the U.S. Revolutionary War regarding the international border between Spanish America and Georgia. In both the 1790s and 1820s boundary disputes, the primary source of disagreement was the point of origin of the Saint Marys River. See Morton, "Boundaries of Georgia." In a message to the president, then-governor John Forsyth of Georgia not only explained the state's position on the border but also suggested that the only reason the United States and Spain were able to agree on a boundary in 1802 was their desire to "produce an immediate good effect on the Indians." John Forsyth, "Boundary Line," *Macon Telegraph*, April 21, 1828, Georgia Historic Newspapers, https://gahistoricnewspapers.galileo.usg.edu /lccn/sn82014386/1828-04-21/ed-1/seq-1/.

4. U.S. Department of State, *Treaty of San Lorenzo*, 2. Ellicott ran the line in 1800 when it was the Spanish Florida–Georgia border. In his journal, published in 1803, he wrote that "the astronomical part of the boundary" was complete, and all that was left was to "make out the report, with the maps or charts of the line." U.S. Department of State, 15. In his letter to the Department of State, Ellicott provides further detail on his troubles running the line in 1800. His writings show that Indigenous people, likely from various communities, collectively worked together to thwart the survey and demanded a meeting with the Spanish governor of Florida, at which they expressed their disagreement with the endeavor. Ellicott's frustration is palpable in his journal, and his description of the incident evidences that Indigenous people in the region were keenly aware that the survey was a project that would in no way benefit Indigenous communities. Their collective efforts to circumvent the project were fairly successful for decades. U.S. Department of State, 2–9.

5. From the 1820s to the 1840s, Florida newspapers publicly staged debates about statehood. Affluent white settlers, especially plantation owners, denounced any form of statehood because they felt it would increase taxation. East Florida papers based out of St. Augustine and Jacksonville, like the *News, Courier*, and *Republican*, also ran editorials suggesting that East Florida was more "advanced" and economically better off than middle and West Florida, and single statehood would be to the political and economic detriment of East Floridians.

6. These wars are often called the Seminole Wars—the First U.S.-Seminole War (1816–18), Second U.S.-Seminole War (1835–42), and Third U.S.-Seminole War (1855–58)—but the fighting they denote simplifies the combatants into two distinct sides. I cite these conflicts as "U.S.-Seminole" rather than "Seminole" following the same rationale that leads scholars to prefer "U.S.-Mexico War"—the United States' aggression is stated and not simply an absent presence.

7. Manu Karuka's emphasis on the power of the rumor helps us think through the limits of certain kinds of archival work and fields of study. Karuka suggests that "rumors, as they appear in colonial archives, often share more than a critique of colonial power; they also outline a field of possible responses." Karuka, *Empire's Tracks*, 4.

8. King, *Black Shoals*, 42.

9. To reiterate, I use the term "Black Seminole" to describe Seminole-enslaved people because that has been a term preferred by community members. While this can complicate terminology, as I use "Freedperson" to describe formerly enslaved people from multiple nations in Indian Territory in chapter 4, the mess invites us to agitate U.S.-based racial categories that are and always have been anti-Black and anti-Indigenous. I err on the side of confusion over simplicity to amplify the beautifully textured lives that come to the fore in Afro-Native histories. Seminole people of African descent blur distinct lines between Seminole and Black Seminole as well.

10. "Seminole Tribune: Voice of the Unconquered," Seminole Tribe of Florida website, accessed July 14, 2021, www.semtribe.com/stof/seminole-tribune/about-us.

11. The No-Transfer Resolution was a U.S. response to fears that Spain would turn Florida over to Great Britain. The possibility of British rule in Florida for a second time raised great anxieties for U.S. politicians—a mere year before formal hostilities broke out between the two countries—but it also signaled an imperial struggle over Florida that stretched back to 1763. With the end of the Seven Years' War, Britain agreed to return Havana if Spain would grant Britain control of its Florida territory. Upon gaining the territory, Britain split the space into two—East Florida and West Florida. Twenty years later, Spain regained control of the territory, but U.S. interest in the Floridas increased after independence from Britain.

12. Eleven years before Florida officially became U.S. territory and twelve years before the Monroe Doctrine, Congress asserted the right to invade the "said territory":

> Taking into view the peculiar position of Spain and her American provinces; and considering the influence which the destiny of the territory adjoining the southern boundary of the United States may have upon their security, tranquility, and commerce: Therefore, *Resolved, by the Senate and House of Representatives of the United States of America in Congress assembled,* that the United States, under the peculiar circumstances of the existing crisis, cannot without serious inquietude see any part of the said territory pass into the hands of any foreign Power; and that a due regard to their own safety compels them to provide under certain contingencies, for the temporary occupation of the said territory; they, at the same time, declare that the said territory shall, in their hands, remain subject to a future negotiation. ("No-Transfer Resolution," quoted in Belko, "Epilogue to the War," 57)

Of interest in the statement is its emphasis on the "peculiarity" of conflict over Florida and its assertion of a preordained future as part of the United States. We see the United States avow power based on its "peculiar" proximity to territory.

13. This rhetoric is repeated in later conflicts across the continent and beyond. Manifest Destiny becomes a speculative discourse undergirding U.S. colonial expansion, but also a remapping of space through a model of territoriality that imagines U.S. continental control as a teleological project of incorporation. In these efforts to distinguish the United States from "foreign" powers, we also see an early trace of the paradoxical foreign-domestic logic used by Chief Justice John Marshall in *Cherokee Nation v. Georgia* (1831), in which the Supreme Court argued the Cherokee Nation (and all Native nations) were domestically dependent on the United States.

14. One of the most colorful schemes for wresting control of Florida, however, did acknowledge the influence and power of Native peoples in the Southeast—at least initially. William August Bowles led an unlikely alliance of various Native, Maroon, and white groups that wrought havoc on plantations and settlements. He also attempted to appropriate a sense of Native national sovereignty in his state-making efforts, "United Nations of Creeks and Cherokees" and "State of Muskogee." In 1805, however, Bowles died in a Spanish prison in Havana after a group of Muscogees turned him over to the Spanish. They were tired of his plundering and skirmishes in their territory. See Landers, *Atlantic Creoles*, 100–110.

15. U.S. interventions, including the annexation of West Florida in 1810, the War of 1812, the U.S.-Creek War of 1813–14, Andrew Jackson's occupation in 1814 (and again in 1818), and the destruction of the Negro Fort in 1816, were all part of a long-term campaign to gain U.S. control of Florida. Seminole Wars historian John Mahon argues that the U.S. government attempted to "drape its activity in rectitude" throughout the repeated invasions into Florida. Mahon, *History of the Second*, 26.

16. This is the earliest issue of the newspaper I have been able to find. Since the "Historical Sketch of Florida" is printed as a continuation, it seems safe to assume the July 28 edition is not the first.

17. I use "Hispanic" to describe Hernández here because of his liminal position as an agent both of Spain and of the United States in a moment of geopolitical flux that also inflected categories of identification.

18. In passing, the sketch briefly mentions the Seminoles, describing them as a temporary nuisance quelled during the First U.S.-Seminole War.

19. We cannot be sure who Democritus was. They may have been the newspaper's editor. But the authenticity and veracity of Democritus are less significant to me than the way the editorial discursively contributes to the territorial narrative told by the paper as a whole.

20. Editorial, *Florida Gazette* (East Florida), September 15, 1821, Nineteenth-Century U.S. Newspapers, https://link.gale.com/apps/doc/GT3014121801/NCNP?u=ucsandiego&sid =bookmark-NCNP&xid=3932a91f.

21. See Hogarth, *Medicalizing Blackness*.

22. For a sense of how early Spanish-English bilingual newspapers published by Latinos differed, see Kanellos and Martell, *Hispanic Periodicals*, 77–78.

23. It also seems of significance that in President Monroe's justification for U.S. oversight in the Americas, he lists the proliferation of statehood as *the* primary warrant to justify the overarching claims of the doctrine. His assertion of a paternalistic reach across the many nations and peoples of the Americas also echoes the rhetoric of James Gadsden's speech to the Seminoles. U.S. military and economic strength and a growing U.S. population enable the settler nation to stretch across disparate peoples and lands. Monroe, "President's Message," 22–23.

24. Americanus, "For the Florida Gazette. To the Spanish Inhabitants of St. Augustine," *Florida Gazette*, September 8, 1821, Nineteenth-Century U.S. Newspapers, https://link.gale .com/apps/doc/GT3014121782/NCNP?u=ucsandiego&sid=bookmark-NCNP&xid =e3383c96. "Free male inhabitants" is the language used in the official notice from territorial governor Andrew Jackson calling for Spanish inhabitants to voluntarily apply for U.S. citizenship, which appears in the same issue as Americanus's editorial.

25. Hymen, "For the Florida Gazette," *Florida Gazette*, September 15, 1821.

26. Moses Jumper, "Major Dade," in *Echoes in the Wind*, 33.

27. Jumper, 33.

28. Jumper, 33. It should again be noted that Jumper himself served as editor of the Seminole Tribe of Florida's newspaper the *Seminole Tribune* for years.

29. As Deborah Rosen observes of the war's signature conflicts, "Like the 1816 attack on the Prospect Bluff fort, the Florida invasion of 1818 attempted to eliminate safe havens for self-emancipated people and put an end to cross-border attacks by Black and Seminole raiders. It was not a coincidence that it was Andrew Jackson who initiated both incursions." Rosen, *Border Law*, 164.

30. Blomley, "Law, Property," 134. For additional analyses of the role of the survey in the United States, see Hubbard, *American Boundaries*; and Johnson, *Order upon the Land*.

31. Mahon writes that little was known of Florida Territory's interior in 1835 at the start of the Second U.S.-Seminole War: "No white man had seen the greater part of its 58,560 square miles, nor did anyone then know its area. Maps accurately showed the outlines of the peninsula, but the interior, south of the little town of Micanopy, was either incorrectly shown or else left blank." Mahon, *History of the Second*, 129.

32. "East Florida—Alligators—Seminoles, etc.," *Knickerbocker: or, New York Monthly Magazine*, August/September 1836, 150, https://babel.hathitrust.org/cgi/pt?id=mdp.39015011269829&view =1up&seq=164.

33. Allewaert, *Ariel's Ecology*, 34. While Allewaert provides a compelling argument about how the "dense networks" of the ecological world worked against the plantation zone, she only cursorily discusses Indigeneity.

34. Navakas, "Island Nation," 263.

35. Many of the people who served in the wars, especially the Second U.S.-Seminole War, wrote and published poetry and fiction as a way to describe (and often capitalize on) their experiences. Florida was both a space imagined by soldiers and a space experienced by them, and the two were often incongruous.

36. James Leitch Wright, *Creeks and Seminoles*, 275.

37. Sprague, *Origin, Progress, and Conclusion*, 310. The preface to the 1964 reprinting of the memoir calls the Second U.S.-Seminole War the "Seminole-Negro war." Patrick, "Editorial Preface" in *Origin, Progress, and Conclusion*, xi–xii.

38. Missall and Missall, *Seminole Wars*, xv. It was also costly for Florida Territory, which had to fund the territorial militia throughout that time.

39. James Cusick was generous enough to share with me his presentation to the Florida Historical Society on the difference between the various versions, as well as the provenance of the imagery. The full title of the first edition was *An Authentic Narrative of the Seminole War: Its Cause, Rise, and Progress, and a Minute Detail of the Horrid Massacres of the Whites, by the Indians and Negroes, in Florida, in the Months of December, January, and February; Communicated to the Press by a Gentleman Who Has Spent Eleven Weeks in Florida, Near to the Scene of the Indian Depredations, and in a Situation to Collect Every Important Fact relating Thereto.* The second edition was published just a few months later by the same publisher: *An Authentic Narrative of the Seminole War: And of the Miraculous Escape of Mrs. Mary Godfrey, and Her Four Female Children. Annexed Is a Minute Detail of the Horrid Massacres of the Whites; by the Indians and Negroes in Florida in the Months of December, January, and February.*

The third: *A True and Authentic Account of the Indian War in Florida, Giving the Particulars Respecting the Murder of the Widow Robbins, and the Providential Escape of Her Daughter Aurelia, and Her Lover, Mr. Charles Somers, after Suffering Almost Innumerable Hardships. The Whole Compiled from the Most Authentic Sources* (New York: Saunders and Van Welt, 1836). In his paper, Cusick clarifies the differences between the three publications of *An Authentic Narrative* and their repurposing of other sources. Cusick, "Public Viewpoint."

40. I describe the man as a Maroon in order to attend to how he, as a character, is committed to Black freedom outside the United States. *Authentic Narrative*, 10.

41. Cusick persuasively offers context for both pamphlets in a blog post for the Smathers Libraries. Cusick, "Hidden Meanings."

42. Cusick, "Hidden Meanings."

43. King, *Black Shoals*, 75.

44. Cusick, "Hidden Meanings."

45. "Mary Godfrey," in Derounian-Stodola, *Women's Indian Captivity Narratives*, 211–34.

46. *Authentic Narrative*, 3.

47. *Authentic Narrative*, 10.

48. Fielder, *Relative Races*, 170. For other scholarly readings of this scene, see Burnham, *Captivity and Sentiment*; and Navakas, *Liquid Landscape*.

49. Before spotting the Seminoles, he offers to show them "to a path" to "the plantation of some of their friends." *Authentic Narrative*, 10.

50. *Narrative of the Life*, 13.

51. *Narrative of the Life*, 10.

52. The final paragraph of *An Authentic Narrative of the Seminole War*, for example, begins with the following bleak commentary: "There has been a fatal error on the part of the Government in relation to the strength of these Indians, and the facilities they have for procrastinating the war." *Authentic Narrative*, 24.

53. A comment from the memoir of John Bemrose, who served as an enlisted man during the Second U.S.-Seminole War, expresses the disgust many felt about the conflict: "My reader will be ready to ask why all this strife and bloodshed between the mercenaries of a great nation and one small tribe of Indians located in a wilderness so inaccessible to white men. All I can answer is that it is the natural heart of [the] white man filled with sin and craving for more than is good for him. The government of the United States is not so much to blame as at first sight appears, but the citizens and squatters are generally the first intermeddlers and it is they which invite the government to take the matter in hand." Bemrose, *Reminiscences*, 53. He calls out the violence and greed undergirding U.S. colonial warfare in Florida. He also reveals the multiscalar work of statehood and territorial acquisition, which relies on *both* official campaigns of the federal government, the recruitment of militias and volunteers from across the region, *and* the vigilantism of white settlers operating outside the interests of the U.S. legal system.

54. He in fact makes an appearance in *An Authentic Narrative*, where Osceola is described as even more successful than Black Hawk at "frustrat[ing] measures of our government, for the removal of the Indians." *Authentic Narrative*, 4.

55. F. Evan Nooe convincingly argues that the Second U.S.-Seminole War was hugely influential in shaping a regional "Southern" identity, and newspapers played a vital role in the discourse and in the recruitment of white male volunteers to fight in Florida. Nooe, "'Zealous in the Cause.'"

56. Mahon, *History of the Second*, 132. Myer M. Cohen describes the production and circulation of newspapers among soldiers in his memoir. Cohen, *Notices of Florida*. Cusick compiled an extensive historiography of nineteenth-century Florida that includes publications during the wars. See Cusick, "Historiography."

57. Aldrich and Anderson, *Echoes from a Distant Frontier*, 84.

58. John M. Coward offers the following as an explanation of how news and misinformation about Florida were disseminated in the United States:

> The Seminole Wars of the 1820s and 1830s provided many examples of confusion and rumor in the news. Newspapers throughout the country reported the story, but few had reliable sources of information. Instead, news reports slowly made their way back from travelers, soldiers, and sailors who told what they knew to newspapermen in Florida or neighboring states. Such stories were subject to exaggeration, misstatement, and a host of other errors. Once published, however, these stories could be picked up by exchange papers, repeating whatever errors appeared in the original published accounts. And in the news-gathering era before the telegraph, editors had no timely way of verifying such reports. (Coward, *Newspaper Indian*, 54)

59. For a discussion of the rise of party papers, see Nerone, "Newspapers," 234.

60. Miles, *Ties That Bind*, 78–83.

61. Virginia Bergman Peters, *Florida Wars*, 159.

62. Missall and Missall, *Seminole Wars*, 137.

63. The name Osceola was a transcription created by members of the American military who had heard his name spoken by other Native people. Other iterations of his name include Asi Yoholo and Asin Yahola. I use "Osceola" because it is the version used on the Seminole Tribe of Florida's website. "Historic Seminole," Seminole Tribe of Florida website, accessed September 3, 2020, www.semtribe.com/STOF/history/historic-seminole.

64. Virginia Bergman Peters, *Florida Wars*, 95.

65. Cohen, *Notices of Florida*, 126. The verity of Cohen's text is suspect, but as with the early Florida newspapers, I am less interested in Cohen as a truthteller and more interested in him as a storyteller—more specifically, as a storyteller capitalizing on a particular historical moment.

66. Mahon, *History of the Second*, 214. At the end of the century, Native resistance fighters, including Geronimo, were forcibly Removed east and incarcerated at Fort Marion. Captain Richard Henry Pratt, who worked as a jailer during this time, based much of his approach to Native education at Carlisle Boarding School on his experiences at Fort Marion, and some of his first students were previously incarcerated at the fort.

67. Mahon, *History of the Second*, 217–18.

68. O'Brien, *Firsting and Lasting*, 109. In these literary accounts one can also read Osceola, as Osceola became a figure of what Gordon M. Sayre calls the "Indian chief as tragic hero," which he says was consistent with tragedy's sociocultural functions in the eighteenth and nineteenth centuries. Sayre explains that "only catharsis reconciles the contradictory reactions of enmity and admiration, pity, fear, and censure and articulates the responses of both historical agents and distant audiences." Sayre, *Indian Chief*, 5–6.

69. The Osceola narratives that circulated in the first half of the century included the following: Buntline, *White Wizard*; Mayne Reed, *Osceola the Seminole*; and Ransom, *Osceola*.

Some examples of Osceola poetry include [Anonymous], "Osceola," *Waldo Patriot* (Belfast, Maine), March 23, 1838, Early Visions of Florida, https://earlyfloridalit.net/anonymous -oseola/; James Henry Carleton, "The Death of Osceola," *Gentleman's Magazine* (Philadelphia), May 1838, American Periodical Series II, www.proquest.com/magazines/death-osceola /docview/124737183/se-2?accountid=14524; [Josephine], "Osceola," *Hudson River Chronicle*, April 4, 1838, Early Visions of Florida, https://earlyfloridalit.net/josephine-osceola/; Leslie, "Osceola: Dirge of the Indian Braves," *Ladies' Companion* (New York City), March 1838, American Periodical Series II, www.proquest.com/magazines/osceola/docview /136949715/se-2?accountid=14524; L. H., "Osceola," *New-York Mirror*, March 24, 1838, American Periodical Series II, www.proquest.com/magazines/original-outline-sketches/docview /136451433/se-2?accountid=14524; Theta, "Osceola," *American Monthly Magazine* (New York City), June 1838, American Periodical Series II, www.proquest.com/magazines/osceola /docview/89576120/se-2?accountid=14524; and P. H. M., "Osceola's Soliloquy," *Knickerbocker; or New York Monthly Magazine*, July 1838, American Periodical Series II, www.proquest .com/magazines/osceolas-soliloquy/docview/137183478/se-2?accountid=14524.

70. Catlin was not the only artist to depict Osceola. For a discussion of the various contemporaneous portraits, see Wickman, "Through the Eyes of Those Who Saw Him," in *Osceola's Legacy*.

71. See Wickman, "The Weedon Family," in *Osceola's Legacy*.

72. Catlin, *Letters and Notes*, 220.

73. Catlin, 220.

74. Mahon, *History of the Second*, 218.

75. In *An Authentic Narrative*, discussed earlier, Osceola's murder of Thompson is a pivotal scene in which Osceola feigns friendship so he can get close enough to kill Thompson. Indian scouts were perceived as trying to do good and help the Seminoles; murdering scouts ostensibly demonstrated just how little the Seminoles appreciated what was perceived as white benevolence. Moreover, the suggestion that Osceola could trick a U.S. official raised anxiety about the efficacy of outsmarting the Indian Other. *Authentic Narrative*, 5.

76. Following Osceola's death, the *Niles' National Register* said that he "will long be remembered as the man that with the feeblest means produced the most terrible effects." Virginia Bergman Peters, *Florida Wars*, 161. In his memoir, O. O. Howard refers to Osceola as "brave, wary, revengeful and able." Howard, *My Life and Experiences*, 568. The compiled memoir of the Second Dragoons describes him as "young and ambitious, eloquent in council, and brave in action" and says "he proved a formidable enemy." Rodenbough, *From the Everglades*, 18.

77. Even with Catlin's portrait, Osceola did have some control over his image, including what he wore and how he chose to pose. While there were attempts to separate the man from his portrait, he still disrupted the portraiture narrative in subtle ways.

78. Renato Rosaldo understands this desire for mythmaking as "imperialist nostalgia" in which one simultaneously announces one's innocence by declaring what one has destroyed, a "nostalgia at play with domination. . . ." For Rosaldo, all "ideological discourses work more through selective attention than outright suppression," and we see this in the cultural-literary elegy that followed Osceola's death. Rosaldo, *Culture and Truth*, 87.

79. Such revisioning perhaps helps explain how I have discussed Walt Whitman's depiction of Osceola elsewhere. See Walkiewicz, "Portraits and Politics."

80. Walt Whitman published his "Osceola" poem in *Munyon's Illustrated World in 1890* (and later included it in his "Second Annex" section of *Leaves of Grass*).

81. Albery Whitman held a strong stance on the political and aesthetic power of poetry. In *The Rape of Florida*'s dedicatory address, he argues that, unlike newspapers, government documents, or other forms of print and narration that claimed verity, poetry is "a secret interpreter, she waits not for data, phenomena, and manifestations, but anticipates and spells the wishes of Heaven." Whitman, "Dedicatory Address" in *Rape of Florida*, 5.

82. Sandler, *Black Revolution*, 159.

83. "In the eighteenth century, a series of migrations brought in three of the groups of towns that would form the Seminole Nation. The fourth group arrived in the nineteenth century. By the outbreak of the war with the Americans in 1835, those four groups of towns—the Apalachees (Mekusukeys), Alachuas, Apalachicolas, and Redsticks—appear to have been four largely autonomous regional chiefdoms that began merging into a single Seminole nation not long before the war and the removal." Miller, *Coacoochee's Bones*, 9.

84. For further reading on Seminole, Afro-Seminole, and Black alliances during the Seminole wars, see Kly, "Gullah War"; and Twyman, *Black Seminole Legacy*.

85. Other events that exacerbated tensions leading up to the war were Andrew Jackson's brazen desire to take West Florida from Spain, his punishment of Native people who fled from his invasions into Muscogee communities in Alabama and Georgia, and an alliance between Black people and Seminoles to thwart white enslavers searching for formerly enslaved self-emancipated people in the territory.

86. Porter, *Black Seminoles*, 16.

87. Jackson ordered Brigadier General Edmund P. Gaines to destroy the fort, and he and his troops did so on July 27, 1816. For a discussion of the Negro Fort, see James Leitch Wright, *Creeks and Seminoles*, 197–99.

88. In reflecting on the Negro Fort, I am also reminded of the opening scene in Harney and Moten's *The Undercommons*, which asks us to rethink the spatial and political positioning the image of the settler fort presents. See Harney and Moten, *Undercommons*, 17.

89. Sandler argues that in the poem, "Whitman casts racial mixture as a sublime counterpoint to the sexual violence at the center of the New World contact narrative." Sandler, *Black Revolution*, 175.

90. Sandler, 156, 157.

91. Whitman, *Not a Man*. Whitman's poem "Custer's Last Ride" also depicts General Custer as a martyr. Whitman, "Custer's Last Ride," in *At the Dusk*, 244–45.

92. Ivy Wilson writes that "Whitman's belief in the United States was unduly, almost blindingly, strident, so much so that he seldom made reference to other locales and countries to which black Americans might have held an affinity." Wilson, "Introduction," 12–13.

93. Whitman, *Rape of Florida*, canto 3, stanza 45, lines 1–9.

94. Porter, *Black Seminoles*, 4.

95. Miller, "Seminoles and Africans," 190.

96. Miller, 190.

97. Maillard, "Redwashing History," 96.

98. While the Seminoles in Oklahoma and Florida have strong cultural and historical ties, they are separate nations and do not share consensus on tribal membership or sub-

scribe to the same enrollment procedures. For further reading, see Miller, "Seminoles and Africans"; Maillard, "Redwashing History"; and Mulroy, *Seminole Freedmen*.

99. Melinda Micco provides a nuanced analysis of how anti-Blackness became incorporated into the Five Tribes' autonomy in the twentieth century but also interrogates U.S. complicity in such anti-Blackness even when the federal government denounced the Seminole Tribe of Oklahoma's decision to remove Seminole Freedmen from tribal enrollment. See Micco, "'Blood and Money.'"

100. Delany, *Blake*, 88.

101. Klos, "Blacks and the Seminole," 138. As Kevin Mulroy further explains, "It emerges that Africans and Indians were joined in a close military alliance in opposition to American expansionism. The two groups needed each other—the blacks to preserve their freedom and the Seminoles their land. Joint military ventures tended to be well organized and usually were successful." Mulroy reinscribes the dialectic of Indigeneity/land and Blackness/bodies in ways that simplify Florida combat, but he persuasively argues why the Florida coalitions were such a powerful force. Mulroy, *Freedom on the Border*, 17.

102. Clavin, "'It Is a Negro,'" 182, 199.

103. Cohen, *Notices of Florida*, 46. Congressman Joshua Giddings's *Exiles of Florida* served as an abolitionist tract that emphasized the relationship between enslavement and the Second U.S.-Seminole War. Moreover, John and Mary Lou Missall note Giddings's use of the war to break the congressional gag rule on slavery: "On one occasion, in response to the protest of a fellow congressman, Giddings informed the Chair, 'I will, however, assure this gentleman from South Carolina that I shall abide to the subject of slavery so far as it stands connected with the Florida War.' He then continued on with his harangue, 'alluding' to the subject of slavery no less than 267 times." Missall and Missall, *Seminole Wars*, 180–82.

104. Littlefield, *Africans and Seminoles*, 10.

105. Whitman, *Rape of Florida*, canto 3, stanza 52, lines 1–9.

106. Mahon, *History of the Second*, 321.

107. Whitman, *Rape of Florida*, canto 4, stanza 49, lines 1–2.

108. Gumbs, *Spill*; McKittrick, *Demonic Grounds*, 17–18; Moten, *In the Break*. Leanne Betasamosake Simpson also draws specific connections between Nishnaabeg and Maroon ontologies. She argues that *biiskabiyang*, which she understands as "the embodied process of freedom," is a form of marronage. She also acknowledges Gumbs's emphasis on presentness and fugitivity in an interview for *Spill*. Simpson, *As We Have Always Done*, 17.

109. Missall and Missall, *In Their Own Words*, 8. Tukose Emathla's mention of the book echoes the "talking book" trope in African American literature. See Gates, "The Trope of the Talking Book," in *Signifying Monkey*, 139–83.

110. "Seminole Tribune: Voice of the Unconquered," Seminole Tribe of Florida website, accessed July 14, 2021, www.semtribe.com/stof/seminole-tribune/about-us. Today the paper is called the *Seminole Tribune*.

111. Margo Harakas, "The Story of Betty Mae Jumper—Living History—a Nurse, an Author, a Mother, a Survivor, Betty Mae Jumper Is a Bridge Linking Two Eras of Seminole Culture," *Fort Lauderdale Sun-Sentinel*, March 23, 1997, NewsBank: Access World News—Historical and Current, https://infoweb.newsbank.com/apps/news/document-view?p=WORLDNEWS&docref=news/0EB5160C4B1E999E.

112. Betty Mae Tiger Jumper and West, *Seminole Legend*, 7.

113. Missall and Missall, *Seminole Wars*, 209. However, the motto was controversial enough that the flag never became an official state flag.

114. In 1957 the Seminole Tribe of Florida established a constitution, gained federal recognition, and established a business charter for the Seminole Tribe of Florida, Inc. Following these changes, the Seminole Tribe began vigorously pursuing economic possibilities in the state, becoming the first federally recognized tribe to establish a high-stakes casino. For more on the Seminole Tribe of Florida and gaming, see Cattelino, *High Stakes*.

Chapter Three

1. Sandler, *Black Revolution*, 159; Whitman, "Dedication," in *Twasinta's Seminoles*, 3. Robinson was governor of Kansas Territory and then the state of Kansas. Proslavery Kansas settlers challenged his territorial term because they said the Topeka Constitution (1856) under which he was elected was illegal. Whitman lived in Kansas for a significant period, which also helps explain his choice of Robinson. For more on the influence of Kansas on Whitman's writing, see Sandler, *Black Romantic*, 177–80.

2. Sundquist, *To Wake the Nations*, 174.

3. Clara Sue Kidwell explains, "Indian Territory in the early 1850s ostensibly covered the entire Midwest, but the federal government easily forced land cession treaties in 1854 with the tribes in what became the new states of Kansas and Nebraska. It had become perfectly apparent by 1855 that the integrity of the much-diminished Indian Territory was under attack." Kidwell, *Choctaws in Oklahoma*, 88.

4. Anne F. Hyde writes, "The Kansas-Nebraska Act opened up land for settlement when not one acre was actually available," thus "rewriting . . . nearly a century's work of Indian policy to make Kansas and Nebraska into white settler states." Hyde, *Empires, Nations, and Families*, 479.

5. Murphree, "Kansas," 382–85.

6. The final section of the Kansas-Nebraska Act specifically addresses Indian treaties. Section 37 states, "And be it further enacted, That all treaties, laws, and other engagements made by the government of the United States with the Indian tribes inhabiting the territories embraced within this act, shall be faithfully and rigidly observed, notwithstanding anything contained in this act; and that the existing agencies and superintendencies of said Indians be continued with the same powers and duties which are now prescribed by law, except that the President of the United States may, at his discretion, change the location of the office of the superintendent." An Act to Organize the Territories of Nebraska and Kansas, *United States Statutes at Large*, 33rd Cong., 1st Sess. (1854), chap. 59, https://catalog.archives.gov/id/1501722.

7. Warrior cites John Joseph Mathews at the end of this passage: "(Mathews, *The Osages: Children of the Middle Waters*, 624, 645–66)." Warrior, *People and the Word*, 65.

8. "155 Anniversary of Treaty of 1867," Citizen Potawatomi Nation website, February 4, 2022, https://www.potawatomi.org/blog/2022/02/04/155th-anniversary-of-treaty-of-1867/.

9. All three state capitals were colonial intrusions on Native land. Hyde, *Empires, Nations, and Families*, 482–83.

10. As evidenced by the paper's name, it was an antislavery publication printed out of Lawrence.

11. For further discussion of the map, see Miner and Unrau, *End of Indian Kansas*, 7–8.

12. As I discussed more extensively in chapters 1 and 2, surveys are not benign projects of scientific inquiry but are essential to mapping and narrating U.S. colonial space.

13. Byrd, *Transit of Empire*, 27.

14. For more on Brown playing Indian, see Trodd, "Writ in Blood."

15. Philip Deloria, *Playing Indian*, 5.

16. "Legislative Action Relative to the Kansas Election Fraud," *Liberator* (Boston), May 4, 1855, 71, American Periodicals Series II, https://proquest.com/magazines/narcisso-lopez-his-companions/docview/126362668/se-2?accountid=14524.

17. For a discussion of the gendering of the West, see Kolodny, *Lay of the Land*.

18. Tompkins, *Racial Indigestion*.

19. Wynter, "1492," 36.

20. Before "filibuster" gained hold as a cultural meme, the phrase "buffalo hunt" was employed, further highlighting an awareness that what happened in the so-called West was connected to what was happening in the Caribbean and throughout the Americas. May, *Manifest Destiny's Underworld*, 1. Robert May argues that press phrases such as "Missouri filibusters in Kansas" and "Kansas filibusters" demonstrate the term's pervasiveness as a way to denote insurrectionist acts of individuals or groups without government affiliation. May, *Manifest Destiny's Underworld*, 77–78.

21. Robert May argues that press phrases such as "Missouri filibusters in Kansas" and "Kansas filibusters" demonstrate the term's pervasiveness as a way to denote insurrectionist acts of individuals or groups without government affiliation. May, 77–78.

22. Judith Madera also analyzes how 1850s maps rendered proximity between the United States and Cuba. See Madera, "This House of Gathering: *Axis Americanus*," in *Black Atlas*.

23. Pérez, *On Becoming Cuban*, 22.

24. Pérez, 22.

25. Guterl, "American Mediterranean," 100.

26. Chapters 28–30 were published in January, and the magazine then published chapters 1–23 until July 1859. See McGann's "Editor's Note" to *Blake*, xxxiii.

27. Spires, *Practice of Citizenship*, 178.

28. Spires, 178. See also Ball, *To Live an Antislavery Life*, 109–31.

29. Martin R. Delany, "Blake: Or, The Huts of America: A Tale of the Mississippi Valley, the Southern United States, and Cuba," *Anglo-African Magazine* (New York), January 1859, 20.

30. It is possible that Mr. Culver is meant to depict a member of the prominent Colbert family from the Chickasaw Nation.

31. Delany, *Blake*, 87.

32. Delany, 87.

33. Krauthamer, *Black Slaves, Indian Masters*, 32.

34. For further discussion of 1441's significance, see King, *Black Shoals*, 40.

35. See Krauthamer, *Black Slaves, Indian Masters*, 74–76, 92–97.

36. Delaney, *Blake*, 88.

37. Xine Yao describes moments like this one as "Black-Indigenous counterintimacies." Yao, *Disaffected*, 70–106.

38. The 1854 "Treaty with the Choctaw and Chickasaw" deemed the Choctaws and Chickasaws two separate nations.

39. Byrd, *Transit of Empire*, xv.

40. Gerrity, "Freedom on the Move," 3.

41. Diouf, *Slavery's Exiles*; Neil Roberts, *Freedom as Marronage*.

42. Delany, *Blake*, 90.

43. Delany, 90.

44. Ifeoma Nwankwo understands Delany's use of Cuba in the novel as twofold. It serves as a "synecdoche for all people of African descent everywhere" and "allows Delany to play on the fears of the Africanization of Cuba that were rampant throughout the nineteenth century." U.S. annexation sits in the background, amplifying the significance of both. Nwankwo, *Black Cosmopolitanism*, 12, 13.

45. Throughout her book, Finch convincingly argues that, while Plácido served as a prominent symbol of La Escalara and large-scale Black organizing efforts against enslavement and racism in Cuba, focusing on a singular (male) revolutionary martyr obscures broader, communal uprising efforts, especially the work done by women, the poor, and the enslaved. Finch, *Rethinking Slave Rebellion*.

46. Brickhouse, *Transamerican Literary Relations*, 128. For more on Delany's use of Plácido in the novel, see Nwankwo, "The View from Next Door," in *Black Cosmopolitanism*, 48–80.

47. Delany, *Blake*, 197.

48. Delany, 287.

49. Delany, 246.

50. Delany, 246

51. Delany, 246. Nwankwo points out that some of Delany's representations of race in Cuba flatten Blackness in ways that are not entirely representative of 1850s Cuba. Nwankwo, *Black Cosmopolitanism*, 92–95.

52. Delany, *Blake*, 247.

53. Yaremko, *Indigenous Passages to Cuba*, 2. For a discussion of the Caste War of 1847 and its influence on Mayans in Cuba, see Kazanjian, *Colonizing Trick*, chap. 4.

54. Anna Brickhouse provides possible historical context for Mayan enslavement. However, her analysis also reinforces Taíno extinction on the island by asking, "How could there be Indians in nineteenth-century Cuba, where the indigenous population had long since been destroyed?" Brickhouse, *Transamerican Literary Relations*, 211.

55. Lowe, *Intimacies of Four Continents*.

56. For a discussion of the origin and history of the derogation "coolie," particularly its use in Cuba, see Yun, introduction to *Coolie Speaks*.

57. Yun, *Coolie Speaks*, 7. In addition, Yun offers a nuanced discussion of how midcentury contract labor and enslavement wove together, constructing a deeply complex network of power and agency that was influenced not simply by race but also by mobility, the plantation system, and urbanization. Yun, 11.

58. In an attempt to increase the ratio of white people on the island, Chinese immigrants and Indigenous Yucatánian Mayans were classified as white, and by 1874 both groups together totaled almost 130,000 people. This racializing policy says less about the actual lived experiences of many Chinese laborers, who often suffered under conditions of severe exploitation, than it does about the changing social fabric of Cuba and its participation in a global economy, including its mutually beneficial economic relationship with the United States. Reid-Vazquez, *Year of the Lash*, 155.

59. For more on the multiracialism of Cuba's three rebellions, see Ferrer, *Insurgent Cuba*, 3.

60. For a discussion of the tension between an emerging "raceless" nation and the maintenance of inherently racialist institutional structures and practices in Cuba, see Pérez, *On Becoming Cuban*, 91.

61. Delany, *Blake*, 248. The Star of Hope may reference Venus.

62. Delany, 248; Madera, *Black Atlas*, 142.

63. In Langston Hughes's *Not without Laughter*, published seventy years after Kansas statehood (and Harper's story), the denouncement of Kansas's emancipatory statehood narrative comes from a Black matriarch, Aunt Hager Williams. Hers is the voice in the novel that imagines other spaces of freedom beyond the state. Upon realizing that Kansas is no better than the South for Black people, the main character Sandy asks Aunt Hager, "They don't like us here either do they?" Aunt Hager responds to him through song:

> But Aunt Hager gave him no answer. In silence, they watched the sunset fade from the sky. Slowly the evening star grew bright, and, looking at the stars, Hager began to sing, very softly at first:
>
>> From this world o' trouble free,
>> Stars beyond!
>> Stars beyond!
>
> And Sandy, as he stood beside his grandmother on the porch, heard a great chorus out of the black past—singing generations of toil-worn Negroes, echoing Hager's voice as it deepened and grew in volume: "There's a star fo' you an' me, / Stars beyond!" (Hughes, *Not without Laughter*, 213)

Aunt Hager responds to Sandy through a collectivity that spans time and space. While Aunt Hager is a character created by yet another male writer, her response to state belonging is a powerful one that refuses the terms of the conversation—she offers Sandy no clear answers. Instead, she sings of a collective dream of a world beyond the confines of the terrestrial, not unlike Delany's Star of Hope, that holds space for both of them. Unlike Sandy, she has no illusions about the failures of Kansas to hold her.

64. One reason Delany wrote *Blake* was to raise money for his African emigration plans. McGann, introduction to *Blake*, xxiv.

65. Rollin, *Life and Public Services*, 86–87. Stephanie LeMenager argues that "one of the most interesting aspects of John Brown's (provisionally) emplaced utopia is its fluidity, the fact that it was to be both 'state' and, as its earlier name suggests, 'pass way,' nominal and adverbial, an *it* and a *through*, in other words not at all a proper place." LeMenager, "Marginal Landscapes," 50.

66. Rollin, *Life and Public Services*, 87.

67. Rollin, 89.

68. Rollin, 88–89.

69. Rollin, 89.

70. For further reading, see *Doc. No. I. Governor's Message and Reports of the Public Officers of the State, of the Boards of Directors, and of the Visitors, Superintendents, and Other Agents of Public Institutions or Interests of Virginia* (Richmond: William F. Ritchie, 1859), 49–155, in "'His Soul Goes Marching On': The Life and Legacy of John Brown," West

Virginia Archives and History, August 3, 2020, http://129.71.204.160/history/jbexhibit /virginiadocuments61.html.

71. While the Cherokee Nation had some landholdings in Kansas Territory at this time, the majority of the Nation was located in Indian Territory.

72. Rollin, *Life and Public Services*, 84.

73. Jackson, *Creole Indigeneity*, 30.

74. Arvin, *Possessing Polynesians*, 15.

75. Mathews, *Osages*, 624.

76. In *Wayward Lives, Beautiful Experiments*, Saidiya Hartman offers up one potential method, whereby she provides "an archive of the exorbitant, a dream book for existing otherwise," imagining beyond archival evidence to narrate Black femme and queer social life in the early twentieth century. Hartman, *Wayward Lives, Beautiful Experiments*, xv.

77. Windell, *Transamerican Sentimentalism*, 204. Throughout *Rethinking Slave Rebellion in Cuba*, Aisha Finch contextualizes the insurgencies of the 1840s in a broader legacy of slave uprisings across the Americas. She argues for the necessity of reflecting on the significant role of women, rural communities, and spiritual practices in uprisings in the Americas and calls for new historical methods that take account of these voices. See also Finch, *Rethinking Slave Rebellion*.

78. Pyle, "Prairie Potawatomi."

79. Rustic, "Chit Chat," 42.

80. Rustic, 42.

81. Harper's short story "Zombi, or Fancy Sketches" (1860), also published in the *Anglo-African Magazine*, details the Maroon community of Quilombo dos Palmares. Derrick Spires reads the story as evidence of Harper's skepticism about emigration and her belief in the usefulness of Maroon and African models of emancipation. Additionally, "Zombi" argues for the necessity of struggle and sacrifice: "Jane makes an argument for 'Zombi' as a constitutive narrative for the whole of African America and those fighting for greater freedom—a community that is sieged by an ostensibly overwhelming force and from which, in Jane and Ballad's view, sacrifices on multiple fronts will be required: liberty until death." Spires, *Practice of Citizenship*, 235.

82. For further reading about La Escalera, see Finch, *Rethinking Slave Rebellion*. She writes, "To learn about La Escalera, then, is to learn intimately about the Spanish colonial state—its ideological power, its expansive reach, its capacity for pain. This knowledge mirrors intelligence that black people gathered throughout the Americas about white racial power—its endless capacity for humiliation, its recurring promise of violation, its chronic and yet unpredictable intrusions. These two strands of knowledge woven together—the lengths to which the colonial state would go to contain its threats and the endless possibilities for black degradation under slavery—might be said to reflect the enduring historical lessons of La Escalera." Finch, 2.

83. The O'Donnell administration in Cuba incentivized Black migration to tamp down uprising plots. Reid-Vazquez, *Year of the Lash*, 47–53.

84. Thomas Jefferson to James Monroe, October 24, 1823.

85. O'Sullivan's interest in Cuba arose after his sister married Cristóbal Madan, a Club de la Habana leader. In 1846 O'Sullivan decided to travel with his new wife to Cuba, and there,

his brother-in-law introduced him to other members of the club. See Chaffin, *Fatal Glory*, 12–13, 22.

86. Chaffin, *Fatal Glory*, 46.

87. "Cuban Affairs," *Christian Advocate and Journal* (New York), September 11, 1851, 146, American Periodicals Series II, www.proquest.com/magazines/cuban-affairs/docview/125998333 /se-2?accountid=14524.

88. "Last of the Filibusters," *New York Observer and Chronicle*, September 11, 1851, 294, American Periodicals Series II, www.proquest.com/magazines/last-flibustiers/docview /136575778/se-2?accountid=14524.

89. "General Lopez," *Gleason's Pictorial Drawing-Room Companion* (Boston), September 27, 1851, 352, American Periodicals Series II, www.proquest.com/magazines/general -lopez/docview/124060493/se-2?accountid=14524.

90. "Narciso Lopez and His Companions," *United States Magazine and Democratic Review* (New York), October 1851, 291, American Periodicals Series II, www.proquest.com /magazines/narciso-lopez-his-companions/docview/126362668/se-2?accountid=14524.

91. Charles Brown, *Agents of Manifest Destiny*, 129.

92. For more on Brougham, see Detsi-Diamanti, "Burlesquing 'Otherness'"; and Hawes, "John Brougham as Playwright."

93. "Cuba," *Child's Friend and Family Magazine* (Boston), January 1, 1856, 185, American Periodicals Series II, www.proquest.com/magazines/cuba/docview/125195897/se-2?accountid =14524.

94. The manifesto's plan fell through, however, when there was public outrage. Moreover, it became one of the rallying cries for the uprisings surrounding slavery termed Bleeding Kansas.

95. "The Southern Press: Mr. Buchanan and Cuba," *National Era* (Washington, D.C.), April 23, 1857, 68, American Periodicals Series II, www.proquest.com/magazines/southern -press/docview/137616621/se-2?accountid=14524.

96. Jackson, *Creole Indigeneity*, 29.

97. The figure of Columbia also plays a vital role in the play. Before Columbus sets sail, she awakens him in his quarters and informs him she will join him on his journey. Columbia identifies herself as both his child and the niece of Uncle Sam (whom he has yet to meet). Brougham, *Columbus el Filibustero!*, 14.

98. Bartosik-Vélez, *Legacy of Christopher Columbus*, 11.

99. See Horsman, *Race and Manifest Destiny*, 282–83.

100. In the case of Cuba, the United States did not annex but instead deployed a paternalistic occupation and intervened in the production of a state and economic infrastructure fashioned after its own. Unlike with the other Spanish colonies, the United States could not gain complete territorial control of Cuba due to the 1898 Teller Amendment. To somewhat remedy this bind, Congress passed the Platt Amendment in 1901, a year before the United States formally pulled its military forces out of Cuba. The amendment gave the United States a carte blanche ability to enter Cuba whenever it so chose to preserve the nascent nation-state and outline compulsory economic practices and foreign relations. It was a move that, according to historian Jana Lipman, "fundamentally compromised Cuban sovereignty." To ensure complicity with the amendment, the United States demanded Cuban officials sign the agreement

before the United States would formally recognize Cuba as an independent nation. Lipman, *Guantánamo*, 23.

101. Walker's ventures into Nicaragua and his brief reign as the president of the Republic of Nicaragua from 1856 to 1857 were widely publicized and granted him celebrity status in the U.S. press.

102. The term "filibuster" is an Anglicization of the Spanish term "filibustero" that came into common use in the seventeenth century to describe pirates plundering the West Indies. Rodrigo Lazo offers a more detailed etymology and a rich discussion of the term's use in nineteenth-century America. See Lazo, introduction to *Writing to Cuba*.

103. Lazo, *Writing to Cuba*, 7.

104. Lazo, 22.

105. For more on the significance of New York City for Cubans, see Mirabal, "Rhetorical Geographies," in *Suspect Freedoms*, 25–60.

106. Brougham, *Columbus el Filibustero!*, 17.

107. Brougham, 23.

108. Brougham, 22.

109. These characters are not even individually listed in the play's cast of characters.

110. Brougham, 22.

111. Brougham, 23.

112. All of the states are described as "beautiful young ladies." Brougham, 22.

113. Tompkins, *Racial Indigestion*, 90.

114. Tompkins, 90. Tompkins further elaborates: "Vernacularity gestures to regional identity in the same way that vernacular food—intimately connected to local and everyday ways of being—describes the boundaries of, and differences between, identities. In *Uncle Tom's Cabin*, the use of the vernacular marks the intersection between the body and language, as the discursively constructed hyperembodiedness of the 'lower orders'—those peoples who are represented as food—by definition influences and shapes the language of middle- and upper-class whites." Tompkins, 106.

115. Brougham, *Columbus el Filibustero!*, 24.

116. For further discussion of racialization, whiteness, and U.S. empire in the Pacific, see Arvin, *Possessing Polynesians*; Isaac, *American Tropics*; and Rodríguez, *Suspended Apocalypse*.

117. McKittrick, *Demonic Grounds*, xiv.

Chapter Four

1. The Five Tribes, also called the Five Civilized Tribes, were forcibly Removed from the Southeast to Indian Territory in the first half of the nineteenth century.

2. "Black" and "Native" were not simple signifiers. They gestured toward a broad spectrum of identity in the territories. Even when individuals saw themselves as part of both or either group, the machinations of settler colonialism, legacies of enslavement, and racial capitalism relentlessly demanded individuals be pigeonholed as one *or* the other. However, when I use "Black" and "Native," I imagine them as far more fluid, to account for how both terms attend to different assemblages of people—sometimes the same individuals—in different contexts. I use "Black" to gesture toward Afro-Native, African American, and other people of African descent. When I use "Native," I include Afro-Native, unless noted other-

wise. Throughout most of this chapter, I shorten "Muscogee (Creek)" to "Creek" because that was the self-identified name used at that time, rather than the rebranded "Muscogee Nation" of the twenty-first century. This is one of the only times in the book that I do not use the current terminology of a Native nation. This is a complicated choice and was not an easy one to make, but I made it to stay consistent with the terms Muscogee (Creeks) used to describe themselves and their nation in this era. Native nations' names, like the identity categories I just described, have sometimes been fluid because of the ongoing violence of settler colonialism and its role in controlling language, including Indigenous language use. For further elaboration on my word choice, please see "A Note on Terminology" at the start of the book.

3. The *Oklahoma!* musical is based on Cherokee playwright Lynn Riggs's *Green Grow the Lilacs* (1930).

4. Land runs, also called land rushes, occurred when land previously owned by a Native nation was opened for non-Native settlement. Runs typically had a start line and start time from which prospective settlers would run (or rush) to stake a land claim. Much of Oklahoma Territory was colonized by non-Native settlers in this way.

5. Benjamin Fagan makes a similar argument about Black newspapers. See Fagan, "Chronicling White America."

6. Foreman, *Oklahoma Imprints*, xx–xxi.

7. Foreman, xiii.

8. In her study of nineteenth-century newspapers, Grace Ernestine Ray observes, "The newspapers, controlled by their tribal governments or by churches or schools, were in a measure independent of their subscribers and advertisers. Under this plan of operation, the editors shaped their editorial policies to conform to the best interests of the tribes which they were sponsoring. This freedom of the press is a distinctive characteristic of the early newspapers in the Indian Territory." Ray offers a detailed account of the earliest newspapers in the territory (those established between 1844 and 1871)—six in total: the *Cherokee Messenger, Cherokee Advocate, Choctaw Telegraph, Cherokee Rosebud, Choctaw Intelligencer,* and *Halaquah Times.* She also describes the publication history, content, and political bent (if there was one), as well as material aspects of the publications, such as size and layout. Ray, *Early Oklahoma Newspapers*, 10.

9. The choice to do so may have been made for a number of reasons and not necessarily the same for all editors. Because Indian Territory was home to a number of nations that did not all speak the same language, English became the lingua franca used across Native communities. Some Native readers could only read in English, and at least a few Cherokee papers could not acquire Sequoyan typeface because it was not always easy or cost effective. Additionally, the use of English made the papers accessible to non-Native settlers in the region, which invariably helped increase sales and financial stability. Finally, the use of English ensured the broadest possible audience of both Native and non-Native readership and circulation across tribes and beyond the territories.

10. See Justice, *Our Fire Survives*, pt. 1; Womack, "Alexander Posey's Nature Journals."

11. The sway newspapers held over readers was demonstrated in a letter sent to Principal Chief Samuel Houston Mayes in 1895 by the Cherokee delegation in Washington, D.C. The delegation believed the Dawes Commission's assessment of self-government in the territory was shaped by inaccurate newspaper reporting from non-Native papers. The delegation's

concerns also touched on the practice of selective citation in determining what was happening on the ground. Debo, *And Still the Waters*, 27–30.

12. Editors of the *Cherokee Advocate* consistently expressed a belief that the paper's job was to educate U.S. citizens illiterate in Indian affairs and remind readers of the United States' obligation to uphold treaty agreements with the Cherokee Nation. Cullen Joe Holland, "Cherokee Indian Newspapers," 399–400.

13. From the 1870s until the 1889 Land Run, the term "Boomer" describe white squatters who felt that the so-called Unassigned Lands in Indian Territory were rightfully theirs for settlement and did not belong to the tribes. The Unassigned Lands were those land holdings tribes were required to cede to the United States following the U.S. Civil War. After 1889, the term "Boomer" described people who participated in the Oklahoma land runs.

14. Ray, *Early Oklahoma Newspapers*, 81.

15. See Debo, *Road to Disappearance*, 211. For further reading on Boudinot's rationale for establishing his own railroad company, see Julie Reed, *Serving the Nation*, 97.

16. Debo, *Road to Disappearance*, 211.

17. According to Cullen Joe Holland, "Very few of the new publications were owned and edited by Cherokees. The new publishers arrived from surrounding states with their presses and type cases and quickly began issuing newspapers in support of allotment of lands for the Cherokees. The Indians were helpless to stop the flood, and only the *Advocate*, *Indian Chieftain*, *Indian Arrow*, and a few others supported the Cherokees' early refusals to sell their homeland within the Nation proper." Holland, "Cherokee Indian Newspapers," 499. L. Edward Carter also observes of this era, "In the Cherokee Nation, newspapers could be found in practically every town. The Nation contained a highly literate population because of the ease with which the Cherokee Indians learned to read their own language printed in Sequoyah's syllabary. More than 125 newspapers were published between 1844 and 1907 in the Cherokee Nation, but almost all of these were established after the 1890s." Carter, *Story of Oklahoma Newspapers*, 30.

18. As one example, a February 2, 1900, letter to the editor thanked the *Chieftain* for being "the only newspaper that has taken a brave stand and raised a voice on behalf of the poor Indian people." Whether truth, advertising, or both, the *Chieftain* published multiple pieces like this in editorials written for the paper and letters to the editor (ostensibly written by readers). "COMMENDATORY WORDS: The Chieftain Is Proud to Be Regarded as the Indian's Friend," *Daily Chieftain* (Vinita), February 2, 1900. For a period of time the *Chieftain* published daily issues (*Daily Chieftain*) as well as a weekly issue that collected the most significant news of the week (*Weekly Chieftain*). The paper changed its name to the *Vinita Weekly Chieftain* (1902–1904), switching exclusively to a weekly format, and then to the *Weekly Chieftain* (1905–1913).

19. In *The Third Space of Sovereignty*, Kevin Bruyneel traces the Senate Indian Affairs Committee's 1865 attempt to organize Indian Territory and consolidate the tribes. See Bruyneel, *Third Space of Sovereignty*, 37–38.

20. Julie Reed discusses some of the ways Cherokee leaders delayed negotiations, as well as the ways Cherokees continued to fight for social services to support Cherokee people during and after allotment. See Reed, *Serving the Nation*, chap. 8.

21. It should be noted that tribal recordkeeping meant that significant portions of these rolls were already compiled, and these earlier rolls proved invaluable to the Dawes Com-

mission. For a discussion of the Dawes Commission's statements, see Debo, *And Still the Waters*, 23–26. Debo also notes that when Dawes Commission members arrived in Indian Territory and experienced "concerted resistance" to negotiation, they "advised Congress to disregard the treaties and abolish the tribal status without waiting for the Indians' consent." Debo, 23–24.

22. The history of the now legendary corruption of the Dawes Commission has been extensively studied by scholars. Angie Debo was one of the first historians to write a lengthy history of the commission. She was given access to Indian Affairs documents previously inaccessible to historians and famously described her research for *And Still the Waters Run* as an investigation into horrifying corruption: "When I knew what they [grafters] did and what honest people who had tried to check it were up against, I had a feeling of fear as I went through those dark corridors and basements and so on." Angie Debo, interview in *Indians, Outlaws, and Angie Debo*, quoted in Fitzpatrick, *History's Memory*, 137.

23. In a footnote to their collected volume of Alex Posey's Fus Fixico letters, Daniel F. Littlefield Jr. and Carol A. Petty Hunter explain how and why allotment owners publicized the sale of their lands in the *Muskogee Phoenix* and other territorial papers. They write,

> Under federal law, white and Freedmen citizens of the Indian nations could sell their allotments outright. Inherited land could also be sold. The owner could apply to advertise the sale. Bidders submitted sealed bids and certified checks for one-fifth of their bids. Sixty days after the land was advertised, the bids were opened, the land went to the highest bidder if the bid was at least market value and if the bidder paid the remainder of the price. Of the many tracts advertised, few sold each week. Indians could also apply for removal of restrictions on the sale of their surplus allotments. If the application was approved, the Indian could make a warranty deed. (Posey, *Fus Fixico Letters*, 194n5)

24. It is also worth noting that Tams Bixby, chairman of the Dawes Commission from 1897 until 1907, had influence over the *Muskogee Phoenix*, and many newspaper editors would allege the paper was "Bixby's paper." For example, a 1903 editorial from the *Vinita Weekly Chieftain* suggested that Bixby influenced the *Phoenix*'s official position on statehood: "Tams Bixby's paper, the Muskogee Daily Phoenix, is opposed to single statehood or perhaps more properly speaking any sort of statehood for the Indian Territory." Editorial, *Vinita Weekly Chieftain*, May 28, 1903. In 1906 Bixby "bought controlling interest in the *Phoenix*. When he resigned as acting chairman in 1907, he became publisher-editor of the paper." The paper later bought the *Muskogee Times-Democrat*. Before working for the Dawes Commission, Bixby had run his own paper, further highlighting nineteenth-century affinities between newspaper publishing and colonial projects. L. Edward Carter, *Story of Oklahoma Newspapers*, 33.

25. For more on the complexity of allotment, see Kent Carter, *Dawes Commission*.

26. Dawes Commission corruption was covered extensively by Indian Territory newspapers. As one example: "A few papers in this territory are seeking to shield and cover up the shortcomings of the Dawes commission and other federal officials under fire. This is not creditable to an intelligent and an untrammeled press. Everyone who is familiar with conditions here must know that there has been unwarranted and vexatious delays, and that speculation and grafting has taken place of honest labor in the performance of the duties

assigned the officials. The sycophant whining of a few newspapers that in the face of a mountain of evidence contend that the Dawes commission is immaculate is disgusting. The public fortunately knows better." Editorial, *Vinita Weekly Chieftain*, September 24, 1903.

27. The war reignited tensions already at play in Indian Territory. In the Cherokee Nation, the decades following Removal were a time of instability and division because many felt the Treaty of New Echota (1835), which authorized Cherokee Removal, was made without the consent of the people. These tensions boiled over into assassinations and violent conflict. The U.S. Civil War revived Removal-era divisions and fomented civil war within the Nation. Even though he signed a Confederacy treaty on behalf of the Nation, John Ross supported the Union cause. Nonetheless, a sizable number of Southern Cherokees aligned with Stand Watie and fought for the Confederacy. For further reading on the impact of the U.S. Civil War on the Cherokee Nation and Cherokee autonomy, see Julie Reed, *Serving the Nation*, chap. 3.

28. For a discussion of the Civil War in Indian Territory and the treaties of 1866, see Abel, *American Indian*; Bailey, *Reconstruction in Indian Territory*; Krauthamer, *Black Slaves, Indian Masters*; Naylor, *African Cherokees*; and Alaina Roberts, *I've Been Here*.

29. Muriel Wright, *Story of Oklahoma*, 164–65.

30. The intertribal councils required by the Reconstruction Treaties were the first space where Native leaders organized a statehood campaign. While the congressional goal with the councils was to increase U.S. surveillance of Native nations, putting numerous tribes in conversation with one another actually strengthened intertribal alliances and provided a forum for Native leaders to strategize ways to protect their sovereignty, including the threat U.S. statehood posed. In 1870 a group of tribal leaders met at Okmulgee in the Muscogee Nation and developed a constitution proposing an Indian Territory government. See Hoxie, *This Indian Country*, 130–35. The Five Tribes wielded a great deal of power as some of the most populous nations. However, according to Vine Deloria Jr. and Clifford M. Lytle, there were efforts to maintain "a semblance of political integrity for the smaller tribes" and use the meeting "to adopt an organic document that would preserve the tribal rights and cultural traditions of the tribes while enabling the territory as a whole to move toward statehood." Deloria and Lytle, *Nations Within*, 24.

31. Alaina E. Roberts succinctly describes these tensions when she explains that U.S. Republicans were able to enact their ambitions for Reconstruction in Indian Territory in ways they could not elsewhere because Native people had no (voting) congressional representation. She writes, "The land cession in these treaties were a clear violation of Indigenous sovereignty. And yet, this violation gave people of African descent the freedom and rights they may otherwise never have attained in the Five Tribes without U.S. intervention." Roberts, *I've Been Here*, 49–50.

32. Roberts, 45–71.

33. The Unassigned Lands, those lands opened for settlement during the 1889 land run, were initially intended as lands for Removed Native nations and Freedpeople following the treaties of 1866, but the federal government prioritized white settlement over Freedpeople's allotments; U.S. support for Freedpeople would quickly vanish whenever it threatened white settlers' economic opportunities. Arthur Tolson also importantly notes that Choctaw and Chickasaw leaders pushed for the Removal of Freedpeople from their territory following the 1866 treaties: "Choctaw and Chickasaw leaders appealed to the United States

Secretary of the Interior and Congress in the 1870's that their former slaves be settled there, but no action was taken." The desire to Remove Freedpeople reproduced the Removal trauma they experienced just a few decades earlier with their Native enslavers. Tolson, *Black Oklahomans*, 88.

34. It is important to note that people challenged this approach; some hired lawyers to fight their case. Freedpeople also hired lawyers to advocate for their rights to allotted land in the process.

35. See Cherokee Nation principal chief Chuck Hoskin Jr., "CHIEF CHAT: Commemorating 100 Years since the Tulsa Race Massacre," *Tahlequah Daily Press*, June 4, 2021, www .tahlequahdailypress.com/news/tribal_news/chief-chat-commemorating-100-years-since -thetulsa-race-massacre/article_9a08f2bd-21b5-5493-929f-3c53cc22eed9.html.

36. I find Jodi Byrd's discussion of the denaturalizing of colonial borders and maps a beneficial reminder of the need to spatially orient away from an imperial vantage point. Byrd, *Transit of Empire*, xxx.

37. Littlefield and Parins, "Short Fiction Writers," 24.

38. Here I am reminded of Noenoe K. Silva's work on Hawaiian-language newspapers and her assertion that they served a political purpose for Kanaka Maoli at the time but also were self-consciously created as archives for future Kanaka Maoli. These archives embedded Hawaiian cosmologies and epistemologies into their content and recorded for future generations the ways their ancestors vigorously fought colonialism. Like Kanaka Maoli writers, Native writers in Indian Territory knew that "when the stories can be validated, as happens when scholars read the literature in Hawaiian and make findings available to the community, people begin to recover from the wounds caused by that disjuncture in their consciousness." Silva, *Aloha Betrayed*, 3.

39. It is difficult to pinpoint the exact subscription numbers for Indian Territory newspapers. However, the September 1, 1905, issue of the *Muskogee Democrat*, one of the most widely read newspapers in the territory at the time, cited subscriptions at 2,801 for daily circulation. For July 1905, the *Indian Journal* ran a full-page advertisement claiming a 5,000-person readership and identified itself as "the medium for advertisers" because "it reaches the people." The *Journal* was a weekly, not a daily, which might explain why its numbers would be greater than those of the *Democrat* (if we believe that figure), but these numbers were also run three years before the *Democrat*'s. The fact that the *Journal*'s claim to be one of the most popular newspapers was made in an era of accelerated immigration and occupation in which the population increased rapidly year to year leads me to believe that was true.

40. Foreman, *Oklahoma Imprints*, 174. The paper later moved to Eufaula, Muscogee (Creek) Nation.

41. As one example, Cherokee historian Julie Reed explains that the Cherokee Nation felt railroad development in the territory was inevitable, so in 1866 it proactively lobbied with the federal government, with limited success, to have as much autonomy as possible over where tracks were built, the right to buy stock in the railroads, and some say on railroad boards. See Reed, *Serving the Nation*, 96–97. See also Thompson, *Closing the Frontier*, 31–32.

42. The use of newspapers to circulate governmental documents evokes what Phillip Round describes as Native "print constitutionalism." Round, *Removable Type*, 46–47.

43. Charles Gibson, about thirty years Posey's senior, was a nephew of the well-known Creek chief Opothleyahola, who fought against the United States during the First U.S.-Seminole War and then led a faction of Creeks with Union sentiments during the Civil War. According to Bernd Peyer, Gibson was largely self-educated but received some training at the Methodist Asbury Mission near Eufaula and at Creek common schools. Throughout the 1880s and 1890s, he worked at Grayson Brothers store (often advertised in the pages of the *Journal*), and in 1896, a few years before he began writing prolifically in territorial newspapers and magazines, he opened his own store in Eufaula. For a short time during the spring of 1903, Gibson ran for principal chief of the Creek Nation and, as his longtime friend, Posey used the pages of the *Journal* to advocate for Gibson's election, even using his Fus Fixico letters as a campaign venue. Gibson has become canonized, to the extent that such a canon exists, as an important Indian Territory writer and nineteenth-century Native American writer, but discussion of his essays and short fiction is sparse. While his work often contains humor and irony like Posey's, he makes temporal links that differ from Posey's. His essays and fables often follow oral storytelling conventions that hark back to Creek stories or histories and explicitly comment on the current moment in Eufaula, the Creek Nation, and the larger Indian Territory. See Womack, *Red on Red*, 135; Littlefield, *Alex Posey*, 118–21; and Peyer, "Charles Gibson Biography," in *American Indian Nonfiction*, 173.

44. Emphasis in the original. W. C. Grayson's Grocery Advertisement, *Indian Journal* (Eufaula), July 25, 1902.

45. Littlefield, *Alex Posey*, 148.

46. One of the county names drafted for the State of Sequoyah was Spokogee as well.

47. Littlefield, *Alex Posey*, 146.

48. Kent Carter, *Dawes Commission*, 130.

49. Terms like "fullblood," "pullback," and "traditional" were stereotypical, often derogatory, ways to describe Native people who wanted to maintain long-standing Indigenous cultural, spiritual, linguistic, and political practices and were resistant to assimilation, adoption of Western values or cultural practices, or increased cooperation with the U.S. federal government. These epithets were often contrasted with "progressive," which denoted individuals often racialized as of mixed white-Native ancestry who were more open to innovation and change in tribal practices and the adoption of U.S. or Western cultural, spiritual, linguistic, and political practices.

50. Two characters, Doc and J. N., take their boat on the Oktahutche, a beloved spot for Posey. Matthew Wynn Sivils reprints "The Cruise of the Good Vrouw" in his edited collection of Posey's collected journals. See Posey, *Lost Creeks*, 102–4.

51. See Littlefield, *Alex Posey*, 185.

52. James A. Norman (Cherokee Nation) seems to have initiated use of the name Sequoia in one of a series of editorial pieces he published in the *Muskogee Democrat* advocating a separate statehood movement. J. A. Norman, "State of Sequoia," *Muskogee Democrat*, April 2, 1905.

53. By many accounts, Ayoka (sometimes written as Ayokeh) was essential to creating the syllabary and to the Cherokee Nation's decision to take it up as the national language. Not only did she help Sequoyah develop the syllabary, but she helped him persuade the National Council of its essential contribution. She was the one who demonstrated its effectiveness when they presented their invention to other Cherokees.

54. Too-Qua-Stee, "Sequoyah," *Vinita Weekly Chieftain,* June 2, 1904. For a discussion of Too-Qua-Stee's life and work, see Parins, *Literacy and Intellectual Life,* chap. 7. Robert Dale Parker offers a reprint of the poem in his anthology as well. See Parker, *Changing Is Not Vanishing,* 210–11. There are various ways of spelling Too-Qua-Stee's name. I use the spelling most prevalent in his *Chieftain* publications.

55. David J. Brown, "Sequoyah," *Cherokee Advocate* (Tahlequah), February 26, 1879. Robert Dale Parker offers a reprint of the poem in his anthology. See Parker, *Changing Is Not Vanishing,* 140. The poem was reprinted twice, once in the *Indian Chieftain* (March 25, 1886) and again in *Twin Territories* (June 1900). Littlefield and Parins, *Biobibliography* (1981), 23.

56. Joshua Ross, "Sequoyah," in Parker, *Changing Is Not Vanishing,* 133.

57. Littlefield, *Alex Posey,* 114.

58. Introduction to "Ode to Sequoyah," by Alexander Posey, *Twin Territories* (Muskogee), April 1899.

59. Introduction to "Ode to Sequoyah."

60. Quoted in Littlefield, *Alex Posey,* 117.

61. Alexander Posey, "Ode to Sequoyah," *Twin Territories,* April 1899.

62. The third stanza of the poem, which is not included in the excerpt, details Sequoyah's perseverance in developing the syllabary. This is not the only Sequoyah poem that Posey wrote. Matthew Wynn Sivils includes another in his collection of Posey's poetry. Also, the version of "Ode to Sequoyah" reprinted by Sivils and Robert Dale Parker does not include an exclamation mark after "nay" in the second stanza. Posey's wife Minnie may have made this change when she edited a collection of his poetry in 1910. Posey, *Song of the Oktahutche,* 76, 167.

63. Editorial, *Muskogee Cimeter,* June 8, 1905.

64. Franklin, *Journey toward Hope,* 174–75.

65. Spires, *Practice of Citizenship,* 4. Spires's introduction provides an excellent method for engaging early African American print's theoretical and political work. He also discusses the ways state conventions of the 1840s "developed as collective and dialogic institutions in which black political thought emerged not just as an intellectual project but as a set of citizenship practices enacted through print." His analysis of the conventions helps us think about how the Sequoyah discussions and the statehood debates reflected and refracted earlier Black engagements with state politics. See Spires, chap. 2.

66. Boley was organized as a Freedpeople's community in the Muscogee Nation. It was perhaps the most famous Black community in either of the territories during this era. According to Linda Williams Reese, most of the agents for the paper were Black women who traveled throughout the South advertising the paper and encouraging Black Southerners to emigrate. Reese, *Trail Sisters,* 132.

67. Alaina Roberts, *I've Been Here,* 86.

68. "Come to Boley," *Boley Progress,* March 9, 1905.

69. "Come to Boley."

70. For a discussion of late nineteenth-century Black newspapers, see Washburn, *African American Newspaper,* chap. 3.

71. Miles and Holland, "Introduction," 4.

72. Fields, "'No Such Thing,'" 696.

73. Before the 1889 land run, McCabe lived in Nicodemus, Kansas, one of many Black colonies established in Kansas after an influx of Black settlers in the 1870s. Sometimes referred to as "Exodusters," these African Americans migrated in response to failed Reconstruction policies following the Civil War. McCabe also helped establish Langston University, which today is the only historically Black college in so-called Oklahoma. Some sources refer to him as Edwin McCabe, but I have been unable to determine why.

74. McCabe was not the only person to advocate for a Black state, but as historian Jimmie Lewis Franklin observes, "he best symbolized the sentiment for black statehood." Franklin, *Journey toward Hope*, 13.

75. He also met with President Benjamin Harrison in 1890 to discuss his proposal for a Black state.

76. "Oklahoma," *Indian Chieftain*, March 6, 1890.

77. See Tolson on the Black statehood movements. Tolson, *Black Oklahomans*, 88.

78. Tolson, 65. The fact that the *Oklahoma Guide*, which often functioned more like a recruitment pamphlet than a newspaper, included this in its pages indicates just how seriously Black residents took the incident and the danger it posed.

79. However, Kendra Fields explains that railroad investors and allotment also played a role in their creation: "In the name of racial uplift, the vast majority of the celebrated 'all-black' towns of Oklahoma were built upon Indian allotments and were publicized by motivated white railroad investors who hired African American men as town promoters to recruit black southerners." Fields, "'No Such Thing,'" 703.

80. Fields further writes, "Between 1890 and the admission of Oklahoma to the United States in 1907, African Americans entered Indian Territory by the tens of thousands, and the African American population nearly quadrupled; their presence quickly overwhelmed the numbers of African-descended Creeks and the Indian population as a whole." Fields, 702–3.

81. Chang, *Color of the Land*, 101. Fears that African Americans and Freedpeople were unfairly eroding tribal landholdings by claiming allotments or purchasing Native land only exacerbated already-present anti-Black sentiments prevalent across Indian Territory. In response to Freedman lawsuits against the Cherokee Nation, the *Cherokee Advocate* (the *Phoenix*'s Indian Territory successor) tersely commented, "We can[']t see what more the negroes want than they are getting right about now, unless they want the Cherokee people to give them this country and move out. They are filing and on just as much land to [t]he head as an Indian. No other people that ever existed were forced to do more than the Indians of this territory are doing by their former slaves." Editorial, *Cherokee Advocate*, February 4, 1905. Racist concerns about Freedpeople trying to exploit allotment for their own interests, and insinuations that many of the individuals who claimed to be Freedpeople had no actual ties to Indian communities, were repeatedly expressed in papers of the era.

82. The rolls also ignored previous citizenship practices of some Native nations, including community adoption outside blood relations. For further reading on race and the Dawes rolls, see Chang, *Color of the Land*; and Sturm, *Blood Politics*.

83. Perceived blood quantum also informed if and when a person could sell their land. "Fullblood" people were viewed by the Dawes Commission as not civilized enough to understand how to sell their land, and it was believed that maintaining the land would help assimilate them until they were competent enough to sell, if they chose to do so.

84. As Celia Naylor notes in her study of Afro-Cherokees in Indian Territory, some Afro-Native people asserted their distinct identities as Afro-Native members of specific Indigenous nations. Naylor, *African Cherokees*, 199.

85. See Pascoe, *What Comes Naturally*.

86. Chang writes of Porter that he was the "son of a white planter and his Creek wife who owned one of the most impressive plantations worked by enslaved people in the nation. He was educated in mission schools, fought for the Confederacy, and then built a ranching empire that came to encompass thousands of head of cattle and tens of thousands of acres." Chang, *Color of the Land*, 85. For a discussion of Posey's views on Porter, especially Porter's negotiation of the supplemental agreement to the Creek allotment treaty and his statehood campaigns, see Littlefield, *Alex Posey*, 148–53.

87. Debo, *Road to Disappearance*, 376.

88. In 1902, the same year the Creek Nation signed an allotment agreement with the U.S. government, Porter organized the first in a series of conventions that would advocate for Indian Territory statehood as the best way to perpetuate Native political presence. Again in 1903, leaders of the Five Tribes met to discuss a separate statehood plan. Principal Chief of the Choctaw Nation Green McCurtain called the meeting. Kidwell, *Choctaws in Oklahoma*, 185–86.

89. Allen, *"Sequoyah" Movement*, 20.

90. It should be noted that many white settlers who settled before the 1890s had done so at the behest of tribal governments to work for wealthy landowners, ostensibly farming as sharecroppers. This perceived racial role reversal angered eastern non-Native white people who perceived these economic arrangements as a threat to the fantasy of the Jeffersonian yeoman farmer. By the end of the nineteenth century, some U.S. politicians argued, as a means of rationalizing U.S. trampling of treaty negotiations (especially Removal treaties) with Native nations in Indian Territory, that Native people had brought the rush of non-Native settlers upon themselves.

91. Settlers who did not wait until the official start times and instead claimed plots of land illegally in advance were called "Sooners." Sooners became the University of Oklahoma's mascot and thus entrenched another form of Indigenous land dispossession into a state institution.

92. The word "Oklahoma" harks back to the Treaties of 1866. During the Choctaw-Chickasaw treaty negotiations in Washington, D.C., there was discussion about what to name a new Indian Territory commonwealth when it was organized. According to Oklahoma historian Muriel Wright, her grandfather, Rev. Allen Wright, was the first to propose the name "Oklahoma" for the region. In previous treaties with the U.S. government, the Choctaw Nation was referred to as "the Choctaw Nation of Red People," and in Choctaw, the phrase "red people" could be rendered as "Okla" (people) and "homma" (red). Reverend Wright suggested the name "Oklahoma" for any organized territorial moves in the future because it echoed the language of previous Choctaw-U.S. negotiations. The phrase continued to be used whenever there were proposals for organized territory (like that of Oklahoma Territory) or an organized commonwealth (like that of the state of Oklahoma). Thoburn and Wright, *Oklahoma*, 1:397–98. While the phrase has commonly come to be understood as "the red people's land" or "land of the red people," it is tethered to territorial and statehood projects that continued to erode Native self-determination and control of the region and perpetuated a reminder of the bitter history of Native-U.S. relations.

93. These included the Moon bill and the Knox bill, which never made their way past the House of Representatives. The Hamilton Bill was passed in 1906 as the Oklahoma Enabling Act and authorized joint statehood. For a discussion of the Moon and Knox bills, see Jeffrey Burton, *Indian Territory*, 247.

94. For a discussion of how party politics shaped Oklahoma Territory and fueled divisions between the twin territories, see Scales and Goble, *Oklahoma Politics*, 3–19.

95. Wynn, "'Miss Indian Territory,'" 185.

96. Piatote, *Domestic Subjects*, 12.

97. In her essay "'Miss Indian Territory' and 'Mr. Oklahoma Territory,'" Wynn unpacks how intercultural marriage was sometimes understood as a way to assert Cherokee sovereignty and determine who was included in the Nation. Wynn, "'Miss Indian Territory,'" 173–79.

98. Cushman, *Cherokee Syllabary*, 149.

99. Julie Reed, *Serving the Nation*, 265.

100. There was some dissent within the Chickasaw Nation about whether separate statehood would be the best choice for them. Therefore, Johnson sent a delegate instead of attending himself in an attempt to curtail all-out conflict in the Nation. He was not an avid supporter of the movement.

101. Too-Qua-Stee [DeWitt Clinton Duncan], "A Plea for Separate Statehood," *Weekly Chieftain*, November 2, 1905. Sentiments expressed in a 1905 *Cherokee Advocate* article speak to this: "In all the old treaties the government promised that never would they extend the lines of any state around us without our consent, and that when we desired it we should have a state of our own—an Indian state. Now does it seem right and just for congress to include us with Oklahoma when the Indian population desire separate statehood? WE think not. Give us an Indian state to perpetuate the Indian's name." Editorial, *Cherokee Advocate*, July 29, 1905.

102. Despite having a white, non-Cherokee editor at the time, the *Indian Chieftain* appears to have been relatively Native friendly (although pro-allotment) until around 1903, when the paper became far more critical of Cherokee resistance to tribal dissolution and allotment. It also vocally (and emphatically) endorsed single statehood in the 1903–5 *Weekly Chieftain* issues.

103. The Nighthawk Keetowah Society was a spiritual group that advocated returning to Cherokee ways and rejecting colonial influences.

104. For a discussion of newspaper efforts to deter voters, see Mize, "Black, White, and Read," 233–35. Both Mize and Angie Debo argue that the endorsement for Sequoyah was "light." See Mize, 235; and Debo, *And Still the Waters*, 163–64. C. M. Allen has a different interpretation of the numbers, however: "The election took place on November 7. For the Constitution, 56,279 votes were cast and against it 9,073. The vote for the four congressmen was about the same. The day following the election the *Muskogee Phoenix* announced this as a 'Waterloo' Election. Looking at it from our standpoint it appears as a remarkably good vote. Regarding the voting strength as one-seventh of the population, a proportion that holds for Kansas, Oklahoma and Texas, we conclude that seventy-five per cent, or more of the votes of the territory were cast on this day and eighty-five per cent of them for the Constitution." Allen, *"Sequoyah" Movement*, 54.

105. According to Joseph B. Thoburn and Muriel Wright,

The proposed constitution divided the Indian Territory into forty-eight counties. Twenty of these counties were given Indian names; eight were names for prominent Federal officials or non-citizen politicians; two (Washington and Jefferson) were named for Presidents of the United States; four received geographic names which perpetuated the old tribal districts or counties; the other fourteen were christened in honor of as many prominent men of families among the several tribes. It is worthy of note, also, that nine of the counties thus proposed were approximately recreated, under the same names respectively, but the Oklahoma Constitutional Convention, namely, Jefferson, Garvin, Johnson, McCurtain, Sequoyah, Okmulgee, Muskogee, Mayes, and Seminole. (Thoburn and Wright, *Oklahoma*, 2:629)

106. At this time, women's suffrage had only been adopted in four other states: Wyoming, Colorado, Utah, and Idaho. However, many Native people in the territory saw the citizenship requirement as problematic because it conceded citizenship to the United States to maintain geographic and political autonomy. U.S. citizenship was also compulsorily tied to allotment. Voting rights were added in an amendment to the Dawes Act on March 3, 1901: "*Be it enacted* . . . that section six of chapter one hundred and nineteen of the United States Statutes at Large numbered twenty-four, page three hundred and ninety, is hereby amended as follows, to wit: After the words 'civilized life,' in line thirteen of said section six, insert the words 'and every Indian in Indian Territory.'" Prucha, *Documents of United States*, 198; Allen, "*Sequoyah*" *Movement*, 92.

107. Editorial, *Muskogee Cimeter*, August 3, 1905. The use of the term "pow wow" clarifies how the territorial press was complicit in fueling racialized stereotypes.

108. Cartoon, *Muskogee Cimeter*, October 26, 1905.

109. Editorial, *Muskogee Cimeter*, October 26, 1905.

110. The editorial on page 4 reads, "We have many letters from different parts of the territory asking what to do on election day and we have advised our boys against double statehood if they vote at all, but we real[l]y think it best not to vote at all because that constitution was not made by the people of I. T. [Indian Territory], and because the statehood that Owen, Thomas, et. al. want." Editorial, *Muskogee Cimeter*, October 26, 1905."

111. Also included in the October 26 issue is a reprinted article in which "Bishop Turner" responds to the mayor of Carrolton that the "Negro was not seeking social equality with the white race," because while Black people are "just as brainy and as intelligent as men of the white race," "the American whites were the meanest, and the devil of hell could not begin to compare with them." "Bishop Turner's Reply to Mayor of Carrolton, MO," *Muskogee Cimeter*, October 26, 1905.

112. The 1906 Enabling Act was also accompanied by a congressional compromise that New Mexico and Arizona be entered as one state into the United States if both territories' populations consented. While history has demonstrated this was not the case for Arizona and New Mexico, it was for Oklahoma and Indian Territory, and by June 1906, Oklahoma statehood was all but guaranteed. Debo, *And Still the Waters*, 278.

113. Konkle, *Writing Indian Nations*, 26.

114. Too-Qua-Stee regularly published in the Vinita *Chieftain*.

115. Too-Qua-Stee, "IMPERIALISM: Abandonment of the Monroe Doctrine," *Indian Chieftain*, August 9, 1900.

116. Too-Qua-Stee, "Indian Territory at World's Fair," *Muskogee Democrat*, October 1, 1904. Robert Dale Parker reprints the poem in his collection. See Too-Qua-Stee, "Indian Territory at World's Fair," in Parker, *Changing Is Not Vanishing*, 214–15.

117. Again, the Five Tribes had been inhabitants of the area for less than one hundred years, but Too-Qua-Stee seems to speak more generally about Native people's indigenous ties to the land. Nonetheless, it is necessary to remember that the Five Tribes were not the only nations Removed to the territory.

118. Too-Qua-Stee, "IMPERIALISM."

119. Leeds, "Defeat or Mixed Blessing." For a differing opinion on Sequoyah, see Russell, *Sequoyah Rising*.

120. As Claudio Saunt observes, a critical element of the state of Oklahoma's constitutional convention was to racially classify everyone as Black or white to deal with the "Indian's anomalous status." Saunt, *Black, White, and Indian*, 194. See also Wickett, *Contested Territory*, 41. It should also be noted that the new state legislation included an antimiscegenation clause that categorized all non-Black residents as white. For a discussion of segregation debates in drafting the Oklahoma constitution and Senate Bill No. 1, which segregated public transportation, see Franklin, *Journey toward Hope*, 34–59.

Conclusion

1. Sean "Sticks" Larkin, one of *Live PD*'s three main hosts, also served as a Tulsa police officer before cohosting, adding an air of local flavor to the program.

2. This was the second time the city and *Live PD* had cut ties. The first time was after season 1.

3. This is not the first time Tulsa, and so-called Oklahoma, has been a site of cultural existentialism during a moment of national "crisis." In the 1930s, Oklahoma circulated as a symbol of the Great Depression and migration, through fiction and film (John Steinbeck's *Grapes of Wrath*) and the folk music of Woody Guthrie. However, it also registered imperial nostalgia for a bygone era of western cowboys and westward expansion, as depicted in Edna Ferber's *Cimarron* and *Oklahoma!* the musical.

4. "Syllabus" in *Oklahoma v. Castro-Huerta*, 597 U.S. ___ (2022), 3, accessed August 11, 2022, https://www.supremecourt.gov/opinions/21pdf/21-429_806a.pdf.

5. "Gorsuch, J., dissenting" in *Oklahoma v. Castro-Huerta*, 597 U.S. ___ (2022), 1, accessed August 11, 2022, https://www.supremecourt.gov/opinions/21pdf/21-429_806a.pdf.

6. I am thinking of the upcoming *Haaland v. Brackeen* case, for example.

7. The case was first titled *Sharp v. Murphy*, but the title changed with a change in leadership at the Oklahoma State Penitentiary.

8. In the podcast, Nagle outlines the case's significance for tribal nations and also contextualizes the case as part of a long legacy of Indian Removal and dispossession, allotment, slavery, and genocide.

9. Hartman, *Lose Your Mother*, 6.

10. Edwards, Lee, and Esposito, "Risk of Being Killed"; Elise Hansen, "The Forgotten Minority in Police Shootings," CNN, November 13, 2017, www.cnn.com/2017/11/10/us/native-lives-matter/index.htm; Harvey, "Fatal Encounters." According to Harvey, most fatal encounters occur outside tribal jurisdictions.

11. "Oklahoma Profile," Prison Policy Initiative, accessed August 12, 2021, www .prisonpolicy.org/profiles/OK.html. However, both of these graphs are deeply fraught and naturalize state identity and a particular global order. Using NATO countries as a contrast implies that states like Oklahoma are less "advanced"—code for logics of modernity that have always positioned Black and Indigenous peoples as less than human.

12. Deer talks about the *McGirt* decision's potential impact on Indigenous women when interviewed by Amy Goodman. "'Most Important Indian Law Case in Half a Century': Supreme Court Upholds Tribal Sovereignty in OK," transcript, *Democracy Now*, July 10, 2020, www .democracynow.org/2020/7/10/scotus_oklahoma_muscogee_creek_nation#transcript.

13. This includes migrants and refugees (some of whom are Indigenous and/or Black).

14. The significance of Vernon was discussed in a piece for the *McAlester News*. See Mike Cathey, "Vernon at the Center of U.S. Supreme Court Case," *McAlester News*, October 26, 2019, www.mcalesternews.com/news/local_news/cathey-vernon-at-center-of-u-s-supreme -court-case/article_3e6596f7-0e08-5782-959d-31d4bc9411ea.html. Vernon, established in 1911, was named after William Tecumseh Vernon, an African Methodist Episcopal bishop who served for a time as supervisor of Indian and Black schools in the new state of Oklahoma. Williamson, *Crucible of Race*, 358.

15. King, *Black Shoals*, 21. I am thinking here in particular of King's articulation of "shoaling" work and Leanne Betasamosake Simpson's description of "radical resurgence." Leanne Betasamosake Simpson, *As We Have Always Done.*

16. Spires, *Practice of Citizenship*, 3.

17. Cherokee Nation, "ᏣᎳᎩ: Wherever We Are, 2022 Cherokee Freedmen Edition," YouTube, streamed live on February 19, 2022, video, 1:01:23, https://youtu.be/JXfqobnoelM.

18. Kauanui, *Paradoxes of Hawaiian Sovereignty*, 195.

19. The most prominent Native character is a young child adopted by Angela and Cal Abar. Given that the adoption of Native children outside their tribal communities continues to be weaponized by individuals and groups who want to see the erosion of tribal sovereignty, the depiction is a charged one, even if unintentionally so. I would also note that the show's representation of Asian Americanness reinscribes stereotypes of women of Asian descent and does not account for the significant history of Vietnam-Oklahoma affinities. Many Vietnamese refugees, and other refugees from the United States' military interventions into the Pacific and the Arab world, resettled in Oklahoma in the late twentieth century. Oklahoma is home to many vibrant Vietnamese communities.

20. Stark, "Making of a Savage," 10.

21. Kassell, *Watchmen*, episode 1.

22. Art Burton, *Black Gun, Silver Star*, 11.

23. Littlefield, foreword to Burton, *Black Gun, Silver Star*, xiii.

24. Wynter, "How We Mistook."

25. Walker, Brown, and Greene, *Bitter Root*, 11.

26. I am thinking of a few examples that also foreground Tulsa or Indian Territory, including Tom Holm's novel *The Osage Rose* (2008), which attempts to bring together the Tulsa Massacre and the Osage oil murders, as well as the television series *Lovecraft Country* (2020), critiqued for its offensive representation of a Two-Spirit character, and *Reservation Dogs* (2021), which was critiqued for anti-Blackness in season 1.

Bibliography

Primary Sources

ARCHIVES

American Antiquarian Society, Worcester, Mass.
Hargrett Rare Book and Manuscript Library, University of Georgia, Athens
Oklahoma Historical Society, Oklahoma City
Smathers Libraries Special Collections, University of Florida, Gainesville

PERIODICALS

Anglo-African Magazine (New York)
Athenian (later the *Southern Banner*)
  (Athens)
Boley Progress (Boley)
Cherokee Advocate (Tahlequah)
Cherokee Phoenix (New Echota)
Columbus Enquirer (Columbus)
Constitutionalist (Augusta)
Daily Indian Chieftain (Vinita)
Florida Gazette (East Florida)
Freedom's Journal (New York)
Georgia Courier (Augusta)

Georgia Journal (Milledgeville)
Indian Chieftain (later the *Vinita Weekly Chieftain* and then the *Weekly Chieftain*)
  (Vinita)
Indian Journal (Muskogee and Eufaula)
Muskogee Cimeter (Muskogee)
Muskogee Democrat (Muskogee)
Muskogee Phoenix (Muskogee)
Seminole Tribune (Hollywood)
Southern Recorder (Milledgeville)
Twin Territories (Muskogee)
Weekly Anglo-African (New York)

GOVERNMENT DOCUMENTS AND REPORTS

Georgia General Assembly. *Report of the Committee to Whom Was Referred So Much of the Governor's Message, as Relates to the Enforcement of the Law Making It Penal, under Certain Restrictions, for White Persons to Reside within the Limits of the Cherokee Nation.* Milledgeville, Ga.: Office of the Federal Union, 1832.

Harvey, Matthew. "Fatal Encounters between Native Americans and the Police." Center for Indian Country Development, March 2020. www.minneapolisfed.org/~/media/assets/articles/2020/fatal-encounters-between-native-americans-and-the-police/fatal-encounters-between-native-americans-and-the-police_march-2020.pdf?la=en.

Haynes, Charles Eaton. "Remarks of Mr. Haynes, of Georgia, in the House of Representatives, June 27, 1836." Hargrett Rare Book and Manuscript Library, University of Georgia.

———. *Speech of Mr. Haynes, of Georgia, on the Bill Making Appropriations for Suppressing Indian Hostilities: Delivered in the House of Representatives of the United States, May 28 and 29, 1838.* Washington, D.C.: Globe Office, 1838.

Jefferson, Thomas. Thomas Jefferson to James Monroe, October 24, 1823. In *Founders Online*,
   National Archives. https://founders.archives.gov/documents/Jefferson/98-01-02-3827.
Kappler, Charles J., ed. *Indian Affairs: Laws and Treaties*. Vol. 2. Washington, D.C.:
   Government Printing Office, 1904. https://avalon.law.yale.edu/18th_century/chr1791.asp.
Monroe, James. "President's Message." In *A Century of Lawmaking for a New Nation: U.S.
   Congressional Documents and Debates, 1774–1875*, 23–24. Washington, D.C.: Senate,
   18th Congress, 1st Session, 1823. http://memory.loc.gov/cgi-bin/ampage?collId
   =llac&fileName=041/llac041.db&recNum=3.
Peters, Richard. *The Case of the Cherokee Nation against the State of Georgia Argued and
   Determined at the Supreme Court of the United States, January Term 1831*. Philadelphia:
   John Grigg, 1831.
Smith, James F. *The Cherokee Land Lottery, Containing a Numerical List of the Names of
   the Fortunate Drawers in Said Lottery, with an Engraved Map of Each District*. New York:
   Harper and Brothers, 1838.
U.S. Department of State. *Treaty of San Lorenzo el Real: Letter from the Secretary of State,
   Transmitting Copies of Certain Letters of Andrew Ellicot, Commissioner, &c., Relating to
   the Head or Source of St. Mary's River*. Washington, D.C.: Gales and Seaton, 1829.

BOOKS

Aldrich, Corinna Brown, and Ellen Brown Anderson. *Echoes from a Distant Frontier:
   The Brown Sisters' Correspondence from Antebellum Florida*. Edited by James M. Denham
   and Keith L. Huneycutt. Columbia: University of South Carolina Press, 2004.
*An Authentic Narrative of the Seminole War; Its Cause, Rise and Progress, and a Minute Detail
   of the Horrid Massacres of the Whites, by the Indians and Negroes, in Florida, in the Months
   of December, January and February*. Providence: D. F. Blanchard, 1836.
Brougham, John. *Columbus el Filibustero! A New and Audaciously Original Historico-
   plagiaristic, Ante-national, Pre-patriotic, and Comic Confusion of Circumstances, Running
   through Two Acts and Four Centuries*. New York: S. French, 1858.
Buntline, Ned [E. Z. C. Judson]. *The White Wizard, or The Great Prophet of the
   Seminoles: A Tale of Strange Mystery in the South and North*. 1858. New York: Beadle
   and Adams, 1879.
Catlin, George. *Letters and Notes on the Manners, Customs, and Condition of the North
   American Indians*. Vol. 2. London: Tosswill and Meyers, 1841.
Cohen, Myer M. *Notices of Florida and the Campaigns*. Charleston: Burges and Honour,
   1836.
Dana, Richard Henry. *To Cuba and Back: A Vacation Voyage*. London: Smith, Elder, 1859.
Delany, Martin R. *Blake; or, The Huts of America*. Corrected ed. Edited by Jerome
   McGann. Cambridge, Mass.: Harvard University Press, 2017.
———. *Martin R. Delany: A Documentary Reader*. Edited by Robert S. Levine. Chapel
   Hill: University of North Carolina Press, 2003.
Ellison, Ralph. *The Collected Essays of Ralph Ellison*. Rev. ed. Edited by John Callahan.
   New York: Modern Library, 2003.
Evarts, Jeremiah. *Cherokee Removal: The "William Penn" Essays and Other Writings*. Edited
   by Francis Paul Prucha. Knoxville: University of Tennessee Press, 1981.

Giddings, Joshua R. *The Exiles of Florida, or The Crimes Committed by Our Government against the Maroons: Who Fled from South Carolina and Other Slave States, Seeking Protection under Spanish Law.* Columbus, Ohio: Follett, Foster, 1858.

Howard, O. O. *My Life and Experiences among Our Hostile Indians: A Record of Personal Observations, Adventures, and Campaigns among the Indians of the Great West, with Some Account of Their Life, Habits, Traits, Religion, Ceremonies, Dress, Savage Instincts, and Customs in Peace and War.* Hartford, Conn.: A. T. Worthington, 1907; repr., New York: Da Capo, 1972. Citations refer to the Da Capo edition.

Hughes, Langston. *Not without Laughter.* New York: Alfred A. Knopf, 1930. https://hdl .handle.net/2027/uiuc.3004694.

Lumpkin, Wilson. *The Removal of the Cherokee Indians from Georgia.* 2 vols. New York: Arno Press, 1969.

Missall, John, and Mary Lou Missall, eds. *In Their Own Words: Selected Seminole "Talks," 1817–1842.* Vol. 1. Dade City, Fla.: Seminole Wars Foundation, 2009.

A Narrative of the Life and Sufferings of Mrs. Jane Johns, Who Was Barbarously Wounded and Scalped by Seminole Indians, in East Florida. Baltimore: Jas. Lucas and E. K. Deaver, 1837.

Occom, Samson. *The Collected Writings of Samson Occom, Mohegan: Leadership and Literature in Eighteenth-Century Native America.* Edited by Joanna Brooks. Oxford: Oxford University Press, 2006.

Parker, Robert Dale, ed. *Changing Is Not Vanishing: A Collection of American Indian Poetry to 1930.* Philadelphia: University of Pennsylvania Press, 2011.

Peyer, Bernd C., ed. *American Indian Nonfiction: An Anthology of Writings, 1760s–1930s.* Norman: University of Oklahoma Press, 2007.

Posey, Alexander Lawrence. *The Fus Fixico Letters.* Edited by Daniel F. Littlefield Jr. and Carol A. Petty Hunter. Lincoln: University of Nebraska Press, 1993.

———. *Lost Creeks: Collected Journals.* Edited by Matthew Wynn Sivils. Lincoln: University of Nebraska Press, 2009.

———. *Song of the Oktahutche: Collected Poems.* Edited and with an introduction by Matthew Wynn Sivils. Lincoln: University of Nebraska Press, 2008.

Prucha, Francis Paul, ed. *Documents of United States Indian Policy.* 3rd ed. Lincoln: University of Nebraska Press, 2000.

Ransom, James Birchett. *Osceola; or, Fact and Fiction: A Tale of the Seminole War by a Southerner.* New York: Harper and Brothers, 1838.

Reed, Mayne. *Osceola the Seminole; or, The Red Fawn of the Flower Land.* New York: Robert De Witt, 1858.

Rollin, Frank [Frances] A. *Life and Public Services of Martin R. Delany, Sub-assistant Commissioner Bureau Relief of Refugees, Freedmen, and of Abandoned Lands, and Late Major 104th U.S. Colored Troops.* Boston: Lee and Shepard, 1883.

Ross, John. *The Papers of Chief John Ross.* Edited by Gary E. Moulton. Vol. 1, *1807–1839.* Norman: University of Oklahoma Press, 1985.

Rustic, Jane [Frances Ellen Watkins Harper]. "Chit Chat, or, Fancy Sketches." *Anglo-African Magazine* 1, no. 11 (November 1859): 42.

Sprague, John T. *The Origin, Progress, and Conclusion of the Florida War.* Facsimile reproduction of the 1848 edition. Gainesville: University of Florida Press, 1964.

Stowe, Harriet Beecher. *First Geography for Children*. Boston: Phillips, Sampson, 1855.

A True and Authentic Account of the Indian War in Florida, Giving the Particulars Respecting the Murder of the Widow Robbins, and the Providential Escape of Her Daughter Aurelia, and Her Lover, Mr. Charles Somers, after Suffering Almost Innumerable Hardships. New York: Saunders and Van Welt, 1836.

Walker, David. *David Walker's Appeal to the Coloured Citizens of the World*. Edited by Peter P. Hinks. University Park: Pennsylvania State University Press, 2000.

Whitman, Albery Allson. *At the Dusk of Dawn: Selected Poetry and Prose of Albery Allson Whitman*. Edited by Ivy G. Wilson. Boston: Northeastern University Press, 2009.

———. *Not a Man, and Yet a Man*. Upper Saddle River, N.J.: Literature House, 1970.

———. *The Rape of Florida*. Miami: Mnemosyne, 1884.

———. *Twasinta's Seminoles; or, Rape of Florida*. Saint Louis: Nixon-Jones, 1885.

Secondary Sources

BOOKS

Abel, Annie Heloise. *The American Indian and the End of the Confederacy, 1863–1866*. Lincoln: University of Nebraska Press, 1993.

Ahmed, Sara. *Living a Feminist Life*. Durham, N.C.: Duke University Press, 2017.

Allen, C. M. *The "Sequoyah" Movement*. Oklahoma City: Harlow, 1925.

Arvin, Maile. *Possessing Polynesians: The Science of Settler Colonial Whiteness in Hawai'i and Oceania*. Durham, N.C.: Duke University Press, 2019.

Allewaert, Monique. *Ariel's Ecology: Plantations, Personhood, and Colonialism in the American Tropics*. Minneapolis: University of Minnesota Press, 2013.

Bacon, Jacqueline. *Freedom's Journal: The First African American Newspaper*. Lanham, M.D.: Lexington Books, 2007.

Bailey, M. Thomas. *Reconstruction in Indian Territory, 1865–1877*. Port Washington, N.Y.: Kennikate, 1972.

Ball, Erica L. *To Live an Antislavery Life: Personal Politics and the Antebellum Black Middle Class*. Athens: University of Georgia Press, 2012.

Bartosik-Vélez, Elise. *The Legacy of Christopher Columbus in the Americas: New Nations and a Transatlantic Discourse of Empire*. Nashville: Vanderbilt University Press, 2014.

Beer, Samuel H. *To Make a Nation: The Rediscovery of American Federalism*. Cambridge, Mass.: Harvard University Press, 1993.

Belcourt, Billy-Ray. *NDN Coping Mechanisms: Notes from the Field*. Toronto: House of Anansi Press, 2019.

———. *This Wound Is a World*. Minneapolis: University of Minnesota Press, 2019.

Belko, William S., ed. *America's Hundred Years' War: U.S. Expansion to the Gulf Coast and the Fate of the Seminole, 1763–1858*. Gainesville: University Press of Florida, 2011.

Bemrose, John. *Reminiscences of the Second Seminole War*. Edited by John K. Mahon. Gainesville: University Press of Florida, 1966.

Benítez-Rojo, Antonio. *The Repeating Island: The Caribbean and the Postmodern Perspective*. Translated by James E. Maraniss. Durham, N.C.: Duke University Press, 1996.

Brady, Mary Pat *Extinct Lands, Temporal Geographies: Chicana Literature and the Urgency of Space*. Durham, N.C.: Duke University Press, 2002.

Brannon, Frank. *Cherokee Phoenix: Advent of a Newspaper: The Print Shop of the Cherokee Nation, 1828–1834, with a Chronology.* Tuscaloosa: SpeakEasy, 2005.

Brickhouse, Anna. *Transamerican Literary Relations and the Nineteenth-Century Public Sphere.* New York: Cambridge University Press, 2004.

brown, adrienne maree. *Emergent Strategy: Shaping Change, Changing Worlds.* Chico, Calif.: AK Press, 2017.

brown, adrienne maree, and Walidah Imarisha, eds. *Octavia's Brood: Science Fiction Stories from Social Justice Movements.* Chico, Calif.: AK Press, 2015.

Brown, Charles H. *Agents of Manifest Destiny: The Lives and Times of the Filibusters.* Chapel Hill: University of North Carolina Press, 1980.

Brückner, Martin. *The Geography Revolution in Early America: Maps, Literacy, and National Identity.* Chapel Hill: University of North Carolina Press, 2006. Published for the Omohundro Institute of Early American History and Culture, Williamsburg, Va.

Bruyneel, Kevin. *The Third Space of Sovereignty: The Postcolonial Politics of U.S.-Indigenous Relations.* Minneapolis: University of Minnesota Press, 2007.

Burnett, Christina Duffy, and Burke Marshall, eds. *Foreign in a Domestic Sense: Puerto Rico, American Expansion, and the Constitution.* Durham, N.C.: Duke University Press, 2001.

Burnham, Michelle. *Captivity and Sentiment: Cultural Exchange in American Literature, 1682–1861.* Hanover, N.H.: University Press of New England, 1997.

Burton, Art T. *Black Gun, Silver Star: The Life and Legend of Frontier Marshal Bass Reeves.* Lincoln: University of Nebraska Press, 2006.

Burton, Jeffrey. *Indian Territory and the United States, 1866–1906: Courts, Government, and the Movement for Oklahoma Statehood.* Norman: University of Oklahoma Press, 1997.

Butrick, D. S., and D. Brown. *Tsvlvki sqclvclv: A Cherokee Spelling Book.* Knoxville: F. S. Heiskell and H. Brown, 1819.

Byrd, Jodi A. *The Transit of Empire: Indigenous Critiques of Colonialism.* Minneapolis: University of Minnesota Press, 2011.

Carretta, Vincent. *Phillis Wheatley: Biography of a Genius in Bondage.* Athens: University of Georgia Press, 2011.

Carter, Kent. *The Dawes Commission and the Allotment of the Five Civilized Tribes, 1893–1914.* Orem, Utah: Ancestry.com, 1999.

Carter, L. Edward. *The Story of Oklahoma Newspapers, 1844 to 1984.* Muskogee: Western Heritage Books, 1984. Published for the Oklahoma Heritage Association.

Castronovo, Russ. *Propaganda 1776: Secrets, Leaks, and Revolutionary Communications in Early America.* New York: Oxford University Press, 2014.

Cattelino, Jessica R. *High Stakes: Florida Seminole Gaming and Sovereignty.* Durham, N.C.: Duke University Press, 2008.

Chaffin, Tom. *Fatal Glory: Narciso López and the First Clandestine U.S. War against Cuba.* Charlottesville: University Press of Virginia, 1996.

Chang, David A. *The Color of the Land: Race, Nation, and the Politics of Landownership in Oklahoma, 1832–1929.* Chapel Hill: University of North Carolina Press, 2010.

Chen, Mel Y. *Animacies: Biopolitics, Racial Mattering, and Queer Affect.* Durham, N.C.: Duke University Press, 2012.

Coleman, Aaron N. *The American Revolution, State Sovereignty, and the American Constitutional Settlement, 1765–1800.* Lanham, Md.: Lexington Books, 2016.

Coronado, Raúl. *A World Not to Come: A History of Latino Writing and Print Culture.* Cambridge, Mass.: Harvard University Press, 2013.

Coulthard, Glen Sean. *Red Skins, White Masks: Rejecting the Colonial Politics of Recognition.* Minneapolis: University of Minnesota Press, 2014.

Coward, John M. *The Newspaper Indian: Native American Identity in the Press, 1820–90.* Urbana: University of Illinois Press, 1999.

Cushman, Ellen. *The Cherokee Syllabary: Writing the People's Perseverance.* Norman: University of Oklahoma Press, 2011.

Debo, Angie. *And Still the Waters Run: The Betrayal of the Five Civilized Tribes.* Princeton, N.J.: Princeton University Press, 1940.

———. *The Road to Disappearance.* Norman: University of Oklahoma Press, 1941.

Deer, Sarah. *The Beginning and End of Rape: Configuring Sexual Violence in Native America.* Minneapolis: University of Minnesota Press, 2015.

Deloria, Philip J. *Playing Indian.* New Haven, Conn.: Yale University Press, 1998.

Deloria, Vine, Jr., and Clifford M. Lytle. *The Nations Within: The Past and Future of American Indian Sovereignty.* Austin: University of Texas Press, 1984.

Denson, Andrew. *Monuments to Absence: Cherokee Removal and the Contest over Southern Memory.* Chapel Hill: University of North Carolina Press, 2017.

Derounian-Stodola, Kathryn Zabelle, ed. *Women's Indian Captivity Narratives.* New York: Penguin Books, 1998.

Diouf, Sylviane A. *Slavery's Exiles: The Story of the American Maroons.* New York: New York University Press, 2016.

Dimaline, Cherie. *The Marrow Thieves.* Toronto: DCB Press, 2017.

Elden, Stuart. *The Birth of Territory.* Chicago: University of Chicago Press, 2013.

———. *Terror and Territory: The Spatial Extent of Sovereignty.* Minneapolis: University of Minnesota Press, 2009.

Ferrer, Ada. *Insurgent Cuba: Race, Nation, and Revolution, 1868–1898.* Chapel Hill: University of North Carolina Press, 1999.

Fielder, Brigitte. *Relative Races: Genealogies of Interracial Kinship in Nineteenth-Century America.* Durham, N.C.: Duke University Press, 2020.

Finch, Aisha K. *Rethinking Slave Rebellion in Cuba: La Escalera and the Insurgencies of 1841–1844.* Chapel Hill: University of North Carolina Press, 2015.

Fitzpatrick, Ellen. *History's Memory: Writing America's Past, 1880–1980.* Cambridge, Mass.: Harvard University Press, 2002.

Forbes, Jack D. *Africans and Native Americans: The Language of Race and the Evolution of Red-Black Peoples.* Urbana: University of Illinois Press, 1993.

Foreman, Carolyn Thomas. *Oklahoma Imprints, 1835–1907: A History of Printing in Oklahoma before Statehood.* Norman: University of Oklahoma Press, 1936.

Franklin, Jimmie Lewis. *Journey toward Hope: A History of Blacks in Oklahoma.* Norman: University of Oklahoma Press, 1982.

Gates, Henry Louis, Jr. *The Signifying Monkey: A Theory of African-American Literary Criticism.* New York: Oxford University Press, 1988.

Glymph, Thaviola. *Out of the House of Bondage: The Transformation of the Plantation Household.* New York: Cambridge University Press, 2008.

Goeman, Mishuana. *Mark My Words: Native Women Mapping Our Nations*. Minneapolis: University of Minnesota Press, 2013.

Goldstein, Alyosha, ed. *Formations of United States Colonialism*. Durham, N.C.: Duke University Press, 2014.

Griffith, Louis Turner, and John Erwin Talmadge. *Georgia Journalism, 1763–1950*. Athens: University of Georgia Press, 1951.

Gruesz, Kirsten Silva. *Ambassadors of Culture: The Transamerican Origin of Latino Writing*. Princeton, N.J.: Princeton University Press, 2002.

Gumbs, Alexis Pauline. *Spill: Scenes of Black Feminist Fugitivity*. Durham, N.C.: Duke University Press, 2016.

———. *Undrowned: Black Feminist Lessons from Marine Mammals*. Chico, Calif.: AK Press, 2020.

Harney, Stefano, and Fred Moten. *The Undercommons: Fugitive Planning and Black Study*. New York: Minor Composition, 2013.

Hartman, Saidiya V. *Lose Your Mother: A Journey along the Atlantic Slave Route*. New York: Farrar, Straus, and Giroux, 2007.

———. *Scenes of Subjection: Terror, Slavery, and Self-Making in Nineteenth-Century America*. New York: Oxford University Press, 1997.

———. *Wayward Lives, Beautiful Experiments: Intimate Histories of Riotous Black Girls, Troublesome Women, and Queer Radicals*. New York: W. W. Norton, 2019.

Harvey, David. *The New Imperialism*. Oxford: Oxford University Press, 2003.

———. *Social Justice and the City*. Rev. ed. Athens: University of Georgia Press, 2009.

Hinks, Peter P. *To Awaken My Afflicted Brethren: David Walker and the Problem of Antebellum Slave Resistance*. University Park: Pennsylvania State University Press, 1997.

Hogarth, Rana A. *Medicalizing Blackness: Making Racial Difference in the Atlantic World, 1780–1840*. Chapel Hill: North Carolina Press, 2017.

Horsman, Reginald. *Race and Manifest Destiny: The Origins of American Racial Anglo-Saxonism*. Cambridge, Mass.: Harvard University Press, 1981.

Hoxie, Frederick E. *This Indian Country: American Indian Activists and the Place They Made*. New York: Penguin, 2012.

Hsu, Hsuan L. *Geography and the Production of Space in Nineteenth-Century American Literature*. New York: Cambridge University Press, 2010.

Hubbard, Bill, Jr. *American Boundaries*. Chicago: University of Chicago Press, 2009.

Hyde, Anne F. *Empires, Nations, and Families: A History of the North American West, 1800–1860*. Lincoln: University of Nebraska Press, 2011.

Isaac, Allan Punzalan. *American Tropics: Articulating Filipino America*. Minneapolis: University of Minnesota Press, 2006.

Jackson, Shona N. *Creole Indigeneity: Between Myth and Nation in the Caribbean*. Minneapolis: University of Minnesota Press, 2012.

Jeffers, Honorée Fanonne. *The Age of Phillis*. Middleton, Conn.: Wesleyan University Press, 2020.

Jennison, Watson W. *Cultivating Race: The Expansion of Slavery in Georgia, 1750–1860*. Lexington: University of Kentucky Press, 2012.

Johnson, Hildegard Binder. *Order upon the Land: The U.S. Rectangular Land Survey and the Upper Mississippi Country*. New York: Oxford University Press, 1976.

Jones-Rogers, Stephanie E. *They Were Her Property: White Women as Slave Owners in the American South*. New Haven, Conn.: Yale University Press, 2019.

Jumper, Betty Mae Tiger, and Patsy West. *A Seminole Legend: The Life of Betty Mae Tiger Jumper*. Gainesville: University Press of Florida, 2001.

Jumper, Moses, Jr. *Echoes in the Wind: Seminole Indian Poetry*. Boca Raton: Boca Raton Printing, 1990.

Justice, Daniel Heath. *Our Fire Survives the Storm: A Cherokee Literary History*. Minneapolis: University of Minnesota Press, 2007.

———. *Why Indigenous Literatures Matter*. Waterloo, ON: Wilfrid Laurier University Press, 2018.

Kanellos, Nicolás, and Helvetia Martell. *Hispanic Periodicals in the United States, Origins to 1960: A Brief History and Comprehensive Bibliography*. Houston: Arte Público, 2000.

Kaplan, Amy. *The Anarchy of Empire in the Making of U.S. Culture*. Cambridge, Mass.: Harvard University Press, 2002.

Karuka, Manu. *Empire's Tracks: Indigenous Nations, Chinese Workers, and the Transcontinental Railroad*. Berkeley: University of California Press, 2019.

Kauanui, J. Kēhaulani. *Paradoxes of Hawaiian Sovereignty: Land, Sex, and the Colonial Politics of State Nationalism*. Durham, N.C.: Duke University Press, 2018.

Kazanjian, David. *The Colonizing Trick: National Culture and Imperial Citizenship in Early America*. Minneapolis: University of Minnesota Press, 2003.

Khalili, Laleh. *Time in the Shadows: Confinement in Counterinsurgencies*. Stanford, Calif.: Stanford University Press, 2013.

Kidwell, Clara Sue. *The Choctaws in Oklahoma: From Tribe to Nation, 1855–1970*. Norman: University of Oklahoma Press, 2007.

King, Tiffany Lethabo. *The Black Shoals: Offshore Formations of Black and Native Studies*. Durham, N.C.: Duke University Press, 2019.

Kly, Y. N., ed. *The Invisible War: The African American Anti-slavery Resistance from the Stono Rebellion through the Seminole Wars*. Atlanta: Clarity, 2006.

Kolodny, Annette. *The Lay of the Land: Metaphor as Experience and History in American Life and Letters*. Chapel Hill: University of North Carolina Press, 1975.

Konkle, Maureen. *Writing Indian Nations: Native Intellectuals and the Politics of Historiography, 1827–1863*. Chapel Hill: University of North Carolina Press, 2004.

Krauthamer, Barbara. *Black Slaves, Indian Masters: Slavery, Emancipation, and Citizenship in the Native American South*. Chapel Hill: University of North Carolina Press, 2013.

LaCroix, Alison L. *The Ideological Origins of American Federalism*. Cambridge, Mass.: Harvard University Press, 2016.

Landers, Jane G. *Atlantic Creoles in the Age of Revolutions*. Cambridge, Mass.: Harvard University Press, 2010.

Lazo, Rodrigo. *Writing to Cuba: Filibustering and Cuban Exiles in the United States*. Chapel Hill: University of North Carolina Press, 2005.

Limerick, Patricia. *The Legacy of Conquest: The Unbroken Past of the American West*. New York: W. W. Norton, 1987.

Lipman, Jana. *Guantánamo: A Working-Class History between Empire and Revolution.* Berkeley: University of California Press, 2008.

Littlefield, Daniel F., Jr. *Africans and Seminoles: From Removal to Emancipation.* Westport, Conn.: Greenwood, 1977.

———. *Alex Posey: Creek Poet, Journalist, and Humorist.* Lincoln: University of Nebraska Press, 1992.

Littlefield, Daniel F., Jr., and James W. Parins. *A Biobibliography of Native American Writers, 1772–1924.* Metuchen, N.J.: Scarecrow, 1981.

———. *A Biobibliography of Native American Writers, 1772–1924: A Supplement.* Metuchen, N.J.: Scarecrow, 1985.

Loughran, Trish. *The Republic in Print: Print Culture in the Age of U.S. Nation Building, 1770–1870.* New York: Columbia University Press, 2007.

Lowe, Lisa. *The Intimacies of Four Continents.* Durham, N.C.: Duke University Press, 2015.

Madera, Judith. *Black Atlas: Geography and Flow in Nineteenth-Century African American Literature.* Durham, N.C.: Duke University Press, 2015.

Mahon, John K. *History of the Second Seminole War, 1835–1842.* Gainesville: University Presses of Florida, 1991.

Massey, Doreen. *For Space.* London: Sage, 2005.

Mathews, John Joseph. *The Osages: Children of the Middle Waters.* Norman: University of Oklahoma Press, 1961.

May, Robert E. *Manifest Destiny's Underworld: Filibustering in Antebellum America.* Chapel Hill: University of North Carolina Press, 2002.

McGill, Meredith. *American Literature and the Culture of Reprinting, 1834–1853.* Philadelphia: University of Pennsylvania Press, 2003.

McHenry, Elizabeth. *Forgotten Readers: Recovering the Lost History of African American Literary Societies.* Durham, N.C.: Duke University Press, 2002.

McKittrick, Katherine. *Dear Science and Other Stories.* Durham, N.C.: Duke University Press, 2021.

———. *Demonic Grounds: Black Women and the Cartographies of Struggle.* Minneapolis: University of Minnesota Press, 2006.

Merritt, Keri Leigh. *Masterless Men: Poor Whites and Slavery in the Antebellum South.* New York: Cambridge University Press, 2017.

Miles, Tiya. *The House on Diamond Hill: A Cherokee Plantation Story.* Chapel Hill: University of North Carolina Press, 2012.

———. *Ties That Bind: The Story of an Afro-Cherokee Family in Slavery and Freedom.* Berkeley: University of California Press, 2005.

Miles, Tiya, and Sharon P. Holland, eds. *Crossing Waters, Crossing Worlds: The African Diaspora in Indian Country.* Durham, N.C.: Duke University Press, 2006.

Miller, Susan A. *Coacoochee's Bones: A Seminole Saga.* Lawrence: University Press of Kansas, 2003.

Miner, H. Craig, and William E. Unrau. *The End of Indian Kansas: A Study of Cultural Revolution, 1854–1871.* Lawrence: Regents Press of Kansas, 1978.

Mirabal, Nancy Raquel. *Suspect Freedoms: The Racial and Sexual Politics of Cubanidad in New York, 1823–1957.* New York: New York University Press, 2017.

Missall, John, and Mary Lou Missall. *The Seminole Wars: America's Longest Indian Conflict.* Gainesville: University Press of Florida, 2004.

Moreton-Robinson, Aileen. *The White Possessive: Property, Power, and Indigenous Sovereignty.* Minneapolis: University of Minnesota Press, 2015.

Moten, Fred. *In the Break: The Aesthetics of the Black Radical Tradition.* Minneapolis: University of Minnesota Press, 2003.

Mulroy, Kevin. *Freedom on the Border: The Seminole Maroons in Florida, the Indian Territory, Coahuila, and Texas.* Lubbock: Texas Tech University Press, 1993.

———. *The Seminole Freedmen: A History.* Norman: University of Oklahoma Press, 2007.

Navakas, Michele Currie. *Liquid Landscape: Geography and Settlement at the Edge of Early America.* Philadelphia: University of Pennsylvania Press, 2018.

Naylor, Celia E. *African Cherokees in Indian Territory: From Chattel to Citizens.* Chapel Hill: University of North Carolina Press, 2008.

Norgren, Jill. *The Cherokee Cases: Two Landmark Federal Decisions in the Fight for Sovereignty.* Norman: University of Oklahoma Press, 2004.

Nwankwo, Ifeoma Kiddoe. *Black Cosmopolitanism: Racial Consciousness and Transnational Identity in the Nineteenth-Century Americas.* Philadelphia: University of Pennsylvania Press, 2005.

O'Brien, Jean M. *Firsting and Lasting: Writing Indians Out of Existence in New England.* Minneapolis: University of Minnesota Press, 2010.

Parins, James W. *Literacy and Intellectual Life in the Cherokee Nation, 1820–1906.* Norman: University of Oklahoma Press, 2013.

Pascoe, Peggy. *What Comes Naturally: Miscegenation Law and the Making of Race in America.* Oxford: Oxford University Press, 2009.

Perdue, Theda. *Cherokee Women: Gender and Cultural Change, 1700–1835.* Lincoln: University of Nebraska Press, 1998.

Perdue, Theda, and Michael D. Green. *The Cherokee Nation and the Trail of Tears.* New York: Viking, 2007.

Pérez, Louis A., Jr. *On Becoming Cuban: Identity, Nationality, and Culture.* Chapel Hill: University of North Carolina Press, 1999.

Peters, Virginia Bergman. *The Florida Wars.* Hamden, Conn.: Archon Books, 1979.

Piatote, Beth H. *Domestic Subjects: Gender, Citizenship, and Law in Native American Literature.* New Haven, Conn.: Yale University Press, 2013.

Porter, Kenneth Wiggins. *The Black Seminoles: History of a Freedom-Seeking People.* Edited by Alcione M. Amos and Thomas P. Senter. Gainesville: University Press of Florida, 1996.

Raustiala, Kal. *Does the Constitution Follow the Flag? The Evolution of Territoriality in American Law.* New York: Oxford University Press, 2009.

Ray, Grace Ernestine. *Early Oklahoma Newspapers: History and Description of Publications from Earliest Beginnings to 1889.* Norman: University of Oklahoma, 1928.

Reed, Julie L. *Serving the Nation: Cherokee Sovereignty and Social Welfare, 1800–1907.* Norman: University of Oklahoma Press, 2016.

Reese, Linda Williams. *Trail Sisters: Freedwomen in Indian Territory, 1850–1890.* Lubbock: Texas Tech University Press, 2013.

Reid-Vazquez, Michele. *The Year of the Lash: Free People of Color in Cuba and the Nineteenth-Century Atlantic World.* Athens: University of Georgia Press, 2011.

Roberts, Alaina E. *I've Been Here All the While: Black Freedom on Native Land*. Philadelphia: University of Pennsylvania Press, 2021.

Roberts, Neil. *Freedom as Marronage*. Chicago: University of Chicago Press, 2015.

Robinson, Cedric J. *Black Marxism*. Chapel Hill: University of North Carolina Press, 2000.

Rodenbough, Theo F. *From the Everglades to Cañon with the Second United States Cavalry*. Norman: University of Oklahoma Press, 2000.

Rodríguez, Dylan. *Suspended Apocalypse: White Supremacy, Genocide, and the Filipino Condition*. Minneapolis: University of Minnesota Press, 2009.

Rosaldo, Renato. *Culture and Truth: The Remaking of Social Analysis*. Boston: Beacon, 1993.

Rosen, Deborah A. *American Indians and State Law: Sovereignty, Race and Citizenship, 1790–1880*. Lincoln: University of Nebraska Press, 2007.

———. *Border Law: The First Seminole War and American Nationhood*. Cambridge, Mass.: Harvard University Press, 2015.

Round, Phillip H. *Removable Type: Histories of the Book in Indian Country, 1663–1880*. Chapel Hill: University of North Carolina Press, 2010.

Russell, Steve. *Sequoyah Rising: Problems in Post-Colonial Tribal Governance*. Durham, N.C.: Carolina Academic Press, 2010.

Saldaña-Portillo, María Josefina. *Indian Given: Racial Geographies across Mexico and the United States*. Durham, N.C.: Duke University Press, 2016.

Saler, Bethel. *The Settlers' Empire: Colonialism and State Formation in America's Old Northwest*. Philadelphia: University of Pennsylvania Press, 2015.

Sandler, Matt. *The Black Romantic Revolution: Abolitionist Poets at the End of Slavery*. London: Verso, 2020.

Saranillio, Dean Itsuji. *Unsustainable Empire: Alternative Histories of Hawai'i Statehood*. Durham, N.C.: Duke University Press, 2018.

Saunt, Claudio. *Black, White, and Indian: Race and the Unmaking of an American Family*. New York: Oxford University Press, 2005.

Sayre, Gordon M. *Indian Chief as Tragic Hero: Native Resistance and the Literatures of America, from Moctezuma to Tecumseh*. Chapel Hill: University of North Carolina Press, 2005.

Scales, James R. and Danney Goble. *Oklahoma Politics: A History*. Norman: University of Oklahoma Press, 1982.

Schoolman, Martha. *Abolitionist Geographies*. Minneapolis: University of Minnesota Press, 2014.

Schulten, Susan. *Mapping the Nation: History and Cartography in Nineteenth-Century America*. Chicago: University of Chicago Press, 2012.

Schweiger, Beth Barton. *A Literate South: Reading before Emancipation*. New Haven, Conn.: Yale University Press, 2019.

Scott, James C. *Seeing like a State: How Certain Schemes to Improve the Human Condition Have Failed*. New Haven, Conn.: Yale University Press, 1998.

Sharpe, Christina. *In the Wake: On Blackness and Being*. Durham, N.C.: Duke University Press, 2016.

Silva, Noenoe K. *Aloha Betrayed: Native Hawaiian Resistance to American Colonialism*. Durham, N.C.: Duke University Press, 2004.

———. *The Power of the Steel-Tipped Pen: Reconstructing Native Hawaiian Intellectual History*. Durham, N.C.: Duke University Press, 2017.

Simpson, Audra. *Mohawk Interruptus: Political Life across the Borders of Settler States.* Durham, N.C.: Duke University Press, 2014.

Simpson, Leanne Betasamosake. *As We Have Always Done: Indigenous Freedom through Radical Resistance.* Minneapolis: University of Minnesota Press, 2017.

Soja, Edward. *Postmodern Geographies: The Reassertion of Space in Critical Social Theory.* London: Verso, 1989.

Spires, Derrick R. *The Practice of Citizenship: Black Politics and Print Culture in the Early United States.* Philadelphia: University of Pennsylvania Press, 2019.

Stoler, Ann Laura, ed. *Haunted by Empire: Geographies of Intimacy in North American History.* Durham, N.C.: Duke University Press, 2006.

Sturm, Circe. *Blood Politics: Race, Culture, and Identity in the Cherokee Nation of Oklahoma.* Berkeley: University of California Press, 2002.

Sundquist, Eric J. *To Wake the Nations: Race in the Making of American Literature.* Cambridge, Mass.: Belknap Press of Harvard University Press, 1993.

Thoburn, Joseph B., and Muriel Wright. *Oklahoma: A History of the State and Its People.* 4 vols. New York: Lewis Historical, 1929.

Thompson, John. *Closing the Frontier: Radical Response in Oklahoma, 1889–1923.* Norman: University of Oklahoma Press, 1986.

Tolson, Arthur L. *The Black Oklahomans: A History, 1541–1972.* New Orleans: Edwards, 1966.

Tompkins, Kyla Wazana. *Racial Indigestion: Eating Bodies in the 19th Century.* New York: New York University Press, 2012.

Twyman, Bruce Edward. *The Black Seminole Legacy and North American Politics, 1693–1845.* Washington, D.C.: Howard University Press, 1999.

Walker, David F., Chuck Brown, and Sanford Greene. *Bitter Root.* No. 7. Portland, Ore.: Image Comics, 2020.

Warrior, Robert. *The People and the Word: Reading Native Nonfiction.* Minneapolis: University of Minnesota Press, 2005.

Washburn, Patrick S. *The African American Newspaper: Voice of Freedom.* Evanston, Ill.: Northwestern University Press, 2006.

Weisman, Brent Richards. *Like Beads on a String: A Culture History of the Seminole Indians in North Peninsular Florida.* Tuscaloosa: University of Alabama Press, 1989.

Wickett, Murray R. *Contested Territory: Whites, Native Americans and African Americans in Oklahoma, 1865–1907.* Baton Rouge: Louisiana State University Press, 2000.

Wickman, Patricia R. *Osceola's Legacy.* Tuscaloosa: University of Alabama Press, 1991.

Williams, Heather Andrea. *Self-Taught: African American Education in Slavery and Freedom.* Chapel Hill: University of North Carolina Press, 2007.

Williamson, Joel. *The Crucible of Race: Black-White Relations in the American South since Emancipation.* New York: Oxford University Press, 1984.

Windell, Maria. *Transamerican Sentimentalism and Nineteenth-Century U.S. History.* Oxford: Oxford University Press, 2020.

Womack, Craig S. *Red on Red: Native American Literary Separatism.* Minneapolis: University of Minnesota Press, 1999.

Wright, James Leitch, Jr. *Creeks and Seminoles: The Destruction and Regeneration of the Muscogulge People.* Lincoln: University of Nebraska Press, 1990.

Wright, Muriel H. *The Story of Oklahoma*. Edited by Joseph B. Thoburn. Oklahoma City: Webb, 1929.

Yao, Xine. *Disaffected: The Cultural Politics of Unfeeling in Nineteenth-Century America*. Durham, N.C.: Duke University Press, 2021.

Yaremko, Jason M. *Indigenous Passages to Cuba, 1515–1900*. Gainesville: University of Florida Press, 2016.

Yun, Lisa. *The Coolie Speaks: Chinese Indentured Laborers and African Slaves in Cuba*. Philadelphia: Temple University Press, 2008.

JOURNAL ARTICLES, BOOK CHAPTERS, ENCYCLOPEDIA ENTRIES, AND DISSERTATIONS

Asukile, Thabiti. "The All-Embracing Black Nationalist Theories of David Walker's Appeal." *Black Scholar* 29, no. 4 (1999): 16–24. https://doi.org/10.1080/00064246.1999 .11430981.

Anderson, William L. "Sequoyah." In *Encyclopedia of Oklahoma History and Culture*. Accessed September 8, 2021. https://www.okhistory.org/publications/enc/entry.php ?entry=SE020.

Barker, Joanne. "For Whom Sovereignty Matters." In *Sovereignty Matters: Locations of Contestation and Possibility in Indigenous Struggles for Self-Determination*, edited by Joanne Barker, 1–31. Lincoln: University of Nebraska Press, 2005.

———. "Territory as Analytic: The Dispossession of Lenapehoking and the Subprime Crisis." *Social Text* 36, no. 2 (June 2018): 19–39. https://doi.org/10.1215/01642472 -4362337.

Belko, William S. "Epilogue to the War of 1812: The Monroe Administration, American Anglophobia, and the First Seminole War." In *America's Hundred Years' War: U.S. Expansion to the Gulf Coast and the Fate of the Seminole, 1763–1858*, edited by William S. Belko, 54–102. Gainesville: University Press of Florida, 2011.

Blomley, Nicholas. "Law, Property, and the Geography of Violence: The Frontier, the Survey, and the Grid." *Annals of the Association of American Geographers* 93, no. 1 (March 2003): 121–41. www.jstor/com/stable/1515327.

Brooks, Joanna. "'This Indian World': An Introduction to the Writings of Samson Occom." In *The Collected Writings of Samson Occom, Mohegan: Leadership and Literature in Eighteenth-Century Native America*, edited by Joanna Brooks, 3–40. Oxford: Oxford University Press, 2006.

Callahan, John. Introduction to *The Collected Essays of Ralph Ellison*, rev. ed., edited by John Callahan, xvii–xxix. New York: Modern Library, 2003.

Chiles, Katy. "Within and Without Raced Nations: Intertextuality, Martin Delany, and *Blake; or the Huts of America*." *American Literature* 80, no. 2 (June 2008): 323–52. https://doi.org/10.1215/00029831-2008-005.

Clavin, Matthew. "'It Is a Negro, Not an Indian War': Southampton, St. Domingo, and the Second Seminole War." In *America's Hundred Years' War: U.S. Expansion to the Gulf Coast and the Fate of the Seminole, 1763–1858*, edited by William S. Belko, 181–208. Gainesville: University Press of Florida, 2011.

Crocket, Hasan. "David Walker's *Appeal* in Georgia." *Journal of Negro History* 86, no. 3 (Summer 2001): 305–18. www.jstor/org/stable/1562449.

Cusick, James G. "Hidden Meanings in a Second Seminole War Pamphlet." *Special and Area Studies Collections Blog,* Smathers Libraries, University of Florida, January 2020. https:// ufsasc.domains.uflib.ufl.edu/hidden-meanings-second-seminole-war-pamphlet -florida/.

———. "Historiography of Nineteenth-Century Florida." *Florida Historical Quarterly* 94, no. 3 (Winter 2016): 295–319. www.jstor.org/stable/24769274.

———. "Public Viewpoint and Moral Compass: An Analysis of Three Tracts on the Second Seminole War." Paper presented at the Annual Meeting of the Florida Historical Society. Sarasota, Fla., 2018.

Daut, Marlene L. "Before Harlem: The Franco-Haitian Grammar of Transnational African American Writing." *Journal of Nineteenth-Century Americanists* 3, no. 2 (Fall 2015): 385–92. https://doi.org/10.1353/jnc.2015.0023.

Detsi-Diamanti, Zoe. "Burlesquing 'Otherness' in Nineteenth-Century American Theatre: The Image of the Indian in John Brougham's *Met-a-mora; or, The Last of the Pollywogs* (1847) and *Po-Ca-Hon-Tas; or, The Gentle Savage* (1855)." *American Studies* 48, no. 3 (Fall 2007): 101–23. https://doi.org/10.1353/ams.0.0058.

Dinius, Marcy J. "'Look!! Look!!! At This!!!!': The Radical Typography of David Walker's *Appeal.*" *PMLA* 126, no. 1 (January 2011): 55–72. www.jstor.org/stable/41414081.

Doolen, Andy. "'Be Cautious of the Word "Rebel"': Race, Revolution, and Transnational History in Martin Delany's *Blake; or the Huts of America.*" *American Literature* 81, no. 1 (March 2009): 153–79. https://doi.org/10.1215/00029831-2008-054.

Edwards, Frank, Hedwig Lee, and Michael Esposito. "Risk of Being Killed by Police Use of Force in the United States by Age, Race–Ethnicity, and Sex." *PNAS* 116, no. 34 (August 20, 2019): 16793–98. https://doi.org/10.1073/pnas.1821204116.

Fagan, Benjamin. "Chronicling White America." *American Periodicals* 26, no. 1 (2016): 10–13. https://muse.jhu.edu/article/613375.

Fields, Kendra T. "'No Such Thing as Stand Still': Migration and Geopolitics in African American History." *Journal of American History* 102, no. 3 (2015): 693–718. https://doi .org/10.1093/jahist/jav510.

Gerrity, Sean. "Freedom on the Move: Marronage in Martin Delany's *Blake; or, The Huts of America.*" *MELUS: Multi-ethnic Literature of the U.S.* 43, no. 3 (Fall 2018): 1–18. https://muse.jhu.edu/article/708193.

Goldstein, Alyosha. "Introduction: Toward a Genealogy of the U.S. Colonial Present." In *Formations of United States Colonialism,* edited by Alyosha Goldstein, 1–30. Durham, N.C.: Duke University Press, 2014.

Gruesz, Kirsten Silva. "America." In *Keywords for American Cultural Studies,* edited by Bruce Burgett and Glenn Hendler, 16–22. New York: New York University Press, 2007.

Guterl, Matthew Pratt. "An American Mediterranean: Haiti, Cuba, and the American South." In *Hemispheric American Studies,* edited by Caroline F. Levander and Robert S. Levine, 96–115. New Brunswick, N.J.: Rutgers University Press, 2007.

Harris, Cheryl I. "Whiteness as Property." *Harvard Law Review* 106, no. 8 (June 1993): 1707–91. https://doi.org/10.2307/1341787.

Hawes, David S. "John Brougham as Playwright." *Educational Theatre Journal* 9, no. 3 (October 1957): 184–93. https://doi.org/10.2307/3203527.

Hinks, Peter P. Introduction to *David Walker's Appeal to the Coloured Citizens of the World*, edited by Peter P. Hinks, xi–xliv University Park: Pennsylvania State University Press, 2000.

Holland, Cullen Joe. "The Cherokee Indian Newspapers, 1828–1906: The Tribal Voice of a People in Transition." PhD diss., University of Minnesota, 1956.

Holland, Sharon P., and Tiya Miles. "Afro-Native Realities." In *The World of Indigenous North America*, edited by Robert Warrior, 524–48. New York: Routledge, 2015.

Klos, George. "Blacks and the Seminole Removal Debate, 1821–1835." In *The African American Heritage of Florida*, edited by David R. Colburn and Jane L. Landers, 128–56. Gainesville: University of Florida Press, 1995.

Kly, Y. N. "The Gullah War, 1739–1858." In *The Invisible War: The African American Anti-slavery Resistance from the Stono Rebellion through the Seminole Wars*, edited by Y. N. Kly, 50–99. Atlanta: Clarity, 2006.

Leeds, Stacy L. "Defeat or Mixed Blessing—Tribal Sovereignty and the State of Sequoyah." *Tulsa Law Review* 43, no. 5 (2007): 5–16. https://digitalcommons.law.utulsa.edu/tlr/vol43/iss1/2.

LeMenager, Stephanie. "Marginal Landscapes: Revolutionary Abolitionists and Environmental Imagination." *Interdisciplinary Literary Studies* 7, no. 1 (Fall 2005): 49–56. www.jstor.org/stable/41209929.

Leroy, Justin. "Black History in Occupied Territory: On the Entanglements of Slavery and Settler Colonialism." *Theory and Event* 19, no. 4 (2016). https://muse.jhu.edu/article/633276.

Littlefield, Daniel F., Jr. Foreword to *Black Gun, Silver Star: The Life and Legend of Frontier Marshal Bass Reeves*, by Arthur T. Burton, xi–xv Lincoln: University of Nebraska Press, 2006.

Littlefield, Daniel F., Jr., and James W. Parins. "Short Fiction Writers of the Indian Territory." *American Quarterly* 23, no. 1 (Spring 1982): 23–38.

Maillard, Kevin Noble. "Redwashing History: Tribal Anachronisms in the Seminole Nation Cases." *Freedom Center Journal* 96 (2008): 96–115.

Maynard, Robyn, and Leanne Betasamosake Simpson. "Towards Black and Indigenous Futures on Turtle Island: A Conversation." In *Until We Are Free: Reflections on Black Lives Matter Canada*, edited by Rodney Diverlus, Sandy Hudson, and Syrus Marcus Ware, 75–93. Regina, SK: University of Regina Press, 2020.

McGann, Jerome. Editor's note to *Blake; or The Huts of America*, corrected ed., by Martin R. Delany, edited by Jerome McGann, ix–xxxiii–xxxviii. Cambridge, Mass.: Harvard University Press, 2017.

———. Introduction to *Blake; or The Huts of America*, corrected ed., by Martin R. Delany, edited by Jerome McGann, ix–xxxii. Cambridge, Mass.: Harvard University Press, 2017.

McNair, Glenn M. "The Elijah Burritt Affair: David Walker's *Appeal* and Partisan Journalism in Antebellum Milledgeville." *Georgia Historical Quarterly* 83, no. 3 (Fall 1999): 448–78. www.jstor.org/stable/40584109.

Micco, Melinda "'Blood and Money': The Case of Seminole Freedmen and Seminole Indians in Oklahoma." In *Crossing Waters, Crossing Worlds: The African Diaspora in Indian Country*, edited by Tiya Miles and Sharon P. Holland, 121–44. Durham, N.C.: Duke University Press, 2006.

Miles, Tiya, and Sharon P. Holland. "Introduction: Crossing Waters, Crossing Worlds." In *Crossing Waters, Crossing Worlds: The African Diaspora in Indian Country*, edited by Tiya Miles and Sharon P. Holland, 1–23. Durham, N.C.: Duke University Press, 2006.

Miller, Susan A. "Seminoles and Africans under Seminole War: Sources and Discourses of Tribal Sovereignty and 'Black Indian' Entitlement." In *Native Historians Write Back: Decolonizing American Indian History*, edited by Susan A. Miller and James Riding In, 187–206. Lubbock: Texas Tech University Press, 2011.

Mize, Richard. "Black, White, and Read: The Muskogee Daily Phoenix's Coverage of the Sequoyah Statehood Convention of 1905." *Chronicles of Oklahoma* 82, no. 2 (Summer 2004): 222–39.

Morton, William J. "Boundaries of Georgia." In *New Georgia Encyclopedia*, last edited July 27, 2017. www.georgiaencyclopedia.org/articles/history-archaeology/boundaries -georgia.

Moten, Fred. "The Case of Blackness." *Criticism* 50, no. 2 (Spring 2008): 177–218. https:// doi.org/10.1353/crt.0.0062.

Murphree, Daniel S. "Kansas." In *Native America: A State-by-State Historical Encyclopedia*, edited by Daniel F. Murphree, 1:369–92. Santa Barbara, Calif.: Greenwood, 2012.

Navakas, Michele Currie. "Island Nation: Mapping Florida, Revising America." *Early American Studies* 11, no. 2 (Spring 2013): 243–11. https://doi.org/10.1353/eam.2013.0012.

Nerone, John. "Newspapers and the Public Sphere." In *The Industrial Book, 1840–1880*, vol. 3 of *A History of the Book in America*, edited by Scott E. Casper, Jeffrey D. Groves, Stephen W. Nissenbaum, and Michael Winship, 230–47. Chapel Hill: University of North Carolina Press, 2007.

Nooe, F. Evan. "'Zealous in the Cause': Indian Violence, the Second Seminole War, and the Formation of a Southern Identity." *Native South* 4 (2011): 55–81. https://doi.org/10 .1353/nso.2011.0000.

Noonan, Mark J. "Printscape." *American Periodicals* 30, no. 1 (2020): 9–11. https://muse.jhu .edu/article/751776.

Nyong'o, Tavia. "Race, Reenactment, and the 'Natural-Born Citizen.'" In *Unsettled States: Nineteenth-Century American Literary Studies*, edited by Dana Luciano and Ivy G. Wilson, 76–102. New York: New York University Press, 2014.

Patrick, Rembert W. "Editorial Preface." In *The Origin, Progress, and Conclusion of the Florida War*, John T. Sprague, xi–xii. Facsimile reproduction of the 1848 edition. Gainesville: University of Florida Press, 1964.

Perez, Craig Santos. "Transterritorial Currents and the Imperial Terripelago." *American Quarterly* 67, no. 3 (September 2015): 619–24. https://doi.org/10.1353/aq.2015.0044.

Pyle, Kai. "Prairie Potawatomi Two-Spirit Survivance in the Early Reservation Era." Paper presented at the biannual C19: Society of Nineteenth-Century Americanists Conference, Coral Gables, Fla., April 2, 2022.

Rogers, Melvin L. "David Walker and the Political Power of the Appeal." *Political Theory* 43, no. 2 (April 2015): 208–33. www.jstor.org/stable/24571663.

Schweiger, Beth Barton. "The Literate South: Reading before Emancipation." *Journal of the Civil War Era* 3, no. 3 (September 2013): 331–59. https://doi.org/10.1353/cwe.2013.0049.

Scott, David. "The Re-enchantment of Humanism: An Interview with Sylvia Wynter." *Small Axe* 8, no. 120 (2000): 119–207.

Spillers, Hortense. "Mama's Baby, Papa's Maybe: An American Grammar Book." *Diacritics* 17, no. 2 (Summer 1987): 64–81. www.jstor.org/stable/464747.

Stark, Heidi Kiiwetinepinesiik. "The Making of a Savage in a Lawless Land." *Theory and Event* 19, no. 4 (2016). https://muse.jhu.edu/article/633282.

Trodd, Zoe. "Writ in Blood: John Brown's Charter of Humanity, the Tribunal of History, and the Thick Link of American Protest." *Journal for the Study of Radicalism* 1, no. 1 (2007): 1–29. https://doi.org/10.1353/jsr.2008.0020.

Tuck, Eve, and K. Wayne Yang. "Decolonization Is Not a Metaphor." *Decolonization: Indigeneity, Education, and Society* 1, no. 1 (2012): 1–40.

Walkiewicz, Kathryn. "Portraits and Politics: The Specter of Osceola in *Leaves of Grass*." *Walt Whitman Quarterly Review* 25, no. 3 (Winter 2008): 108–15. https://doi.org/10.13008/2153-3695/1842.

Wilson, Ivy G. "Introduction: Reconstructing Albery Allson Whitman." In *At the Dusk of Dawn: Selected Poetry and Prose of Albery Allson Whitman*, edited by Ivy G. Wilson, 1–15 Boston: Northeastern University Press, 2009.

Womack, Craig S. "Alexander Posey's Nature Journals: A Further Argument for Tribally-Specific Aesthetics." *SAIL* 13, no. 2–3 (Summer/Fall 2001): 49–66. www.jstor.org/stable/20737013.

Wynn, Kerry. "'Miss Indian Territory' and 'Mr. Oklahoma Territory': Marriage, Settlement, and Citizenship in the Cherokee Nation and the United States." In *Moving Subjects: Gender, Mobility, and Intimacy in an Age of Global Empire*, edited by Tony Ballantyne and Antoinette Burton, 172–89. Urbana: University of Illinois Press, 2009.

Wynter, Sylvia. "1492: A New World View." In *Race, Discourse, and the Origin of the Americas: A New World View*, edited by Vera Lawrence Hyatt and Rex Nettleford, 5–57. Washington, D.C.: Smithsonian Institution Press, 1996.

———. "How We Mistook the Map for the Territory, and Reimprisoned Ourselves in Our Unbearable Wrongness of Being, of *Desêtre*: Black Studies toward the Human Project (2005)." In *I Am Because We Are: Reading in Africana Philosophy*, edited by Fred Lee Hord, Mzee Lasama Okpara, and Jonathan Scott Lee, 267–80. Amherst: University of Massachusetts Press, 2016.

TELEVISION SHOWS

Kassell, Nicole, dir. *Watchmen*. Episode 1, "It's Summer and We're Running Out of Ice." Aired October 20, 2019, on HBO.

PODCASTS

Nagle, Rebecca. *This Land*. Season 1. Podcast. Crooked Media, 2019. https://crooked.com/podcast-series/this-land/#all-episodes.

Index

abolitionism, 36, 49, 135, 206, 210, 239n103;
  Black, 52–53, 138; in British colonies, 142;
  in Kansas, 114, 117; in Mexico, 13; white,
  53, 112
Adams, John Quincy, 83
Adams-Onís Treaty, 76, 83
Africa, 26, 49, 100, 115, 125, 128, 130, 135,
  163, 180–81
African Americans, 11, 99, 130, 138, 158, 192,
  254n73, 254n79; and economic security,
  164; in Indian Territory, 180–85,
  254nn80–81; and print culture, 36, 177,
  253n65; terminology for, xv, 246n2
African Methodist Episcopal Church, 99,
  259n14
Afro-Cherokees, 22, 39, 60, 65, 211, 255n84
Afro-Chickasaws, 128
Afro-Choctaws, 128
Afro-Indigeneity, 17, 21, 85, 205
Afro-Native people: alliances, 16, 21, 85, 106,
  152; beyond the state, 6, 26–28, 74–75; in
  Blake, 125, 127, 129–30; definitions of,
  xv–xvi, 246n2, 255n84; in Florida, xvii,
  81, 85–93, 96, 98–104, 106, 112, 129; and
  Freedpeople, 165, 178, 184–85, 206, 209;
  and intermarriage, 219; and statehood,
  192; subjectivity of, 16, 18
Aguinaldo, Emilio, 10
Ahmed, Sara, 213n9
Alabama, 95, 169, 238n85
Alamo myth, 13
Alaska, 10–11, 149, 217n61
All-Black towns, 30, 151, 156, 158, 176–78,
  180–84, 190, 196–97, 205–6, 254n79
Allen, C. M., 256n103
Allewaert, Monique, 84, 234n33
allotment: and Black people, 18, 165, 184,
  250, 254n79, 254n81; in Creek Nation,

169, 172, 255n86, 255n88; in Indian
  Territory, 16, 30, 64, 105, 116–17, 159, 165,
  178, 191, 197; in print culture, 151, 153,
  158–62, 170, 248n17, 249n23; and
  statehood, 184, 190, 256n102; and
  women, 184, 187, 257n106
American Board of Commissioners for
  Foreign Nations, 40, 221n34, 222n43
Anglo-African Magazine, 125–26, 131, 138,
  177, 244n81
Anglo-Cherokee War, 37
animacy, 8–12, 23, 57, 111, 147, 185, 187.
  See also anthropomorphization
Anishinaabe people, 138
anthropomorphization, 14, 57, 59–60,
  101, 123, 150, 187, 228n90. *See also*
  feminization
anti-Blackness, 1, 15, 22, 33, 40; and
  anti-Indigeneity, 113–14, 147, 176, 204,
  208; definition of, xvi; and enslavement,
  57, 60, 104, 125, 138, 197; Indigenous, 103,
  164, 176, 181, 192, 195–96, 206, 221n27,
  239n99, 254n81; logics of, 17–18, 31; in
  print culture, 49, 56, 158, 177, 181; and
  statehood, 35, 56, 70, 81, 151, 180, 192,
  195–96, 200, 204; and violence, 39, 114,
  137, 162, 180, 182, 184, 202. *See also* Jim
  Crow; lynchings; racism
anticolonialism, 34, 43, 47, 85, 101, 113, 126,
  128, 131, 145, 219n15
anti-Indigeneity, xvi, 1, 42, 70, 81, 104–5, 128,
  199, 232n9; and anti-Blackness, 113–14,
  147, 176, 204, 208. *See also* racism
Apache people, 13, 133, 162
apishness, 139
Arizona, 10–11, 257n112
Arkansas, 130–31, 209, 218n66
Arkansas Territory, 37, 43

Arvin, Maile, 4, 18, 137
Athenian, 56, 219n16, 226n80, 227n86, 229n101
Atlanta, GA, 68–70
Augusta, GA, 50
Authentic Narrative of the Seminole War, An, 86–93, 98, 234–35n39, 235n52, 235n54, 237n75
Ayoka, 43–44, 172, 188, 222n43, 252n53

Baltimore Morning Chronicle, 76
Barbour, James, 107
Barker, Joanne, 3–4, 24
Barnum, P. T., 146
Beecher, Catherine, 14
Belcourt, Billy-Ray, 211
Bemrose, John, 235n53
Benítez-Rojo, Antonio, 144
biopolitics, 6, 8, 213–14n11, 217n58
Bitter Root, 211–12
Bixby, Tams, 190, 249n24
Black Hawk War, 87, 90, 101
Black Lives Matter movement, 201, 206, 208
Black-Native alliances, 26, 127, 129, 131–33, 209–10, 212. *See also* Afro-Native people
Blackness, 202; and Asianness, 134; criminalization of, 29; and Indigeneity, 2, 15–19, 21, 26, 29, 35, 60, 81, 85, 199–200; in print culture, 89–90, 131, 212, 219n11; as property, 17–18, 127, 215n39, 239n101; racialization of, xvi, 17, 132, 150, 185; and Removal, 19, 60, 85, 162; and Spanish-ness, 148–49, 242n51; and whiteness, 16, 60, 113, 121, 123, 203, 213n2
Black newspapers. See *Anglo-African Magazine; Boley Progress; Douglass' Monthly; Frederick Douglass' Paper; Freedom's Journal; Liberia Herald; Provincial Freeman; Weekly Anglo-African*
Black people, terminology for, xv–xvii, 246–47n2
Black Seminole people, 28, 73–75, 83–85, 91, 93, 98, 100, 102–5, 108; terminology for, xvi, 232n9

Black statehood campaigns, 28–29, 113–15, 136, 180–85, 193, 197, 254n74–75
Black studies, 4, 17, 25
Black towns. See All-Black towns
Black Wall Street, 21. *See also* Tulsa Race Massacre
Blake, or, The Huts of America. See Delany, Martin, R.
Blomley, Nicholas, 83
blood quantum, 16–18, 65, 161, 165, 184–85, 254n83
Boley, Indian Territory, 178–79, 185, 211, 253n66
Boley Progress, 178–80, 196
Bonin, Gertrude Simmons. *See* Zitkala-Ša
Boomers, 156–57, 248n13
Boone, Daniel, 13
Border Ruffian settlements, 121–22
Boucicault, Dion, 143
Boudinot, Elias, 36–51, 56, 157, 174, 221n34, 221n36–37, 223n47, 223n55, 224n58, 224n62
Boudinot, Elias C., 157
Bowlegs, Billy, 93
Bowles, William August, 233n14
Brainerd Mission, 222n43
Brand, Dionne, 211
Brannon, Frank, 223–24n55
Brickhouse, Anna, 242n54
Brougham, John: *Columbus el Filibustero!*, 28, 115, 142–48, 245n97; *Met-a-mora; of, The Last of the Pollywogs*, 143
brown, adrienne maree, 139, 211
Brown, Charles H., 142
Brown, Corinna, 94, 136
Brown, David, 222n43
Brown, David J., 173
Brown, John (abolitionist), 28, 112, 115, 121, 135–39, 142, 243n65
Brown, John (governor), 188
Bruyneel, Kevin, 216n53
Buchanan, James, 122–23, 143
Burritt, Elijah, 53, 226n77
Burton, Art T., 209
Butler, Octavia, 25

Butrick, David, 222n43

Byrd, Jodi, 17, 121, 130, 213n2, 251n36

Byrd County, 190

cacophony, 17, 121

Caddo people, 162

Cadmus, 174

Calhoun, John C., 141, 148

California, 8, 10, 13, 217n61

Canada, 16, 125, 130, 135, 141, 209

Candy, John, 41

capitalism, 64, 80, 126, 128, 131, 146–47, 149, 170, 199; capitalist accumulation, 2, 139; racial, 12, 246n2

Caribbean, 5, 76, 78, 82, 84, 113–14, 142–47, 149, 241n20

Carlisle Boarding School, 236n66

Carpenter v. Murphy, 203, 205–6

Carter, L. Edward, 248n17

Cass, Lewis, 122–23, 229n102

Castronovo, Russ, 2–3

Catlin, George: *Letters and Notes*, 96; *Osceola, the Black Drink, a Warrior of Great Distinction*, 96–98, 237n70, 237n77

Chang, David, 184, 255n86

Chen, Mel Y., 8

Cherokee (language), 41–46, 156, 172–73, 188, 222n41–44, 223n47, 223n49, 247n9, 248n17, 252n53. *See also* Sequoyah

Cherokee Advocate, 156–57, 248n12, 254n81, 256n101

Cherokee County, GA, 61–64, 66–67, 190

Cherokee Keetowah Society, 190

Cherokee Nation, 9, 27, 155, 202; artists from, xiii, 30, 173, 190; cosmologies of, 25–26, 64; elites of, 220n21–23; enslavement by, 16, 18–19, 30–31, 39–40, 49–50, 103, 221n28; and federal government, 37, 198, 220–21n19; and Five Tribes, xv, 1, 27, 152; and Freed-people, 18–19, 30, 165, 207–8, 215n43; and Georgia, 27, 31–33, 37–38, 46–51, 56, 61–68, 190, 227n85, 228n96, 229n100–1; matriliny in, 5, 38–40, 43, 66, 68, 188, 199, 220n24; newspapers in, 27, 32–37,

40–42, 44–51, 157–58, 225n67, 248n17; Removal of, 31–39, 48–49, 56–60, 63–67, 117, 136, 210, 227n86, 230n113, 250n27; scholars from, 5–6, 22, 156, 188, 192, 197, 199, 203; and Sequoyah movement, 172–75, 185, 188, 199; women in, 38–39, 48, 51, 66, 199, 220n19, 224n58, 224n64, 229n101

Cherokee National Council, 38, 40, 44, 172, 220n22, 252n53

Cherokee Nation v. Georgia, 27, 32–33, 46–47, 50–51, 63, 223n53, 227n85, 232n13

Cherokee Phoenix: bilingualism in, 34, 42–46, 222n41–42, 223n47, 223n49; and Cherokee sovereignty, 33–37, 48, 66, 178; circulation of, 33, 46–47, 223n55; founding of, 36, 39–42, 219n12, 221n34; and Georgia newspapers, 26, 33–35, 37, 48–51, 53, 56, 68, 79, 224n61, 225n66; masthead of, 68–69

Chicago Defender, 177

Chicago Sun-Times, 157

Chickasaw Nation: in *Blake*, 103, 126, 127–30; and the Civil War, 163; and Five Tribes, xv, 1, 27, 152; and Freedpeople, 250n33; scholars from, 17, 121; slavery in, 16, 19; and State of Sequoyah, 188, 190, 256n100

Chiles, Katy, 126

China, 197

Chinese Exclusion Act (1882), 11

Chinese people: "coolie" laborers, 133–34, 242n58

Choctaw (language), 156

Choctaw-Chickasaw Nation, 130

Choctaw Intelligencer, 156

Choctaw Nation: in *Blake*, 103, 127–30; and *Cherokee Phoenix*, 50; and the Civil War, 163; and Five Tribes, xv, 1, 27, 152; and Freedpeople, 250n33; slavery in, 16, 19; and State of Sequoyah, 188, 190; treaties with, 255n92

Christian Advocate and Journal, 141

Christianity, 20, 46

Christian Recorder, 99

Civil War (U.S.), 18, 117, 162–64, 185, 248n13, 250n27, 252n43; and Florida, 71, 101; and Kansas, 149, 254n73; and states' rights, 6, 57–58, 110

Clavin, Matthew, 104

Clinch, Duncan Lamont, 95

Cohen, M. M., 95, 104, 236n65

colonialism. *See* settler colonialism

Columbus, Christopher, 132, 142–48

Columbus el Filibustero!. See Brougham, John

Columbus Enquirer, 50, 225n67

Comanche people, 13, 162

Confederacy, 11, 68, 142, 163–64, 185, 250n27, 255n86

Connecticut Gazette; and the University Intelligencer, 20

Coulthard, Glen Sean, 25

COVID-19 pandemic, 207

Coward, John M., 236n58

Creek Nation. *See* Muscogee (Creek) Nation

Creole people, 131, 133–34, 140–41; Guyanese, 144

criminalization, 29, 202–4, 208. *See also* incarceration

Crittenden, William, 141

Cuba: in *Blake*, 125–26, 130–31, 133–34, 242n44, 242n51; Chinese people in, 133–34; Indigenous people in, 126, 133, 242n54; and Kansas, 28, 113–15, 125, 142, 148–50; in print culture, 9, 113, 123–25; and slavery, 115, 123–24, 130, 134, 142, 242n45, 242n54; and the U.S., 7, 28, 113–14, 125, 139–45, 148–49, 245n100

Curtis, Charles, 190

Curtis Act, 159

Cushman, Ellen, 44

Cusick, James, 89–90, 234–35n39

Dahlonega, Cherokee Territory, 62, 229n97

Daily Chieftain. See Indian Chieftain (Vinita)

Dalrymple, Louis, 9

Daut, Marlene, 126

Dawes Commission, 159, 161–62, 169, 184–85, 196, 247–48n11, 248–49nn21–22, 249n24, 249–50n26, 254n83

Dawes Rolls, 215n43

Dawes Severalty Act, 105, 159, 257n106

Debo, Angie, 185, 249n22

decolonization, 1, 6, 21, 26, 99, 114, 135, 204, 206–7, 210

Deer, Sarah, 204, 205

Delany, Martin, R., 28, 36, 86, 115, 135–36, 181; *Blake*, 103, 115, 125–39, 242n44, 242n51

Delaware (Lenape) people, 3, 115, 136, 153, 190–91

Deloria, Philip J., 121

Deloria, Vine, Jr., 250n30

democracy: liberal, 6, 126; participatory, 150; U.S., 144, 146, 204

Democratic Party, 113, 121–24, 182, 185, 187, 192

de Onís, Luis, 83

Dimaline, Cherie, 211

Diouf, Sylviane, 130

Doolen, Andy, 126

Douglas, Stephen, 122–23, 140–41

Douglass, Frederick, 36. *See also Douglass' Monthly; Frederick Douglass' Paper*

Douglass' Monthly, 128

Dred Scott decision, 143

Duncan, DeWitt Clinton. *See* Too-Qua-Stee

DuVal, William Pope, 104

Eastern Band of Cherokee Indians, 31

Eastern Shawnee people, 153, 191

Eddleman, Ora V., 173–74

Edes, Richard, 79

education, 12–15, 107, 117, 155–56, 164, 192–93, 196, 214n19; boarding schools, 19, 236n66; mission schools, 40, 222n43. *See also* 1836 Project (Texas)

1866 treaties. *See* Reconstruction Treaties

1836 Project (Texas), 13

Elden, Stuart, 216n52

El Filibustero, 145

Ellicott, Andrew, 71–72, 231n4

Ellison, Ralph, 29

Emathla, Tukose, 107–8

Enabling Act (Hamilton Bill), 196, 257n112

England, 12, 85, 141. *See also* Great Britain

English (language): in *Cherokee Phoenix*, 34, 41–46, 222n41, 223n49; in *Florida Gazette*, 78–80; in Indian Territory, 155–56, 174, 247n9; in *La Patria*, 222n40; and Seminole people, 107, 109

Enlightenment era, 2, 61, 90, 124, 129, 135, 212

enslavement: in *Blake*, 126–30, 132; and Cuba, 115, 123–25, 130, 133–34, 140, 142–43, 242n45, 242n54; in Five Tribes, xv, 5, 163–64; in Florida, 98, 100–1, 110; in Georgia, 27, 35, 52, 56–61, 66, 68, 218–19n10, 227–28n89, 228n93; and Indigenous dispossession, 13, 28, 32, 120, 148, 206; in Kansas, 112, 114–15, 117, 122–24, 135, 137–38, 150, 245n94; in Muscogee Nation, 16, 19, 103, 193–95, 206; and Removal, 4, 26, 71, 81, 87, 124, 130, 162, 226n77; and Seminole people, 16, 19, 75, 82–83, 85, 92, 102–5, 127, 232n9, 238n85; and settler colonialism, 13, 15, 86, 91–92, 215n30, 228n89–90; uprisings against, 30, 85, 86, 89–91, 104, 130–31, 245n94, 244n77; and U.S. Congress, 123, 239n103, 251n33; and women, xvi, 60, 128. *See also* abolitionism; plantation economy; slavocracy

Eufaula, OK, 170, 252n43

Everglades, FL, 105, 108–9

Explore Georgia, 31

Fanon, Frantz, 135

federalism, 8, 84, 229n103

Federal Road, 63, 230n105

Federal Union, 53–55

feminism, 5, 188; Black, 139, 211; Indigenous, 211

feminization: of Indian Territory, 167, 185, 187–88, 197–99; of states, 59–60, 101, 123, 228n90. *See also* anthropomorphization

Ferdinand, King of Spain, 142, 146

Fielder, Brigitte, 91–92

Fields, Kendra T., 181, 254n79–80

Fields, Yatika Starr, 30

filibusterism, 124, 126, 131, 139–41, 143, 145–46, 148, 241n20–21, 246n102

Finch, Aisha, 138, 140, 242n45, 244n77

First U.S.-Seminole War, 83, 100, 231n6, 233n18, 252n43

Five Tribes: and allotments, 64, 159, 161; enslavement by, xv, 5, 163–64; and Freedpeople, 19, 164, 192, 207, 209; in Indian Territory, 10, 64, 153, 186; and *McGirt* ruling, 1, 18, 204, 206–7; and railroads, 166; Removal of, 2, 5, 64, 190, 246n1, 258n117; schools of, 10, 155, 192; and statehood campaigns, 28, 151, 186–87, 191, 255n88. *See also* Cherokee Nation; Chickasaw Nation; Choctaw Nation; Muscogee (Creek) Nation; Seminole people

Five Tribes Act, 196

flags, xiii, 30, 110

Fleming, John, 155

Florida: Afro-Native resistance in, 28, 73–75, 81, 85–93, 104, 129, 152; and Georgia border, 71–72, 231n3–4; and print culture, 73–74, 76–79, 86–94, 108, 156, 231n5, 236n58; Removal in, 28, 73–74, 81, 85, 96, 98, 106, 117; and Seminole wars, 21, 28, 74, 100, 104–6, 110, 187, 235n53, 236n58; U.S. acquisition of, 28, 73, 76, 78–85, 100, 110–11, 232n11–12, 233n14–15. *See also* Seminole Tribe of Florida

Florida Gazette, 76–81, 233n16, 233n19

Florida Territory, 28, 72, 78, 90, 234n31, 234n38

Florida War. *See* Second U.S.-Seminole War

Forsyth, John, 224n64

Foucault, Michel, 213–14n11

France, 76, 78, 85

Franklin, Jimmie, 177

Frederick Douglass' Paper, 128

freedom (Black and Indigenous), definition of, 15, 24, 26, 210–12

Freedom's Journal, 36, 50, 52, 177, 219n12

Freedpeople: Afro-Native, xvi, 165, 209; and allotments, 165, 184, 250–51n33–34, 254n81; and Black Lives Matter, 206; and Black towns, 165, 178, 182–84, 190, 253n66; and Cherokee Nation, 18–19, 30, 165, 207–8, 215n43; definition of, xv–xvi, 185, 232n9; and Reconstruction Treaties, 164, 192; and Seminole Nation, 75, 103; and statehood, 192

Free-Soilers, 114, 123

Fugitive Slave Act, 130

Gadsden, James, 233n23

Gaines, Edmund, 87, 238n87

Garveyism, 181

genocide: in *Columbus el Filibustero!*, 148; and Florida, 74, 90, 92; and Georgia, 57–59, 67; and Kansas, 114, 116–17, 149–50; and Removal, 6, 35, 57, 90, 96, 117, 128, 163, 218n6, 258n8; and statehood, 15, 33, 35, 112, 206

Georgia: Atlanta, 68–69; Cherokee County, 190; and enslavement, 60, 66, 227–28n89; and Florida, 71–72, 231n3–4; land lotteries in, 56, 61, 63–68, 71; newspapers in, 27, 33–37, 42, 44, 47–58, 63–65, 219n16, 224n59, 226n80, 227n85; Removal in, 32, 38, 57–58, 95, 117, 220n25, 227n85; statehood of, 33, 38, 57, 59–60, 62, 70, 156, 227n87, 228n90, 228n93, 229n100, 230n113; white migrants to, 230n108. *See also* Cherokee Nation; *Cherokee Nation v. Georgia*

Georgia Courier, 219n16, 227n86

Georgia Department of Economic Development, 31

Georgia General Assembly, 31, 227n85, 228–29n96

Georgia Guard, 35, 219n16, 224n64, 230n105

Georgia Historic Newspapers, 53

Georgia Journal, 47, 225–26n74, 226n80

Georgia State Route, 225, 31–32; Chieftains Trail, 31–32, 34, 70, 218n2–3

Georgia Supreme Court, 59

Gerrity, Sean, 130

Gibson, Charles, 167, 169–70, 186, 252n43

Giddings, Joshua, 239n103

Gilmer, George, 62

Gleason's Pictorial Drawing-Room Companion, 141

Godfrey, Mary, 87, 89–92, 98

Goeman, Mishuana, 4, 24

Goenpul people, 15

Gold, Harriet, 40

Goldstein, Alyosha, 214n12

Gorsuch, Neil, 202–3

Grayson, W. C., 169–70

Great Britain, 47, 76, 140, 224n56, 232n11; colonies of, 11, 60, 100, 120, 141–42, 144, 146, 228n93. *See also* England

Great Dismal Swamp, 130

Griggs, Sutton E., 181

grounded normativity, xvi

Gruesz, Kirsten Silva, 4, 222n40

Guam, 7, 217n61

Gumbs, Alexis Pauline, 106, 139, 211, 239n108

Guterl, Matthew Pratt, 125

Guthrie, Oklahoma Territory, 181

Guthrie, Woody, 258n3

Haaland, Deb, 215n43

Haiti, 139; Revolution, 81, 131

Hamilton, Thomas, 125–26

Harjo, Chitto, 169

Harney, William S., 93

Harper, Frances Ellen Watkins, 126, 138–39, 244n81

Harpers Ferry raid, 136

Harris, Cheryl, 16, 215n39

Harris, Isaac N., 41

Hartman, Saidiya, 59, 204, 225n72, 244n76

Haskell, Charles N., 192

Havana, Cuba, 131–32, 232n11, 233n14

Hawai'i, 7, 9–10, 149, 217n58, 217n61, 219n15, 251n38. *See also* Kānaka Maoli

Haynes, Charles Eaton, 60, 220n25, 228n90
Henry, Patrick, 51
Herald, 181
Hernández, Joseph Marion, 78, 233n17
heteronormativity, 39, 81, 95, 129, 169, 187
Hicks, John. *See* Emathla, Tukose
Holdenville Times, 170
Holland, Cullen Joe, 248n17
Holland, Sharon P., 17, 180
Holm, Tom, 259n26
homesteading, 156, 206
Hoskin, Chuck, Jr., 207
Hughes, Langston, 243n63
Hunter, Carol A. Petty, 249n23

Illinois Territory, 90
incarceration, 19, 204, 208–10. *See also* criminalization
Indian Chieftain (Vinita), 158, 173, 181, 191, 248n17–18, 256n102
Indian Intercourse Act, 218n66
Indian Journal, 165–73, 251n39
Indian Progress, 157
Indian Removal Act, 59
Indians, use of term, xvi
Indian Territory, 15, 208; allotment in, 16, 30, 64, 105, 116–17, 159, 165, 178, 191, 197; Black people in, 176–85, 193, 195–96, 205–11, 254n80–81; Cherokee Nation in, 43, 48, 214n19, 224n58; feminization of, 167, 185, 187–88, 197–99; Five Tribes in, 10, 64, 153, 186–87; and Kansas, 111–21, 149, 163; Muscogee Nation in, 1, 201, 203; and print culture, 10–11, 26, 28, 151–59, 163, 165–67, 171, 197, 247n8–9, 251n38–39; Removal in, 29–30, 109–10, 149, 162–65, 169, 172, 250–51n33; Seminole people in, 103–5, 129–30, 188; and statehood, 6, 137, 162, 185–86, 190, 196–99, 249n24, 250n30, 255n88, 255n92; use of term, 213n2, 217n66. *See also* Sequoyah, State of
Indigeneity, 113, 132: and Blackness, 2, 15–19, 21, 26, 29, 35, 60, 81, 85, 199–200, 202; definition of, xvi; in media, 208–10; and nation-building, 144, 148; in print

culture, 89–90, 123, 128, 136, 212, 219n11; and Removal, 162; and territory, 10, 149, 239n101; and whiteness, 31–32, 123, 150, 185, 203
Indigenous newspapers. See *Cherokee Phoenix*; *Choctaw Intelligencer*; *Indian Chieftain* (Vinita); *Indian Journal*; *Indian Progress*; *Oklahoma War-Chief*; *Seminole News*; *Seminole Tribune*
Indigenous peoples, terminology for, xv–xvii
Insular Cases, 7
Intercourse Act, 60
Isabella, Queen of Spain, 147

Jackson, Andrew, 63, 229–30n103–4, 233n24, 238n87; in Florida, 76, 78, 82–85, 94, 100, 233n15, 234n29, 238n85
Jackson, Shona, 4, 137, 144
Jacobs, George, 205–6
Jacobs, Patsy, 205
Jeffers, Honorée Fanonne, 20
Jefferson, Thomas, 30, 66, 116, 140, 257n105
Jesup, Thomas, 82, 85, 87, 94–95, 104
Jim Crow, 32, 105, 138, 153, 162, 181, 192, 197
Johns, Jane, 86, 91–92, 98
Johnson, Douglas, 188, 256n100
Jumper, Betty Mae Tiger, 75, 109–10
Jumper, Moses, Jr., 75, 82, 106, 234n28
Junta Cubano, 140, 141
Justice, Daniel Heath, 26, 156, 220n20, 222n42

Kānaka Maoli, 3, 18, 219n15, 251n38. *See also* Hawai'i
Kansas: Black people in, 243n63, 254n73; Bleeding, 112–14, 117, 119, 147, 245n94; in *Columbus el Filibustero!*, 142, 146–48; and Cuba, 28, 113–15, 125, 142, 148–50; and enslavement, 112, 115, 122–24, 135, 137–38, 150, 245n94; filibusters in, 148, 241n20–21; and Indian Territory, 111–21, 149, 163; Indigenous people in, 15, 117, 137, 149; in print, 117–24, 139, 156; statehood campaigns in, 28, 113–15, 120–23, 142, 149, 156, 240n1, 240n3

Kansas Free State, 117–19

Kansas-Nebraska Act, 112–13, 115–17, 142, 240n4, 240n6

Kansas Territory, 112–13, 115–17, 121, 136–38, 142–43, 240n1, 244n71

Kansas Tribune, 117

Karuka, Manu, 231n7

Kauanui, J. Kēhaulani, 3–4, 25, 207, 217n58

Kavanaugh, Brett, 202

Kaw people, 115, 136

Kentucky, 13, 79

Khalili, Laleh, 216n54

Kickapoo people, 115–16, 136

Kidwell, Clara Sue, 240n3

King, Tiffany Lethabo, 4–5, 19–20, 25, 59, 74–75, 89, 206

Kingsbury, Cyros, 50

Kiowa people, 162, 182

Knickerbocker Magazine, 83–84

Knox, Henry, 219n19

Krauthamer, Barbara, 16, 127

Kumeyaay people, 22

La Escalera, 140, 242n45, 244n82

La Flesche (Tibbles), Susette, 36

La Grange, FL, 94

Laguna Pueblo people, 215n43

land allotment. *See* allotment

land lotteries. *See* lotteries (printed)

Land Run (1889), 13, 248n13

land runs, 153, 178, 181, 184, 186, 247n4, 248n13, 250n33, 254n73

land surveys. *See* surveys

land theft, 1, 19, 30, 115–16, 137, 139, 156, 206, 208

Langston City, OK, 181

La Patria, 222n40

lasting narratives, 95–96

Latin America, 124, 131, 145–46, 148–49

Latin American studies, 7

Latinx studies, 7

Lawrence City, KS, 119

Lawson, Oklahoma Territory, 182

Lazo, Rodrigo, 145

Leeds, Stacy L., 199

LeMenager, Stephanie, 243n65

Lenape people. *See* Delaware (Lenape) people

liberalism: and democracy, 6, 126, 130, 216n53; and freedom, 134, 139; and individualism, 141; and statehood, 112; and subjectivity, 4, 12, 16–17, 36, 53, 101, 124, 138, 159, 205

Liberator, 122

Liberia, 49, 128, 135

Liberia Herald, 128

Liliuokalani, Queen of Hawai'i, 10

Lipman, Jana, 245n100

literacy: Black, 35, 56, 218n10; Indigenous, 10, 44, 56, 107–9, 172, 188, 222n41; Southern, 34, 37, 56

lithographs, 121–25

Littlefield, Daniel, Jr., 166, 249n23

Live PD (TV show), 29, 201, 207–9, 258n1–2

López, Narciso, 126, 139–41, 145

lotteries (printed), 3, 33, 42, 56–58, 62–68

Loughran, Trish, 215n28, 222n38

Louisiana, 218n66

Lovecraft Country, 259n26

Lowe, Lisa, 12, 133

Lumpkin, Joseph, 227–28n89

Lumpkin, Wilson, 33, 37, 56–63, 65, 67, 70, 227–28n88–90, 230n104, 230n108, 230n112–13

Lumpkin County, 57, 229n97

lynchings, 6, 30, 57

Lytle, Clifford M., 250n30

Madera, Judith, 126, 135, 241n22

Madison, James, 76

Magee, J. L., 121–25, 138, 193

Mahon, John K., 97, 233n15, 234n31

Maillard, Kevin Noble, 103

Manifest Destiny, 28, 80–81, 86, 101, 116, 122, 147, 232n13

maps: of Cherokee territory, 32–34, 56–57, 59, 61, 63–66; of Florida, 72–73, 86, 108, 234n31; of Indian Territory, 151, 154, 184;

of Kansas, 117–21, 149; of Sequoyah, 174, 190–92; of Texas, 13–14; of U.S., 3, 24, 72, 90, 206, 211, 217n61. *See also* lotteries (printed); surveys

Marcy, William L., 121–22

Maroons: in *Blake*, 129–30; definition of, xvii; in Florida, 21, 28, 71–74, 81, 83–87, 91–93, 98, 103–4, 108, 233n14; ontologies of, 239n108; in Quilombo dos Palmares, 244n81; in *Rape of Florida*, 99, 101–2

marriage, 40, 80–81, 127, 169, 187, 216n49, 219n11, 256n97

marronage, 75, 99–100, 102, 106, 130, 239n108

Marrs, D. M., 158

Marshall, John, 63, 229n103

Martí, José, 134, 144

Maryland, 79

Mason-Dixon Line, 71, 119–20

Mathews, John Joseph, 137–38

matriliny: Cherokee, 5, 38–40, 43, 66, 68, 188, 199, 220n24; and citational approaches, 5; Muskogean, 95, 109; Seminole, 109–10

May, Robert, 241n20

Mayans. *See* Yucatánian Mayans

Maynard, Robyn, 211

McCabe, Edward, 181–82, 254n73–74

McCurtain, Green, 188, 255n88

McCurtain County, OK, 190

McGirt v. Oklahoma, 1, 6, 18, 29, 151–52, 201–7, 210, 259n12

McHenry, Elizabeth, 36

McKittrick, Katherine, 25, 106, 150, 213n9

McNair, Glenn M., 226n77

Merritt, Keri Leigh, 218–19n10

Mexico, 13–15, 99, 105, 133, 215n30, 219n15

Miami people, 115, 136, 153, 191

Miccosukee Tribe, 111

Michi Saagiig Nishnaabeg, xvi, 106

Miles, Tiya, 16–17, 31, 49, 180, 218n3–4, 219n11, 221n28, 229n100

Milledgeville, Georgia, 47, 53–54, 56, 226n75

Miller, Susan A., 100, 102

Mississippi River, 48, 57, 62, 163, 217n66

Missouri, 122, 218n66

Missouri Compromise, 112, 120

Modoc people, 153, 191

Monroe, James, 80, 233n23

Monroe Doctrine, 80, 197, 232n12

Montgomery, Hugh, 63, 229n102

Moreton-Robinson, Aileen, 15–16, 213–14n11

Moten, Fred, 25, 106, 238n88

Mulroy, Kevin, 239n101

Murphy, Patrick, 205

Murray, William H., 188, 192

Muscogee (Creek) Nation: and allotments, 168–72, 184, 255n86, 255n88; artists from, xiii, 30; and the Civil War, 164; in Cuba, 133; and the Five Tribes, 1, 27; in Florida, 233n14–15, 252n43; and Freedpeople, 253n66; in Georgia, 49, 58, 61, 210, 229n101, 238n85; and *McGirt* ruling, 1, 201–3; and *Murphy* ruling, 205–6; newspapers in, 165–67, 171, 196, 252n43; and Osceola, 94–95; scholars from, 21, 156, 204; and Sequoyah movement, 152, 185–86, 188; slavery in, 16, 19, 103; and the Snakes, 169–70; terms for, xv, 247n2; and Tulsa, 208

Muskogee, OK, 166, 169, 176, 180, 188, 196

Muskogee Cimeter, 176–77, 180, 193–96, 257n110, 257n111; "Ring Master and His Slave," 193–95, 196

Muskogee Democrat, 251n39

Muskogee Phoenix, 159–60, 185, 249n23–24, 256n103

Mvskoke (language), 104, 155

Nagle, Rebecca: *This Land*, 203, 258n8

Narrative of the Life and Sufferings of Mrs. Jane Johns, A, 86, 91–92

Nashville Banner, 50

Native peoples, terminology for, xvi, 246–47n2

Native South studies, 27

Native studies, 17

Navakas, Michele Currie, 84

Naylor, Celia E., 16, 221n27, 255n84

Nebraska, 240n3

Negro Fort, FL, 100–1, 233n15, 238n88

Netherlands, 128

New Echota, Cherokee Nation, 31, 35, 41, 48, 221n34, 221n37, 223n55

New England, 17, 144, 215n28, 215n30, 218n7

New Mexico, 10–11, 257n112

newspapers. *See* Black newspapers; Indigenous newspapers; *other individual papers*

New York City, NY, 142–43, 145, 211, 219n12, 222n40

New York Journal of Commerce, 226n75

New York Observer and Chronicle, 141

Nicaragua, 246n101

Niger Valley Exploring Party, 135, 181

Nighthawk Keetowah Society, 256n103

Niimiiipuu: people, 187

Nooe, F. Evan, 235n55

Northwest Ordinance of 1787, 7

No-Transfer Resolution, 76, 232n11–12

Nwankwo, Ifeoma Kiddoe, 126, 242n44, 242n51

O'Brien, Jean M., 95, 216n49, 218n7

Occom, Samson, 20

Ojibwe people, 208

Okefenokee Swamp, 71–72

Oklahoma: Black people in, 114, 182–83, 192, 200, 204–6, 208, 254n79–80, 258n120, 259n14; flag of, xiii, 30; Indigenous people in, 15, 109, 199–200, 204, 208; and *McGirt* ruling, 1, 29, 201–5; newspapers in, 156, 166; origin of word, 255n92; statehood of, 151–54, 157, 165, 185–92, 196–99, 203–5, 208–9, 257n112; as symbol of Depression, 258n3; Vietnamese people in, 259n19. *See also* Indian Territory

Oklahoma!, 153, 247n3, 258n3

Oklahoma City, OK, 186

Oklahoma Enabling Act, 256n93

Oklahoma Guide, 182, 254n78

Oklahoma Territory, 180–82, 185–87, 193, 247n4, 255n92; and Indian Territory, 10, 153, 159, 162–63, 198, 209

Oklahoma v. Castro-Huerta, 202–3, 205

Oklahoma War-Chief, 156–57

Osage murders, 208, 259n26

Osage people, xiii, 30, 115–17, 136–37, 162, 208, 211, 259n26

Osceola, 73, 86, 93–99, 109–11, 187, 235n54, 236n63, 237n70, 237n76–77

Osceola, Alice, 75, 109

Ostend Manifesto, 143

O'Sullivan, John, 140, 244–45n85

Ottawa people, 115, 136, 153, 191

Owen, Robert L., 192–93

Parins, James, 166, 222n42, 224n62

patriarchy: possessive logics of, 16, 142; settler, 18, 81; Southern, 4; and statehood, 138, 188; white, 2, 5, 16, 25, 30, 65, 114, 138, 185, 205. *See also* heteronormativity

Pawnee people, 162

Payne, David L., 156–57

Pensacola, FL, 76, 78

Peoria people, 153, 191

Perez, Craig Santos, 217n61

Pérez, Louis A., Jr., 125

Philadelphia, PA, 143

Philadelphia Press, 174

Philippines, 7, 9

Phoenix. See Cherokee Phoenix

Piatote, Beth, 187

Pierce, Franklin, 113, 122, 123

Plácido, 131, 242n45

plantation economy, 40, 66, 71, 85, 87, 92, 125, 130, 147, 149. *See also* enslavement

Platt Amendment, 245n100

Pocahontas, 146–48

poetics, 101–2, 106–7, 172–76

poetics of landscape, 106

Polk, James K., 140

Porter, Kenneth Wiggins, 102

Porter, Pleasant, 167, 169–70, 185–86, 188, 190, 255n86, 255n88

Posey, Alexander, 165, 167, 169–72, 186, 249n23, 252n43, 255n86; "Ode to Sequoyah," 173–75, 253n62

possessive logics, 16–17, 31, 139

Potawatomi people, 115, 136, 138

Powell, William, 95

Pratt, Richard Henry, 236n66

print culture: Black and Native, 29–30, 52, 155, 158, 176–77, 181, 196; Cherokee, 33, 41, 51, 66; Cuba, 134; Florida, 86; Georgia, 33, 52–53, 56; Indian Territory, 28, 151–59, 163, 165, 197; nineteenth century, 4–5, 20, 108, 222n38; Northern, 225n67; Seminole, 107; Southern, 34, 37, 218–19n10; territorial, 3, 36, 76–81, 188; U.S., 74, 84, 166, 222n38

printscapes: Black sovereign, 126, 131, 195–96; colonial, 3, 33, 93, 115, 117, 119; definition of, xi, 2–3; imperial, 11; Indigenous, 98, 167; nineteenth-century, 210; sovereign, 2–3, 33, 42, 48, 67, 73, 152–53, 158, 176–78, 180

Provincial Freeman, 177

Puck magazine: "School Begins" cartoon, 9–12, 15

Puerto Rico, 7, 9

Puritanism, 144

Qualla Boundary, 31

Qualls, F., 195

Quapaw Nation, 1, 153, 162, 190–91

queer people, 30, 138, 211

queer studies, 5

race, taxonomies of, xvi, 16–18, 85, 92, 150, 232n9. *See also* blood quantum

racial geographies, 12

racial indigestion, 148

racism: anti-Asian, 11–12; anti-Black, 17, 79, 101, 129, 164, 177, 181–82, 192, 195, 208; and the filibuster, 148; and labor, 133–34, 242n57–58; and literacy, 27, 56, 218–19n10; and matriliny, 40; in print culture, 10–11;

35, 52, 143; and property, 39, 161, 254n81; and states' rights, 212. *See also* anti-Blackness; anti-Indigeneity

railroads, 115, 157, 161, 164, 166, 170, 251n41, 254n79

Rape of Florida, The. See Whitman, Albery Allson

Ray, Grace Ernestine, 157, 247n8

Reconstruction, 101, 164, 181, 250n31, 254n73

Reconstruction Treaties, 18, 164–66, 192, 196–97, 204, 206, 250n30, 250n33, 255n92

redface, 121, 136, 142

Redstick Muscogee, 94, 238n83. *See also* Muscogee (Creek) Nation

Red Stick War, 94

Reed, Julie, 188

Reese, Linda Williams, 253n66

Reeves, Bass, 209–10

Removal, 9, 27, 172, 202; and Blackness, 19, 60, 85, 162; of Cherokee Nation, 31–39, 48–49, 56–60, 63–67, 117, 136, 210, 227n86, 230n113, 250n27; in Cuba, 140; definition of, 1–2, 19, 207; and enslavement, 26, 71, 87, 124, 130; of Five Tribes, 2, 5, 64, 190, 246n1, 258n117; in Florida, 28, 73–74, 81, 83–85, 96, 98, 100, 106, 117; and genocide, 6, 35, 57, 74, 90, 96, 117, 128, 163, 218n6, 258n8; in Georgia, 32, 38, 57–58, 95, 117, 220n25, 227n85; in Indian Territory, 29–30, 149, 162–65, 169, 250–51n33; in Kansas, 112, 115–17, 128; and policing, 204, 210; of Seminole people, 82, 90–91, 93, 96, 103–6, 109–11, 117, 238n83; and states' rights, 4, 19, 57–59, 61. *See also* Trail of Tears

Republican Party, 181–82, 185, 187, 193, 201, 250n31

Reservation Dogs, 259n26

revolutionary sentimentalism, 138

Revolutionary War (U.S.), 37, 100, 231n3

Reynold's Political Map of the United States, 119–20

Ridge, John, 40, 48, 225n67

Ridge, Major, 48

Rigg, Lynn, 247n3
Roberts, Alaina E., 16, 250n31
Roberts, Neil, 130
Robertson, William, 50
Robinson, Charles, 112, 240n1
Rogers, W. C., 188
Roosevelt, Theodore, 167, 187, 192, 196
Rosaldo, Renato, 237n78
Rosen, Deborah, 228n93, 234n29
Ross, John, 37–38, 40–41, 47–48, 56, 63, 67, 221n34, 224n62, 229n102, 250n27
Ross, Joshua, 173

Sac and Fox people, 115–16, 136
Saint Louis World's Fair, 198
Saint Marys River, 71–72, 92, 231n3
Saldaña-Portillo, María Josefina, 12
Saler, Bethel, 214n12
San Diego, CA, 22
Sandler, Matt, 101
Saranillio, Dean Itsuji, 6, 10
Saunt, Claudio, 258n120
Sayre, Gordon M., 236n68
scalping, 92, 122–23
Schweiger, Beth, 56, 218–19n10
Scott, Winfield, 82, 87
Second U.S.-Seminole War, 28, 104–6, 109, 234n31, 234n35, 234n37, 235n53, 235n55, 239n103; and Jackson, 83, 100; and Osceola, 73, 93–99; terminology for, 231n6
segregation, 6, 30, 133, 164–65, 192–93, 199, 258n120
Selu, 199
Seminole Nation of Oklahoma, 103, 238n98
Seminole News, 75, 109
Seminole people: and Cuba, 133; enslavement by, 16, 19, 75, 82–83, 85, 92, 102–5, 127, 232n9; and Five Tribes, xv, 1, 27, 152; and Freedpeople, 163–64, 239n99, 239n101; in Indian Territory, 103–5, 129–30, 188; and Osceola, 94–98, 111, 237n75; in print, 74, 78, 84, 86–90, 107–9; in *Rape of Florida*, 99–102, 105, 107; Removal of, 82, 91, 93, 96, 103–6, 109–11, 117, 238n83; resistance in Florida, 21, 28,

71, 73–74, 76, 82–111, 234n29; and surveys, 71, 91; women, 109–10. *See also* Black Seminole people; Seminole Nation of Oklahoma; Seminole Tribe of Florida
Seminole Tribe of Florida, 75, 109, 234n28, 238n98, 240n114
Seminole Tribune, 75, 234n28
Seminole Wars. *See* First U.S.-Seminole War; Second U.S.-Seminole War; Third U.S.-Seminole War
Seneca-Cayuga people, 153, 191
Sequoyah, 43, 172–76, 188, 197, 199, 222–23n43–45, 248n17, 252n53, 253n62. *See also* Cherokee (language)
Sequoyah, State of, 6, 28–29, 151–53, 171–72, 185–86, 188, 190–97, 199, 253n65, 256n104
settler colonialism: and anti-Blackness, 17; and enslavement, 15, 91–92, 228n89–90; and flags, xiii; and Indigeneity, xvi, 121, 128, 213n2; and occupation of territory, 16, 23, 25–26, 65, 176; and policing, 203; in print, 12, 71, 78, 80, 91, 101, 144, 152; and statehood, 8, 57, 136, 188, 199, 204, 206–7; and white supremacy, xviii, 71, 85–86, 162
Seven Years' War, 232n11
sexual violence, 12, 18, 51, 57, 101, 109–10, 208, 238n89
Shadd, Isaac, 135
Shadd Cary, Mary Ann, 36, 126, 177
Sharpe, Christina, 25
Sharp v. Murphy. See Carpenter v. Murphy
Shawnee Indian Mission, 117
Shawnee people, 115–17, 136. *See also* Eastern Shawnee people
Silva, Noenoe K., 4, 251n38
Simpson, Audra, 25
Simpson, Leanne Betasamosake, xvi, 25, 106, 139, 211, 239n108, 259n15
slavery. *See* enslavement
slavocracy, 58, 66, 91, 114, 125
Smith, Chad, 215n43
Smith, James F., 64, 66
Smith, James McCune, 36, 126
Snakes, 169–70, 190

South Carolina, 58, 60, 95, 226n74, 227n87, 228n93

Southern Recorder, 219n15, 225n65–66

sovereign printscapes, 2–3, 33, 42, 48, 67, 73, 152–53, 158, 176–78, 180

Spain: in *Columbus el Filibustero!*, 142, 146–47; in Cuba, 113, 125, 140–41, 143–45, 149, 232n11, 233n14, 244n82, 245n100; in Florida, 72, 76, 79–83, 85, 100, 231n3–4, 232n11, 238n86; in *Rape of Florida*, 99, 105

Spanish (language), 79–80, 104, 145, 222n40

Spanish-American War, 7, 10, 114, 149

Spires, Derrick R., 4, 126, 177–78, 207, 244n81, 253n65

Spokogee people, 169

Sprague, John, 85–86, 234n37

Standing Rock Sioux, 121

Stark, Heidi Kiiwetinepinesiik, 208–9

Starks, Amber, 21

statehood campaigns. *See* Black statehood campaigns; Sequoyah, State of

Stateman and Patriot. *See* *Federal Union*

State of Sequoyah. *See* Sequoyah

states (U.S.). *See* Florida; Georgia; Kansas; Oklahoma; *other individual states*

states' rights: and the federal state, 8, 58, 229n103; in Florida, 110; in Georgia, 31–35, 42, 49–50, 58–59, 68, 70, 227n86; and print culture, 4–5, 27–28, 34–35, 42, 49–50, 68, 151, 227n86; and racism, 1, 6, 21, 57–58, 149, 151, 202, 204–6, 212, 264; and Removal, 4, 19, 57–59, 61; and Sequoyah movement, 199

St. Augustine, FL, 76, 78–80, 95, 231n5

Steinbeck, John, 258n3

Stephens, Alexander H., 142

Stitt, Kevin, 1, 202–3, 205

Stone Mountain, GA, 68, 70, 230n114

Stowe, Harriet Beecher: *First Geography for Children*, 14–15, 214–15n27–28, 215n30, 217n61; *Uncle Tom's Cabin*, 246n114

Sturm's Statehood Magazine, 188–89

Subterranean Pass Way, 135

Sundquist, Eric, 113

Supreme Court (U.S.), 63, 136, 223n53, 227n85, 229n100, 232n13; on sovereignty, 1, 7, 27, 33, 46–47, 51, 56, 202–3; on territories, 7, 23. *See also individual cases*

surveys, 91, 131, 161, 169, 231n4; and dispossession, 2–4, 32–34, 42, 56, 62–74, 83, 93, 116, 153, 241n12. *See also* allotment; lotteries (printed); maps

Sylvester, Walter, 211

Taínos, 126, 133, 242n54

Tariff Bill, 58

Taylor, Zachary, 82

Teller Amendment, 245n100

terra nullius, 7, 117, 123, 144, 149

territorial hermeneutics, 4, 23–24, 73, 89, 151

territory, definitions of, 7, 23–26, 216n52, 217n61, 217n65

Texas, 10, 13–15, 163, 215n30, 256n104

Theumba, Inshata. *See* La Flesche (Tibbles), Susette

Third U.S.-Seminole War, 143, 231n6

Thompson, Wiley, 95, 97–98, 237n75

Tolson, Arthur, 182, 250n33

Tompkins, Kyla Wazana, 123, 147–48, 246n114

Tonawanda Band of Seneca, 24

Too-Qua-Stee, 190, 253n54; "Imperialism: Abandonment of the Monroe Doctrine," 197; "Indian Territory at World's Fair," 198–99, 258n117; "Sequoyah poem," 173, 197

Topeka Constitution, 240n1

Trail of Tears, 31–32, 48, 130, 136, 218n6

treaties. *See individual treaties*

Treaty of Greenville, 217–18n66

Treaty of Holston, 219n19

Treaty of Hopewell, 219n18

Treaty of New Echota, 48, 250n27

Tulsa, OK, 29–30, 165, 201–2, 208–11, 211, 258n3, 259n26

Tulsa Race Massacre, 21–22, 30, 165, 182, 202, 208, 211, 216n51, 259n26

Turner, Nat, 87, 90

Turtle Island, xvi, 15

Turtle Mountain Ojibwe, 208

Twasinta's Seminoles. See Whitman, Albery Allson

Twine, William Henry, 176, 195–96

Twin Territories: The Indian Magazine, 173–74

Two-Spirit people, 5, 30, 138, 203, 211, 259n26

Uncle Sam, 9–10, 12, 188

Underground Railroad, 135

Union Mission, 155

United States Magazine and Democratic Review, 140–41

U.S. Civil War. *See* Civil War (U.S.)

U.S. Congress: and Cuba, 245n100; and the filibuster, 148; and Florida, 71, 76, 78, 232n12; and Georgia, 227n85; and Kansas, 116; and Removal, 57; and slavery, 123, 239n103, 251n33; and statehood, 73, 157, 162, 166, 187, 190, 196, 214n13, 256n101

U.S. Constitution, 23, 46, 141

U.S.-Mexico War, 14, 231n6

U.S.-Seminole wars. *See* First U.S.-Seminole War; Second U.S.-Seminole War; Third U.S.-Seminole War

U.S. Supreme Court. *See* Supreme Court (U.S.)

Vann, James, 230n105

Vann House plantation, GA, 31

Vann's Valley, 229n101

Vernon, OK, 205–6, 259n14

Vietnamese people, 259n19

Villaverde, Cirilo, 141

Vinita Weekly Chieftain. See Indian Chieftain (Vinita)

violence. *See* genocide; racism; settler colonialism; sexual violence

Walker, David: *Appeal,* 27, 33, 35, 42, 50–54, 56, 68, 226n74–75

Walker, William, 145

Warrior, Robert, 116

Watchmen (TV show), 29, 201, 207–11, 259n19

Waters, Sally, 43

Watie, Buck. *See* Boudinot, Elias

Watie, Stand, 48, 174, 250n27

Weedon, Frederick, 96

Weekly Anglo-African, 125, 131, 134

Weekly Chieftain. See Indian Chieftain (Vinita)

Wells-Barnett, Ida B., 36

Westphalian sovereignty, 23, 216n52

Wheatley (Peters), Phillips, 20

Wheatley, Susanna, 20

Wheeler, John Foster, 41

White Earth Nation, 95

white supremacy: and Blackness/Indigeneity, 16–17, 21, 26, 31, 40, 163, 176, 203; and print culture, 3, 35, 50, 52, 55, 71, 126, 195; resistance to, 89, 98, 101, 128–30, 134, 195, 207, 211; and settler colonialism, xviii, 71, 85–86, 142; and statehood, 29, 70, 138, 152, 184; and territorial hermeneutics, 4, 25; in the U.S., 5, 28, 65, 98, 112, 114, 201, 210; and whiteness, xvii, 22, 31, 184

Whitman, Albery Allson, 99, 101, 137–38, 238n92, 240n1; *Not a Man, and Yet a Man,* 101; *Rape of Florida, The,* 75, 99–102, 105–7, 112, 127, 238n81, 238n89

Whitman, Walt, 98, 238n80

Wichita people, 162

Wilde, Richard, 71

Williamson, William, 67

Windell, Maria, 138

Wirt, William, 223n53, 227n85, 228n94

Wise, Henry A., 136

Womack, Craig, 156

women: Afro-Native, 91, 129; Black, 93, 123, 129, 138–39, 205, 213n9, 253n66; Cherokee, 38–39, 48, 51, 66, 199, 220n19, 224n58, 224n64, 229n101; enslaved, xvi, 60, 128; Indigenous, 30, 92, 93, 123, 129, 138, 147, 187, 205; and literacy, 56; Maroon, 99; and marriage, 40, 80, 188; and print culture, 188; and racial taxonomies, 18, 40, 80, 259n19; Seminole, 109–10; violence against, 30, 51, 123, 203, 205, 209, 224n64; voting

rights of, 192, 257n106; white, 40, 57, 59–60, 91–92. *See also* feminization
Worcester, Samuel A., 36, 155, 221n34, 223n51, 226n75
Worcester v. Georgia, 63, 202, 221n34
World War I, 22
World War II, 22
Wright, Allen, 255n92
Wurteh, 43
Wyandotte people, 115, 136, 153, 191

Wynn, Kerry, 187, 256n97
Wynter, Sylvia, 2, 16, 24, 124, 129, 210–11, 226–27n81

Yorubaland, 137
Yucatánian Mayans, 133, 242n54, 242n58
Yun, Lisa, 133, 242n57

Zitkala-Ša, 36

Printed in the USA
CPSIA information can be obtained
at www.ICGtesting.com
LVHW090747011023
757987LV00069B/191